THE DICTIONARY OF FORESTRY

THE DICTIONARY OF FORESTRY

John A. Helms, editor

The Society of American Foresters

Copyright © 1998 by the Society of American Foresters

Published by
The Society of American Foresters
5400 Grosvenor Lane
Bethesda, MD 20814-2198
www.safnet.org
Tel: (301) 897-8720
Fax: (301) 897-3690
ISBN 0-939970-73-2

International orders (outside North and
Central America, Guam, Puerto Rico,
and the Caribbean) should be directed to
CABI Publishing
A Division of CAB International
Wallingford
Oxon OX10 8DE, UK
Tel: +44(0)1491 832111
Fax: +44(0)1491 833508
E-mail: cabi@cabi.org
ISBN 0-85199-308-7

Definitions of selected terms are reprinted or adapted from other sources, with the kind
permission of the publishers. See page 207.

*White birch, balsam, and
maples near Amnicon
Falls, Wisconsin.*
© Jeff Martin

Printed in the United States of America

10   9   8   7   6   5   4   3

Library of Congress Cataloging-in-Publication Data
The Dictionary of Forestry/John A. Helms, editor.
p. cm.
ISBN 0-939970-73-2
1. Forests and forestry–Dictionaries. I. Helms, John A.
SD126.D535   1998
634.9–dc21   98-30365
                                                                  CIP

CONTENTS

Preface   vii

Explanatory Notes   ix

The Dictionary of Forestry   1

Acknowledgments   205

Reprint Permissions   207

The Dictionary of Forestry is a revision of the 1971 *Terminology of Forest Science, Technology, Practice, and Products,* published by the Society of American Foresters and edited by F.C. Ford-Robertson under the authorization of the Joint FAO/IUFRO Committee on Forest Bibliography and Terminology. Since 1971, there have been substantial changes in the forestry profession—from a focus on multiple use and sustained yield of forest products to a broader, more complex context of sustaining diverse forest uses and values. These changes have modified the use of existing terms, introduced new terms, and created the need for an up-to-date dictionary that permits consistent use of professional language.

The recommendation to revise the Ford-Robertson *Terminology* was made by the Society of American Foresters' Forest Science and Technology Board and endorsed by SAF's Council. SAF's 29 working groups were asked to contribute to the revision. Provided with subsets of terms within their fields of interest, they determined whether to retain, revise, retire, or add terms. Technical editing was done by a subcommittee of the board, whose suggested changes were returned to the working groups. Once the submissions were compiled, the subcommittee resolved issues of duplicate definitions of the same term by different working groups, and the compilation of all terms was returned to the working groups for final review.

We hope this dictionary will help students, professionals, and the public—all those interested in the science, management, and conservation of forests—communicate technically with precision, clarity, and consistency. As with all language, the vocabulary of forestry is dynamic, and the terms and definitions compiled here reflect current professional acceptance and use. Realizing that this work is ongoing, the editor and publisher welcome your general comments and questions as well as information on perceived errors and omissions.

This dictionary seeks to strike a balance between being too inclusive and being too exclusive of both general and specialist terms. The general guidelines for development of the dictionary included (1) not duplicating the depth of more specialized, disciplinary dictionaries and glossaries in the various fields of forest science, (2) avoiding terms that are either self-explanatory or contained in standard dictionaries, (3) not providing taxonomic details or classification systems, (4) amplifying definitions by providing notes that help users interpret the definitions or provide examples of use, and (5) providing cross references to allied terms.

Those guidelines were necessarily interpreted subjectively. The terms included and the information provided in definitions were largely at the discretion of the scientists and practitioners who developed them. Consequently, this dictionary presents the terms and definitions that the science and technology leaders of the Society of American Foresters recognize as being used currently in the profession of forestry.

Terms are printed in lowercase letters unless they are commonly or always capitalized. Definitions for terms with more than one sense are numbered with bold arabic numerals. The disciplinary or other context for a term with multiple senses is given in italic before the numbered definitions; if the context applies to only one sense, it appears after the numeral for that definition. Technical words used to define a term are cross-referenced in bold; at the ends of some definitions are related terms, also cross-referenced in bold. Certain out-of-date terms have been included so that readers can use older literature; these terms are marked *obsolete*. Where appropriate, synonyms and antonyms are given at the ends of the definitions.

The following abbreviations are used:

Å	ångstrom	km	kilometer(s)
ac	acre(s)	kPa	kilopascal(s)
C	Celsius	l	liter(s)
ch	chain(s)	lb	pound(s)
cm	centimeter(s)	m	meter(s)
F	Fahrenheit	mb	millibar(s)
ft	foot (feet)	mi	mile(s)
g	gram(s)	mm	millimeter(s)
gal	gallon(s)	MPa	megapascal(s)
GIS	geographic information system	psi	pound(s) per square inch
ha	hectare(s)	sec	second(s)
in	inch(es)	sp.	species (singular or plural)
kg	kilogram(s)		

A

abiotic pertaining to the nonliving parts of an **ecosystem,** such as soil particles, bedrock, air, water

abiotic disease a disease resulting from nonliving agents, such as temperature or air pollution

ablation the combined processes, e.g., **sublimation,** melting, and evaporation, that remove snow or ice from the surface of a glacier, snowfield, etc.

ablation till the loose, relatively permeable material, either contained within or accumulated on the surface of a glacier deposited during the downwasting of nearly static glacial ice

abney level a hand-held instrument used to determine slopes, elevations, and heights —*note* abney levels have commonly been replaced by more modern **clinometers**

absolute map accuracy the accuracy of a map in relationship to the earth's geoid —*note* the accuracy of locations on a map that are defined relative to the earth's geoid are considered absolute because their positions are global in nature and accurately fix a location that can be referenced to all other locations

absolute stand density —*see* **stand density**

absorptivity the amount of radiant energy absorbed by a given substance of definite dimensions; the ratio of the amount of radiant energy absorbed to the total amount incident on that substance

abundance *ecology* the number of organisms in a **population,** combining density within inhabited areas and number and size of inhabited areas

acaricide a **pesticide** used against mites and ticks —*see* **miticide**

accelerated annual cut —*see* **allowable cut effect**

accelerated erosion —*see* **erosion**

accelerator *economics* **1.** a change in the demand for finished goods that produces larger changes in the demand for capital equipment used to make them, e.g., a relatively small rise in the demand for housing may necessitate a large outlay on new sawmills **2.** the ratio of such a change, i.e., change in investment to change in consumer expenditure —*see* **multiplier**

acceptance test *GIS* a set of particular activities performed to evaluate a hardware or software system's performance and conformity to specifications

accessibility *recreation* the degree to which a **recreation site** can accommodate visitors who may be physically challenged

accessory species a species of less value than the principal species but sometimes useful in assisting the development of the latter and likely to influence in some degree the method of treatment —*note* accessory and secondary species are collectively termed associated species

acclimation a reversible change in the morphology or physiology of an organism in response to environmental change, i.e., a temporary increase in resistance to stress —*see* **hardening off**

acclimatization the adaptation of an organism or a **population** to climatic change, generally considered the result of genetic change via **natural selection** —*see* **adaptation**

accounting variable a **slack variable** representing the weighted sum of an ordinary **decision variable** in a **mathematical programming** problem —*note* an accounting variable may ultimately be used to define new **constraints**

accreditation 1. *forestry* a peer-review program, first established by the Society of American Foresters in 1935, that evaluates and certifies that specific US first-degree (bachelor's or higher) educational curricula meet standards established by the profession for those who practice **forestry** —*note* a list of current forestry majors and curriculum options accredited by SAF may be obtained from the Society of American Foresters —*see* **certify, forest technology recognition, forester 2.** the process used to determine whether organizations have their forest management certified under the Forest Stewardship Council's forest certification system —*see* **certify**

accretion 1. an increment, usually of trees rather than **stand**s, generally applied to the more rapid growth, in diameter or volume, of trees given more growing space during the latter part of the **rotation** —*see* **increment 2.** the accumulation of sediment (a land-building process) in a river delta

accuracy 1. the closeness of computations or estimates to the true (i.e., exact), standard, or accepted values —*note* accuracy refers to quality of data **2.** the degree of obtaining the correct value, especially when the measure is repeated —*see* **precision, root mean square error**

ACE —*see* **allowable cut effect**

ACEC —*see* **area of critical environmental concern**

acid equivalent (a.e.) the amount of active principle in a pesticide expressed in terms of the parent acid

acid precipitation an atmospheric deposition composed of the hydrolyzed by-products from oxidized halogen, nitrogen, and sulfur substances

acid rain the deposition of a variety of acidic pollutants in either wet (e.g., rain, fog, or snow) or dry forms (e.g., gas or dust particles)

acid soil a soil with a **pH** value < 7.0 —*see* **soil reaction**

acquired character a modification developed during the lifetime of an organism as the result of environmental influences —*note* acquired characters are not inherited —*see* **character, phenotype**

acre-foot the volume of water or solids that will cover 1 acre to a depth of 1 foot (43,560 ft^3 or 1,233.5 m^3)

acre-inch the volume of water or solids that will cover 1 acre to a depth of 1 inch (3,630 ft^3 or 102.7 m^3)

actinorhizal plant a plant in which the root system is symbiotically associated with nitrogen-fixing actinomycetes, such as *Frankia* sp. —*note* actinorhizal plants include several *Alnus* sp.

actionable fire any fire requiring suppression, especially a fire started or allowed to spread in violation of law, ordinance, or regulation —*see* **statistical fire**

action threshold the density of a **pest** population, or extent of its injury, at which control or management measures should be initiated to prevent serious damage to the crop or resource value

activator a material added to a **pesticide** to increase toxicity

active ingredient (A.I.) the constituent of a **pesticide** formulation that is toxic to the **pest** for which it is recommended —*note* other constituents of pesticides include **additive, adjuvant, carrier, stabilizer,** and **surfactant** —*synonym* active principle

activity *management* a specific job or task that is a component of a project —*note* activities are represented by arcs in a **program and evaluation review technique (PERT)** or a **critical path method (CPM)**

activity fuel —*see* **fuel type**

activity plan a document that describes management objectives, actions, and projects to implement decisions of the resource management plan or other planning documents —*note* an activity plan is usually prepared for one or more resources in a specific area

activity schedule *management* the timing, placement, and intensity of treatments over a **forest**

actual use *range management* the use made of forage on any area by livestock or game animals without reference to permitted or recommended use —*note* generally expressed in **animal unit months** or **animal units**

adaptation 1. the process of permanent, evolutionary (genetic) adjustments in structure, form, or function that fit individuals, populations, or species to their environment **2.** the process(es) whereby individuals (or parts of individuals), populations, or species change to better survive under given environmental conditions **3.** the changed structure or function itself —*see* **acclimation, ecotype, evolution, mutation**

adaptive management a dynamic approach to **forest management** in which the effects of treatments and decisions are continually monitored and used, along with research results, to modify management on a continuing basis to ensure that **objectives** are being met —*see* **land management planning, monitoring**

additive any solid or liquid substance contributing to the formulation of a pesticide, e.g., a **stabilizer** or an **adjuvant**

additive gene a gene conveying small, incremental changes or effects —*note* additivity is the basis for most quantitative inheritance theory and for most breeding efforts —*see* **additive gene action, additive genetic variation, polygene, quantitative inheritance**

additive gene action the effects of **alleles** combining in a linear, incremental fashion to produce genetic variation —*see* **additive gene, additive genetic variation**

additive genetic variation the proportion of genetic variation that is due to the effects of additive **genes** and which responds to **natural selection, mass selection,** or **pick-the-winner selection** —*note* additive gene variation is the basis of a parent's breeding value or **general combining ability (GCA)** —*see* **additive gene, additive gene action, dominance genetic variation, nonadditive genetic variation**

additivity the sum of the contributions of each **activity**; the contribution of all activities to the **objective function** —*note* additivity is a requisite **assumption** of linear **programming** models

address matching *GIS* a mechanism for relating two files using an address as the key **column** —*note* geographic coordinates and attributes subsequently can be transferred from one address to another

adelgid a member of the family Phylloxeridae (Homoptera), including **gall adelgid**s, pine adelgids, and **woolly adelgid**s —*note* adelgids are closely related to aphids but are found only on conifers

adiabatic gradient —*see* **lapse rate**

adjacency restriction a rule governing the **allocation** of silvicultural activities (usually clearcutting) over the landscape such that adjacent **stands** are not treated at the same time but are separated by a minimum period to allow the first-harvested area to regenerate

adjuvant any substance that, when added to a **pesticide** formulation, increases its effectiveness —*note* adjuvants include a solvent, **diluent, carrier,** emulsifier, **spreader,** or **sticker** —*see* **synergist**

administratively withdrawn area a land area removed from the suitable timber base through management direction and land management planning

adsorption complex a collection of various organic and inorganic substances in soil that are capable of adsorbing ions and molecules

adult a fully grown, usually sexually mature individual —*note* an adult insect is the final **instar, stage,** or form —*see* **larva, nymph, pupa**

adult phase —*see* **maturity**

ad valorem tax the annual tax assessed on the basis of land value —*note* in some cases the tax is based on the value of land plus timber —*see* **severance tax, specific tax, yield tax**

advanced very high resolution radiometer (AVHRR) a multispectral imaging system carried by the TIROS-NOAA family of meteorological satellites that is neither advanced nor of very high spatial **resolution** but that provides a very high (10 **bit**s per **pixel**) radiometric resolution

advance felling 1. any cutting that has taken place prior to the prescriptions presented in a **forest management** plan **2.** a preparatory cutting

advance regeneration seedlings or **saplings** that develop or are present in the understory —*synonym* advance growth, advance reproduction

advection the process of transport of an atmospheric property solely by the mass motion (velocity field) of the atmosphere

adventitious pertaining to a plant part that develops outside the usual order of time, position, or tissue —*note* e.g., an adventitious bud arises from any part of a stem, leaf, or root but lacks vascular connection with the pith; an adventitious root arises from parts of the plant other than a preexisting root, e.g., from a stem or leaf

adverse land use land use that is not in conformity with the planning or social requirements of the community

advocacy planning planners working directly with socioeconomically defined special interest groups to translate their aspirations for a living environment into formal planning goals and a set of procedures for attaining those goals

a.e. —*see* **acid equivalent**

aeciospore an asexual **spore** produced in an **aecium** in the **rust fungi** —*synonym* aecidiospore

aecium *plural* **aecia** a cuplike or blisterlike structure bearing **aeciospore**s in the **rust fungi** —*synonym*

aecidium, **cedar-apple rust, Gymnosporangium rust, primary host, white pine blister rust**

aerenchyma parenchyma tissue in leaves and in the **cortex** of roots containing large intercellular air spaces

aerial fuel —*see* **fuel type**

aerial ignition device (AID) —*see* **ignition tool**

aerial logging a **yard**ing system employing aerial means, e.g., helicopters or balloons, to lift logs

aerial photo coverage a set of **aerial photograph**s completely depicting a region, having stereoscopic overlap between exposures along the line of flight and sidelap between photographs on adjacent lines of flight

aerial photograph, oblique an aerial photograph taken with some angular deviation from the vertical —*note* a high oblique includes the apparent horizon of the earth; a low oblique does not show the horizon

aerial photograph, vertical an aerial photograph made with the optical axis of the camera approximately perpendicular to the earth's spheroid and with the film as nearly horizontal as practical

aerial reconnaissance *fire* the use of aircraft for observing **fire behavior, values at risk,** suppression activity, and other critical factors

aerial seeding the broadcast **seeding** of seeds, seed pellets, etc., from aircraft

aerial torch —*see* **ignition tool**

aerobic 1. occurring in the presence of free oxygen **2.** growing only in the presence of molecular oxygen, as aerobic organisms **3.** occurring only in the presence of molecular oxygen —*note* the term is used to describe certain chemical or biochemical processes, such as aerobic decomposition —*see* **anaerobic**

aerobiology the study of the distribution of living organisms, e.g., microorganisms and some insects, seeds, and spores freely suspended in the atmosphere, and some consequences of this distribution

aeroplankton the small living organisms, ranging from minute arthropods and seeds to microscopic fungal spores and bacteria, that are suspended in the atmosphere

aerosol a colloidal suspension in which the dispersed phase is either solid or liquid particles (less than 4μ diameter) and the dispersion medium is a gas, usually air

afforestation the establishment of a **forest** or **stand** in an area where the preceding vegetation or land use was not forest — *see* **deforestation, reforestation, regeneration, stand establishment**

afromontane forest —*see* **montane**

aftermath *range management* the plant residue or plant regrowth after a crop has been grazed or harvested —*note* includes **coppice** —*see* **stubble**

afterripening a biochemical or physical change occurring in seeds, bulbs, tubers, and fruits after harvesting when ripe, generally promoted by a combination of moisture, oxygen, and weak acids, with various temperature regimes —*note* afterripening is often necessary for seed germination —*see* **dormancy, stratification, vernalization**

age 1. the mean age of the trees constituting a **forest**, crop, or **stand** — *note* in practice, in even-aged forests, the mean age of **dominant** and sometimes also **codominant** trees is taken, and the age of a **plantation** is generally taken, from the year in which it was formed, i.e., exclusive of the age of the nursery stock then brought to it 2. of a tree, the time elapsed since germination of the seed or the budding of, e.g., the sprout or cutting from which it developed —*see* **effective age**

age class 1. one of the intervals into which the age range of trees is divided for classification or use 2. a distinct aggregation of trees originating from a single natural event or **regeneration** activity, or a grouping of trees, e.g., 10-year age class, as used in inventory or management —*see* **cohort, effective age**

age-class distribution the location or proportionate representation, or both, of different age classes in a **forest**

age-class period the number of years within the limits of a given age class

aggradation 1. the geologic process in which inorganic materials carried downstream are deposited in streambeds, floodplains, and other water bodies, resulting in a rise in elevation 2. one of four phases of forest biomass accumulation beginning soon (approximately five to 15 years) after a harvest and dependent on species —*see* **degradation**

aggregated retention —*see* **variable retention harvest system**

aggregate emphasis the combining of many land units or **stands** into a larger, contiguous area for development or forest (project) planning —*note* for each area, alternative management directions are evaluated by considering alternative mixes of land types and **prescriptions**

aggregation *soils* the process whereby primary soil particles (**sand, silt, clay**) are bound together, usually by natural forces and substances derived from root exudates and microbial activity

aging a physiological or morphological change in the life of an organism or its parts, generally irreversible and typically associated with a decline in growth and reproductive vigor —*see* **maturation**

agroforestry a land-use system that involves deliberate retention, introduction, or mixture of trees or other woody perennials in crop and animal production systems to take advantage of economic or ecological interactions among the components —*see* **agrosilviculture, agrosilvopastoralism, farm forestry, forestry, parkland system**

agrosilviculture a form of **agroforestry** consisting of tree (woody perennial) and crop components

agrosilvopastoralism a form of **agroforestry** consisting of tree (woody perennial), crop, and pasture and livestock components —*synonym* agrosilvopasture —*see* **silvopastoralism**

agrostology the study or the taxonomy of grasses —*note* agrostology may include the study of forage legumes for **livestock** nutrition

A horizon —*see* **horizon**

AHP —*see* **analytic hierarchy process**

A.I., AI 1. active ingredient 2. artificial intelligence

air attack the use of aircraft in **fire suppression** —*synonym* aerial attack —*see* **helitack**

air base the line joining two locations of the center of perspective of one camera, or the centers of perspective of a pair of cameras, at the moments of exposure

airborne GPS a method of computing an airborne platform position using a **global positioning system (GPS)**

airborne imaging spectrometer (AIS) an along-track pushbroom, multispectral scanner developed by the Jet Propulsion Laboratory with spatial **resolution** of 40 ft (12 m) at a flying altitude of 3.7 mi (6 km) used for geochemistry, mineral identification, mineralized zones, and geobotany

air coordinator (AIRCO) an experienced fire officer in a light, fixed-wing aircraft who serves as coordinator of **air attack** on a fire **incident**

air drainage the gravity-induced, downslope flow of relatively cold air —*note* winds produced by air drainage are called **gravity wind**s

air layering a procedure to induce root development on an undetached aerial portion of a plant —*note* air layering is commonly induced by wounding or girdling the undetached aerial portion of a plant, treating it with root stimulant, and wrapping it in moist material so that the treated portion grows roots and becomes capable of independent growth after separation from the mother plant —*see* **cutting, layering**

airshed a geographical area that shares the same air mass due to topography, meteorology, and climate

air tanker a fixed-wing aircraft fitted with tanks and equipment for releasing water or **fire retardant** —*synonym* fire bomber, water bomber

air temperature inversion the condition of the atmosphere when the environmental lapse rate is less negative than the (dry-) adiabatic lapse rate, resulting in an increase in air temperature with altitude, i.e., $\delta T/\delta z > -9.77°C/1,000$ m $(-5.4°F/1,000$ ft), where T is the air temperature and z is height —*note 1.* the term inversion commonly denotes a condition where $\delta T/\delta z > 0.0$ —*note 2.* the layer in which this condition occurs is called the inversion layer, and the lowest altitude at which the departure is found is called the base of the inversion

AIS —*see* **airborne imaging spectrometer**

alate winged; having wings

albedo the ratio of the amount of electromagnetic radiation reflected by a body to the amount incident on it, commonly expressed as a percentage

albic horizon —*see* **horizon, soil**

albinism a condition caused by **homozygosity** for a **recessive gene** resulting in the complete or nearly complete absence of pigment in part or all of a plant —*note* the affected parts are white or nearly so and the plant usually soon dies —*see* **chimera, lethal gene**

algorithm a step-by-step procedure for solving a mathematical problem —*note* the conversion of data from one map projection to another requires that the data be processed through an algorithm of precisely defined rules or mathematical equations

alidade a surveying instrument consisting essentially of a straight-edge rule with two vertical sights whose alignment is parallel with its edge —*see* **firefinder**

alignment chart —*see* **nomogram**

alkaline soil soil with a **pH** value > 7.0 —*see* **soil reaction**

alkaloid a complex alkaline organic compound found in many plants —*note* many alkaloids have powerful toxic or pharmacological actions

all-aged stand a **stand** with trees of all or almost all age classes, including those of exploitable age —*see* **stand, two-aged stand, uneven-aged stand**

allele an alternative form of a **gene** (at a given **locus**) differing in **DNA** sequence —*note* multiple alleles of a gene arise by repeated **mutations** in the gene's DNA sequence —*see* **epistasis, homologous chromosomes, hybrid, xenia**

allelopathy the inhibitory or stimulatory effects of released organic chemicals by one plant on the germination, growth, or metabolism of a different plant

alley cropping growing food, forage, or other crops between **hedgerows** or rows of planted shrubs or trees —*synonym* alley farming, avenue cropping, hedgerow intercropping

alliance *ecology* a physiognomically uniform group of community associations sharing one or more diagnostic (dominant, differential, indicator, or character) species which, as a rule, are found in the uppermost stratum of vegetation

allocation **1.** *fire* the process of distributing a resource through a **network** based on demand —*note* firefighters and equipment (the resources) need to be delivered to fires (the demand) by using roads (the network) **2.** *physiology* the process of distributing carbon to different plant tissues, e.g., roots, stem, or foliage **3.** *planning* committing a given area of land or resource to one or more specific uses —*note* allocation is necessary when there are limitations on either the amount of resources available or on the way in which they can be used, such that each separate activity cannot be performed in the most effective way **4.** *utilization* the process of accumulating a resource from a network based on capacity —*note* the resource (logs) needs to go to mills (having adequate capacity) by using roads (the network)

allochthonous pertaining to food organisms, organic matter, and nutrients originating outside and transported into a system —*note* the term usually refers to organic material of terrestrial origin transported into streams and lakes but can include material deposited by wind, carried by animals, etc. —*see* **autochthonous**

allochthonous flora organisms that are not indigenous to the soil but enter in precipitation, diseased tissues, manure, sewage, etc. —*note* these organisms may persist but do not notably contribute to ecologically significant transformations or interactions

allogenic originating external to a system —*see* **succession**

allomone a **semiochemical** emitted by one organism to another of a different species that incites a response favorable to the emitting organism —*see* **kairomone, pheromone**

allopatric pertaining to races or populations of the same or similar species that occupy separate, nonoverlapping geographic ranges or adjacent but different **habitats**, and that are genetically isolated from each other —*see* **sympatric**

allopolyploid a **polyploid** resulting from the union of different sets of **chromosomes** usually from different **species** —*see* **autopolyploid**

allowable burned area the maximum average area burned over a specified period of years that is considered an acceptable loss for a specified area under organized **fire suppression** —*synonym* acceptable burn

allowable cut the volume of timber that may be harvested during a given period (usually a year) that is specified by a **sustained-yield** forest plan —*synonym* **allowable sale quantity** (ASQ, a USDA Forest Service term) —*see* **allowable cut effect, allowable sale quantity**

allowable cut effect (ACE) the **allocation** of anticipated future timber **yields** to the present **allowable cut** —*note* the allowable cut effect is employed to increase current harvest levels (especially when constrained by **evenflow**) by spreading anticipated future growth over all the years in the rotation — *see* **allowable cut, allowable sale quantity**

allowable defect any blemish that does not exclude a piece of timber, lumber, or log from a specific grade —*note* allowable blemishes and imperfections are generally included in allowable defects

allowable sale quantity (ASQ) the quantity of timber that may be sold from an area covered by a **forest plan** during a time period specified by the plan —*note* the term is used by the USDA Forest Service and is usually expressed as the average annual allowable sale quantity —*synonym* **allowable cut** —*see* **allowable cut effect**

allowable use *range management* **1.** the degree of utilization considered desirable and attainable on various parts of a ranch or allotment considering the present nature and condition of the resource, management **objective**s, and levels of management **2.** the amount of forage planned to be used to accelerate **range** improvement —*see* **proper use factor**

all-terrain vehicle (ATV) a gasoline-powered, off-road vehicle used for accessing remote areas for recreational and work-related activities —*note* all-terrain vehicles generally have high clearance, high traction, high maneuverability, and low speed — *see* **off-road vehicle**

alluvial soil a soil developing from recently deposited water-borne sediments and exhibiting essentially no **horizon** development or modification of the recently deposited materials —*see* **soil order**

alluvium all sediment deposits resulting directly or indirectly from sediment transport within streams deposited in riverbeds, floodplains, lakes, fans, and estuaries

alpha diversity the variety of organisms occurring in a particular place or **habitat;** often called local diversity

alternate host one of two or more unlike **host** species without which a **heteroecious** insect or pathogen cannot complete its life history —*see* **alternative host**

alternative host one of two or more **host** species that may form the food base for a **parasite** but is not essential for the completion of the latter's life history —*see* **alternate host**

alternative rate of return the **opportunity cost** rate attached to the use of capital which guides a firm in its choice of investments —*note* those investments are rejected which, after due allowance for differences of **risk**, etc., promise a return of less than the alternative rate —*synonym* **time-preference rate,** guiding rate of return

alterne one of two or more plant communities that alternate with each other in space

ambrosia beetle a member of the family Scolytidae and all members of the family Platypodidae (both Coleoptera) whose small cylindrical adults make or initiate small round (1 to 3 mm, or 0.04 to 0.12 in) tunnels (appearing in cross-section as **shotholes** or pinholes) in green timber and living but generally unhealthy, damaged, or dying trees —*synonym* ambrosia borer, pinhole borer, **shothole** borer, keyhole borer —*see* **powderpost beetle, wood borer**

amensalism an interaction in which one organism or population adversely affects a second organism or population, but the second has no effect on the first

ament a structure of apetalous flowers, either **staminate** or **pistillate** —*see* **catkin**

American National Standards Institute (ANSI) an institute that specifies computer system standards —*note* the abbreviation is often used as an adjective to computer systems that conform to these standards

American Standard Code for Information Interchange (ASCII) a set of codes for representing alphanumeric information —*note 1.* a byte with a value of 77 represents a capital M —*note 2.* text files, such as those created with a computer system's text editor, are often referred to as ASCII files

AM/FM —*see* **automated mapping and facilities management**

ammonification the biological release of NH_3 from organic compounds during breakdown, often with the subsequent formation of NH_4^+ (ammonium ions)

amortization 1. *economics* the process of repaying a principal sum and interest on the unpaid balance in periodic installments over a predetermined period of time **2.** *accounting* writing off the value of an asset over a period of years, generally its expected working life

AMS —see **analysis of the management situation**

anabatic wind an upslope wind resulting from local surface heating as distinct from the effects of larger-scale circulation —*note* the most common type of anabatic wind is the **valley wind** —*antonym* **katabatic wind**

anadromous fish fish that are born and reared in freshwater, move to the ocean to grow and mature, and return to freshwater to reproduce, e.g., salmon, steelhead, shad

anaerobic 1. occurring in the absence of free oxygen —*see* **anoxic 2.** living in the absence of molecular oxygen **3.** growing in the absence of molecular oxygen (such as anaerobic bacteria) **4.** occurring in the absence of molecular oxygen (such as a biochemical process) —*see* **aerobic**

analog map any directly viewable printed map on which graphic symbols portray features and values—*note* most analog maps are printed on paper, but the medium can also be film, Mylar™, etc. —*see* **digital map**

analysis area a collection of land areas, not necessarily contiguous, sufficiently similar in character that they can be treated as if they were identical —*synonym* management unit, land type, **stand** type, analysis unit

analysis of covariance (ANCOVA) an extension of the **analysis of variance** procedure that statistically eliminates the effect of variables irrelevant to the question of interest (i.e., the test of the **null hypothesis**); specifically, this procedure applies to the case where the dependent variable (i.e., the variable being analyzed) is a function of one or more independent variables (covariates) that have not been controlled in the experimental design but have been observed on each experimental or sampling unit —*note* the analysis seeks to discover whether the variation of the dependent variable between classes is due to class effects or to its dependence on the other variates that themselves vary between classes; class effects are determined by adjusting values of the dependent variable to a common level of the covariates

analysis of the management situation (AMS) a document that summarizes information about resource conditions, uses, demands, and existing management activities and provides the baseline for subsequent steps in the planning process, such as the design of alternatives and affected environment

analysis of variance (ANOVA) a statistical procedure by which (a) total **variance** is separated into components attributable to defined sources (e.g., treatments, sites, families), and (b) mean square ratios are calculated and compared to determine the probability that differences among treatments or populations are too large to be due to chance —*see* **generalized linear models**

analysis unit —*see* **analysis area**

analytical watershed a drainage basin subdivision used in planning for analyzing **cumulative effects** on resources

analytic hierarchy process (AHP) an approach to multicriteria **decision making** based in part on pairwise comparisons for elements in a hierarchy

anchor point *fire* an advantageous location, generally a fire barrier, from which to start constructing a **fireline** —*note* an anchor point is used to minimize the chance of being outflanked by the fire while the line is being constructed

andic *soils* related to materials of volcanic origin

andr-, andro *prefix* male —*see* **gyn-, gyno-**

anemophily pollination by wind —*see* **entomophily, ornithophily**

aneroid barometer a portable instrument used in the field to determine differences in ground elevation —*note* this instrument registers the effect of atmospheric pressure on an evacuated, flexible capsule and not on a fluid column (e.g., mercury)

aneuploid having a **chromosome** number deviating from an exact multiple of the **haploid** number —*see* **chromosome number, polyploid**

Angiospermae the group of vascular flowering plants that produce seeds enclosed in an ovary —*note 1.* this botanical group includes hardwoods, bamboos, and palms but not softwoods —*note 2.* Angiospermae are divided into the Monocotyledonae and the Dicotyledonae —*synonym* angiosperm —*see* **Gymnospermae**

angle count method —*see* **cruise, point sampling, prism cruising, relaskop, three-P sampling**

angle of attachment the angle with which a limb attaches to the trunk of a tree —*note* in **urban forestry**, the preferred angle of attachment is U-shaped, wide, or > 45° to enable urban trees to better withstand ice loads in winter

animal damage the result of any kind of animal activity that reduces the growth or causes mortality of trees or forests —*note* in general, any effect of animal feeding deemed deleterious to some management **objective**(s)

animal month one month's tenure on a **range** by one animal —*note 1.* the kind and class of animal must be specified —*note 2.* animal month is not synonymous with **animal-unit month**

animal unit (AU) a measure of **livestock** concentration on a **range**; considered to be one mature cow of approximately 1,000 lb (453.6 kg), either dry or with a calf of six months of age or less, consuming about 26 lb (11.8 kg) of forage on an oven-dry basis —*note* animal unit may be used to describe other kinds and classes of grazing animals expressed as an equivalent —*see* **animal month, animal-unit conversion factor, animal-unit equivalent, animal-unit month**

animal-unit conversion factor a number expressing the forage requirements of a particular kind or class of animal relative to the requirement for an animal unit —*note* a conversion factor determines the amount of forage required to maintain an animal but may not be applicable in determining **stocking** rates for **range** use for particular kinds or classes of animals because of different grazing preferences

animal-unit equivalent (AUE) a number relating the forage dry matter intake (oven-dry basis) of a particular kind or class of animal relative to one **animal unit** —*note* if intake is not known, it can be estimated from the ratio of the metabolic rate of the animal to the metabolic rate of one animal unit (450 kg to the 0.75 power) —*see* **animal month, animal-unit conversion factor, animal-unit month**

animal-unit month (AUM) the amount of forage necessary for the sustenance of one cow or its equivalent for one month based on a forage allowance of 26 dry lb (11.8 kg) per day —*note 1.* animal-unit month is not synonymous with **animal month** —*note 2.* the term is commonly used in three ways: (a) stocking rate, as in X ac/AUM; (b) forage **allocations**, as in X AUMs in allotment A; (c) utilization, as in X AUMs taken from unit B —*see* **animal month, animal unit, animal-unit conversion factor**

anion exchange capacity the sum total of exchangeable anions that a soil can absorb

annosum root disease a root disease caused by the **white rot** fungus *Heterobasidion annosum* mostly on conifers, characterized by a light-yellowish stringy decay of the roots and butt, **thinning** crowns, and windthrow —*note* the fungus spreads from tree to tree by root contact; the disease tends to occur in patches of trees that enlarge progressively with **infection** centers often beginning in freshly cut stumps

annotation *GIS* descriptive text used to label geographic data

annual flood the highest peak discharge of a stream or river in a **water year** —*see* **flood**

annual ring —*see* **discontinuous ring, false ring, growth ring**

ANOVA —*see* **analysis of variance**

anoxic characterized by lack of oxygen —*see* **anaerobic**

ANSI —*see* **American National Standards Institute**

antagonism interference with, or inhibition of, the growth of a living organism by another living organism due either to creation of unfavorable conditions (e.g., exhaustion of food supplies) or to production of a specific antibiotic substance (e.g., penicillin) —*note* antagonism includes **allelopathy** —*antonym* synergism

antecedent precipitation index a weighted summation of daily **precipitation** amounts —*note* this index is used as an index of soil moisture

antecedent soil moisture the amount of water stored in soil on the day of a storm —*note* the amount is determined by the total rainfall accumulating during a specified time

antenna *plural* **antennae** a pair of segmented appendages on the head of all insects except the Protura —*note* the primary function of antennae is sensory (humidity, auditory, olfactory, tactile, thermal); the size and shape of antennae are commonly used as taxonomic characteristics in identifying insects

anther the part of the male **flower,** usually borne on a stalk (filament), that bears pollen

anthesis the period or stage of expansion of a **flower** —*note* anthesis often refers to the bursting of the pollen sacs with subsequent release of pollen —*see* **dehisce, receptivity**

anthracnose a type of disease characterized by numerous sharply defined necrotic **lesions** on leaves and twigs and the formation of acervuli

anthropic epipedon a surface layer of mineral soil that has the same requirements as the **mollic epipedon** with respect to color, thickness, organic carbon content, consistence, and **base saturation** but has > 110 mg P kg^{-1} soluble in 0.05 M citric acid, or is dry > 300 days (cumulative) during the period when not irrigated

anthropogenic of human origin or influence

antibiotic a metabolic product of one organism that has inhibitory or toxic effects on another organism —*note* the association between the two organisms is termed antibiosis or, in plants, **allelopathy**

apatite a naturally occurring complex of calcium phosphate that is the original source of most phosphate fertilizers

aphid a small (1 to 6 mm or 0.04 to 0.24 in), soft-bodied, often pear-shaped insect of the family Aphididae (Homoptera) that sucks sap from leaves, stems, or roots —*note* aphids excrete the processed sap as **honeydew** —*see* **gall adelgid**

aphytal lacking plants, e.g., the plantless zone of a lake bottom —*see* **hypolimnion, profundal**

apical dominance the upward growth of terminal shoot meristem(s) at the expense of lateral shoots below them whose development they inhibit —*note* differences in degree of apical dominance often determine differences in growth habit among plants

apical meristem a group of **meristem**atic cells at the apex of a shoot or root that gives rise to primary tissues through cell division followed by cell differentiation

apogamy a form of **apomixis** in which the reproductive function of the **gamete**s is taken over by unspecialized cells —*see* **apospory**

apomixis any form of asexual reproduction that tends to substitute for sexual regeneration —*see* **asexual reproduction, clone, ortet, parthenocarpy, parthenogenesis**

apoplast the network of connected dead cells and cell walls that acts as the framework holding the **symplast** in place —*note* the apoplast holds free and bound water

apospory a form of **apomixis** in which the reproductive function of the spores is taken over by unspecialized cells —*see* **apogamy**

apothecium *plural* **apothecia** an open, cup-, disk-, or saucer-shaped **ascocarp** in which the asci are borne —*see* **ascus**

apparent lignin —*see* **lignin**

application *GIS* a program or specially defined procedure, generally in addition to the standard set of basic software functions supplied by a **GIS** —*note 1.* an application is usually developed by the vendor or by a third party and purchased separately —*note 2.* developed to perform a series of steps, these applications may create specialized reports or complex map products, or lead an operator through a decision process —*note 3.* some of the more common applications are now becoming part of basic software functions

appraisal 1. *forestry* the determination by a competent authority of value, or the value so determined, of property or goods, e.g., **forest** land or **timber** –*see* **forest valuation** 2. *range management* —see **range appraisal**

apterous *entomology* wingless

aquic a mostly reducing soil moisture regime nearly free of dissolved oxygen due to saturation by groundwater or its capillary fringe and occurring at periods when the soil temperature at 50 cm (19.6 in) below the surface is > 5°C (41°F)

aquifer a saturated, permeable geologic unit of sediment or rock that can transmit significant quantities of water under ordinary hydraulic gradients

aquitard a subsurface rock unit, with relatively low permeability, that retards the flow of water

arbor the shaft on which a circular **saw** is mounted (including the bearings) —*synonym* saw mandrel, saw mandril, saw shaft, saw spindle

arboretum a place where primarily trees are grown for scientific and educational purposes

arboriculture the planting, care, and scientific cultivation of trees and woody vegetation in a nonforest context, usually in relation to orchards or for their ornamental or aesthetic values

arborist one who possesses the technical skills, through experience and related training, to care for individual trees and related woody plants in the residential, commercial, and public landscape —*note* some states have programs that license arborists or certify or require bonding of arborists

arbuscle a specialized extension of an intracellular **endomycorrhizal** fungal hyphae that increases the exchange surface for the transfer of resources from fungus to plant and vice versa

arc 1. a continuous portion of a mathematically defined curve 2. a string of x,y coordinate pairs (vertices) that begin at one location and end at another —*note* connecting the arc's vertices creates a line

arch *harvesting* a supporting device towed behind or mounted on a skidding vehicle —*note* an arch is used to lift one end of a log or logs to reduce sliding resistance or transfer the weight of the load to a skidding vehicle —*see* **skidder**

archegonium the flask-shaped female sex organ that contains the egg cell of most gymnosperms, liverworts, mosses, and ferns

arching skidding logs or trees using a mounted or trailing **arch**

architecture 1. *computers* the form in which a computer is seen by someone who understands its internal commands and instructions and the design of its interface hardware 2. *genetics—see* **genetic architecture** 3. *landscape* —*see* **landscape architecture** 4. *trees* the shape of the tree crown

archive *genetics* a preservation area for genetic conservation; an *ex situ* collection of **germplasm**

arc-node topology *GIS* the coordinate and topological data structure used by some software to represent linear features and polygon boundaries —*see* **topology, vector data**

ARD —*see* **automated resource data**

area *GIS* 1. a closed figure (**polygon**) that has a specific measurement in, e.g., square meters or hectares 2. a homogeneous area bounded by one or more **arc** features, e.g., states, counties, lakes, land-use areas, and census tracts

area command —*see* **incident command system**

area ignition —*see* **ignition pattern**

area kill the **hunter kill** per unit area in a given period

area of critical environmental concern (ACEC) land where special management attention is needed to protect and prevent irreparable damage to important historic, cultural, or scenic values, fish, and wildlife resources

area regulation —*see* **forest regulation**

argillic horizon —*see* **horizon**

aridic a soil moisture regime that has no water available for plants for more than half the cumulative time that the soil temperature at 50 cm (19.6 in) below the surface is > 5°C (41°F)

arithmetic mean the average value of a series or set of observations, obtained by dividing the algebraic sum of all observations in the set by the number of observations; often referred to as a measure of central location or central tendency —*note* the adjective "arithmetic" is frequently omitted —*see* **geometric mean, mode**

arithmetic(al) mean diameter —*see* **mean diameter**

Armillaria **root disease** a root disease caused by *Armillaria* species —*note 1.* in colonized trees, the fungus forms bioluminescent mycelial fans in the inner bark of stems and roots, reddish brown to black rhizomorphs (common name **shoestring root rot**), and honey-colored mushroom **sporocarps** (common names **honey fungus** and **honey mushroom**) —*note 2.* many species of *Armillaria* are **secondary pathogen**s, but some are serious **primary pathogen**s that can attack, colonize, and kill apparently healthy trees or predispose trees to **bark beetle** attack —*note 3.* stumps or dead trees serve as root disease (**infection**) centers that can expand to cover several hectares

army worm —*see* **cutworm**

artesian involving water that rises to the earth's surface under hydrostatic pressure from an aquifer that is confined between two impermeable strata

articulated hinged at the center for turning, e.g., a wheeled **skidder**

artificial intelligence (A.I.) the use of computers and program design to perform operations analogous to human abilities of learning and **decision making** —*note* artificial intelligence is used in the development of **expert system**s

artificial regeneration a **group** or **stand** of young trees created by direct **seeding** or by planting seedlings or cuttings —*synonym* artificial reproduction

ASCII —*see* **American Standard Code for Information Interchange**

ascocarp a structure in or on which asci are produced —*see* **apothecium, ascus**

ascospore a sexual **spore** produced by means of free-cell formation (nuclear fusion) in an **ascus**

ascus *plural* **asci** a saclike specialized hypha borne on **ascocarp**s containing **ascospore**s and produced in the **perfect stage** —*see* **apothecium**

asexual reproduction the process of reproduction without fertilization —*note* new individuals may develop from vegetative parts such as tubers, bulbs, or rooted stems, or from sexual parts such as unfertilized eggs or other cells in the ovule —*see* **apomixis, clone, parthenogenesis, propagule, vegetative propagation**

aspect 1. a position facing a particular direction —*note* aspect is usually expressed as a compass direction in degrees or cardinal directions **2.** *ecology* the seasonal appearance of a community, e.g., the spring aspect

ASQ —*see* **allowable sale quantity**

assembly *ecology* the smallest of plant or animal community units, e.g., aphid colonies on particular plants

assessment a procedure used by certifying organizations to determine whether forestry operations meet certification standards —*see* **certify**

assignment problem a **network analysis** problem that often involves the assignment of agents (e.g., logging trucks, helicopter landings, global positioning system receivers, people) to tasks —*note* an assignment problem can be formulated as a linear program and is a special case of the transportation problem —*see* **programming**

associated species a species found to be numerically more abundant in a particular forest successional stage or type compared with other areas

association *ecology* a plant community of some particular kind or grade —*note 1.* usage of the term varies greatly from one ecological school to another: (a) in most non-British schools, an association is the fundamental unit of plant ecology and is the equivalent of **species** in taxonomy, includes many local subassociations and facies (roughly equivalent to subspecies and varieties respectively in taxonomy), and defined mainly by floristic composition not by **habitat,** (b) in most of North America and Britain, the term follows Clements and refers to a major subdivision of formation restricted to (the presumed) **climax** communities —*note 2.* in both (a) and (b), an association may have several dominants, either mixed together or occurring in different places —*see* **society**

assortative mating the sexual recombination among individuals similar (positive) or dissimilar (negative) to each other

assortment table a type of volume table in which the figures for average cubic content are resolved into categories (assortments), mainly by size, in general relation to markets

assumption a judgmental decision used in planning to supply missing values, relationships, or societal preferences in order to proceed with the planning process toward a final decision

atmospheric pressure the pressure exerted by the atmosphere as a consequence of gravitational attraction exerted on the column of air lying directly above the point in question —*synonym* barometric pressure —*note* the most common unit of atmospheric pressure is the millibar (1 mb equals 1,000 dynes/cm^2)

attack time —*see* **elapsed time**

attenuation 1. *ecology* the reduction in light intensity though a forest canopy **2.** reduction in light intensity in water because of absorption by water molecules, suspended particles, and dissolved substances

at the base *timber* at ground level —*note* the term is used when specifying tree diameters in sales of standing timber, in contrast to the usual custom of measuring **at the stump** or at **breast height**

at the stump the level at which the stems are severed from the stump —*note* the term is used when specifying stem diameters in sales of standing timber —*see* **at the base, stump height**

attractant a substance that elicits a positive directive response, particularly a chemical having positive attraction for animals such as insects —*note* an attractant is usually effective in low concentration and at considerable distances —*see* **repellent**

attribute 1. a qualitative characteristic (variable) of an individual or group **2.** *GIS* a numeric, text, or image data field in a **relational database** table that describes a spatial feature such as a **point, line, node, area,** or **cell 3.** *GIS* a characteristic of a geographic feature described by numbers or characters, typically stored in tabular format and linked to the **feature** by an identifier, e.g., attributes of a well (represented by a point) might include depth, pump type, location, and gallons per minute **4.** a **column** in a database

attribute sampling sampling where the characteristics under consideration are **attribute**s —*synonym* sampling for attribute

ATV —*see* **all-terrain vehicle**

AU —*see* **animal unit**

AUE —*see* **animal-unit equivalent**

auguring standard *urban forestry* a tree protection rule that requires building contractors to tunnel or augur at a depth of 2.5 ft (0.76 m) under trees to avoid the damage to roots and other negative impacts on tree health caused by trenching

AUM —*see* **animal-unit month**

autecology 1. the ecology of an individual organism or taxonomic group **2.** the study of environmental factors and their effects on plants

autochthonous 1. pertaining to organic substances, materials, or organisms originating within a particular stream or river and remaining in that watercourse **2.** pertaining to rocks, mantle rock, peat, soils, or their constituents, formed at the site —*see* **allochthonous**

autocorrelation the internal correlation between members of a series of observations ordered in time or space

autoecious a type of life cycle in **rust fungi** in which all **stages** occur on one **host** —*see* **heteroecious**

autogenic originating from within a system —*see* **succession**

automated mapping and facilities management (AM/FM) a GIS technology focused on the specific segment of the market concerned with specialized infrastructure and geographic facility information applications and management, such as roads, pipes, and wires

automated resource data (ARD) computerized map data used for the management of resources

autopolyploid a **polyploid** resulting from the multiplication of a single set of **chromosome**s —*see* **allopolyploid**

autotrophic pertaining to organisms that manufacture their own energy (food) exclusively from inorganic substances or from sunlight, e.g., green plants and primary producers —*see* **heterotrophic**

auxin a natural organic compound formed in actively growing parts of plants, particularly in the growing points of shoots, which in minute concentrations regulates cell expansion and other developmental processes —*see* **plant-growth regulator**

available fuel that portion of the total wildland **fuel** that would actually be consumed under specified burning conditions

available nutrients the amount of soil nutrients in chemical forms accessible to plant roots or compounds likely to be convertible to such forms during the growing season

available water that portion of soil water which plants can extract, generally measured per unit of soil volume and usually estimated in freely draining soils as the amount of water between **field capacity** and the **permanent wilting point** —*synonym* available water capacity

average yarding distance the total **yard**ing distance for all **turn**s divided by total number of turns for a particular setting

AVHRR —*see* **advanced very high resolution radiometer**

axenic sterile, e.g., tissue culture cells that are free from contaminating organisms —*see* **tissue culture**

axil the angle formed between a plant stem and any organ developing from it, e.g., a leaf axil

axis *GIS* a reference line in a coordinate system

azimuth the horizontal angle of a point, measured clockwise from true (astronomic) north —*note* the azimuth plus 180° is termed the back azimuth —*see* **bearing**

azimuth circle a circle or protractor graduated in 360° in a clockwise direction from true (astronomic) north

azonal soil *obsolete* a soil without distinct **horizons** —*note* this term is not used in the current US system of soil taxonomy; azonal soils include Alluvial, Lithosol, and Regosol —*see* **soil order**

azygospore a **spore** that is morphologically like a **zygospore** but forms parthenogenetically

B

BA —*see* **basal area**

back-blading *engineering* the smoothing of earth or gravel or a road surface by using the back side of a bulldozer blade as the tractor moves in reverse

backcountry byway a road segment designated as part of the National Scenic Byway System

backcountry campsite a **campsite** in a relatively unmodified backcountry area, usually accessible only by foot, horse, or watercraft, providing accommodation for those engaged in backcountry experiences; may be within a designated backcountry **campground**

backcross to cross a **hybrid** to either one of its parental types —*note* backcrossing is particularly effective in transferring simply inherited characters from a donor parent to a deficient but otherwise valuable recurrent parent —*see* **cross-pollination, hybridization, introgression**

backcut the final cut in felling a tree, made on the opposite side of the direction of fall

backfiring —*see* **ignition pattern**

background luminance the brightness of the background against which a target is viewed

back guy *harvesting* one of several lines behind the **spar** opposite the **main line** or **skyline** that oppose most of the pull when **yard**ing logs

backing a change in wind direction in an anticlockwise sense (e.g., south to southeast to east) in either hemisphere of the earth —*antonym* **veering**

backing fire —*see* **fire behavior**

back-sawn —*see* **flat-sawn**

backup a computer process by which a copy of data or programs that are on hard drives is produced on other media, such as computer tapes —*note* the copy is then stored as insurance in case the computer disk drive fails or in case of operator error

bacterium *plural* **bacteria** a single-cell microorganism lacking chlorophyll, mitochondria, and a true nucleus that reproduces by fusion

badlands more or less barren, rough, broken land that is strongly dissected or gullied by streams —*note* badlands are most common in semiarid regions where streams have entrenched themselves in soft, erodible materials, e.g., clays, soft shales, limestones

bag *wildlife* the animals, particularly game birds, killed or captured, usually by hunting —*note 1.* the bag limit is the maximum, generally by species, that a hunter may legally take from an area in a specified period (e.g., daily, seasonally) —*synonym* permitted bag, permitted kill —*note 2.* for fish, the proper term is catch

bagworm a defoliator of numerous woody plant species whose **larvae** spin individual silk cases or bags —*note 1.* the bags generally incorporate fragments of leaves, twigs, and other vegetable matter in which the larval developmental period is passed —*note 2.* bagworms are seldom serious forest defoliators but are sometimes a **pest** on **plantation** or ornamental trees —*synonym* evergreen bagworm, casemoth

bait to provide food, food plants (bait crop), shelter, water, or other essentials to attract animals to an area to study or harvest them, to control their numbers, or to modify their normal routine —*note* a small block of wood, etc., having a hole bored in it for the bait, is termed a bait block —*see* **covert, food patch**

balance of payments *international trade* the difference (surplus or deficit) between one country's total payments to all other countries and its total receipts from them, as periodically assessed, constituting a sort of statement of income and expenditure on international account —*note* such a statement for imports and exports of goods is termed the balance of trade; because the value of services is commonly excluded from computations of the balance of trade, and because payments for services represent an increasing share of the transactions between countries, the balance of trade has become a less useful statistic for setting trade policy than in previous decades

ball planting setting out young trees after enclosing their roots in rough balls of earth

band 1. *entomology* to encircle a tree stem with a band of any material such as grease or pesticide that protects it against the passage of insects —*note* occasionally, bandings such as burlap bands are used to create shelters in which insects aggregate and are useful in estimating population density **2.** *GIS* a wavelength interval in the electromagnetic spectrum —*note* in **digital image**s, the bands designate specific wavelength intervals at which **images** are acquired, e.g., C band (6 cm) and L band (23 cm) **3.** *GIS* user-specified wavelength values derived by manipulation of original image bands —*note 1.* a standard color display of multispectral image has three bands, one each for red, green, and blue —*note 2.* satellite imagery such as Landsat™ and SPOT provide multispectral images of the earth, some containing seven or more bands **4.** *range management* any number of sheep handled as a unit attended by a herder —*see* **band day 5.** *wildlife* to mark wildlife for studying their movement and other behavior

band day tenure by a **band** of sheep of a given size and class for one day

band dendrometer a tensioned metal band encircling a tree stem, measuring increasing diameter or circumference (girth) with a gauge, vernier scale, or recording pen —*note* the continuous record is termed a dendrograph

band girdling —*see* **girdle**

band saw —*see* **saw**

bankfull discharge the rate of flow of a stream or river when flow is sufficient to fill the channel to the level of the floodplain —*see* **discharge**

bank storage the water absorbed by the bed and banks of a stream, reservoir, or channel and returned in whole or in part as the water level falls

bareroot(ed) seedling a seedling lifted from a nursery with its roots freed from the soil in which it had been grown —*see* **container seedling**

bark the outer layer of a tree stem outside the vascular cambium derived from cell division of the **phellogen** —*note 1.* the anatomical structure of bark is more complex than that of wood and has higher **lignin** and lower **cellulose** content —*note 2.* in older trees, bark is generally divisible into inner bark and outer bark and, in any growing season, into early bark consisting typically of sieve tubes with **companion cell**s or sieve cells (soft bark), and late bark consisting typically of **parenchyma** and a few small sieve cells (hard bark) —*see* **bark thickness, periderm**

bark allowance a measured, conventional, or statutory deduction generally as a percent of the outside bark volume of a stem —*note* with diameter of circumference (girth) measurements, the difference for bark thickness is generally termed a bark deduction, as between diameter outside bark (DOB) and diameter inside bark (DIB)

bark beetle a member of the family Scolytidae (Coleoptera), particularly species in the genera *Dendroctonus*, *Ips*, and *Scolytus* whose adults and **larvae** tunnel in the cambial region (either in the bark only or in the bark and xylem) of living, dying, and recently dead or felled trees —*note* bark beetles do immense damage to forests all over the world; some species are carriers of disease, e.g., Dutch elm disease; a few species attack roots, twigs, cones, and solid wood

bark gauge an instrument used to measure the thickness of bark

bark slip(ping) the separation of the bark from the wood at an active **cambium** layer

bark thickness a measure of the width of the bark at **DBH**, unless otherwise specified —*note 1.* it is measured from the inside of the cambium layer to the outside of the exterior bark —*note 2.* at least two measurements of bark thickness are usually taken to obtain an average reading

barrier 1. *fire* any obstruction to the spread of fire, typically an area or strip devoid of combustible material —*see* **control line, firebreak, fuelbreak, scratch line 2.** *wildlife* any physical, physiographic, or biological obstacle to **migration** or dispersal of animals

basal area (BA) 1. the cross-sectional area of a single stem, including the bark, measured at **breast height** (4.5 ft or 1.37 m above the ground) —*note* the international symbol for basal area is g **2.** the cross-sectional area of all stems of a species or all stems in a **stand** measured at breast height and expressed per unit of land area **3.** *range management* the cross sectional area of the stem or stems of a plant or of all plants in a stand —*note* herbaceous and small woody plants are measured at or near ground level, and larger woody plants are measured at breast or other designated height —*synonym* basal cover

basal area regulation —*see* **forest regulation**

basal spray the application of a pesticide, usually an herbicide for controlling brush or weed trees, directed at the base of the stem

basal till unconsolidated material deposited and compacted beneath a glacier and having a relatively high bulk density

base 1. *engineering* the layer of load-bearing material that distributes the weight of the traffic over the formation —*note* an underlying layer laid to prevent moisture invading the base from the formation is termed the sub-base —*synonym* base course, road base **2.** *timber* —*see* **at the base**

base flow 1. the typical flow rate for a given stream at a particular time of the year **2.** the contribution that **groundwater** flow makes in sustaining water yields in a watercourse during periods of no rainfall

base/height ratio the ratio of the length of an **air base** to the average altitude at which a stereoscopic pair of photographs was taken

base length the distance on an aerial photo between the **principal point** and the **conjugate principal point**

baseline 1. *management* the starting point for analysis of environmental consequences —*note* a baseline may be the conditions at a point in time (e.g., when inventory data are collected) or the average of a set of data collected over a specified period of years **2.** *surveying* a line used as a datum for further work —*note* a baseline can be a measured distance forming one of the sides of a triangulation survey

base map a map showing **planimetric,** topographic, geologic, political, or cadastral information that may appear in many different types of maps —*note*

1. the base map information is drawn with other types of changing thematic information —*see* **cadastre** —*note 2.* base map information may be as simple as major political boundaries, major hydrographic data, and major roads —*note 3.* the changing thematic information may be bus routes, population distribution, caribou **migration** routes, etc.

base population the set of plants from which selections will be taken to form advanced-generation breeding or production **population**s

base sale schedule a timber sale schedule formulated on the basis that the **quantity** of timber planned for sale and harvest for any future decade is equal to or greater than the planned sale and harvest for the preceding decade, and this planned sale and harvest for any decade is not greater than the long-term **sustained yield** capacity

base saturation the ratio of the quantity of exchangeable bases to the **cation exchange capacity,** often expressed as a percent —*note* the value of base saturation varies according to whether the cation exchange capacity includes only the salt-extractable acidity or the total acidity determined at pH 7 or 8 —*see* **soil reaction**

basicole a plant that lives on highly basic soils —*see* **basiphile, calcicole, calciphile**

basic slag a by-product in the manufacture of steel, containing lime, phosphorus, and small amounts of other plant nutrients such as sulfur, manganese, and iron

basidiocarp a fruiting body bearing or containing basidia in fungi —*see* **basidium**

basidiospore a sexual **spore** produced by means of hyphal fusion on the **primary host,** and subsequently infecting the **secondary host,** which is often a conifer

basidium *plural* **basidia** a club-shaped hyphal structure formed on the perfect fruiting body of a fungus on which the sexual **spores** (**basidiospore**s) are borne —*see* **promycelium**

basifuge a plant that tends to avoid highly basic soils —*see* **calcifuge**

basin *ecology* an area in which the margins dip toward a common center or depression, and toward which surface and subsurface channels drain

basin program a state administrative rule that establishes types and amounts of water uses allowed in the state's major river basins and that forms the basis for issuing water rights

basiphile a plant that tends to be restricted to basic soils —*see* **basicole, calcicole, calciphile**

basis the set of nonzero valued **decision variable**s in a mathematical **programming** solution and the values of the reduced costs and **dual prices** associated with that solution —*note* the variables that make up the basis are termed basic variables, and the remaining variables are called nonbasic variables

bast —*see* **cells (wood)**

batter *engineering* **1.** an inclined surface, e.g., earth bank or a retaining wall —*synonym* battering **2.** the slope of such a surface, expressed as a ratio of horizontal to vertical, e.g., 1/3 or one-in-three, or in degrees from the vertical

bayou **1.** a bay, inlet, backwater, river channel slough, oxbow lake, channel in coastal marshes and sluggish creeks, arm, outlet, or tributary of a lake, river, etc. **2.** any stagnant or sluggish creek, marshy lake, or the like

bearing *surveying* the acute angle that a line makes with the **meridian,** measured from the north-south line and never exceeding 90° —*note* bearings are expressed, e.g., as N5°E

bearing strength the amount of weight that a soil or subgrade can safely support

bearing tree a tree marked to identify the nearby location of a survey corner —*synonym* witness tree

beating up restocking failed areas in a stand by further plantings or sowings —*synonym* beating, blanking —*note* the term is not used in the United States —*see* **refilling**

Beaufort wind scale a system for estimating and reporting wind speeds —*note* the scale was invented in the early 19th century by Admiral Beaufort of the British Navy

bed **1.** *ecology* the bottom of a lake, pond, river, stream, or other body of water **2.** *harvesting* to raise mounds on the ground with a tractor along the line on which a large tree is to be felled, to minimize shattering of the log **3.** *agriculture* to prepare seedbeds for row crop culture **4.** *range, wildlife* an area where animals sleep and rest

bedding **1.** *silviculture* to raise mounds in potentially wet areas with a plow during site preparation on which seedlings are planted **2.** *soil engineering* to drain or irrigate the ground surface by constructing narrow-width plowlines in which the furrows run parallel to the prevailing land slope —*synonym* crowning, ridging **3.** *engineering* to lay a drain or conduit in a trench and tamp the earth around it **4.** *geology* the arrangement of sediment and sedimentary rock in layers or strata more than 1 cm (0.39 in) thick —*see* **bed**

bed-ground an area where animals sleep and rest

bed load **1.** the sediment that moves by sliding, rolling, or bounding on or very near the streambed **2.** the sediment moved mainly by tractive or gravi-

tational forces or both, but at velocities less than the surrounding flow

bedrock the solid rock that underlies the soil and other unconsolidated material that is exposed at the surface

bench **1.** a shelflike area with steeper slopes above and below **2.** *in the floodplain* a series of level areas remaining as a result of periodic deposition and **erosion**

benchmark tests various standard tests, easily duplicated, for assisting in measurement of product performance under typical conditions of use

benefit-cost ratio the ratio obtained by dividing the anticipated benefits of a project by its anticipated costs (or realized benefits by realized costs) to obtain a measure of expected (or realized) benefits per unit of cost —*note 1.* a benefit-cost ratio is usually based on discounted incomes and costs (or compounded incomes and costs) —*note 2.* a benefit-cost ratio should include all benefits and costs borne by society as well as the individual firm, but in practice this is rarely achieved, which can lead to investment and production levels that differ from true social equilibria —*see* **cost-benefit ratio, discounted cash flow**

benthic pertaining to the plant and animal life whose **habitat** is the bottom of a sea, lake, or river

benthos the plants and animals that inhabit the bottom substrate of a body of water

berm **1.** the outside or downhill side of a ditch or trench **2.** the shoulder of a road **3.** a natural or constructed levee, shelf, ledge, groyne, or bench along a stream bank that may extend laterally into the channel to partially obstruct the flow, or parallel to the flow to contain the flow within its stream banks **4.** *fire* a ridge of soil and debris along the edge of a **fireline** resulting from line construction —*note* a berm is often created on the downhill side to stop burning or potentially burning material from rolling

best management practice(s) (BMP) a practice or usually a combination of practices that are determined by a state or a designated planning agency to be the most effective and practicable means (including technological, economic, and institutional considerations) of controlling point and nonpoint source pollutants at levels compatible with environmental quality **goal**s —*note* BMPs were conceptualized in the 1972 US Federal Water Pollution Control Act —*see* **pollution**

beta-diversity **1.** the diversity between or among more than one community or along an environmental gradient **2.** the variety of organisms within a region arising from turnover of species among **habitat**s

better face *lumber grading* the surface (**face**) containing the lesser amount of defective material, not necessarily fewer defects —*note 1.* lumber is generally graded on this face —*note 2.* a **cant** with four faces has a best face —*note 3.* hardwood lumber is commonly graded on the **worse face**

B horizon —*see* **horizon**

bias the difference between the expected value of a sample **statistic** known as an estimator and the **population** parameter, or the true population value that the statistic is intended to estimate —*note* bias implies systematic distortion, as distinct from random error, which balances out on average; a sampling process involving such a distortion is said to be biased

Biltmore stick a graduated rule used to estimate tree diameters by holding it at right angles to the axis of the stem and comparing the graduations cut by lines of sight tangential to either edge of the stem —*note* the graduations assume observations at a specified distance of the stick from the eye

binary large object (BLOB) the data type of a column in a **relational database management system (RDBMS)** table that can store large images or text files as attributes

binary search a one-dimensional **heuristic** search technique based on splitting the search region into two parts —*note* when a binary search is applied to harvest scheduling, there are only one **decision variable** per period (the amount of harvest) and two choices: to increase or decrease harvest

bind *of a saw* to become stuck as the sides of the cut pinch together —*note* wedges are used to alleviate the situation

binder a tensioning device used to tighten chain or **wire rope** (wrapper) in securing logs on a truck

binding constraint a **constraint** that limits the **objective function** value in a **mathematical programming** problem —*note* these constraints can be identified in the solution as having nonzero **dual prices** and no **slack;** if relaxed (by changing the right-hand-side values), the objective function value could be improved

binomial distribution a discrete probability dispersion which, when a chance event has only two possible outcomes (i.e., a dichotomous or binary response, often termed success and failure), each with fixed probabilities of occurring, gives the probabilities of the number of successes in a given number of independent trials of the event

bioc(o)enology the study of communities of living organisms, i.e., of **biocoenoses**

bioc(o)enose any community of plants and animals —*note 1.* Sukachev's biogeoc(o)enose implies that locality factors are to be included as an inseparable

part of the community concept, the whole forming an **ecosystem** —*note 2.* a phytocoenose = phyocoenosis —*note 3.* this term is used mainly by Central and Eastern European ecologists

biochemical oxygen demand (BOD) **1.** the amount of dissolved oxygen removed from water by aquatic microorganisms in the process of biological decomposition of organic matter —*note* BOD_5 is a standard value, measured in mg/l, indicating the amount of oxygen utilized by microorganisms in a five-day period when incubated at a temperature of 20°C (68°F) **2.** the amount of molecular oxygen required to stabilize decomposable matter by aerobic biochemical action —*synonym* biological oxygen demand

biodiversity **1.** the variety and abundance of life forms, processes, functions, and structures of plants, animals, and other living organisms, including the relative complexity of **species,** communities, gene pools, and **ecosystems** at spatial scales that range from local through regional to global —*synonym* biological diversity, diversity **2.** an index of richness in a community, ecosystem, or landscape and the relative **abundance** of these species —*note 1.* there are commonly five levels of biodiversity: (a) genetic diversity, referring to the genetic variation within a species; (b) species diversity, referring to the variety of species in an area; (c) **community** or **ecosystem** diversity, referring to the variety of communities or ecosystems in an area; (d) landscape diversity, referring to the variety of ecosystems across a landscape; and (e) regional diversity, referring to the variety of species, communities, ecosystems, or landscapes within a specific geographic region —*note 2.* each level of biodiversity has three components: (a) compositional diversity or the number of parts or elements within a system, indicated by such measures as the number of species, genes, communities, or ecosystems; (b) structural diversity or the variety of patterns or organizations within a system, such as **habitat** structure, population structure, or species morphology; and (c) functional diversity or the number of ecological processes within a system, such as disturbance regimes, roles played by species within a community, and nutrient cycling within a **forest**

biogenic resulting from activity of living organisms; necessary for continuation of life processes

biological control **1.** the artificial application of a natural control agent to regulate **pest** species —*note* the **objective** of biological control is to conserve or augment the natural or exotic enemy complex (**predators, parasites,** and disease) of the pest **species** by introducing **pheromones, hormones,** sterilization techniques, genetic manipulations, or plant resistance, as opposed to **chemical control** **2.** interference in the pest's environmental status through management of the physical or biotic environment associated with the pest organism or population to reduce disease —*synonym* biocontrol, cultural control

biological corridor —*see* **corridor**

biological diversity —*see* **biodiversity**

biological diversity values the intrinsic, ecological, genetic, social, economic, scientific, educational, cultural, recreational, and aesthetic values of biological diversity and its components —*see* **biodiversity**

biological growth potential the average net growth attainable in a fully stocked, natural forest **stand**

biological index a measure of **ecosystem** health or condition using biological or physical characteristics —*see* **diversity index, index of biotic integrity**

biological legacy an organism, a reproductive portion of an organism, or a biologically derived structure or pattern inherited from a previous **ecosystem** —*note* biological legacies often include large trees, **snags,** and down logs left after harvesting to provide refugia and to structurally enrich the new stand —*see* **forest management, legacy tree, regeneration method, sustainable forest management, variable retention harvest system**

biological opinion —*see* **jeopardy biological opinion**

biological oxygen demand (BOD) —*see* **biochemical oxygen demand**

biomagnification the increasing concentration of a compound in the tissues of organisms as the compound is transferred from lower to higher **trophic levels** through consumption

biomass 1. *ecology* the total dry organic matter at a given time of living organisms of one or more species per unit area (species biomass) or of all the species in the **community** (community biomass) **2.** the living or dead weight of organic matter in a tree, **stand,** or **forest** in units such as living or dead weight, wet or dry weight, ash-free weight, etc. **3.** *harvesting* the wood product obtained (usually) from in-woods chipping of all or some portion of trees including limbs, tops, and unmerchantable stems, usually for energy production

biomass tree a rapidly growing tree having a form that may not be suitable for timber production, but having wood that provides fiber for biomass or composite products

biome a regional **ecosystem** with a distinct assemblage of vegetation, animals, microbes, and physical environment often reflecting a certain climate and soil

biosphere 1. the portion of the earth comprising the lower atmosphere, the seas, and the land surface (mantle rock) in which living organisms exist **2.** the part (reservoir) of the global carbon cycle that includes living organisms (plants and animals) and life-derived organic matter (litter, detritus) —*note* the terrestrial biosphere includes the living **biota** (plants and animals) and the litter and soil organic matter on land; the marine biosphere includes the biota and detritus in the oceans

biosystematics taxonomic studies involving morphology, cytogenetics, ecology, and phytogeography

biota the animal and plant life (fauna and flora) of a given area

biotic pertaining to living organisms and their ecological and physiological relations

biotic climax a community maintained by biotic factors and therefore differing from any other **climax** community —*note* such a community maintained by humans or livestock is termed disclimax —*synonym* plagioclimax

biotic factor any environmental influence of living organisms, e.g., shading by trees, trampling by heavy animals, burning by humans, in contrast to inanimate, i.e., abiotic, particularly climatic and **edaphic** influences —*note* the influence of humans alone is termed **anthropogenic**

biotic pesticide a pathogenic microorganism that is applied in the same manner as conventional pesticides to control **pest** (usually insect) species

biotic potential the unrestricted growth rate of a species under ideal conditions —*note 1.* biotic potential depends on the number of live, fertile offspring produced at each reproduction, the frequency of reproduction, and the sex ratio —*synonym* reproductive potential, (gross) reproductive capacity, biological potential, (gross) biological capacity —*note 2.* biotic potential is the difference between the rate at which new individuals are being born per individual and the rate at which previously existing individuals are dying per individual —*note 3.* under optimal conditions population growth is typically exponential —*synonym* intrinsic rate of increase, reproductive potential, (gross) reproductive capacity, biological potential, (gross) biological capacity

biotype a group of individuals sharing similar biological attributes, e.g., susceptibility to a particular pathogen

bird's-eye the figure produced on **flat-sawn** and rotary-cut (**peel**ed) surfaces of boards by small conical depressions of the **fiber**s characterized by numerous rounded areas of the grain resembling small eyes —*note* bird's-eye grain is common in *Acer saccharum* —*see* **fiddleback**

bisect a diagram showing whole plants, i.e., roots and shoots, in one or more vertical profiles —*see* **vegetation profile**

bisexual having functional male and female reproductive organs in the same flower or on the same individual; hermaphroditic —*see* **dioecious, emasculation, monoecious**

bit *remote sensing, computers* **1.** contraction of binary digit, which in digital computing represents an exponent of the base 2 **2.** the smallest unit of information that can be stored and processed in a computer —*note* a bit has two possible values, 0 or 1, which can be interpreted as YES/NO, TRUE/FALSE, or ON/OFF —*see* **byte**

Bitterlich method —*see* **point sampling, relaskop, three-P sampling**

bivoltine a **life cycle** in which two generations or **brood**s are produced in a single year —*see* **multivoltine, univoltine**

black-body radiation the electromagnetic radiation emitted by an ideal black body —*note* the theoretical maximum amount of radiant energy of all wavelengths that can be emitted by a body at a given temperature —*see* **Stefan-Boltzmann law**

black line a line formed by preburning wildland **fuel**s, either adjacent to a control line before igniting a **prescribed fire** or along a roadway or boundary, as a deterrent to human-caused fires —*note 1.* a backline is usually made in **heavy fuel**s adjacent to a control line during periods of low **fire danger** to reduce pressure on holding forces —*note 2.* a backline denotes a condition in which there is no unburned fine fuel remaining —*see* **fireline**

blaze a mark on a tree, usually made by painting or cutting the bark —*note* blazes are frequently used to mark the boundaries of forest properties, borders of timber management units, or locations of trails

bleeding —*see* **resinosis**

blight a disease or disease symptom characterized by rapid discoloration, **wilt,** and death of all parts of a plant

blind a place of concealment, rarely completely natural, from which wildlife can be hunted or studied at close **range** without disturbance —*synonym* hide —*see* **stand**

blind area **1.** *fire* the ground or vegetation growing thereon that is not visible to a **lookout** and that either lies below the line of sight or is hidden by cloud, haze, or smoke —*see* **seen area** **2.** *logging* that portion of a harvest area that is inaccessible to cable yarding due to horizontal alignment of the harvest area boundary or vertical alignment of the slope in relation to the yarding location or elevation

blind conk an overgrown, protruding swelling on a tree stem where a **conk** dropped off or was aborted

blister a **vesicle** formed in bark or leaves by a separation and raising of the surface layers —*note* sometimes caused by insect or fungal attack

blister rust a disease caused by **rust fungi** and characterized by the formation of **blister**s —*note* an example is the white pine blister rust, *Cronartium ribicola* —*see* **comandra blister rust**

BLOB —*see* **binary large object**

block **1.** *biometrics* a set of experimental units that have been grouped to minimize initial differences with respect to the variable(s) being studied, e.g., a set of contiguous experimental plots **2.** *harvesting* a metal case enclosing one or more sheaves—*synonym* pulley —*note* a block is used in **wire rope** logging to change the direction of the rope or to increase pulling power —*see* **setting**

blowdown tree or trees felled or broken off by wind —*synonym* windfall, windthrow

blowout a hollow or depression of the land surface, generally saucer or trough shaped, formed by wind **erosion** especially in an area of shifting sand or loose soil, or where vegetation is disturbed or destroyed

blowup —*see* **fire behavior**

blue stain a discoloration in the sapwood of pine due to fungal infection —*note* blue **stain** commonly results in visual defect, but boards or plywood made from wood with blue stain can also be used to provide an interesting interior finish

BMP —*see* **best management practice**

board foot (bd ft, bf) the amount of wood contained in an unfinished board 1 in thick, 12 in long, and 12 in wide ($2.54 \times 30.5 \times 30.5$ cm), abbreviated bd ft —*note* in trees or logs, board-foot volume is a measure of merchantability, and therefore the number of board feet in a cubic foot depends on tree diameter, amount of slab, and saw **kerf;** commonly, 1,000 bd ft is written as 1 MBF and 1,000,000 BF is written as 1 MMBF —*see* **board rule, board-foot:cubic-foot ratio**

board-foot:cubic-foot ratio the number of board feet per cubic foot, nominally 12 —*note* because of the varying proportion of **kerf** and **slab** relative to tree or log diameter, the number commonly varies from about 4 to 8 for 10- to 35-in-diameter stems —*see* **board foot**

board-foot log scale the volume of a log measured in board feet as determined by a board foot **log rule** —*synonym* log-scale board foot

board-foot measure a method of timber measurement in which the unit is the board foot —*note* is commonly used as MBF for 1,000 bd ft

board rule a flat stick on which are engraved board-foot volumes corresponding to length, width, and thickness of sawn or hewn timber so that, with the stick placed on the width dimension of a piece, its board-foot content can be read directly from the figures corresponding to its length and thickness —*synonym* scaling stick, log scaling rule, and lumber scaling rule

BOD —*see* **biochemical (biological) oxygen demand**

bog a wet, poorly drained, highly acid, nutrient-poor, peat-accumulating **wetland** with surface vegetation of acidophilic mosses (particularly *Sphagnum*) and possibly some **shrubs** or **trees** —*see* **marsh, swamp**

bole a trunk or main stem of a tree —*note* seedlings and **saplings** have stems rather than boles

bole area the total stem surface area of a tree or **stand** —*note* tree bole area is computed as the product of some measure of girth and height of the tree (or length of stem); equal to cambial area if girth is inside bark

bole length the merchantable length of the stem of a tree between the top of the stump and the merchantable top

bolt a short piece of pulpwood; a short log

bone-dry ton wood pulp or residue that weighs 2,000 lb (907 kg) at 0 percent moisture content —*synonym* oven-dry ton

bone-dry unit the amount of wood residue that weighs 2,400 lb (1,088 kg) at 0 percent moisture content

Boolean expression a type of statement based on or reducible to a true or false condition —*note 1.* a Boolean operator is a key word that specifies how to combine simple logical expressions into complex expressions; Boolean operators negate a predicate (NOT), specify a combination of predicates (AND), or specify a list of alternative predicates (OR), e.g., the use of AND in the expression DEPTH > 100 AND GPM > 500 —*note 2.* other Boolean operators are available, such as XOR, CAND, COR, and CXOR —*note 3.* loosely, but erroneously, a logical expression such as DEPTH greater than 100

Boolean search a specialized form of searching databases using criteria specified as **Boolean expression**s

bordered pit —*see* **pit**

boreal pertaining to northern latitudes

boreal forest the northern hemisphere, circumpolar, tundra forest type consisting primarily of black spruce and white spruce with balsam fir, birch, and aspen —*note* the boreal forest is the most extensive forest type in the world —*see* **boreal, taiga, tundra**

borer —*see* **bark beetle, wood borer**

botanical pesticide a **pesticide** in which the active ingredient is either a naturally occurring plant chemical or a product thereof, e.g., pyrethrum and nicotine

boundary layer any layer of fluid in the immediate vicinity of a bounding surface, such as the laminar, turbulent, planetary, or surface boundary layer

bound moisture moisture that is intimately associated (not freely available for movement) with the cell wall by molecular sorption

bounty system the legal provision for a fee to be paid on presenting satisfactory proof of destruction of an individual or species declared undesirable, i.e., vermin

Bowen ratio at a water surface, the ratio of the energy flux upward as sensible heat to the energy flux used in evaporation —*note* the Bowen ratio is highly variable and sometimes negative

bow saw —*see* **saw**

bract a modified or much reduced leaf in a **flower** cluster

branch 1. a secondary division of a **tree** or **shrub** trunk —*synonym* limb —see **burl, knot** 2. *computers* any point in a program at which the logic(al) flow is directed according to a logic(al) decision 3. *fire* —*see* **incident command system**

branch-and-bound a solution procedure for integer linear programs that sequentially partitions the set of **feasible solutions** into smaller and smaller subsets until the **optimal solution** is found

branch director —*see* **incident command system**

brand 1. *range management* to mark the skin or wool of an animal in a distinctive pattern by use of a hot or cold iron, chemical, paint, or other means to designate ownership or to identify individual animals for registration or management purposes —*synonym* **mark, tag** 2. *logging* to make a physical impression on the end of a log to identify its owner —*see* **branding hammer** 3. the mark so made

branding hammer a light hammer having a die for stamping letters, figures, or distinctive devices, i.e., marks, on trees and timber —*synonym* marking hammer —*see* **brand**

brashing the removal of live or dead branches (usually with a club) on a tree stem from ground level to as high as a worker can reach (7 to 8 ft or 2.0 to 2.5 m) in a young **stand** —*see* **pruning**

breaking-down saw —*see* **saw**

breakline *GIS* a line that defines and controls the surface behavior of a triangulated irregular network (**TIN**) in terms of smoothness and continuity —*note* physical examples are ridge lines, streams, and lake shorelines

breakover a **fire edge** that crosses a **control line,** or the resultant fire —*synonym* slopover

breast height a standard height from ground level, generally 4.5 ft (1.37 m), for recording diameter, circumference (girth), or **basal area** of a tree —*note 1.* the measurement is usually taken on the uphill side of the tree and includes any duff layer that may be present, but does not include unincorporated woody debris that may rise above the ground line —*note 2.* in Europe, breast height is 4.25 ft (1.30 m) above the ground —*see* **diameter at breast height (DBH)**

breast-high age the number of rings from the pith to the cambium counted at **breast height** —*note* the number is often used in estimating **site index** in order to avoid the indefinite time taken for a tree to reach breast height —*see* **tree age**

breccia a coarse-grained, clastic rock composed of angular fragments (> 2 mm or 0.08 in) bonded by a mineral cement or in a finer-grained matrix of varying composition and origin

breeding the science or art of changing the genetic constitution of a population of plants or animals through sexual reproduction

breeding arboretum (breeding orchard) a collection of selected trees or **species** established for breeding —*note 1.* if the collection is preserved vegetatively, it is sometimes known as a clone bank —*note 2.* spacing, culture, and protection are normally designed to stimulate early and prolific flowering —*see* **arboretum, forest tree breeding, seed orchard**

breeding group —*see* **multiline**

breeding herd the animals retained for breeding purposes to provide for the perpetuation of the herd or band excluding those being prepared for market

breeding population a group of selected parents that are intercrossed to form a **population** for the next cycle of selection

breeding potential the inherent ability of an organism to multiply under natural conditions —*synonym* reproductive potential —*see* **biotic potential, breeding rate, recruitment**

breeding rate the number of live offspring produced by an organism in any given period, generally at some specified stage of its life, under natural conditions —*note* breeding rate is a particular expression of **breeding potential**

breeding value the **narrow-sense heritable** departure of a parent's **progeny test** value from the average of its population (either for one **trait,** or for an index of traits) —*note* breeding value equates to two times the individual's **general combining ability** —*see* **heritability**

broadcast to spread or apply seed, fertilizer, or pesticides more or less evenly over a entire area

broadcast burn a **prescribed fire** allowed to burn over a designated area within well-defined boundaries to achieve some land management **objective**

broad-crested weir an overflow structure for measuring water, often rectangular in cross section, in which the water adheres to the surface of the crest rather than springing clear

broadleaf —*see* **deciduous, hardwood**

broad-sense heritability the ratio of total genetic **variance** to phenotypic variance —*note* broad-sense **heritability** provides an estimate of the degree of genetic control of a **trait** in a **population** and is useful for predicting response to clonal selection —*see* **narrow-sense heritability, phenotype**

broad-spectrum pesticide a nonselective **pesticide** (usually an **insecticide**) that is toxic to many **species** —*see* **narrow-spectrum pesticide**

brood **1.** progeny of the same male or female produced within a certain period **2.** individuals that hatch at about the same time and normally mature at about the same time

brood tree a tree whose wood or bark contains large breeding populations of insects —*note* the term is usually used with respect to **bark beetle** infestations —*see* **trap tree**

brow log a large log laid beside the track or road at a log dump or landing to prevent logs from swinging or kicking back against the railroad cars or logging trucks

brown root rot a root decay caused by the fungus *Phellinus noxius* —*note* brown root rot is a serious problem in forests of Africa, Asia, and Australia

brown rot any decay or rot in wood attacking **cellulose** but not **lignin** —*note* brown rot fungi produce a brown color in wood due to the oxidation of lignin, and a crumbly texture caused by the loss of cellulose; some root decay fungi cause brown rot, but most cause **white rot**

browse **1.** any woody vegetation consumed, or fit for consumption, by livestock or wild animals, mainly ungulates **2.** to forage or graze on the buds, stems, and leaves of woody growth by **livestock** or wildlife —*see* **grazing, range plant, utilization cut**

browse line the height in woody vegetation below which foliage and small twigs have been or would be more or less completely consumed by livestock or wild animals, mainly ungulates —*synonym* browsing level, grazing line, high line —*see* **over-browsing**

browsing preference selection of woody plants, or plant parts, over others by browsing animals —*see* **grazing preference**

brush shrubby vegetation that does not produce commercial timber —*see* **bush, shrub**

brush fire a fire in which the predominant fuel is brush —*see* **forest fire, grass fire**

brush hook —*see* **hand tool**

bryophyte a type of nonvascular plant including mosses, liverworts, and hornworts

buck to saw felled trees into shorter lengths

bucker one who saws (**buck**s) felled trees into required lengths such as logs or **bolt**s —*synonym* **sawyer** —*see* **slasher**

bud 1. a dormancy structure in shoots consisting of external protective scales (cataphylls) and an internal embryonic shoot possessing an apical meristem and leaf primordia in various stages of development 2. to slip a **scion** bud and adjacent cambial tissue under the bark of a **rootstock** plant —*see* **graft**

budbreak the opening of **bud**s and appearance of leaves or needles

bud pruning the removal of lateral buds from a stem to prevent their developing into branches —*note* also called finger budding, disbudding, or debudding —*see* **pruning**

budset the formation of visible buds accompanied by cessation of stem elongation

budworm a **larva** of the family Tortricidae (Lepidoptera) that feeds on and in buds and young shoots —*note* budworms are important forest defoliators that can cause extensive damage, e.g., spruce budworm *(Choristoneura fumiferana),* western spruce budworm *(C. occidentalis),* jack pine budworm *(C. pinus),* black-headed budworm *(Acleris variana),* and large aspen tortrix *(C. conflictana)*

buffer 1. a vegetation strip or management zone of varying size, shape, and character maintained along a stream, lake, road, recreation site, or different vegetative zone to mitigate the impacts of actions on adjacent lands, to enhance aesthetic values, or as a **best management practice** —*synonym* buffer strip, buffer zone, roadside zone, roadside strip, waterfront zone —*see* **riparian zone** 2. *GIS* a zone of a specified distance around features —*note 1.* both constant- and variable-width buffers

can be generated for a set of features based on each feature's attribute values; the resulting buffer zones form **polygon**s that are areas either inside or outside the specified buffer distance from each feature —*note 2.* buffers are useful for proximity analysis, e.g., to find all stream segments within 300 ft (91.4 m) of a proposed logging area 3. an area maintained around an **experimental** or **sample plot** to ensure that the latter is not affected by any treatment applied to the area outside them both —*synonym* isolation strip 4. *wildlife management* habitat that reduces dangers of having sharply contrasting edges of a harvest area next to protected habitat 5. *wildlife management* an animal species that reduces or neutralizes the incidence of predation on another species —*see* **predator** 6. an area of intergradation between two **sympatric** species 7. an area uninhabited by a particular species or related species but likely to be inhabited

buffer power the ability of solid phase soil materials to resist changes in ion concentration in the solution phase, often expressed as $\partial C_s/\partial C_l$ where C_s represents the concentration of ions on the solid phase in equilibrium with C_l, the concentration of ions in the solution phase —*note* buffer power includes **pH** buffering as well as the buffering of other ionic and molecular components —*see* **soil reaction**

building pole a small-diameter **pole** used for the construction of traditional huts and fencing —*note* in some developing countries building poles are the second most important wood product, after fuelwood

buildup *fire* 1. the **cumulative effects** of long-term drying on current **fire danger** 2. the increase in strength of a **fire management** organization 3. the accelerated spreading intensity of a fire with time

bulk density the weight per unit of volume of a material —*note 1.* bulk density of plants is measured at a specified moisture tension —*note 2.* bulk density includes both solid material and pore space and, in wood, generally serves as an indicator of the specific gravity —*see* **porosity**

bull block *harvesting* the main **block** on the spar of the yarder in high-lead logging

bullbuck the supervisor of a number of felling and bucking crews (**set**s)

bulldozer —*see* **tractor**

bulldozer company *fire* any bulldozer operated by at least two persons —*note* bulldozer company is an **ICS** term

bumpup method —*see* **fire suppression**

bunch *harvesting* to gather trees or logs into small piles for subsequent extraction —*synonym* prebunch —*see* **feller-buncher**

bunch grass a grass having the characteristic growth habit of forming a bunch or tussock —*note* bunch grasses lack stolons or rhizomes —*see* **sod grass, stem grass**

bundled *computer software* sold integrated with hardware —*note* in the early days of computers, software products were bundled; today, computer hardware and software are usually sold **unbundled**

bunk a cross beam on which logs rest in a trailer or on a truck

burl an irregular, commonly round growth on a tree **stem** or **branch** resulting from the entwined growth of a cluster of adventitious buds and having contorted grain

burning index (BI) a relative number indicating the contribution that **fire behavior** makes to the amount of effort needed to contain a fire in a specified fuel type —*note* doubling the burning index indicates twice the effort will be required to **contain a fire** in that fuel type as was previously required providing all other parameters are constant

burning period that part of each 24-hour period when fires spread most rapidly, typically from 10 AM to sundown —*synonym* critical burning period

burn out to set out a suppression fire to widen **control line**s during line construction or eliminate unburned **wildland** fuels inside the control lines after **containment** —*synonym* clean burn, fire out

bush all types of forests or **woodland**s, with particular reference to untended, indigenous forest —*see* **brush**

bush fallow an area of secondary woody growth in tropical or subtropical **forests**, developed between periods of field cropping

butt **1.** the base of a tree **2.** the large end of a log

butte a conspicuous, generally craggy and precipitous, isolated hill-mass —*note* a flat-topped butte is termed a mesa, i.e., a miniature tableland

butt log the first log cut above the stump

buttress a ridge of wood developed in the angle between a lateral root and the **butt** of a tree, which may extend up to a considerable height —*note 1.* buttresses are particularly common and well developed in certain tropical rainforest species —*note 2.* a plank buttress is a buttress in which the ridge develops as a relatively thin plate

butt rigging *harvesting* a system of swivels, shackles, and hooks that permits both the hookup between the main and haulback lines and the attachment of **chokers**

butt rot any decay or rot developing in, and sometimes characteristically confined to, the upper root crown and base or lower stem of a tree —*note*

many butt rots occur in both the roots and the butt and are not easily separated into root and butt rots —*synonym* trunk rot, bole rot

byte *computers* a group of contiguous **bits**, usually eight, that is a memory and data storage unit —*note 1.* file sizes are measured in bytes or megabytes (1 million bytes) —*note 2.* bytes contain values of 0 to 255 and are most often used to represent integer numbers or ASCII characters, e.g., a byte with an ASCII value of 77 represents a capital M —*note 3.* a collection of bytes (often four or eight bytes) is used to represent real numbers and integers larger than 255

C

cable *harvesting* a wire rope used in **yard**ing and winching systems

cable log to take logs from the stump to a landing and stationary yarder using winch-driven **cables** that pull **butt rigging**, a block, or a carriage to which logs are attached with **chokers** —*synonym* cable **yard**ing

cable skidder —*see* **skidder**

cable yarding taking logs from the stump area to a landing using an overhead system of winch-driven cables to which logs are attached with chokers —*see* **highlead logging, skyline**

CAD —*see* **computer-aided design**

cadastre a record of interests in land encompassing both the nature and the extent of interests —*note 1.* generally, this means maps and other descriptions of land parcels as well as the identification of who owns certain legal rights to the land (such as ownership, liens, easements, mortgages, and other legal interests) —*note 2.* cadastral information often includes other descriptive information about land parcels —*see* **base map**

CAE —*see* **computer-aided engineering**

CAI —*see* **current annual increment**

calcareous soil soil containing sufficient free $CaCO_3$ and other carbonates to effervesce visibly or audibly when treated with cold 0.1M HCl —*note* these soils usually contain from 10 to almost 1000g kg^{-1} $CaCO_3$ equivalent

calcicole a plant that lives in **calcareous soils** —*see* **calciphile, basiphile, basicole**

calcification the process or processes of soil formation in which the surface soil is kept sufficiently supplied with calcium to saturate the soil cation exchange sites, or the process of accumulation of calcium in some **horizon** of the profile, such as the calcic horizon of some Aridisols and Mollisols —*see* **soil order**

calcifuge a plant that tends to avoid **calcareous soils**

calciphile a plant that tends to be restricted to **calcareous soils** —*see* **calcicole, basiphile, basicole**

calculation of probabilities *fire* the evaluation of all factors pertinent to probable future behavior of a **going fire** and of the potential ability of available forces to perform **fire suppression** operations on a specified time schedule

caliche 1. a zone near the soil surface, more or less cemented by secondary carbonates of Ca or Mg precipitated from the soil solution —*note* caliche may occur as a soft thin soil **horizon**, as a hard thick bed, or as a surface layer exposed by **erosion**

2. alluvium cemented with $NaNO_3$, NaCl, and/or other soluble salts in the nitrate deposits of Chile and Peru

caliper(s) 1. an instrument for determining tree and log diameters by measuring their rectangular projection on a straight, graduated rule via two arms at right angles to (and one of them sliding along) the rule itself **2.** the linear measurement taken with calipers —*note* an optical caliper determines upper, out-of-reach tree diameters through an optical system incorporating two parallel lines of sight separated by a variable baseline

calks *also* **caulks** short spikes in the soles and heels of boots designed to give secure footing while walking on logs or **slash** —*synonym* corks

callus a growth of large, undifferentiated, nonlignified, homogeneous cells produced by the cambial zone on the margin of a wound —*note* callus growth may eventually cover the wound —*see* **occlusion**

CAM —*see* **computer-aided mapping**

cambial initial an individual cell of the **cambium** or **phellogen** that can contribute new cells on either the inside or the outside of the meristematic zone

cambic horizon —*see* **horizon**

cambium —*see* **cells (wood)**

cambium miner an insect whose **larvae** tunnel in the cambial region of living trees —*note* some cambium miners cause a timber defect termed pith fleck

camera station the point in space occupied by the camera lens at the moment of exposure

campaign fire *firefighting* a fire of such size or complexity that it requires a large organization and possibly several days or weeks to extinguish —*synonym* project fire

campfire a fire started for cooking, warmth, or light that has spread sufficiently to require firefighting activity

campground an aggregation of **campsites** providing such facilities as tent spaces (or pads), fireplaces, picnic tables, water, and sanitation for overnight use

campsite a unit of a **campground** providing overnight accommodation and generally developed to include tent or trailer space, parking spur, fireplace, table, garbage receptacle, and toilet facility

candidate species those plants and animals included in the Federal Register "Notice of Review" that are being considered by the Fish and Wildlife Service for listing as threatened or endangered —*see* **endangered species, threatened species**

candle   the growing terminal shoot of certain conifers, notably pines

canker   1. a disease of the **bark** and **cambium** that causes a usually well-defined sunken or swollen necrotic **lesion** —*note 1.* there are several forms of canker based on shape, position of occurrence on the **bole,** and whether produced in one year or several —*note 2.* important canker diseases include chestnut **blight** *(Cryphonectria parasitica),* hypoxylon canker of aspen *(Hypoxylon mammatum),* and beech bark disease *(Nectria* sp.) **2.** a malformation of a **host** stem or branch caused by a disruption of the cambium as a result of dwarf mistletoe **infection 3.** a scar left after canker disease or environmental injury

canonical correlation analysis a technique of **multivariate analysis** (specifically, two-stage principal components analysis) by which two groups of observed variables are transformed so that (a) the transformed members within each group (canonical variates) are linear combinations of the original variables, (b) the simple correlation between the canonical variates is maximized, and (c) successive pairs of canonical variates are orthogonal with preceding pairs —*see* **orthogonality, nonorthogonal data**

canopy 1. the foliar **cover** in a forest **stand** consisting of one or several layers **2.** the overhead branches and leaves of streamside vegetation

canopy class —*see* **crown class**

canopy closure —*see* **crown cover**

canopy cover the proportion of ground or water covered by a vertical projection of the outermost perimeter of the natural spread of foliage or plants, including small openings within the canopy —*note* total canopy coverage may exceed 100 percent because of layering of different vegetative strata —*see* **cover**

canopy density —*see* **crown density**

cant a piece of lumber made from a log by removing two or more sides in sawing —*see* **flitch, saw, breakdown**

cant hook *harvesting* a stout wooden lever with a hinged hook or dog used in rolling logs —*note* a cant hook is similar to a **peavey** but instead of a pointed end, it has a thimble fitted to the end with a bill that bites into the log to provide a grip

canyon wind the **mountain wind** of a canyon —*note* the nighttime down-canyon flow of air caused by cooling at the canyon walls —*see* **chinook, foehn, valley wind**

capability the potential of a land area to produce resources, supply goods and services, and allow resource uses under an assumed set of management practices and at a given level of management intensity —*note* capability depends on current conditions and site conditions such as climate, slope, landform, soils, and geology, as well as the application of management practices such as **silviculture** and protection from fire, insects, and disease

capillary fringe a zone in the soil just above the free water table that remains saturated or almost saturated with water

capillary pore *obsolete* a small pore that holds water in soils against a tension usually greater than 60 cm (23.6 in) of water —*note 1.* the pores are commonly filled with water when the soil is at field capacity —*note 2.* the term capillary pore (based on ability to hold water) has no replacement; pore size is now used as a classification criterion —*see* **macropore, micropore**

capillary water *obsolete* the water held in the capillary pores of a soil usually with a tension of greater than 60 cm (0.03 MPa or 23.6 in) of water

capstan *harvesting* a drum that provides power to a **cable** by friction

carbohydrate a class of organic compounds built of carbon, hydrogen, and oxygen and having the general composition $C_x(H_2O)_y$, —*note* carbohydrates include both simple sugars (glucose, xylose, etc.) and polysaccharides (cellulose, starch, xylan), e.g., hexose, pentose

carbon fixation —*see* **photosynthesis**

carbon offset the planting of trees on nonforested land such that the uptake of carbon dioxide from the growing trees will offset the production of carbon dioxide from industrial effluent —*synonym* carbon certificate, carbon credit —*see* **afforestation, carbon sequestration, deforestation, reforestation**

carbon sequestration the incorporation of carbon dioxide into permanent plant tissues

cardinal direction one of the four principal directions north, south, east, or west

carnivore an organism that consumes living animals or parts of living animals —*see* **herbivore, phytophagous, scavenger**

carpel the basic unit of the **gynoecium** composed of a stigma, style, and ovary —*note* the gynoecium may contain a single carpel and be called simple, or may be composed of many carpels and called compound —*see* **flower**

carpenter ant a large black ant *(Campontus* sp.) that tunnels in dead wood including dead trees, utility poles, and structural timber —*note 1.* these **social** insects excavate large cavities in which the colony, consisting of thousands of individuals, lives and rears its young —*note 2.* carpenter ants do not eat wood but remove it to form galleries that serve as a nest, causing damage termed **honeycomb wood-boring** damage —*note 3.* carpenter ants feed on other insects, aphid **honeydew,** and a variety of organic liquids and materials

carpenter bee a large bee (*Xylocopa* sp.) that tunnels in both sound and slightly decayed dead wood including twigs, branches, wood beams, **poles,** and posts, excavating cavities in which to rear young —*note* carpenter bees are not usually serious **pest**s but cause damage to wood structures

carpenterworm a moth (especially *Prionoxystus robiniae*) whose **larvae** bore in the wood of living trees, seriously degrading the timber but rarely killing the **host** —*note* carpenterworms are a major **pest** of southern hardwoods; the adults are incorrectly referred to as carpenter moths

carr deciduous **woodland** or **scrub** on a permanently wet, organic soil —*note* a carr develops from a **bog, fen,** or **swamp**

carriage *harvesting* **1.** a wheeled mechanical assembly that moves back and forth while suspended above the ground by the **skyline** —*note* logs are attached to the carriage by a skidding line for **yard**ing **2.** a track-mounted vehicle that carries a log through the head saw in a sawmill —*see* **setworks**

carrier **1.** a usually inert ingredient used to dilute a **pesticide** for ease of distribution, as a diluant or vehicle for the **active ingredient** or toxicant, or enhancement of effect **2.** any material, e.g., sawdust, that is mixed with seed, etc., to protect it in transit or to facilitate **seeding** of very small seeds

carrying capacity **1.** *ecology* the maximum number or biomass of organisms of a given species that can be sustained or survive on a long-term basis within an **ecosystem** **2.** *planning* the ability of the land to support any particular maximum level of use or extraction given predetermined **assumptions** about type of use, quality level, or other factors **3.** *range* the number of livestock that a **range** can sustain without over grazing and limited by quality of pasture or availability of water —*see* **animal-unit month** **4.** *recreation* the number of **recreation** users an area can accommodate during a given period of time and still provide protection of the resources and satisfaction of the users

Cartesian coordinate system a system of two or three mutually perpendicular axes along which any point can be precisely located with reference to any other point —*note 1.* often referred to as x, y, and z coordinates; relative measures of distance, area, and direction are constant throughout the system —*note 2.* a concept from French philosopher and mathematician René Descartes (1596–1650)

cartography the art of graphically expressing known physical features of the earth onto a map —*note 1.* by using a **GIS** in conjunction with this

art, the science of computer technology is developed —*note 2.* typically, there is a large component of art needed to communicate information contained in the map product

cascading *fire* the free-fall dropping from an aircraft of uncontained, liquid **fire retardant** or suppressants not in spray form —*see* **retardant drop**

case-hardening **1.** *propagation* the setting of cone scales as a result of superficial drying so that they fail to open and discharge their seed —*see* **serotinous** **2.** *seasoning* a stressed condition in seasoned timber characterized by compression in the outer layers accompanied by tension in the core, the result of too-severe drying conditions

casparian strip the localized thickening within the walls and intercellular space of root endodermal cells containing **suberin** and **lignin** —*note* the casparian strip separates the root **cortex** from the **vascular cylinder,** limiting **apoplast**ic transfer —*see* **endodermis**

catchment **1.** a reservoir, basin, etc., for catching water **2.** the water caught in such a basin —*see* **watershed**

categorical exclusion the exemption for US federal agencies from requirements to prepare an environmental impact statement or an environmental assessment for categories of action that have been determined not to involve significant environmental impacts —*note* categorical exclusion is one of four classes of National Environmental Policy Act of 1969 documentation, the other three being **environmental impact statement, conformance determination record,** and **environmental assessment**

catena a sequence of soils of about the same age, derived from similar **parent material** and occurring under similar climatic conditions, but having different characteristics because of variation in relief and in drainage

caterpillar a **larva** of butterflies, moths, and sawflies

catface a partially healed or grown-over wound on a tree stem resulting from fire or use of equipment —*note* a catface often leads to **rot** —*see* **face**

cation exchange the interchange between a cation in solution and another cation in the boundary layer between the solution and the surface of negatively charged material such as clay or organic matter

cation exchange capacity (CEC) the sum of exchangeable bases plus total soil acidity at a specific **pH,** usually 7.0 or 8.0 —*note 1.* when acidity is expressed as salt extractable acidity, the cation exchange capacity is called the effective cation exchange capacity (ECEC) because this is considered to be the CEC of the exchanger at the native pH value —*note 2*. cation exchange capacity is usually expressed in centimoles of charge per kilogram of exchanger ($cmol_c$ kg^{-1}) or millimoles of charge per kilogram of exchanger —*see* **soil reaction**

catkin a unisexual pendulous **inflorescence** consisting of a central stem, scaly bracts, and sessile **flowers** without petals —*note* the term should not be applied to the male **strobilus** of conifers —*see* **ament**

CCD —*see* **charge coupled device**

CCF a hundred cubic feet —*see* **cubic foot**

CD —*see* **conformance determination record**

cedar-apple rust a disease that forms aecia on *Malus* sp. and basidia on cedar (*Juniperus* sp.) — *note* economic damage occurs to the Rosaceous fruit crop, not to the junipers —*see* **aecium, basidium**

c-effect a nonheritable effect common among individuals that is not due to genetic covariation —*note* c-effects may include **maternal effect**s, a nonrandom common environment, or a common physiological condition of donor tissue used for cloning —*see* **paternal effect**

ceilometer an automatic recording, cloud-height indicator

cell **1.** a physiological unit of living plants forming the structural unit of plant tissues —*note* cells are composed of **cell wall** and **protoplast** when live, and cell wall and inclusions when dead **2.** GIS the basic element of spatial information in a **grid** or **raster** data set —*note* cells are typically square but may be rectangular depending on the software system used

cells, wood types of wood cells include the following:

—**bast** a type of **fiber** that comes from the inner bark on numerous **shrub**s and trees and also **herb**s such as hemp and flax —*note 1*. when the inner bark is separated from the dark outer bark, and in some cases from the woody cores, bast yields long, strong fibers that are excellent for papermaking — *note 2*. inner bark bast fibers usually contain a higher percentage of **hemicellulose** than seed-hair fibers

—**cambium** a layer of living, meristematic cells between the wood (secondary **xylem**) and the innermost bark (secondary **phloem**) of a tree —*note* in each growing season, division of these cells adds a new layer of cells on the wood (**xylem**) already formed as well as a layer of inner bark (**phloem**) on the outer face of the cambium

—**cellulose** a straight-chain polymer built up of a large number of glucose anhydride molecules with

cells, wood *continued*

the empirical formula of $(C_6H_{10}O_5)_n$ —*note* cellulose is the principal chemical constituent of the cell secondary walls of higher plants and occurs (often with other components such as **lignins**, **hemicellulose**s, waxes, and gums) mainly as long, hollow chains called **fibers** —*see* **isotropic**

—**companion cell** a cell in the **phloem** intimately connected with a sieve-tube element and retaining the **nucleus** and dense **cytoplasm** —*note* companion cells may undergo some transverse or other divisions preceding their differentiation

—**fiber** a slender, threadlike component of wood, composed chiefly of **cellulose** —*note 1*. fibers differ from **tracheid**s in being more slender, having simple pits and thicker walls in relation to diameter, and often retaining protoplasm —*note 2*. fibers are used in making pulp for paper and classified according to the part of the plant from which they are taken, i.e., stem, bast, leaf, seed-hair —*see* **defibration, microfibril, tracheid** —*note 3*. a gelatinous fiber has a more or less unlignified inner wall of viscuous appearance —*see* **lignin**

—**hemicellulose** a branched-chain polymer of **cellulose** made up of sugars —*note 1*. the chain length of hemicellulose is shorter than that of cellulose, and hemicelluloses are found in higher proportions in wood fibers and some bast fibers —*note 2*. compared with celluloses, hemicelluloses are less resistant to chemical and atmospheric degradation, bond more readily, and are more desirable for some types of papers

—**holocellulose** **cellulose** plus **hemicellulose**

—**lignin** a complex, high-molecular-weight polymer built on phenylpropane units, that occurs between individual cells and within cell walls, is intimately associated with **cellulose**, and serves to impart rigidity to the cell —*note* apparent lignin is lignin content as determined by a standard procedure, e.g., the Klason determination, without the removal of interfering extraneous substances —*see* **sclerosis**

—**micelle** a crystalline region in bundles of cellulose (**microfibrils**) separated longitudinally by amorphous regions —*note* the term micelle, originally proposed by Nägeli in 1885, is now often replaced by the somewhat different concept of crystallite, but the terms are not synonymous

—**microfibril** a cellulose bundle in which the cellulose molecules are mostly oriented parallel to the axis of the microfibril —*note 1*. the orientation of the microfibrils to the long axis of the fiber is called the microfibril (or micellar) angle; wide angles result in high longitudinal shrinkage of the fiber — *note 2*. because the S_2 layer of the **cell wall** is the

cells, wood *continued*

widest layer, the microfibril angle of the S_2 layer has the greatest influence on longitudinal shrinkage of sawn boards

—**parenchyma** vertically or horizontally arranged living cells of the **xylem** that store food

—**periderm** the secondary tissue of stems or roots consisting of the **phellem, phellogen,** and **phelloderm** —*see* **bark**

—**phellem** cork tissue produced by the **phellogen** in a stem or root on the bark side (outside), nonliving at maturity, and having **suberized** walls —*note* the nontechnical name for phellem is cork; the **bark** of cork oaks, *Quercus suber* and *Q. occidentalis,* produce the commercial forms

—**phelloderm** tissue resembling cortical parenchyma produced by the **phellogen** in a stem or root on the pith side (inner side), radially arranged, and with a shape resembling that of phellogen cells

—**phellogen** secondary cambium that produces the **periderm** —*synonym* cork cambium

—**phloem** a layer of cells just inside the bark of plants that conducts food from the leaves to the stem and roots —*note 1.* the conducting elements of phloem are known as **sieve cells** but may also include companion cells, **parenchyma** cells, **fibers, sclereids,** and **rays** —*note 2.* primary phloem differentiates from derivatives of the apical meristem; secondary phloem is produced by the same vascular cambium that forms the secondary **xylem**

—**pit** an interruption or recess in the secondary cell wall through which fluids or gases pass from one cell to another —*note 1.* pits are usually paired in common walls of contiguous cells —*note 2.* bordered pits have secondary walls that overarch the pit membrane; simple pits do not have secondary walls —*note 3.* scalariform pits are elongated or lineal and are arranged in a ladderlike series

—**pith** the central core of a stem, branches, and some roots representing the first year of growth and consisting mainly of soft tissue

—**pore** —*see* **vessel**

—**ray** a type of wood structural element, one to many cells high but usually only one cell wide (uniseriate, ribbon-shaped), extending radially across the grain, that stores and distributes sap horizontally (radially) —*note 1.* fusiform rays have horizontal resin ducts at their centers; medullary rays (pith rays) are **parenchyma** tissues that provide for lateral transport of liquids and soluble material between the **cortex** and the **pith** —*note 2.* rays are usually readily visible on a **quarter-sawn** surface of a board

—**sclereid** a hard, often branched, strongly lignified,

cells, wood *continued*

nonconducting cell that can occur anywhere in a plant but are most abundant in the phloem, fruits, and seeds

—**sieve cell** a nonlignified cell similar in shape to longitudinal **tracheids** of the xylem but somewhat shorter and having circular to oval areas of very thin walls called sieve areas —*note* the primary function of sieve cells is food conduction

—**tracheid** an elongate, spindle-shaped wood cell that loses protoplasm at maturity when becoming conductive —*note* tracheids account for 90 to 95 percent of softwood volume, much less in hardwoods

—**tyloses** saclike structures of protoplast that balloon through pits into the cavities of adjacent **vessels** of **hardwoods** and sometimes **tracheids** of **softwoods** —*note 1.* tyloses are commonly associated with **heartwood** formation and often partially or completely block vessels —*note 2.* the effect of tyloses on wood quality may be detrimental (making wood difficult to dry) or beneficial (as for barrels made to store liquids)

—**vessel** the principal vascular or water-conducting element of **hardwood** —*note 1.* vessel members differ from **tracheids** in having perforations, usually in the end walls —*note 2.* longitudinal series of vessel members constitute a vessel that can be many centimeters or even meters in length —*note 3.* vessels are sometimes visible as small holes on a cross-section of wood —*synonym* pore

—**xylem** the principal water-conducting tissue and the chief supporting system of higher plants, composed of **tracheids** (for conduction and support), **vessels** (for conduction), **fibers** (for support), and **parenchyma** (for food transport and storage) —*note 1.* xylem and associated **phloem** tissues constitute the conducting system of vascular plants—*note 2.* primary xylem consists of two forms: (a) protoxylem is formed while the organ is still elongating and generally includes cells with extensible secondary wall thickening and relatively few tracheids or vessel elements; (b) metaxylem is formed after growth in length is nearly completed and has cells mostly with nonextensible secondary walls accompanied by parenchyma and fibers —*note 3.* secondary xylem in most woody plants constitutes the bulk of the entire plant and is composed of two interpenetrating systems, radial (**ray**) and vertical (axial)

cellulose —*see* **cells (wood)**

cell wall *plants* a structural membrane enclosing the cell membrane and the contents of the protoplast and consisting of **cellulose** (in bundles of **microfibrils** or micelles), **hemicellulose,** and **lignin** —*note* cell walls of woody plants are organized in four layers: (a) primary wall, which is the wall of the meristematic cell modified during differentiation and which is a more or less random network of microfibrils, and (b) a secondary wall, which contains lignin, provides the plant with rigidity and strength, and consists of three layers, a narrow S_1, a wide S_2, and a narrow S_3, with the microfibrils in these layers having distinct and differing orientation called microfibril (micellar) angle

census a complete counting, with more or less classification, of a population or group at a point in time —*note 1.* in a timber sale, a census may involve scaling all trees —*note 2.* in public administration, a census records population and demographic data

center firing —*see* **firing technique**

central limit theorem a statistical principle stating that as sample size becomes larger, the distribution of sample means converges on a normal distribution, regardless of the original distribution of individual observations

centroid the center of gravity or mathematically exact center of a regularly or irregularly shaped **polygon,** often given as an x,y coordinate of a parcel of land

certify 1. *genetics, silviculture* to attest that commercial seed or **propagules** have been produced in accordance with standards and guaranteed by an official agency —*see* **improved, seed certification 2.** *management* to attest that the management of **forest** land meets approved standards of a designated authority —*see* **chain of custody, sustainable forest management 3.** *utilization* to attest that wood products originate from forest land certified as meeting approved standards of a designated authority **4.** *forestry* to attest that a **forester** meets standards of competence and experience —*see* **accreditation, forest technology recognition**

CGP —*see* **coefficient of genetic prediction**

chain a unit of length equal to 66 ft (20.1 m) and composed of 100 links

chain flail a rotating drum(s) with lengths of chain attached, used as **debarker** or **delimber**

chaining 1. *harvesting* a method of skidding pulpwood on short, steep slopes by wrapping a chain around several small piles of wood and dragging them crosswise down the slope **2.** *site preparation* a method of reducing or clearing undesirable **shrubs** or **saplings** from an area by dragging a heavy chain (generally further weighted by, e.g., concrete cylinders or large steel balls) through it between two tractors —*synonym* cabling, using a thick steel cable

chain of custody *certification* assurance provided by

a seller that a certified forest product has remained identifiable from its origin in the forest to the buyer throughout its production, processing, and marketing —*see* **certify**

chain saw —*see* **saw**

chamaephyte a land plant whose buds or shoot apices survive unfavorable seasons at or near (< 25 cm or < 9.8 in) the ground surface —*note* chamaephyte is one of the (noncryptophytic) **life-form**s of Raunkiaer —*see* **cryptophyte**

change detection the process of comparing a temporal series of **images** to identify change in an object

channel capacity the flow rate of a ditch, canal, or natural channel when flowing full or at design flow —*see* **bankfull discharge, discharge**

channel density the ratio of the length of stream channels in a given basin to the area of the basin —*note* channel density is expressed in ft/ac (m/ha)

channelization the mechanical alteration of a stream that may include straightening or dredging of an existing channel or creating a new channel to which the stream is diverted

channel storage the water temporarily stored in channels while en route to an outlet

chaos the erratic, nonrepeating dynamics that are highly sensitive to initial conditions exhibited by a completely **deterministic** system

chaparral a thicket of low, evergreen oaks or dense tangled brushwood

character 1. *genetics* a distinctive and usually variable feature (e.g., color, size, performance) exhibited by all individuals of a group capable of being described or measured—*note* a character of a given individual will have a certain **phenotype** as determined by the individual's **genotype** and environment —*see* **heterozygous population 2.** *computers* a letter, number, or special graphic symbol (e.g., *, @, -) treated as a single unit of data **3.** *computers* a data type referring to text columns in an attribute table, e.g., NAME —*see* **acquired character, combining ability, trait**

charcoal a form of carbon derived from the incomplete combustion of animal or vegetable matter, e.g., bones or wood

charge coupled device (CCD) an electromagnetic-sensitive, solid-state device that generates a voltage proportional to the intensity of illumination used in remote-sensing scanners and modern video cameras

chasmophyte a plant that grows in a rock crevice —*see* **chromophyte**

check a separation of wood fibers on any surface of

a log, timber, or board resulting from the release of tensile stresses set up during drying

checkerboard ownership a land ownership pattern in which every other section (square mile) is in federal ownership as a result of federal land grants to early western railroad companies —*see* **forest fragmentation**

check(ing) station any point where hunters, anglers, tourists, and other visitors to an area are counted, registered, or given information; where admission fees are collected; or where the catch of fish or the bag of game must be reported or delivered —*synonym* check point

check scaler one who rescales logs to detect errors in the initial scaling —*see* **scale**

chelate an organic chemical with two or more functional groups that can bind with metals to form a ring structure —*note 1.* soil organic matter can form chelate structures with some metals, especially transition metals, but much metal ion binding in soil organic matter probably does not involve chelation —*note 2.* artificial chelating compounds are sometimes added to soil to increase the soluble fraction of some metals

chemical control the application of an **insecticide** as the primary means of controlling a **pest** —*see* **biological control**

chemical girdling —*see* **girdle**

chemical oxygen demand (COD) a measure of the amount of oxygen required to oxidize organic and oxidizable inorganic compounds in water

chemical pulp —*see* **pulp**

chemical thinning a **thinning** in which unwanted trees are killed by chemical poisoning

chemotropism the response of a plant organ in growth or position to a gradient in chemicals —*see* **geotropism, hydrotropism, phototropism**

chevron burn —*see* **firing technique**

chilling requirement the minimum time below some threshold temperature required for development by some plants

chimera 1. a plant or a part of a plant whose tissues are of genetically different layers —*note* chimeras may be sexually reproduced if they are in the lineage of reproductive cells **2.** a bacterial **clone** that has been genetically transformed to contain the donor **DNA** —*see* **albinism, genetic transformation, transgenic**

chinook the high velocity, down-slope wind (**foehn**) on the eastern side of the Rocky Mountains —*see* **canyon wind, mountain and valley winds**

chip a small piece of wood used to make pulp or

wood composites (made either from wood waste in a sawmill or pulpwood operation or from pulpwood specifically cut for this purpose) or fuel (made either from sawmill waste or from chipping trees in the woods)

Chip-n-Saw —*see* **saw**

chipper, portable (mobile) a mobile machine consisting of infeed conveyor, debarker (sometimes), and chipper, with the chips being blown into a chip truck or a pile

chip unit a measure of chip volume equal to one **cord** of pulpwood

chi-square test any test of significance based on the P^2 distribution, but often a test of agreement between expected and observed frequencies, i.e., a test for goodness of fit

chlorophyll a complex of mainly green pigments in the **chloroplast**s, characteristic of most plants (termed green plants), whose light-energy-transforming properties permit **photosynthesis** to take place

chloroplast a structure found in cells of plants and certain algae that is exposed to light, contains photosynthetic pigments, and is the location of **photosynthesis** —*see* **cells (wood)**

chlorosis an abnormal yellowing of foliage —*note* chlorosis is often a symptom of some mineral deficiency, **virus** infection, root or stem girdling, or extremely reduced light —*see* **etiolation**

choker *harvesting* a short length of **wire rope** or chain that forms a noose around the end of a log to be skidded or yarded —*see* **skidder**

choker hook (bell) *harvesting* a fastener on the end of a **choker** that forms the noose

chokersetter a person in a logging operation who places the **choker** around the log to be hauled to the landing

chopper a large cylindrical drum, which may be partially filled with water, with cutting blades mounted parallel to its axis and drawn by a **tractor** or **skidder** across a site to break up slash or crush scrubby vegetation prior to (usually) burning and planting —*synonym* drum chopper —*see* **site preparation**

chord the straight line that joins the end points of any arc —*note* in cable **yard**ing, the chord is a measure of cable deflection —*see* **span**

C horizon —*see* **horizon**

chroma the relative purity, strength, or saturation of a color, directly related to the dominance of the determining wavelength of the light and inversely related to the grayness —*note* chroma is one of the three variables of color used in describing soils —*see* **hue, value, Munsell color system**

chromophyte a plant that grows in a fissure or crevice of a rock (*see* **chasmophyte**) or on ledges where rock debris has accumulated

chromosome a microscopic, generally threadlike or rodlike body consisting of linear segments of **deoxyribonucleic acid (DNA)**, carrying the **genes**, and forming the primary constituent of the cell **nucleus** —*note* chromosomes are individually distinguishable only during nuclear division, and their number, size, and form are generally constant for each **species** —*see* **cytogenetics, cytology, meiosis, mitosis, mutation, nucleus**

chromosome number the number of **chromosomes** characteristic of a **species** —*note* the number of **chromosome sets** associated with this number must also be specified; thus in *Pinus* the chromosome number may be expressed as $n = 12$ or as $2n = 24$, depending on whether the reference is to **haploid** sex cells or normal **diploid** vegetative cells —*see* **aneuploid, gamete, hexaploid, karyotype, polyploid**

chromosome set the number (n) of **chromosomes** inherited as a set from one parent —*note* normal **haploid** sex cells carry only one set of chromosomes that includes one of each chromosome characteristic of the **species** —*see* **chromosome number, diploid, karyotype, meiosis, polyploid, vegetative cell**

cicada a large insect in the Homoptera families Cicadidae and Tettigarctidae —*note 1.* there are no contemporary Tettigarctidae in North America —*note 2.* the male cicada is noted for its sound-producing abilities and two- to 17-year life cycles; the insects are not serious forest **pests** but oviposition damage from high populations can kill twigs and small branches

circular saw —*see* **saw**

clan a small but distinctive community of subordinate importance composed of densely aggregated individuals of one or few species in climax vegetation —*note* a clan frequently results from vegetative propagation

class *GIS* a template for defining the methods and variables for a particular type of **object** —*note* all objects of a given class are identical in form and behavior but contain different data in their variables

classification the grouping of similar types according to criteria considered significant for this purpose

class of fire one of seven size categories of fire determined by the area burned: Class A (< 0.25 ac or < 0.1 ha), Class B (0.25 to 10 ac or 0.1 to 4 ha), Class C (10 to 100 ac or 4 to 40 ha), Class D (100 to 300 ac or 40 to 121 ha), Class E (300 to 1,000 ac or 121 to 405 ha), Class F (1,000 to 5,000 ac or 405 to 2,024 ha), Class G (> 5,000 ac or > 2,024 ha) —*synonym* fire size class, size class

clay 1. a soil separate consisting of particles < 0.002 mm (0.00008 in) in equivalent diameter —*see* **soil separates 2.** a textural class —*see* **soil texture 3.** *clay mineralogy* a naturally occurring material, composed primarily of fine-grained minerals, which is generally plastic at appropriate water contents and will harden when dried or fired —*note 1.* although clay usually contains phyllosilicates, it may contain other materials that impart plasticity and harden when dried or fired —*note 2.* associated phases in clay may include materials that do not impart plasticity and organic matter —*see* **sand, silt**

clay mica —*see* **illite**

clay mineral a phyllosilicate mineral or a mineral that imparts plasticity to clay and that hardens on drying

claypan a dense, compact, slowly permeable layer in the subsoil having a much higher clay content than the overlying material from which it is separated by a sharply defined boundary —*note* a claypan is usually hard when dry but plastic and sticky when wet

clean burn any fire that removes all aboveground vegetation and litter to expose mineral soil

cleaning 1. a release treatment made in an age class not past the **sapling** stage to free the favored trees from less desirable individuals of the same age class that overtop them or are likely to do so —*see* **improvement cutting, liberation, weeding 2.** to carry out such a treatment **3.** a treatment designed to eradicate individual trees infected with **dwarf mistletoe**

clearcut 1. a stand in which essentially all trees have been removed in one operation —*note* depending on management objectives, a clearcut may or may not have reserve trees left to attain goals other than regeneration —*see* **regeneration method (two-aged methods) 2.** a regeneration or harvest method that removes essentially all trees in a stand —*synonym* clearcutting —*see* **regeneration method (clearcutting)**

clearing a considerable open space, natural or artificial, in forest or brushwood

climagram a graphic representation of the elements of **climate**, e.g., wet-bulb temperatures and relative humidities, plotted against each other to provide an index to the general climatic characters of a locality

climate 1. the long-term manifestations of **weather 2.** the statistical collection and representation of weather conditions for a specified area during a specified time interval, usually decades, together with a description of the state of the external system or boundary conditions —*note* properties that characterize climate are thermal (temperatures of the surface air, water, land, and ice), kinetic (wind and ocean currents, together with associated vertical motions and the motions of air masses, aqueous humidity, cloudiness and cloud water content, groundwater, lake lands, and water content of snow on land and sea ice), and static (pressure and density of the atmosphere and ocean, composition of the dry air, salinity of the oceans, and the geometric boundaries and physical constants of the system); these properties are interconnected by various physical processes such as **precipitation,** evaporation, infrared radiation, convection, **advection**, and turbulence —*see* **climagram**

climate change the long-term fluctuations or trends in temperature, **precipitation**, wind, and all other aspects of the earth's **climate** —*note 1.* external processes affecting climate include variation in solar-irradiance, variations of the earth's orbital parameters (eccentricity, precession, and inclination), lithosphere motions, and volcanic activity; internal factors affecting climate include fluctuations in the feedback processes that interrelate the components of the climate system —*note 2.* many believe the earth's climate is warming because of the evolution of anthropogenic-generated gases, particularly CO_2 from the burning of fossil fuels

climax *ecology* the culminating stage of plant **succession** for a given environment; the vegetation conceived as having reached a highly stable condition —*note 1.* some ecologists restrict the term to vegetation of mature sites and soils that they presume to have a high degree of permanence, others apply it to vegetation conceived to be stable only as long as the environment remains unchanged, or to vegetation that changes only in response to changes in climate or soil substrate that are slow relative to the rate of plant succession —*note 2.* Clements argued that, for a given region, there was only one true climax, i.e., stable vegetation on mesic sites determined by climate, and hence termed by him the climatic climax; sites with stable vegetation but influenced by factors other than climate received special names: preclimax (local unfavorable conditions preventing full vegetational complexity), postclimax (local favorable conditions permitting greater complexity), biotic climax (maintained by biotic factors), edaphic climax (maintained by soil factors) —*see* **seral stage, subclimax, climax forest**

climax forest an ecological community that represents the culminating stage of a natural **forest succession** for its locality, i.e., for its environment

cline a continuous gradient of **phenotype**s or **geno-type**s within a species' range —*note* clinal varia-

tion usually results from an environmental gradient —*see* **ecotype, geographic variation, race, taxon**

clinometer an instrument for measuring angles of elevation or depression —*see* **abney level, hypsometer**

clip *GIS* the spatial extraction of those features from one **geodataset** that reside entirely within a boundary defined by another geodataset —*note* a clip works much like a cookie cutter

clod a compact mass of soil caused by disturbance such as plowing —*note* clods are ruptured fragments of **ped**s —*see* **soil structure**

clonal replication a tool of genetic testing in which **ramet**s of a given genotype are replicated across environments in time or space —*see* **clone, genetic replication**

clonal test a genetic test designed to evaluate a set of **clone**s —*note* such tests furnish estimates of respective **genotype**s but do not necessarily provide information on breeding behavior —*see* **certify, elite, heritability, progeny test**

clone 1. a **vegetatively propagated** organism, or a group of such organisms consisting of an **ortet** and its **ramet**s 2. a cell **line** of single-cell origin 3. a **gene** or piece of **DNA** replicated (usually) in a host bacterium —*note* all clones imply genetically (usually) identical material and reproduction by mitotic division; they may occur naturally or be created artificially —*see* **apomixis, asexual reproduction, combined test, graft, mitosis, ortet, parthenocarpy, plus tree**

clone bank a collection of selected **vegetatively propagated** trees established for breeding or gene conservation purposes —*see* **breeding arboretum**

closed basin 1. a basin draining to some depression or pond within its area from which water is lost only by evaporation or percolation 2. a basin without a surface outlet for **precipitation** falling therein

close herding the work of handling a herd in a closely bunched manner, restricting the natural spread of the animals when grazing —*see* **open herding, trail herding**

cloud forest vegetation of tropical mountainous regions where rainfall is often heavy and persistent condensation occurs because of cooling of moisture-laden air currents deflected upward by the mountains —*synonym* montane **rainforest**s —*note* trees in a cloud forest are typically short and crooked; mosses, climbing ferns, **lichen**s, and epiphytes form thick blankets on the trunks and branches of the trees; begonias, ferns, and other herbaceous plants may grow exceptionally large in clearings

clump 1. the aggregate of stems issuing from the same root, rhizome system, stump, or **stool**, with particular reference to aspen, redwood, and sprouting hardwoods **2.** an isolated, generally dense, group of trees

cluster 1. *forest habitat* an area containing habitat capable of supporting several bird or mammal breeding pairs with overlapping or nearly overlapping home ranges **2.** *GIS* a spatial grouping of geographic entities on a map, e.g., incidents of disease, crime, and pollution

cluster sampling a survey design in which the basic sampling unit is to be found in groups or clusters —*note* sampling is carried out by selecting a sample of clusters and observing all the members of each selected cluster

CMAI —see **culmination of mean annual increment**

coancestry the degree of relatedness by descent —*see* **inbreeding**

coarse material wood residues suitable for chipping, such as slabs, edgings, and trimmings —*see* **fine material**

coarse woody debris (CWD) any piece(s) of dead woody material, e.g., dead boles, limbs, and large root masses, on the ground in forest stands or in streams —*synonym* large woody debris (LWD), large organic debris (LOD), down woody debris (DWD) —*note* the type and size of material designated as coarse woody debris varies among classification systems

coastal plain the flatter area, or plain, extending along the coast

cocoon a silken case or envelope spun by (a) an insect **larva** inside which the pupa develops or (b) the adults of some spiders to enclose the eggs

COD —*see* **chemical oxygen demand (COD)**

codominance *genetics* the common state in which each of two **alleles** produces its characteristic effect in the **heterozygote**, e.g., pink flowers resulting from the combination of white and red alleles

codominant 1. *ecology* tree species in a forest that are about equally numerous and exert the greatest influence **2.** *genetics* two **alleles** that are not expressed as dominant or recessive but whose attributes are jointly expressed in the **phenotype 3.** *silviculture* —*see* **crown class**

coefficient of genetic prediction (CGP) a statistical value indicating the change in a **trait** which may be expected by the selection for one standard deviation change in another trait —*note* the CGP of a trait with itself is equal to its **heritability**

coefficient of roughness a factor in fluid flow formulas expressing the character of a surface and its factional resistance to flow

coefficient of variation a measure of relative variability or dispersion computed as the **standard deviation** divided by the mean, and generally expressed as a percent

COGO —*see* **coordinate geometry**

cohort 1. a group of individuals or vital statistics about them having a statistical factor in common, such as age class **2.** *silviculture* a group of trees developing after a single disturbance, commonly consisting of trees of similar age, although it can include a considerable range of tree ages of seedling or sprout origin and trees that predate the disturbance —*see* **age class, effective age, multiaged (multicohort) stand**

cold deck logs piled on a landing or storage area for future loading

cold hardening the process by which plants become resistant to damage from subfreezing temperatures —*note* cold hardening is usually accomplished by subjecting plants to a short photoperiod and low but not necessarily freezing temperatures —*see* **photoperiodism**

cold hardiness resistance or tolerance to subfreezing temperatures —*note* cold hardiness is usually associated with the onset of **dormancy** or chilling to near freezing temperatures

cold stratification the storage of **propagules** under cold temperatures for a period of time sufficient to satisfy the **chilling requirement** for germination

cold trailing —*see* **fire suppression**

collapse the folding in of cell walls, usually during suboptimal **kiln** drying, resulting in boards that cup or develop uneven shrinkage —*note* collapse can be relieved or avoided by injecting steam into the kiln

collar the transition zone between stem and root, sometimes recognizable in seedlings by the presence of a slight swelling

colloidal suspension a suspension in water of particles so finely divided that they will not settle under the action of gravity but will diffuse in quiet water under the random influences of Brownian motion

colluvial pertaining to material or processes associated with transportation or deposition by mass movement (direct gravitational action) and local, unconcentrated runoff on side slopes or at the base of slopes

color composite (multiband imaging) a digital color **image** derived from three **bands** of imagery in which each input band is assigned to red, green, or blue (RGB) —*note 1.* a color composite is based on additive color theory —*note 2.* e.g., Landsat™ **multispectral sensor (MSS)** data bands can be applied to create an RGB additive color composite image similar to **color** infrared aerial photography by assigning band 7 to red, band 5 to green, and band 4 to blue

column 1. *computers* a vertical field in a table **2.** *GIS* a vertical group of **cell**s in a grid or **pixel**s in an image

comandra blister rust a disease characterized by slight fusiform swellings on stems and branches; branch flagging, top kill (which may affect much of the tree), and mortality caused by *Cronartium comandrae* —*note* comandra blister rust is the most common **rust** in western US forests on *Pinus banksiana, P. contorta,* and *P. ponderosa*

combined selection the process of choosing the best families and the best individuals within those families —*see* **individual selection, family selection**

combined test the use of clonal and **family** testing in a single test or carried out in parallel —*see* **clone, sequential testing**

combining ability a statistical value indicating the capacity of a parent to transmit genetic superiority to its offspring —*note* combining ability is usually general or specific depending on the type of inheritance pattern being evaluated —*see* **character, general combining ability, open pollination, phenotype, polycross test, progeny test, specific combining ability**

command 1. *computers* an instruction, usually one word or concatenated words or letters, that performs an action using the software —*note* a command may also have extra options or parameters that define more specific application of the action **2.** *fire* the act of directing, ordering, or controlling firefighting resources by explicit legal, administrative, or delegated authority

command staff —*see* **incident command system**

command team —*see* **incident command system**

commensalism a relationship between two kinds of living organisms whereby one (the commensal) benefits and the other (the host) remains relatively or absolutely unaffected, and which is obligatory for the commensal —*see* **symbiosis, parasitism**

commercial forest land (CFL) land declared suitable for producing timber crops and not withdrawn from timber production by statute or administrative regulation —*note* the minimum level of productivity is often set at 20 ft^3/ac/year (1.4 m^3/ha/year)

commercial forestry the practice of **forestry** with the object of producing timber and other forest produce as a business enterprise or for sale to a business enterprise

commercial thinning any type of **thinning** producing merchantable material at least equal to the value of the direct costs of harvesting

commercial tree species 1. tree species suitable for industrial wood products **2.** conifer or hardwood species used to calculate the commercial forest land **allowable sale quantity (ASQ)**

common cost a cost that may be incurred in support of multiple lines of business, such as the costs of telephone or accounting services that may be difficult to desegregate and charge to specific product lines or units of **output**

common use *range management* the practice of grazing the current year's forage production by more than one kind of grazing animal, either at the same time or at different seasons —*see* **dual use**

communal forest *international forestry* a forest owned and generally managed by a village, town, tribal authority, or local government, the members of which share its benefits in cash or kind —*see* **community forest, social forestry**

community 1. *ecology* an assemblage of plants and animals living together and occupying a given area —*note 1.* with plants, a closed community has components that are so completely utilizing the site that they exclude (or give the appearance of excluding) further entrants —*note 2.* classifying a community as closed is subjective and usually based on one-time measurements or observations —*see* **nodum 2.** *societal* an urban or rural group of human families, as in towns, etc.

community allotment *range management* a grazing allotment on which several **permittee**s graze **livestock** in common

community coefficient a measure of the similarity of the flora or fauna of two areas or of two communities —*note* several mathematical forms have been devised, but all are based on the ratio between the number of species common to the two populations and the total number of species in both populations

community forest a forest owned and generally managed by a community, the members of which share its benefits —*see* **communal forest, social forest**

compaction —*see* **soil compaction**

companion cell —*see* **cells (wood)**

company —*see* **incident command system**

compartment a portion of a **forest** under one ownership, usually contiguous and composed of a variety of forest **stand** types, defined for purposes of locational reference and as a basis for **forest management**

compartment history a regularly maintained record of all events or actions affecting **forest** treatments on an individual **compartment**

compartment line the boundary of a **compartment**

compatible use —*see* **use**

compensation point the light level at which **carbohydrate** breakdown through **respiration** is balanced by carbohydrate gain through **photosynthesis** —*synonym* light compensation point

competence *genetics* the capacity of a cell or tissue to produce certain structures, organs, or entire organisms

competition *ecology* the extent to which each organism maximizes fitness by both appropriating contested resources from a pool not sufficient for all, and adapting to the environment altered by all participants —*note* competition among individuals of the same **species** is termed intraspecific competition; competition between different species is termed interspecific competition —*see* **competitive exclusion**

competitive exclusion the elimination from a **habitat** of one **species** by another through interspecific competition —*see* **competition**

competitive use —*see* **use**

complement one of two goods or services such that when the price of one increases, the quantity demanded of the other falls —*antonym* **substitute**

complementary breeding a technique for genetic improvement that employs more than one mating and testing design to meet overall breeding **objectives**

complementary use —*see* **use**

complex *fire* two or more **incidents** in the same general area that are assigned to a single **incident commander** or unified **command** —*note* complex is an **ICS** term

component analysis —*see* **principal component analysis**

composition 1. the constituent elements of an entity, e.g., the **species** that constitute a plant **community 2.** *silviculture* the proportion of each tree species in a **stand** expressed as a percentage of the total number, **basal area,** or volume of all tree species in the stand

composting toilet a toilet employing aerobic bacteria to digest organic material using cellulose material as a medium

comprehensive planning a traditional planning approach relying on science and quantitative analysis to guide planning activities —*synonym* synoptic planning, rational comprehensive planning —*note* comprehensive planning assumes impartiality and objectivity in the methods chosen for analysis, and one correct answer, and final solutions are often gross oversimplifications —*see* **incremental planning, strategic planning**

compression wood a type of reaction wood formed on the lower sides of branches and leaning or crooked stems of coniferous trees, characterized by heavily lignified **tracheids** that are rounded in cross-section and bear spiral cell wall checks —*note 1.* zones of compression wood typically have denser and darker cell walls than the surrounding tissue, and an abnormally high longitudinal shrinkage tending to cause distortion and splitting during drying —*note 2.* compression wood has lower quality with shorter **tracheids,** less **cellulose,** more **lignin,** and higher longitudinal shrinkage —*see* **tension wood**

computer-aided design (CAD) the application of computer technology to creating graphic documents, often in conjunction with computer-aided manufacturing (CAM) software, as in CAD/CAM procedures

computer-aided engineering (CAE) the integration of computer graphics with engineering techniques to facilitate and optimize the analysis, design, construction, nondestructive testing, operation, and maintenance of physical systems

computer-aided manufacturing (CAM) the application of computer technology to manufacturing procedures and design, often in conjunction with computer-aided design (CAD) software, as in CAD/CAM procedures —*note* computer-aided manufacturing is not to be confused with the obsolete term **computer-aided mapping (CAM)**

computer-aided mapping (CAM) *obsolete* the application of computer technology to automate the map compilation and drafting process —*see* **computer-aided manufacturing**

concentration area any place where animals, particularly herbivores and birds, congregate, often characterized by local overuse of the vegetation —*note* the term is also used in connection with human population pressures

concession 1. *recreation* the private management of a **recreation** area facility developed in part by private capital —*note* a concession may include transportation, lodging, or food service **2.** *management* —*see* **forest concession**

concurrent jurisdiction *recreation* a cooperative arrangement that enables federal, state, or local law enforcement officers to enforce federal, state, or local laws

condensation the physical process by which a vapor becomes a liquid or solid

conductivity 1. a measure of the relative ease of movement of an electric current or heat in material —*note 1.* the electrical conductivity of a solution depends on the total concentration of ionized substances dissolved in water —*note 2.* the thermal conductivity of soil or wood depends on its structure, density, and moisture content

cone the seed-bearing structure of conifers consisting of a central stem, woody or fleshy scales, bracts, and seeds; an aggregation of **sporophylls**

cone borer a moth of the genus *Eucosma* whose **larva**e hatch from eggs laid in immature cones and feed on cones or seeds —*note* cone borers attack all North American **species** of pines —*see* **coneworm**

cone insect —*see* **seed and cone insect**

conelet an immature **cone** (**strobilus**) in conifers —*note* the term is usually applied to the young female cone from the time of scale closure after pollination until the initiation of rapid development of the cone following fertilization a few months before maturity —*see* **flower**

cone midge —*see* **gall midge**

coneworm a moth of the genus *Dioryctria* whose **larva**e feed within the cones and sometimes other structures —*note* coneworms attack all commercially significant North American pines as well as spruce, fir, Douglas-fir, hemlock, and cypress —*see* **cone borer**

confidence limits the upper and lower boundaries of an interval that contains a **population** parameter at a prespecified level of probability (confidence level) —*note* for a given set of data and a particular estimator and error, a higher level of confidence implies a wider confidence interval

configuration *computers* the physical content and arrangement of a computer (e.g., memory, disk, display, network) and the connections to its related peripheral devices both internal and external —*note* configuration can also pertain to many computers and peripherals

confine a fire to allow a **wildland** fire to burn itself out within determined natural or existing boundaries such as rocky ridges, streams, and possibly roads —*note* confining a fire is the least aggressive **wildfire** suppression strategy

confirmed channel a channel in which lateral migration is severely restricted by topographic features, generally steep embankments

conflagration —*see* **fire behavior**

conflation *GIS* a set of functions and procedures that aligns the **arc**s of one **GIS** datafile with those of another and then transfers the attributes of one to the other —*note* alignment precedes the transfer of attributes and is most commonly performed by **rubber-sheeting** operations

conflicting use —*see* **use**

conformality *GIS* the quality of small areas being represented on a map such that their true shapes and angles are preserved —*note* a characteristic of a map projection

conformance determination record (CD) the exemption for federal agencies from requirements to prepare an **environment impact statement** (EIS), or an **environmental assessment** (EA), for actions that have already been covered in existing EAs or EISs —*note 1.* a conformance determination record may be based on the same or another agency's National Environmental Policy Act (NEPA) document that fully covers the proposed action —*note 2.* conformance determination records are one of four classes of NEPA of 1969 documentation, the other three being **environmental impact statement, environmental assessment,** and **categorical exclusion**

confounding a controlled technique, or inadvertent feature, of an **experimental design** that restricts comparisons between some treatments that are applied only in combinations; in confounding, the effects of a treatment within the combination cannot be isolated, or are confounded with other treatment effects —*note* it may be used to increase the **accuracy** of particular comparisons by sacrificing other information, or to reduce the number of experimental units needed

conidiophore a specialized hypha bearing one or more conidia —*see* **conidium**

conidium *plural* **conidia** an asexual fungal **spore** borne on a **conidiophore** —*note* conidia are given many special names according to the type of fruiting body producing them, such as a pycnidium and a **sporangium**

conifer a cone-bearing tree —*note* the term often refers to **gymnosperm**s in general —*see* **nonpored wood**

Coniferales an important group within the Gymnospermae comprising a wide range of trees, mostly evergreens, bearing cones (hence coniferous) and needle-shaped or scalelike leaves, and producing timber known commercially as softwood

conjugate principal point *aerial survey* the **image** on an **aerial photograph** of the **principal point** of the preceding or succeeding photograph in a **flight line**

conk 1. the visible fruiting body of a wood-destroying fungus which projects to some degree beyond the substrate —*note* conks are usually found on tree trunks, branches, and stumps and commonly indicate the presence of **rot** in the underlying wood **2.** a sterile, projecting fungus growth that resembles a fruiting body —*see* **heart decay**

connectivity 1. *wildlife* pertaining to the extent to which conditions exist or should be provided between separate forest areas to ensure **habitat** for breeding, feeding, or movement of wildlife and fish within their home range or **migration** areas —*note* providing connectivity is of particular concern when developing harvesting plans —*see* **corridor, fragmentation 2.** *GIS* the path or trace through a **network** from a source to a given point —*note* connectivity is necessary to find the shortest or best route from a fire station to a fire **3.** a topological construct

conservation 1. protection of plant and animal **habitat 2.** the management of a renewable natural resource with the **objective** of sustaining its productivity in perpetuity while providing for human use compatible with sustainability of the resource —*note* for a forest this may include managed, periodic cutting and removal of trees followed by **regeneration conservation 3.** the process or means of achieving recovery of viable populations

conservation area designated land where conservation strategies are applied for the purpose of attaining a viable plant or animal population

conservation pool the minimum body of water reserved behind a dam for a variety of uses including recreation, wildlife, and fisheries

conservation recommendations opinions by the Fish and Wildlife Service or National Marine Fisheries Service regarding discretionary measures to minimize or avoid adverse effects on a proposed action of federally listed threatened or **endangered species** or designated critical habitat —*see* **threatened species**

constancy *ecology* the relative consistency of occurrence (and therefore degree of dispersal) of a **species** throughout a community or throughout different examples of a given **community** —*note* constancy is often expressed as the proportion of samples in which a species occurs —*see* **frequency**

constant *ecology* a **species** that is present in almost every sample (generally accepted as in > 80 percent of a community)

constrained timber production base the area managed for timber production at less than full intensity in consideration of nontimber resource management objectives

constraint *management, operations research* an equation or inequality that helps define the space containing **feasible solutions**

consumers' surplus the difference between the total value consumers receive from the consumption of a particular good or service and the total amount they pay for the good or service —*note* graphically, consumers' surplus is described as the area beneath the demand curve and above the price line for the entire quantity consumed

contact pesticide a **pesticide** that acts by coming in direct external contact with the target organism rather than by **translocation** or ingestion —*see* **systemic**

contagious dispersion a spatial or temporal distribution in which individual events tend to occur closer together than expected under the **null hypothesis** of complete independence or randomness —*synonym* contagious distribution, aggregated distribution, clustered distribution —*note 1.* the condition of exhibiting a contagious distribution has been termed overdispersion, i.e., hyperdispersion (larger variance or dispersion than expected under complete randomness) —*see* **dispersion** —*note 2.* the condition in which the distribution is more regular or uniform than expected under complete randomness has been termed underdispersion, i.e., hypodispersion

contain a fire to take **fire suppression** action which can reasonably be expected to keep the fire within established boundaries under prevailing conditions

container nursery a facility where seedlings are raised individually in tubes, pots, or other receptacles —see **container seedling, pot planting, tube planting**

container seedling a seedling grown in a receptacle containing the soil, etc., in which it has developed either from seed or as transplants —*see* **bare-root seedling, container nursery, pot planting, tube planting**

contingency table a list of sample frequencies in which samples are classified by two or more categorical variables

continuous data 1. *GIS* **grid** or **raster** data representing surface data such as elevation —*note 1.* in this instance, the data can be any value, positive or negative —*note 2.* continuous data are sometimes referred to as real data —*see* **discrete 2.** data represented by a **TIN** or **lattice,** e.g., surface elevation

continuous forest inventory (CFI) —*see* **dynamic sampling**

continuous grazing the grazing of a specific **range** unit by **livestock** throughout a year or that part of a year that grazing is feasible —*note* the term is not necessarily synonymous with **year-long grazing** since seasonal grazing may be involved —*see* **continuous stocking, rotational grazing, set stocking, year-long range**

continuous stocking a method of grazing livestock on a specific unit of rangeland where animals have unrestricted and uninterrupted access throughout the period when grazing is allowed —*see* **continuous grazing, rotational stocking, set stocking**

continuous variable a variable that may take any value at any level of **precision** in a range

continuum *ecology* an area over which the vegetation or animal population is of constantly changing composition so that homogeneous, separate communities cannot be distinguished

contour a **line** connecting points of equal value —*note* a contour is often in reference to a horizontal datum such as mean sea level

contour furrow a shallow trench made along a contour (i.e., horizontal) line to check runoff and soil loss and conserve moisture in hillside **plantations** —*note* a contour furrow is similar to contour ridge, contour trench, etc.

control the group or groups of experimental units that (a) do not receive a treatment or (b) receive a modified treatment designed to isolate the source of a treatment effect; the group or groups of experimental units that provide a standard of comparison for determining the effects of the treatment(s)

control a fire to complete a **control line** around a fire or **spot fire,** and any interior island to be saved, burn out any unburned area adjacent to the fire side of the control lines, and cool down all **hot spot**s that are immediate threats to the control line, so that the line can be expected to hold under foreseeable conditions —*note* to control a fire implies more thorough suppression than containing a fire

controlled burn —*see* **prescribed burn**

controlled pollination the transfer or permitted transfer of pollen from a known genetic source to receptive **flower**s or female strobili of known seed parents, all other pollen being excluded (e.g., by covering flowers or strobili with isolation bags prior to pollination) —*see* **forest tree breeding, open pollination**, **pollination**, **strobilus**, **wind pollination**

control line a constructed or natural barrier and treated **fire edge** used to control a fire —*see* **firebreak, fireline, fuelbreak, scratch line, secondary line**

control method an approach to **forest management** based on a series of intensive complete or sample inventories of the growing stock to maintain a close check on the progression of size-class distributions (and therefore increments) resulting from silvicultural treatments —*note* a control method employs small, permanent, systematically located sample plots —*synonym* **continuous forest inventory (CFI),** Méthode du Contrôle, examination method, check method, check system, periodic (**forest**) inventory, recurrent (forest) inventory —*see* **dynamic sampling**

control point a surveyed point on the ground that provides a framework on which further survey operations may be based, e.g., vertical control points for contour surveys

control section 1. *soil taxonomy* the arbitrary depths of soil material within which certain diagnostic **horizon**s, features, and other characteristics are used to classify soils —*note* the thickness is specific for each characteristic being considered but may be different for different characteristics **2.** *hydraulics* a constriction or obstruction used in design of hydraulic structures, such as spillways or grade stabilization structures, at which depths upstream are subcritical and depths downstream are supercritical

control time —*see* **elapsed time**

convection mass motions within a fluid resulting in transport and mixing of the properties of that fluid

convection column a thermally produced ascending column of gases, smoke, fly ash, particulate, and other debris produced by a fire —*note 1.* the verticality of a convection column indicates that buoyant forces override the ambient surface wind —*note 2.* more than one convection column may be present on multiple-headed fires

conversion 1. *management* a change from one silvicultural system to another or from one tree species to another (species conversion) **2.** *utilization* the transformation of timber into a product: (a) primary conversion is the initial sawing of the log into lumber, and (b) secondary conversion is any subsequent working or finishing of the lumber into products **3.** *GIS* the changing of data from one format to another, e.g., **TIGER** to DXF, or a map to digital files **4.** *computers* the transfer of data from one system to another, e.g., SUN to IBM —*see* **data automation**

conversion surplus *timber appraisal* the residual amount after all costs of production other than **stumpage** have been subtracted from the sale value of the product —*note 1.* conversion surplus for saw timber is the lumber sale value; that for pulpwood is the sale value of bolts delivered at the mill —*note 2.* the conversion surplus may be divided into two parts (not necessarily equal), an allowance for profit-and-**risk** and stumpage return

cooperating association *recreation* a nonprofit organization established in cooperation with a recreation agency to enhance the recreation area's interpretive program

coordinate the position of a point in space with respect to a **Cartesian coordinate system** (x, y, or z values) —*note* in **GIS**, a coordinate often represents locations on the earth's surface relative to other locations

coordinate geometry (COGO) a computerized surveying-plotting calculation methodology

coordinate system a procedure used to measure horizontal and vertical distances on a **planimetric**

map —*note 1.* a common coordinate system is used to spatially register geographic data for the same area —*note 2.* a coordinate system is usually defined by a map projection, a spheroid of reference, a datum, one or more standard parallels, a central **meridian,** and possible shifts in the x- and y-directions to locate x,y positions of point, line, and area features

coppice 1. the production of new stems from the stump or roots **2.** to cut the main stem (particularly of broadleaved **species**) at the base or to injure the roots to stimulate the production of new shoots for **regeneration 3.** a plant derived by coppicing **4.** any shoot arising from an **adventitious** or dormant bud near the base of a woody plant that has been cut back —*see* **epicormic branch, regeneration method, stool, sucker, vegetative propagation**

coppice forest a **forest** originating from **coppice** shoots, root **sucker**s, or both, i.e., by vegetative means

coppice selection (system) —*see* **regeneration method**

coppice with reserves (standards) —*see* **regeneration method**

coprogenic material soil material that has been modified by being passed through the bodies of soil organisms such as earthworms; remains of excreta and similar materials that occur in some organic soils

cord a stack of fuelwood, pulpwood, or other material that measures $4 \times 4 \times 8$ ft, or 128 ft^3 ($1.2 \times 1.2 \times 2.4$ m, or 3.6 m^3) including wood, bark, and empty space within the stack —*synonym* **rick**

corduroy a road built by cross-laying **sapling**s, small **pole**s, or other material used to strengthen road subgrade

cordwood wood that is cut into short lengths, usually measured in **cord**s and commonly used for pulp or fuel

corks —*see* **calks**

corral an enclosure for handling **livestock**, wild horses and burros, or wildlife

correlation analysis a statistical analysis showing the strength of the linear relationship among two or more variables —*note* the strength of the correlation is expressed by the correlation coefficient (r)

corridor 1. *management* a linear strip of land identified for the present or future location of transportation or utility rights-of-way within its boundaries **2.** *wildlife* a defined tract of land connecting two or more areas of similar management or habitat type that is reserved from substantial disturbance and through which a species can travel to reach **habitat** suitable for reproduction and other

life-sustaining **needs** —*see* **connectivity, woody corridor**

cortex primary plant tissue consisting of large, thin-walled cell tissue separating the vascular system and the **epidermis** in **stem**s and roots

corticolous pertaining to an organism inhabiting or growing on bark —*see* **epiphyllous**

cost-benefit analysis an economic **assessment** of an investment project (either anticipated or accomplished), typically using **benefit-cost ratio**s or **cost-benefit ratio**s as a measure of efficiency

cost-benefit ratio the ratio obtained by dividing the anticipated costs of a project by its anticipated benefits to obtain a measure of expected (or realized) cost per unit of benefit —*note 1.* cost-benefit ratio is usually based on discounted costs and incomes (or compounded costs and incomes) —*note 2.* ideally, costs and benefits include all costs and benefits, which implies a concern for society as a whole, but in practice this is rarely achieved —*see* **benefit-cost ratio**

cost effectiveness the usefulness of specified inputs (costs) to produce specified **output**s (benefits) —*note 1.* in measuring cost effectiveness, some outputs, including environmental, economic, or social impacts, are not assigned monetary values but are achieved at specified levels in the least-cost manner —*note 2.* cost effectiveness is usually measured using present net value, although use of **benefit-cost ratio**s and rates-of-return may be appropriate —*note 3.* the cost effectiveness ratio is the ratio of costs (generally at present value and generally measured as social costs) to a standard measure of performance, which may be related to pollution abatement, mitigation, or some other policy standard

coterminous having the same or coincident boundaries —*note GIS* two adjacent **polygon**s are coterminous when they share the same boundary, e.g., a street centerline dividing two blocks

CO$_2$ compensation point the concentration of carbon dioxide at which the fixing of CO$_2$ by **photosynthesis** balances the release of CO$_2$ by **respiration**

cotyledon an embryonic leaf which often stores food materials —*note* cotyledons are characteristic of seed plants, i.e., Spermatophyta —*see* **dicotyledon, monocotyledon**

covariance the sum of products of differences of two or more correlated variables from their means; if the covariance is estimated from a sample, the sum of products is divided by the number of **degrees of freedom** —*see* **analysis of covariance**

cover 1. an area occupied by vegetation or foliage **2.** vegetation that protects the soil and provides shading to ground vegetation and **regeneration 3.** anything that provides protection for aquatic or terrestrial animals from predators, ameliorates adverse weather conditions, or provides shelter for reproduction —*see* **canopy cover**

cover crop herbaceous plants grown and dug or plowed under while succulent to increase soil fertility with or without supplementary fertilizers —*see* **covert, green manure**

covert any area of vegetation, generally limited in extent (e.g., a thicket), providing natural shelter and sometimes food (e.g., berries) for wildlife, particularly game —*note* where such vegetation provides a refuge from predators and other enemies, it is termed an escape **cover** —*see* **bait, cover crop, food patch, ground cover**

cover type the plant species forming a plurality of composition across a given area, e.g., oak-hickory, northern hardwood, maple-birch

coyote tactics —*see* **fire suppression**

CPM —*see* **critical path method**

cradle knoll the pit and mound microtopography formed as a result of tree uprooting and its attendant displacement of soil; the resulting microrelief —*note 1.* cradle knolls occur in forest areas subject to windthrow with dimensions and general characteristics varying according to tree size, depth to a root-restricting layer, slope, rapidity of creep, or the downslope movement of surface material and soil —*note 2.* the absence of microrelief on sites otherwise suitable for its development is presumptive evidence of former cultivation or other artificial disturbance

crawler —*see* **tractor**

creep 1. *soils* slow mass movement of soil and soil material down slopes, driven primarily by gravity but facilitated by saturation with water and by alternate freezing and thawing **2.** *wood utilization* the deflection in a wood beam after long-term loading

creeping fire —*see* **fire behavior**

creosote a distillate obtained mostly by high-temperature carbonization of bituminous coal and consisting mainly of liquid and solid aromatic hydrocarbons with appreciable quantities of tar acids and tar bases —*note 1.* creosote is heavier than water and has a continuous boiling range of at least 125°C beginning at about 200°C —*note 2.* creosote as a wood preservative has mostly been replaced by other chemicals

crest-stage gauge an instrument designed to delineate the peak stage of a flood, usually at remote or other partial recording stations

crew boss —*see* **large fire organization**

crib 1. a boxlike structure consisting of short logs **2.** stacked logs used as a pier to support a bridge

criteria and indicators *sustainable forest management* a measurement of an aspect of a **criterion;** a quantitative or qualitative **variable** that can be measured or described and that, when observed periodically, demonstrates trends —*see* **monitoring**

criterion *plural* **criteria** *sustainable forest management* a category, condition, or process by which **sustainable forest management** may be assessed —*see* **chain of custody, criteria and indicators**

critical depth the depth of flow in a channel of specified dimensions at which specific energy is a minimum for a given discharge

critical habitat *under the Endangered Species Act, 1976* **1.** the specific areas within the geographic area occupied by a federally listed species on which physical and biological features are found that are essential to the conservation of the species and that may require special management or protection **2.** the specific areas outside the geographic area occupied by a listed species that are determined to be essential for the conservation of the species —*see* **crucial habitat**

critical path method (CPM) a **network analysis** model that seeks to determine the expected times of completion of the total project and its subprojects —*see* **program evaluation and review technique**

critical reach the point in the receiving stream below a discharge point at which the lowest dissolved oxygen level is reached and recovery begins

critical root zone *urban forestry* the area surrounding a tree having a radius extending from the stem to 1 ft (0.30 m) beyond the **dripline** of the crown

critical threshold the point along a gradient in a variable at which a small change produces a rapid change in another variable

critical velocity 1. the velocity at which a given discharge changes from tranquil to rapid flow **2.** that velocity in open channels for which the specific energy (sum of the depth and velocity head) is a minimum for a given discharge

crook an abrupt bend in a tree or log

crop the vegetation growing on a forest area, more particularly the major woody growth having commercial value

crop tree any tree selected to become a component of a future commercial harvest

cross 1. —*synonym* **hybrid 2.** the process of **cross-pollination**

crossability the relative success in obtaining viable offspring from cross-pollinations, especially interspecific ones —*see* **cross-pollination, incompatibility, outcrossing, species hybrid, sterility**

cross-cut saw —*see* **saw**

cross dimensions the length and width of a cross-section of a stack of timber, i.e., a section perpendicular to the sides of the stack

cross ditch —*see* **water bar**

cross-pollination pollination by a genetically different plant —*note* an outcross is a cross between unrelated individuals —*see* **backcross, crossability, emasculation, F₁, F₂, hybrid, outcrossing, polycross test, self-pollination, species hybrid, topcross test**

crown the part of a tree or woody plant bearing live branches and foliage

crown base the height on the tree bole representing the bottom of the live **crown**, defined variously as (a) the lowest live branch; (b) the lowest whorl with live branches in at least three of four quadrants around the stem; (c) in a crown visually reconstructed to have a symmetric base, the point of attachment of the lowest live branch; (d) the lowest whorl with live branches around at least 0.75 of the stem circumference; (e) in hardwoods, the lowest live foliage —*see* **crown height**

crown class a category of tree based on its **crown** position relative to those of adjacent trees —*see* **stem class, thinning grade, wolf tree;** types of crown class are the following:

—**codominant** a tree whose crown helps to form the general level of the main canopy in even-aged **stands** or, in **uneven-aged stands**, the main canopy of the tree's immediate neighbors, receiving full light from above and comparatively little from the sides

—**dominant** a tree whose crown extends above the general level of the main canopy of **even-aged stands** or, in **uneven-aged stands**, above the crowns of the tree's immediate neighbors and receiving full light from above and partial light from the sides

—**emergent** a tree whose crown is completely above the general level of the main canopy, receiving full light from above and from all sides

—**intermediate** a tree whose crown extends into the lower portion of the main canopy of **even-aged stands** or, in **uneven-aged stands**, into the lower portion of the canopy formed by the tree's immediate neighbors, but shorter in height than the **codominant**s and receiving little direct light from above and none from the sides

—**overtopped (suppressed)** a tree whose crown is completely overtopped by the crowns of one or more neighboring trees —*note* the vigor of over-

crown class *continued*

topped (suppressed) trees varies from high to low depending on individual circumstances

—**predominant** a tree whose crown has grown above the general level of the upper canopy

crown closure the point at which the vertical projections of crown perimeters within a canopy touch

crown cover the ground area covered by the **crown**s of trees or woody vegetation as delimited by the vertical projection of crown perimeters and commonly expressed as a percent of total ground area —*synonym* **canopy cover** —*note* crown cover measures the extent to which the crowns of trees are nearing general contact with each other

crown density the amount and compactness of foliage of the **crown**s of trees or **shrub**s —*synonym* canopy density —*see* **shade density**

crown diameter the mean of two or more measurements of the widest part of a tree's live crown —*note* when only two measures are taken, they are usually of the maximum and minimum diameters —*synonym* crown width

crown diameter ratio *of a standing tree* the ratio of the crown diameter (ft or m) to the diameter breast height outside the bark (in or cm)

crown fire —*see* **fire behavior, forest fire**

crown forest or **land** a **forest** (or land) owned by the sovereign or the government of commonwealth countries —*note* in Canada, federal crown lands are held by the federal government and provincial crown lands are held by the provincial governments

crown form *of a standing tree* the general shape of the crown, sometimes quantitatively measured as the ratio of crown length to crown diameter, or mapped by computer

crown gall a tumorlike **gall**, generally on tree roots or root crown, originated by pathogenic bacteria, especially the crown-gall bacterium *Agrobacterium tumefaciens*

crown height the vertical distance from ground level to the **crown** base of a standing tree —*see* **crown base**

crown length (live crown) *of a standing tree* the vertical distance from the tip of the leader to the base of the crown, measured to the lowest live whorl (upper crown length) or to the lowest live branch, excluding **epicormics** (lower crown length) or to a point halfway between (mean crown length) —*see* **live crown ratio**

crown ratio (crown length ratio) —*see* **live crown ratio**

crown thinning —*see* **thinning**

crownwood —*see* **juvenile wood**

crucial habitat habitat which is basic to maintaining viable populations of plants, fish, or wildlife during certain seasons of the year or specific reproduction periods —*see* **critical habitat**

cruise, cruising 1. a **forest** survey to locate and estimate the quantity of timber on a given area according to species, size, quality, possible products, or other characteristics 2. the estimate obtained from such a cruise —*see* **forest inventory, reconnaissance**

crumb structure a structural condition in which most of the **ped**s are small particles or crumbs —*note* crumb structure is replaced in the current US system of soil taxonomy by the term massive or **structure**less

cryptophyte a plant whose buds or shoot apices remain below the ground surface or in the soil under water during unfavorable seasons —*note 1.* cryptophyte is one of the major life-forms of Raunkiaer —*note 2.* cryptophytes include **geophyte**s, **helophyte**s, and **hydrophyte**s —*see* **chamaephyte, phaneroptype, hemicryptophyte**

cubic foot a unit of true volume that measures $1 \times 1 \times 1$ ft ($30.48 \times 30.48 \times 30.48$ cm)

cull 1. any item of production, e.g., trees, logs, lumber, or seedlings, rejected because it does not meet certain specifications of usability or grade 2. logs that are rejected, parts of logs deducted in measurement, or the deduction made from gross timber volume because of defects —*note* in a standing tree, the cull expressed as a percent of the tree's gross volume is termed the cull factor —*see* **live cull**

culmination of mean annual increment (CMAI) the age in the growth cycle of a tree or **stand** at which the **mean annual increment (MAI)** for height, diameter, basal area, or volume is at a maximum —*note* at culmination, MAI equals the **periodic annual increment (PAI)**

cultivar a **clone**, **race**, or product of breeding selected from a population of plants because it has desirable characteristics and is generally more or less genetically uniform —*note* such cultivated plants are given a non-Latin name and designated cv —*see* **variety**

cultural operation the manipulation of vegetation to meet **objective**s of controlling **stand** composition or structure, such as site improvement, **forest tree improvement,** increased **regeneration,** increased growth, or measures to control insects or disease

cumulative effects the combined effects resulting from sequential actions on a given area —*note* significant cumulative effects can result from individ-

ually minor but collectively important actions taking place over a period of time because of their being interconnected or synergistic —*synonym* cumulative impacts —*see* **direct effects, indirect effects**

cumulative use —*see* **use, cumulative**

cunit a unit of volume, usually pulpwood, consisting of 100 ft³ (2.83 m³) of solid wood (not including bark or air volume)

current annual increment (CAI) the growth observed in a tree or **stand** in a specific one-year period —*note* although the current annual increment is strictly that of the year just passing, it is generally taken as the mean of a few preceding years, i.e., a short-term mean annual increment termed a periodic (mean) annual increment —*see* **mean annual increment (MAI), periodic annual increment (PAI)**

cursor *computers* 1. a graphic pointer that indicates a location on a terminal screen 2. an internal pointer to a record in a table —*note* the record to which the cursor points is available for display, query, and update operations

curve fitting *GIS* an automated mapping function that converts a series of short, connected straight lines into smooth curves to represent entities that do not have precise mathematical definitions, e.g., rivers, shoreline, and contour lines

curvilinear model a statistical model that includes higher order terms, e.g., quadratic or cubic, in equations

customary rights a prerogative resulting from a long series of habitual or customary actions, constantly repeated, which have by such repetition and by uninterrupted acquiescence acquired the force of a law within a geographical or sociological unit

cut *harvesting* the output of logs based on **stand,** unit, or season

cuticle 1. *plants* a thin, continuous, waterproof, noncellular film secreted by epidermal and other cells on the external surface of aerial parts of vascular plants —*note* a cuticle tends to prevent desiccation and repels external water —*see* **cutin, epicuticular wax** 2. *insects* the outer noncellular layers of an insect (and other arthropod) integument secreted by the epidermis —*synonym* exoskeleton

cutin a waterproof mixture of waxes, fatty acids, soaps, higher alcohols and resinous material forming the chief ingredient of the **cuticle** of many plants —*see* **suberin**

cut-off drain a ditch constructed to intercept surface and subsurface runoff and lead it away from some construction to be protected, e.g., a road —*synonym* catch-water drain, interception drain, trap drain

cutover land that has previously been logged

cutter a person who fells, limbs, tops, or **bucks** trees —*synonym* **faller**

cutting 1. *logging* the **felling** of an individual tree(s) or stand(s) **2.** *regeneration* a shoot, twig, or other plant part removed from a plant —*note* a cutting is usually made to induce roots and to develop into a new plant —*see* **air layering, vegetative propagation**

cutting cycle the planned interval between partial harvests in an **uneven-aged stand** —*see* **thinning interval**

cutting system *sawmilling* a method of cutting logs (usually hardwoods) that determines the grade and sizes of lumber —*note* the defects that are allowed in the area outside the clear or sound face cuttings vary with different rules and grades

cut-to-length *harvesting* a system in which felled trees are processed into log lengths at the stump before they are carried to the road or landing; an alternative **full-tree** logging

cutworm a member of the moth family, particularly of the genus *Agrotis,* whose soil-inhabiting **larvae** feed on roots of various plants including trees, sometimes on the foliage, or on seedling stems at ground level through which they frequently cut —*note* many species of cutworms are serious agricultural **pests**, but serious problems to trees are usually limited to nurseries, young conifer **plantations**, and young ornamental plantings —*synonym* army worm

cytogenetics the study of cells or cellular inclusions as related to genetics —*see* **chromosome, cytology**

cytology the study of the cell, i.e., its structure, function, development, and reproduction in relation to growth, differentiation, and heredity —*see* **chromosome, cytogenetics**

cytoplasm the living matter within a **cell**, excluding the **nucleus** —*see* **gene**

cytoplasmic inheritance nonnuclear **DNA** inheritance usually associated with transmission of mitochondrial and chloroplast DNA, which in trees is sometimes maternal or paternal depending on **species** —*see* **maternal effect, paternal effect**

D

damping-off the rotting of seedlings, before or soon after emergence, caused by soil fungal species of *Fusarium, Phytophthora, Pythium,* and *Rhizoctonia* attacking at or near soil level —*note 1.* the name is derived from an association with damp weather or damp conditions —*note 2.* damping-off is the most common and probably the most serious nursery disease

danger class a relative **fire danger rating** as determined from burning conditions and other variable factors of **fire danger** —*synonym* fire danger class

danger index a relative number indicating the severity of **fire danger** as determined from burning conditions and other variable factors of fire danger —*synonym* fire danger

Darcy's law an expression of the principle of flow in permeable media as follows: a volume of water passing through a porous medium in unit time is proportional to the cross-sectional area and to the difference in hydraulic head, and inversely proportional to the thickness of the medium —*note* the proportionality constant is called the hydraulic conductivity

dart leader *meteorology* the electrical discharge which typically, after the first stroke, initiates each succeeding stroke of a composite flash of lightning —*see* **stepped leader**

data —*see* **datum**

data automation 1. digitizing **2.** using electronic scanning for data collection —*see* **conversion**

database a collection of data stored in a systematic manner such that the data can be readily retrieved, modified, and manipulated to create information —*note 1.* most databases are computerized and consist of fields and records that are organized by data sets and governed by a scheme of organization, and can be linked to allow complex search-and-compare routines —*note 2.* **hierarchical** and **relational** define two popular structural schemes in use in a GIS, e.g., a GIS database includes data about the spatial location and shape of geographic entities as well as descriptions about those entities

database management system (DBMS) 1. *GIS* the software for managing and manipulating whole data sets, e.g., including the graphic and tabular data **2.** *computers* the software for managing (e.g., inputting, verifying, storing, retrieving, querying, and manipulating) the tabular information —*note* a GIS may use a DBMS made by another software vendor, the GIS interfaces with that software

data conversion the translation of data from one format to another —*note* conversion occurs when data are transferred from one computer system to another

data dictionary *computers* a coded catalog of all data types or a list of **column**s giving data names and structures —*note 1.* a data dictionary may be on-line (referred to as an automated data dictionary), in which case the codes for the data types are carried in the database —*note 2.* a data dictionary is also referred to as a DD/D, for data dictionary/directory

data integration *computers* the combination of databases or data files from different functional units of an organization or from different organizations that collect information about the same entities, e.g., properties, census tracts, street segments —*note* in combining the data, added intelligence is derived

data model 1. a generalized, user-defined view of the data related to applications **2.** a formal method for arranging data to mimic the behavior of the real-world entities they represent —*note* (GIS) fully developed data **model**s describe data types, integrity rules for the data types, and operations on the data types; some data models are **triangulated irregular networks (TIN)**, **image**s, and **georela-tional** or relational **model**s for tabular data

datum *plural* **data 1.** facts, numbers, letters, symbols, line graphics, imagery, or alphanumeric information that refer to or describe an object, idea, condition, situation, or other factor —*note* data connote basic elements of information that can be analyzed, processed, stored, or manipulated by a computer **2.** *geodetics* a reference surface consisting of five quantities: the latitude and longitude of an initial point, the azimuth of a line from this point, and two constants necessary to define the reference spheroid —*note 1.* a datum forms the basis for the computation of horizontal control surveys in which the curvature of the earth is considered —*note 2.* the corresponding datum is the basis for a planar coordinate system, e.g., the North American datum for 1983 (NAD83) is the datum for map projections and coordinates in all of North America —*synonym* horizontal control datum, horizontal datum, horizontal geodetic datum **3.** a level surface to which elevations are referred, usually but not always mean sea level —*synonym* vertical datum, vertical control

DBH *also* **dbh** —*see* **diameter (at) breast height**

DBMS —*see* **database management system**

deadhead a vehicle traveling outbound or inbound without a load

deadman *harvesting* an anchoring device consisting of usually one or more logs buried in the ground to which a guy or anchor line is attached —*synonym* anchor log

debarker a machine designed to remove the bark from trees, logs, or **bolt**s —*note* a debarker may

use rings, drums, flails, or high-pressure water (hydraulic debarker)

debris flow a rapidly moving mass of rock fragments, soil, and mud with over half of the materials being larger than sand size

debris torrent a rapid movement of a large quantity of materials (wood and sediment) down a stream channel during storms or floods —*note* debris torrents generally occur in smaller streams and result in scouring of the streambed

decay 1. the decomposition of wood by fungi and other microorganisms resulting in softening, progressive loss of strength and weight, and often in changes of texture and color —*note* two commonly recognized **stage**s of decay are incipient (primary) and final (complete) **2.** the decomposing or decomposed wood —*see* **heart decay, rot**

deciduous 1. naturally shed, e.g., leaves or fruit **2.** of perennial plants that are normally more or less leafless for some time during the year

deciduous cover a vegetation class in which 75 percent or more of the diagnostic vegetation is made up of tree or shrub species that shed foliage simultaneously in response to an unfavorable season

decision making the process of defining a problem, identifying alternative solutions, determining the criteria, evaluating the alternatives, and choosing a solution

decision support system a set of decision-making rules built into computer **model**s that help the computer resolve complex problems —*note* these rules tell the computer when to accept or reject data and options, and how to proceed as the changes are made

decision tree a graphical representation of a sequential decision problem that facilitates analyses that explicitly incorporate the sequential nature of the decisions

decision variable the decision alternative or input that can be specified or controlled by the decision maker —*note* decision varibles are often used to represent combinations of land types, **silvicultural prescription** alternatives, harvest timing choices, etc., in forest planning problems

deck 1. a pile of logs on a landing **2.** an area or platform on which wood is placed

declination, magnetic (compass) the angle between true north and magnetic north, i.e., the direction of a compass needle, which varies with location and changes gradually over time

decline the decrease in trees, shrubs, and herbs, or **forest health** and vigor, caused by one or more biotic or abiotic factors —*see* **syndrome**

decommission to remove those elements of a road

or buildings that reroute hillslope drainage and present slope stability hazards —*synonym* hydrologic obliteration

decomposition   a large number of interrelated processes by which organic matter is broken down to smaller particles and soluble forms available for plants

decreaser plant species any plant **species** of the original or **climax** vegetation that decreases in relative amounts, especially under continued overuse of a forage crop or in response to other disturbance factors such as fire, heavy defoliation, or drought —*note* some agencies use this term only in response to overutilization —*see* **increaser plant species**

decurrent crown the spreading crown form resulting when lateral branches grow nearly as fast as or faster than the terminal leader, often resulting in repeated forking of the main stem —*note* decurrent crowns are typical of many deciduous species including elms, oaks, and maples —*synonym* deliquescent —*see* **excurrent crown**

deepwater habitat permanently flooded lands lying below the deepwater boundary of **wetland**s —*note* this boundary is at a depth of 2 m (6.6 ft) below low water or at the edge of emergent macrophytes, whichever is deeper

deer yard a wintering area used by deer, primarily white-tailed deer, during severe weather

defect *in timber* any feature (whether intrinsic, e.g., **knot**s, or developing later, e.g., **crook**s, **conk**s, decay, splits, **sweep**, bad sawing, or injury) that lowers the utility or commercial value of timber and may therefore lead to lower grade or rejection as a **cull** —*note 1.* whether a particular feature is classed as a blemish, imperfection, or defect depends on the relevant specifications or grading rules, or the purpose for which the timber is intended —*note 2.* a sound defect is one free from decay

defect deduction *in measuring logs or scaling* the estimated amount of defect material subtracted from gross volume to obtain the amount of wood that meets grading standards

deferment the delay of **livestock** grazing on an area for a time adequate to provide for plant reproduction, establishment of new plants, or **restoration** of vigor of existing plants —*see* **deferred grazing**

deferred grazing the use of **deferment** in **grazing management** of a **management unit,** but not in a systematic rotation including other units —*see* **grazing system**

deferred rotation any **grazing system** which provides for a systematic rotation of the **deferment** among pastures or units

defibration the separation of wood and other plant material into **fibers** or fiber bundles by mechanical or mechanical plus chemical means —*see* **pulp**

deflation the sorting out, lifting, and removal of loose, dry, fine-grained soil particles by turbulent eddies of wind

deflection 1. the amount of bending at the midpoint of a loaded beam 2. the vertical distance between the **chord** and the **skyline,** measured at midspan —*note* deflection is frequently expressed as a percentage of the horizontal span length

deflocculant a material added to a pesticide formulation to prevent aggregation of solid particles

defoliant any chemical that initiates abscission or causes leaves to drop when applied to a plant

defoliator 1. any organism, but more particularly insects, that can cause leaves to drop —*note* many defoliators are significant disturbance agents or **pest**s, e.g., **budworm**s and gypsy moth (*Lymantria dispar*) —*see* **leafcast** 2. a defoliant **herbicide**

deforestation the removal of a forest stand where the land is put to a nonforest use —*see* **afforestation, reforestation, regeneration**

deformation a change in the normal shape or size of a body through either (a) an external **stress,** e.g., by bending (deflection), twisting (torsion), stretching (applying tension), compressing (applying compression), and if this causes fracture, crushing; or (b) an internal stress causing swelling or shrinkage —*note* deformation is a measure of **strain** and sometimes identified with it

degradation 1. the process whereby a compound is transformed into simpler compounds 2. the changing of a soil to a more highly leached and a more highly weathered condition —*note* degradation is usually accompanied by morphological changes such as development of an A_2 **horizon** 3. the erosion of stream beds or banks that occurs when instream sediment loads do not meet a stream's capacity (tractive force) to transport sediment —*note* degradation commonly occurs below reservoirs that trap sediments, when flow rates are increased, or when watershed erosion and sediment delivery rates to streams are significantly reduced —*see* **aggradation**

degrade 1. any **defect** that lowers the grade of a log 2. to lower the grade of a log

degree-day a measure of the departure of the mean daily temperature from a given standard —*note* one degree-day is given for each degree (°C or °F) of departure above (or below) the standard during one day —*see* **heating degree-day**

degrees of freedom the number of independent comparisons that can be made between the items in a sample; commonly, the number of sample observations minus the number of functions of the sample values held constant

dehisce to split open, especially of an anther or fruit structure —*see* **anthesis**

delimber *harvesting* a self-propelled machine designed to remove all limbs from trees with flailing chains or knives —*see* **gate delimber**

deliquescent —*see* **decurrent crown**

Delphi method an iterative technique designed to obtain a consensus among experts concerning the best course of action or what is likely to happen under a specified **scenario** —*note* a structured questionnaire or survey is administered to all experts at the same time, the results are compiled and circulated, and another questionnaire or survey is administered that allows experts to revise their initial estimates in light of the information shared by the others in the group

delta a plain of alluvial deposits between the branches at the mouth of a river, stream, or creek

DEM —*see* **digital elevation model**

demand 1. the functional relationship between the price of a given commodity and the quantity that buyers would be willing and able to purchase in a given market during a specified time period —*note* demand is typically expressed as either a mathematical equation (showing quantity demanded as a function of price) or as a curve showing price per unit plotted over quantity 2. the actual quantity of a commodity or service that buyers are willing to purchase in the market at a given price over a specified time period —*see* **supply**

deme *ecology* an interbreeding subpopulation

demobilization *fire* the release of resources from an incident in strict accordance with a detailed plan approved by the **incident commander** —*see* **mobilization**

demographic relating to density, age, and distribution of individuals in a **population**

dendrochronology the study and interpretation of annual growth rings of trees and their use in dating past variations in climate and in archaeological investigations —*see* **growth ring**

dendrograph —*see* **band dendrometer**

dendrology the study of trees and their identifying characteristics

dendrometer a device for measuring the diameter of a tree stem or logs —*note* dendrometers include a simple tape, a **caliper,** an optical device, a **relaskop,** or a **band dendrometer**

denitrification reduction of nitrogen oxides (nitrate and nitrite) to molecular nitrogen or nitrogen ox-

ides with lower oxidation state of nitrogen by bacterial activity —*note* the reduction of nitrogen oxides by chemical reactions involving nitrite is termed chemodenitrification

densify *GIS* a process of adding **vertices** to **arcs** at a given distance without altering the arc's shape —*see* **spline** for a different method for adding vertices

density 1. the weight (mass), number, or size per unit volume 2. *biology* the size of a population in relation to some unit of space —*note* density is usually expressed as the number of individuals or the population biomass per unit area or volume 3. *range management* the number of individuals per unit area —*note* density is not a measure of **cover** although in the past the term has been used to mean cover —*see* **frequency** 4. *silviculture* —*see* **stand density**

density cycle a completed period of rhythmic fluctuation in the density of a species, e.g., from high to low density and back to high

density dependence the decrease in population growth rate with increasing population density —*note* density dependence theoretically results in a sigmoidal population growth curve

density management the cutting or killing of trees to increase spacing and accelerate growth of remaining trees —*note* density management is used to improve forest health of stands, to open the forest canopy for selected trees, to maintain understory vegetation, to accelerate growth to maintain desired seral condition, or to attain later-successional characteristics for biological diversity

den tree a tree that contains a weather-tight cavity for wildlife

deoxyribonucleic acid (DNA) a double-stranded, self-replicating acid of large molecular weight that is the genetically active portion of the **chromosome**

depauperate *biology* an area that has biodiversity reduced to relatively few plant and animal species

depletion the utilization of a natural **renewable resource** at a rate greater than the rate of accretion

depletion allowance a deduction from taxable income allowed, under specified conditions, by US tax laws to the owners of timber for reduction of an original growing stock through cutting

depletion curve *hydraulics* a graphical representation of water depletion from storage-stream channels, surface soil, and groundwater —*note* the curve can be drawn for base flow, direct runoff, or total flow

deployment the physical movement of seedlings or **propagules** from one site (usually a nursery) to another (usually **plantation**s), including their locational configuration on the recipient site

depreciative behavior *recreation* a human act that tends to diminish the quality of outdoor recreation experiences and degrade the condition of the biophysical environment

depression storage the water stored in surface depressions and therefore not available for production surface runoff

depth-area-duration analysis the determination of the maximum amounts of **precipitation** within various durations over areas of various sizes —*note* this term is used in the prediction of flood events

derived savanna the vegetation existing on sites formerly supporting **high forest** and having developed through cutting and burning (e.g., through shifting cultivation) and being maintained as savanna by annual or frequent grass fires —*note* tree **species** in a derived savanna may differ from those of the original high forest —*see* **savanna**

DESCON —*see* **designated control burn**

descriptive data *GIS* tabular data describing the geographic characteristics of map features —*note* descriptive data can include numbers, text, images, and **CAD** drawings about features

desert a **biome** where the average amount of **precipitation** is erratic and less than 25 cm (9.8 in) per year and where evaporation exceeds **precipitation** —*note* such areas have sparse, highly adapted vegetation, e.g., cacti, succulents, and spiny **shrub**s

desertification the progressive destruction or degradation of vegetative **cover**, especially in arid or semiarid regions bordering existing deserts —*note* overgrazing of **range**lands, large-scale cutting of **forest**s and **woodland**s, drought, and burning of extensive areas all contribute to desertification

desert pavement a natural, residual concentration of wind-polished, closely packed pebbles, boulders, and other rock fragments mantling a desert surface where wind action and sheetwash have removed all smaller particles —*note* desert paving usually protects the underlying, finer-grained material from further **deflation**

desiccation the loss of the internal moisture content necessary to maintain **turgor,** growth, or survival —*synonym* dehydration

design —*see* **experimental design**

designated control burn (DESCON) a management system used in the Southern Region of the USDA Forest Service that permits designated personnel to accept specific **wildfire**s as prescribed fires and handle them accordingly —*note* only fires burning within a specified range of environmental

and fuel conditions and contributing to land management **goal**s may be accepted as DESCON fires

desired future condition (DFC) a description of the land or resource conditions that are believed necessary if goals and objectives are fully achieved

determinate growth 1. growth whose structures are initiated by a **meristem** in one year but do not complete development until the meristem resumes growth in the following year 2. structures whose growth is fixed, such as leaves, **flower**s, and fruits —*see* **indeterminate growth**

deterministic a type of system that can be characterized exactly, with no element of chance or probability —*see* **mechanistic, stochastic**

deterministic model a **model** in which relationships are treated as fixed for a given set of input parameters such that the model output never varies for a given set of inputs

detritivory the consumption of **detritus** or dead organic matter

detritus 1. small pieces of dead and decomposing plants and animals 2. detached and broken-down organic fragments of structure 3. small organic particles such as leaves and twigs —*see* **drift**

development the advancement of the management and use of natural resources to satisfy human **needs** and improve the quality of human life —*note* for development to be sustainable it must take into account the social, ecological, and economic factors of the living and nonliving resource base, and of the long-term and short-term advantages and disadvantages of alternative actions

deviation the difference between any particular observation in a set of observations and the **arithmetic mean** of the set

dew water condensed onto grass and other objects near the ground, the temperatures of which have fallen below the dew point of the surface air due to radiational cooling during the night but are still above freezing —*note* hoarfrost forms if the **dew point** is below freezing

dew point the temperature to which a given parcel of air must be cooled at constant pressure and constant water vapor content in order for saturation to occur

DFC —*see* **desired future condition**

diallel cross 1. *complete diallel cross* a mating design and subsequent **progeny test** resulting from the crossing of *n* parents in all possible n^2 combinations including self and **reciprocal cross**es 2. *incomplete diallel cross* a partial sampling of a complete diallel; any individual family or type of family may be omitted —*see* **polycross test, self-pollination**

diameter, basal the diameter of a **shrub** or seedling measured at the **root collar**

diameter (at) breast height (DBH, dbh) the diameter of the stem of a tree measured at **breast height** (4.5 ft or 1.37 m) from the ground —*note 1.* on sloping ground the measure is taken from the uphill side —*note 2.* DBH usually implies diameter outside bark (DOB) but can be measured as inside bark (DIB) —*synonym* **diameter breast high** —*see* **diameter inside bark, diameter outside bark**

diameter class 1. any of the intervals into which a range of diameters of tree stems or logs may be divided for classification and use —*note* e.g., the 6-in (15.24-cm) diameter class includes diameters from 5.0 to 6.9 in (12.70 to 17.52 cm) **2.** the actual trees or logs falling into such an interval —*see* **stem class**

diameter class limit the upper or lower limits of a diameter class

diameter inside bark (DIB) the diameter of the wood portion of a stem or log cross section —*note* DIB is usually measured on logs or estimated on trees as diameter outside bark minus twice the bark thickness —*see* **diameter (at) breast height**

diameter limit the diameter (minimum or maximum) to which trees or logs are measured, cut (felled), or used —*note* one may, e.g., inventory all trees with a **DBH** above a 4.5 in (11.43 cm) minimum diameter limit

diameter-limit cutting the removal of all merchantable trees above or below a specified **DBH** (possibly varying with species), with or without the cutting of some or all **cull** trees

diameter outside bark (DOB) the diameter of a stem or log cross section that includes both the wood and the bark —*see* **diameter (at) breast height**

diameter, stump the diameter of a tree inside or outside bark at stump height (generally 1 ft or 30.5 cm above the ground on the uphill side)

diameter tape a measure specially graduated so that the diameter can be read directly from the circumference of a tree stem or log

diapause *entomology* **1.** a form of dormancy in which development and activity are arrested and metabolism is greatly decreased, but life is maintained —*note* diapause is common in insects, usually occurring in advance of adverse conditions and permitting survival **2.** the period of arrested development —*see* **quiescence**

DIB —*see* **diameter inside bark**

dibble a tool used to prepare planting holes for seedlings —*note* a dibble is spadelike for bareroot seedlings and cone shaped for container seedlings —*see* **hoedad**

dichogamy the maturation of male and female structures on the same plant at different times —*note* dichogamy fosters natural **cross-pollination** —*see* **monoecious, protandry, protogyny**

dicotyledon a plant whose seedling normally has two seed leaves (**cotyledons**); a division of **Angiospermae** —*note* dicotyledonous trees are commonly called broadleaved trees and constitute the majority of commercial **hardwoods** —*see* **monocotyledon, nonpored wood**

dieback the progressive dying from the extremity of any part of a plant —*note* dieback may or may not result in the death of the entire plant —*synonym* top drying —*see* **top kill**

differentiation the divergence in growth patterns of individual trees due to redistribution of growing space during **stand** development —*note 1.* differentiation is first evident as divergence in diameter growth patterns, then in height —*note 2.* differentiation leads to formation of crown classes

diffuse porous pertaining to wood of **hardwood**s in which the **vessels** are of fairly uniform size and distribution throughout a growth ring, e.g., yellow poplar, birch, and maple —*see* **ring porous**

diffuse radiation the radiant energy propagating in many directions through a given small volume of space —*note* diffuse radiation is contrasted with parallel radiation

diffusion *in air* the exchange of fluid parcels (and hence the transport of conservative properties) between regions in space following the apparently random motions of the turbulent air

digital pertaining to data that are in computer-readable format (e.g., **bit** or **byte** data)

digital elevation model (DEM) *GIS* **1.** a continuous **raster** image in which data file values represent elevation **2.** the format of the US Geological Survey (USGS) elevation data sets **3.** a topographic surface arranged in a data file as a set of regularly spaced x,y,z locations where z represents elevation —*see* **digital terrain model**

digital exchange format (DXF) *computers* **1.** the ASCII text files defined by Autodesk, Inc., at first for **CAD**, now appearing in third-party GIS software **2.** an intermediate file format for exchanging data from one software package to another, neither of which has a direct translation for the other but where both can read and convert DXF data files into their format —*note* this often saves time and preserves accuracy of the data because the original is not reautomated

digital image an **image** for which the incident radiation recorded as a voltage by a detector has been converted from a continuous range of values to a range expressed by a finite number of integers, e.g., recorded as binary codes from 0 to 255 (8 **bits**)

digital image processing the computer-aided manipulation of the digital values or picture elements (**pixels**) in an **image** for the purpose of improved image visualization, analysis, or information extraction

digital line graph (DLG) *GIS* **1.** *data* the geographic and tabular data files obtained from the US Geological Survey (USGS) that may include base categories such as transportation, hydrography, contours, and public land survey boundaries **2.** *format* the formal standards developed and published by the USGS for exchange of cartographic and associated tabular data files —*note* many non-DLG data may be formatted in DLG format

digital map a machine-readable representation of a geographic phenomenon stored for display or analysis by a digital computer —*see* **analog map**

digital orthophotograph a computer-compatible **aerial photograph** or digital **image** that has been geometrically corrected for displacements caused by terrain and camera **tilt** —*note* examples include orthophoto, orthophotoquad, ortho, orthoimagery, and orthorectified imagery

digital photogrammetry the science of applying photographic interpretation and measurement techniques to digital **images** —*see* **softcopy photogrammetry**

digital terrain model (DTM) a computer graphics software technique for converting point elevation data to characterize the shape of the land as a contour map or as a three-dimensional hill-and-valley grid view of the ground surface —*see* **digital elevation model (DEM)** —*note* DTM is sometimes used synonymously with DEM

digitize **1.** to convert or encode map data that are represented in analog form into digital information of x and y coordinates **2.** to employ a digitizing tablet to record x,y or x,y,z values for map features —*note* lines are traced to define their shape; a **digitizer** button, pressed periodically along the line, records x,y coordinates; a digitized line is therefore a series of x,y coordinates —*see* **digitizer, gap, scanning**

digitizer **1.** a device used to capture planar coordinate data, usually as *x* and *y* coordinates, from existing analog maps for digital use within a computerized program such as a GIS —*also* digitizing table **2.** a person who **digitizes** —*see* **scanner**

diluent any liquid or solid substance that serves to reduce the concentration of the active ingredient in a pesticide

dimension lumber —*see* **lumber**

dimorphism a difference in size, form, or color among individuals of the same **species** characterizing two distinct types —*note* many insect species exhibit sexual dimorphism and some exhibit **polymorphism** —*see* **morph**

dioecious pertaining to a **species** having male and female **flowers** (or strobili) produced on separate plants —*see* **bisexual, monoecious, staminate, strobilus, taxon**

diploid having two sets of **chromosomes** (2*n*), usually one set from each parent —*note* the cells of most higher organisms are diploid except for the sex cells and associated reproductive tissue —*see* **chromosome number, chromosome set, gamete, haploid, polyploid, vegetative cell**

direct attack —*see* **fire suppression**

direct effects the effects that result from an action and occur at the same time and place as the action —*see* **cumulative effects, indirect effects**

directional felling the cutting of a tree in a predetermined direction to make skidding efficient or to avoid damage —*note 1.* wedges, jacks or cables may be used if the desired falling direction differs from the natural fall line —*note 2.* when shears are used, the wedge-shaped blade provides a lever that directs the tree into its lay

directory *computers* a location on a disk containing a set of data files and other directories (subdirectories) —*note* operating systems use directories to organize data; directories are organized in a tree structure in which each tree branch represents a subdirectory; the location of a directory is specified by a pathname, e.g., /disk/project_db/til02/soilscov)

direct seeding the manual or mechanical sowing of tree seed on an area, either in spots or broadcast

Dirichlet tessellation —*see* **Thiessen polygon**

discharge the rate of water flowing at a given place, and within a given period of time —*note* discharge is usually expressed as m³/sec, ft³/sec, million gal/day, or gal/min —*see* **bankfull discharge**

discharge coefficient the ratio of actual flow to the theoretical rate of flow through orifices, weirs, or other hydraulic structures

discharge curve **1.** a rating curve showing the relation between stage and rate of flow of a stream **2.** a curve showing the relation of discharge of a pump and the speed, power, and head

discharge formula a formula to calculate rate of flow of fluid in a conduit or through an opening —*note 1.* for steady flow discharge, $Q = AV$, where Q is rate of flow (ft³/sec), A is cross-sectional area (ft²), and V is mean velocity (ft/sec) —*note 2.* it is used to calculate the mean velocity, V, for uniform flow in pipes or open channels —*see* **Manning's formula**

discontinuous ring a growth ring that does not continue completely around the stem because parts of the cambium were dormant —*see* **false ring**

discounted cash flow the various costs and benefits anticipated in future years discounted to the present and their values expressed as (a) the difference, based on their **net present value,** (b) the **benefit-cost ratio,** or (c) the discount rate that equates them, giving the internal rate of return which, in **forestry,** is equal to the financial **yield**

discovery time —*see* **elapsed time**

discrete pertaining to a parameter or random variable that may take only one particular set of values within a range, e.g., **integer** values —*note* discrete data are categorical data (e.g., types of vegetation) or class data (e.g., elevation zones); in geographic terms, discrete data can be represented by polygons —*synonym* integer data —*see* **continuous data**

discriminant analysis the statistical methods used in problems of classification —*synonym* discriminatory analysis —*note* given that an individual may belong to one of a number of **population**s, such analyses allocate it to the correct population with minimum error, generally on the basis of multiple measurements of the individual and a prior set of similar measurements on individuals whose origin is known

discriminant function a function of the observations used for the purpose of a discriminant analysis

disease a harmful deviation from normal functioning of physiological processes —*note* a disease is usually **pathogenic** or **abiotic** in origin

disease cycle the sequence of steps involved in the development of a disease —*note* disease cycles include the life stages of the pathogen, steps or processes (including **inoculum** source, transmission, penetration, colonization, and disease expression), and symptoms in the host —*see* **life cycle**

disjunct the characterization of species distribution by geographically separated populations

disk a plow drawn by a **tractor** or **skidder** having one or more heavy, round, concave, sharpened, freely rotating steel disks angled to cut and turn a furrow —*note* a disk is used in **site preparation** or in the construction of **firelines**

dispatcher a person employed to receive reports of discovery and status of fires, confirm fire locations, identify and locate **firefighter**s and equipment likely to be needed to control a fire in **initial at-**

tack, send them to the proper location, and support them as needed

dispersal the spread, on any time scale, of plants or animals from any point of origin or from one place to another —*see* **drift, inoculation, migration**

dispersal habitat habitat that supports the life needs of an animal for foraging, hiding, movement, and protection from predators

dispersed retention —*see* **variable retention harvest system**

dispersed use recreation taking place outside developed sites

dispersion the degree of variability shown by a set of observations —*see* **contagious dispersion**

dissolve *GIS* the process of removing boundaries between adjacent **polygon**s that have the same values for a specified **attribute**

dissolved organic matter (DOM) organic material capable of passing through a 0.45 µ filter —*synonym* **dissolved organic carbon**

dissolved oxygen the concentration of oxygen dissolved in water, expressed in mg/l or as percent saturation, where saturation is the maximum amount of oxygen that can theoretically be dissolved in water at a given altitude and temperature

dissolved solids the total amount of dissolved material, organic or inorganic, contained in water or wastes —*note* the 10 elements that make up 99 percent of the dissolved materials in streams, lakes, soil moisture, groundwater, and seas are magnesium, sodium, potassium, calcium, hydrogen, silicon, chlorine, oxygen, sulfur, and carbon

dissolving pulp —*see* **pulp**

distributed processing *computers* actions by which computer resources are dispersed or distributed in one or more locations —*note* the individual computers in a distributed processing environment can be linked by a communications network to each other or to a host or supervisory computer

disturbance *ecology* any relatively discrete event in time that disrupts **ecosystem, community,** or population structure and changes resources, substrate availability, or the physical environment

disturbance indicator an early sign of an intrusive factor or factors causing **range** deterioration, e.g., trampling, overutilization, the onset of drought and **pest**s, fire, road and trail building, logging, and recreational use —*synonym* deterioration indicator

disturbance-recovery regime a natural pattern of periodic disturbances, such as fire or flooding, followed by a period of recovery from the disturbance, e.g., regrowth of a forest after a fire

diversity —see **biodiversity**

diversity index 1. a numerical value derived from the number of individuals per taxon —see **abundance** and the number of taxa present —see **richness 2.** the relationship of the number of taxa (richness) to the number of individuals per taxon (i.e., **abundance**) for a given community —see **biological index, Shannon-Weiner diversity index, Simpson's diversity index**

division —see **incident command system**

division boss —see **large fire organization**

division or **group supervisor** —see **incident command system**

DLG —see **digital line graph**

DNA —see **deoxyribonucleic acid**

DOB —see **diameter outside bark**

dog 1. a short piece of steel, bent and pointed at one end and sometimes with an eye or ring at the other **2.** a metal- or plastic-toothed plate on a chain saw to provide firm contact with the log

dominance *ecology* **1.** the influence of a **dominant** species **2.** the extent to which a given **species** or life form predominates in a **community** because of its size, abundance, or **cover,** and effects on the fitness of associated species —*note* dominance is interpreted in two ways for vegetation classification purposes: (a) where one or more vegetation strata or life-forms covers greater than 25 percent, the life form greater than 25 percent constituting the uppermost canopy is referred to as the dominant life form (b) where no vegetation life form covers greater than 25 percent, the life form with the highest percent canopy cover is referred to as the dominant life form; in the case of a tie, the upper canopy is referred to as the dominant life form — see **life form 3.** *genetics* the masking of the action of one **allele** by its alternate allele —*note* if a completely dominant allele for red color appears with a recessive one for white, the phenotype will be red; if this dominance is partial, the color may tend toward deep pink; if there is no dominance, the color will be intermediate —see **dominance, epistasis, genetic variation, heterozygous, lethal gene, phenotype, simple Mendelian inheritance, xenia**

dominance genetic variation the component of **nonadditive genetic variation** due to within-**locus** dominance deviations —*note* dominance genetic variation is often used as shorthand for the portion of nonadditive genetic variation estimated by full-sib/half-sib mating designs —see **additive genetic variation, dominance, half-sib progeny**

dominant 1. *ecology* that component of a community, typically a **species**, exerting the greatest influence on its character because of its life form or great **abundance 2.** *ecology, silviculture* an indi-

vidual or species of the upper layer of the canopy —*see* **crown class, dominance, dominant gene, subdominant**

dominant gene an allelic form of a gene that prevents its alternate **allele**(s) from having a **phenotypic** effect —*see* **dominant, recessive gene**

dominant use a concept in which land and water resources are classified and managed for one main type of use —*note* other uses may be exluded but are always of secondary importance to the optimum development for the dominant use

donkey *harvesting* a portable engine mounted on a vehicle or sled and equipped with cable and winch drums, and used for **yard**ing, **skid**ding, or loading

Doppler shift a change in the observed frequency of electromagnetic or other waves caused by the relative motion between source and detector —*note* Doppler shift is used principally in the generation of synthetic aperture **radar** images

dormancy a condition in the life of an organism or its parts (sometimes termed the resting stage) when a tissue predisposed to proliferate does not do so and visible growth and development are temporarily suspended —*note 1.* in plants the suspension of growth may be imposed dormancy brought about by unfavorable external environmental conditions, e.g., drought or cold, or physiological dormancy due to unfavorable internal physiological conditions which may develop (a) within the plant but outside the dormant organ (correlated inhibition) or (b) within the organ itself (rest, winter dormancy) —*note 2.* dormancy may range from shallow, i.e., readily broken and generally brief to deep and generally prolonged —*note 3.* in dormant seeds or spores, germination may be delayed until they become mature and viable and external conditions are favorable; in dormant plants, the buds or **cambium** may be incapable of developing despite a favorable environment —*see* **afterripening, diapause, estivate, hibernation, secondary dormancy, viability**

dose the amount of active ingredient applied —*note* a dose is expressed generally as weight or volume per unit area, plant, or animal, i.e., as a dosage (rate); a practical distinction is made between the emitted dose and the deposited dose —*synonym* emitted dose, dosage, rate

dots per inch (DPI) the sharpness with which an **image** can be represented —*note* in printing or plotting processes, more dots per inch implies that edges of images are more precisely represented

double-bit(ted) ax —*see* **hand tool, fire**

double-conical saw —*see* **saw**

double fertilization the unique process of angiosperms in which one of the two sperm nuclei from the pollen tube unites with the egg nucleus to form the **diploid zygote,** and the other sperm **nucleus** unites with two of the nuclei of the embryo sac to form the triploid **endosperm** —*see* **fertilization, metaxenia, nucleus, xenia**

double precision a level of numeric representation based on the possible number of significant digits that can be stored for the number —*note* double-precision numbers can store up to 15 significant digits (typically 13 or 14) and therefore retain the precision of much less than 1 m at a global scale —*see* **precision, single precision**

downgrade to relegate timber or other forest products to a lower grade

down tree any tree lying on the ground whether uprooted, stem-broken, or deliberately cut —*synonym* **windfall** —*note* down trees are collectively called down timber

down woody debris (DWD) —*see* **coarse woody debris**

Doyle rule a **log rule** used in the East and South, particularly for **hardwood**s; the formula is V = $[(D-4)/4]^2$ L, where V = board foot volume, D = diameter inside bark at the small end in inches, and L = length in feet —*note* the Doyle rule underestimates board foot volume in small logs and overestimates in large logs —*see* **international 1/4-inch rule**, log scale, Scribner rule

Doyle-Scribner rule a combination log formula derived by using Doyle rule values for logs not greater than 28 in (71 cm) in diameter and Scribner rule for logs greater than 28 in (71 cm) —*note* private operators in the southern United States sometimes use the Doyle-Scribner rule —*see* **Scribner rule, Scribner-decimal C rule**

dozer company —*see* **bulldozer company, incident command system**

DPI —*see* **dots per inch**

drag 1. the frictional impedance offered by air to the motion of bodies passing through it —*synonym* resistance **2.** the component of aerodynamic force parallel to the direction of mean flow

drain *inventory* the decrease in growing stock or all live trees from any cause, e.g., removal by cuttings or by mortality from fire, fungi, insects, or wind — *note* a decrease of merchantable timber is termed removals, commercial drain, or commodity drain

drainage 1. the removal of excess surface water or groundwater from land by surface or subsurface drains **2.** the soil characteristics that affect natural drainage **3.** *landscape* an area (basin) mostly bounded by ridges or other topographic features, encompassing part, most, or all of a **watershed** and enclosing over 5,000 acres (2,024 ha)

drainage basin —*see* **watershed**

drainage class a group of soils possessing a similar moisture regime under natural conditions —*synonym* natural drainage class

drawdown the lowering of water levels stored behind a dam or other control structure; the change in reservoir elevation during a specified time interval

drift 1. the voluntary or accidental dislodgment of aquatic invertebrates from the stream bottom into the water column where they move or float with the current **2.** any detrital material transported by wind or water —*see* **detritus 3.** something washed ashore; a mass of water deposited ashore by wind or water currents —*see* **dispersal 4.** *range management* the natural movement of livestock as they graze or move toward water or bedding sites, etc. —*see* **drive 5.** the unintended movement of a **pesticide** by wind **6.** *soils* sediments or rocks transported by glacial action **7.** *genetics* the movement of plants or animals (genes) within or beyond their natural range

drill seeder a mechanical device for sowing seed in furrowed lines (i.e., in drills)

dripline the line extending vertically from the exterior edge of a tree's live crown to the ground

drip torch —*see* **ignition tool**

drive 1. *wildlife management* causing animals to move in a desired general direction, e.g., towards guns or traps or past census points —*see* **drift, stand 2.** *range management* the moving of **livestock** under human direction —*note 1.* the term **drift** is often used in lieu of **drive** when animals are slowly urged in a certain direction —*note 2.* a strip of country set aside for such a movement is termed a driveway or stock route —*synonym* drove, droving, trailing —*see* **drift, transhumance**

drought crack a radial split in the stem of a tree caused by shrinkage of woody tissue resulting from internal water deficits following drought —*note* the crack may be open to the surface or internal only; frost cracks occur similarly

drought index a number representing the net effect of evapotranspiration and **precipitation** in producing cumulative moisture depletion in deep duff or upper soil layers and in large fuels

drought tolerance the ability of plants to either postpone dehydration or tolerate dehydration during a period of drought such that damage is prevented, reduced, or repaired —*note* drought tolerance is often assessed relative to the plant's natural environment or when plants are placed together in the same environment

drum chopper —*see* **chopper**

dry-adiabatic lapse rate —*see* **lapse rate**

dry band *range management* a band of ewes without young —*antonym* wet band, wet flock, wet herd

dry-bulb temperature the temperature of a shaded thermometer that is equivalent to air temperature —*see* **wet-bulb depression, wet-bulb temperature**

drying the process of reducing the **moisture content** of wood or lumber by exposing it to air or using a kiln —*synonym* seasoning—*note 1.* drying wood improves its serviceability for many uses — *see* **kiln-drying, set, sticker**

dry lightning storm a thunderstorm in which negligible **precipitation** reaches the ground —*synonym* dry storm

dry rot **1.** any **brown rot** of wood **2.** a brown cubical rot caused by specialized fungi able to conduct water (via **rhizomorph**s) to wood, particularly in softwoods, otherwise too dry to be attacked —*note* dry rot is found mainly in buildings

DTM —*see* **digital terrain model**

dual price the improvement in value of the **optimal solution** per unit increase in the value of the right-hand side associated with a **linear programming** constraint —*note* the right-hand side (RHS) is the scalar to the right of the **constraint** sign in the equation

dual use the practice of grazing the current year's forage production by two species of grazing animals at the same time —*see* **common use**

duff the partially decomposed organic material of the **forest** floor beneath the litter of freshly fallen twigs, needles, and leaves —*see* **litter**

duff mull a **forest** humus type, transitional between **mull** and **mor**, characterized by an accumulation of organic matter on the soil surface in friable **Oe horizon**s, reflecting the dominant zoogenous decomposers —*note 1.* duff mulls are similar to mors in that they generally feature an accumulation of partially- to well-humified organic materials resting on mineral soil, and similar to mulls in that they are zoologically active —*note 2.* a duff mull usually has four horizons: Oi (L), Oe(F), Oa(H), and A —*note 3.* duff mulls are sometimes differentiated into the following groups: mormoder, leptomoder, mullmoder, lignomoder, hydromoder, and saprimoder

dwarf mistletoe a parasitic flowering plant of the genus *Arceuthobium* —*note 1.* these plants develop extensive absorption systems in the **host**'s xylem tissue and derive most of their water and nourishment from the host; the endophytic system causes the formation of **witches' broom**s in some species; injury is caused by diversion of nutrients, growth reduction, and mortality —*note 2.* dwarf mistletoe

is the most important disease problem in western coniferous forests —*see* **leafy mistletoe**

DXF —*see* **digital exchange format**

dynamic model a statistical concept that possesses either or both of the following characteristics: (a) at least one variable occurring in the structural equations, with values taken at different points in time, (b) at least one equation containing a function of time

dynamic programming —*see* **programming**

dynamic sampling any form of **forest** sampling designed to discover significant changes with time, particularly seral changes of increment —*synonym* **continuous forest inventory (CFI),** recurrent (forest) inventory —*see* **control method**

dysgenic being detrimental to the genetic qualities of future generations —*note* the term applies especially to human-caused deterioration, such as losses resulting from high-grading a forest stand —*see* **eugenic**

dystrophic pertaining to toxic **habitat**s low in nutrients

E

EA —*see* **environmental assessment**

earlywood that part of the annual ring of wood that is less dense and composed of large-diameter, thin-walled, secondary **xylem** cells laid down early in the growing season —*synonym* springwood —*see* **latewood**

earthflow a slow to rapid, downslope, mass movement of soil or weathered rock (with most of the particles being smaller than sand) over a discrete, basal shear zone

earth observing system or **program (EOS)** a multidisciplinary, interdisciplinary science and observation program designed and implemented by NASA to provide long-term data sets for earth science aimed at understanding the interactions between the atmosphere, lithosphere, hydrosphere, and biosphere including global change processes and human factors contributing to global change

earth resources satellite (ERS) a satellite incorporating a C-**band radar** system operated by the European Space Agency and consisting of C band (6 cm) synthetic aperture radar (SAR) and wind **scatterometer** sensors —*note 1.* ERS SAR **imagery** is designed for monitoring polar sea ice and has been used for terrestrial and oceanic surveys —*note 2.* the ERS wind scatterometer is used for monitoring ocean surface wind and waves

easement the public acquisition, by purchase or donation, of certain rights on private lands or, in some cases, restricting the private owner's use of that land

eastings the x-coordinates in a plane-coordinate system —*see* **northings**

ecdysis *entomology* the shedding of the outer skin or **cuticle** during molting

ecesis the process whereby a plant establishes itself in a new area from germination or its equivalent (e.g., the rooting of some detached portion) to reproduction, whether sexual or asexual —*see* **pioneer**

ECF elemental chlorine-free pulp —*see* **pulp**

eclosion 1. the hatching of a larva from its egg 2. the adult's **emergence** from the pupa case or last larval skin

ecological approach a type of natural resource planning, management, or treatment that ensures consideration of the relationship among all biotic organisms (including humans) and their abiotic environment

ecological classification a multifactor approach to categorizing and delineating, at different levels of resolution, areas of land and water having similar characteristic combinations of physical environment (such as topography, climate, geomorphic processes, geology, soil, and hydrology), biological communities (such as plants, animals, microorganisms, and potential natural communities), and human factors (such as social, economic, cultural, and infrastructure)

ecological niche a localized environment that favors the survival of some particular **population** —*note* such a **habitat** may be discontinuous or may be part of a gradient; unique niches may favor **hybrid**s or mutants that are at a disadvantage in other environments —*see* **ecotype, introgression, mutation**

ecological succession —*see* **succession**

ecological type a category of land having a unique combination of potential natural (**climax**) community, soil, landscape features, climate, and differing from other ecological types in its capacity to produce vegetation and respond to management —*synonym* **habitat type**

economically feasible a transaction having a **present net worth** greater than zero

economic efficiency the competence of a business or the worth of a process, piece of equipment, or machine as judged by **output** per unit cost of resources used —*note* maximum efficiency in the use of resources requires the attainment of three conditions: (a) operation of the firm at the lowest long-run average cost (for a firm operating in a competitive market, the point of greatest efficiency occurs when the price, or marginal revenue, equals the marginal cost at the minimum long-run average cost), (b) use of resources in the least-cost combination, i.e., the best combinations of factors given their prices and technological **constraint**s (at the least-cost combination, the marginal rates of substitution between each set of factors equal the ratios of the prices of the factors), and (c) provision of maximum incentive for developing and introducing new techniques

economic fire protection theory a concept postulating that the object of fire protection is to minimize total cost, i.e., the sum of the costs of fire prevention, **fire presuppression,** fire detection, fire suppression, and net fire damage or benefits —*synonym* least cost plus fire protection theory

economic injury level 1. the lowest **pest** population density that will cause economic damage 2. the pest population density that causes damage equal in cost to the cost of preventing damage —*synonym* economic damage level —*see* **economic threshold**

economic selection cutting a cutting in which selection of trees to be removed is based on their economic value —*see* **high grading**

economic threshold 1. the lowest **pest** population density that will cause economic damage 2. the pest population density at which control measures should be applied to prevent an increasing pest population from reaching the **economic injury level**

ecoregion a contiguous geographic area having a relatively uniform macroclimate, possibly with several vegetation types, and used as an ecological basis for management or planning

ecosystem a spatially explicit, relatively homogeneous unit of the earth that includes all interacting organisms and components of the abiotic environment within its boundaries —*note* an ecosystem can be of any size, e.g., a log, pond, field, forest, or the earth's biosphere

ecosystem management management guided by explicit **goals**, executed by policies, protocols, and practices, and made adaptable by monitoring and research based on the best understanding of ecological interactions and processes necessary to sustain **ecosystem** composition, structure, and function over the long term —*note* the term was initially introduced by the USDA Forest Service —*see* **forest management, sustained yield**

ecotone 1. the transition zone between two adjoining **communities** 2. an edge **habitat**

ecotype 1. a genetically differentiated subpopulation (**race**) that is restricted or adapted to a specific **habitat** —*note 1.* most differences among ecotypes are observed only when different ecotypes are tested in a common environment —*note 2.* ecotypes are generally subdivided into races, e.g., edaphic, climatic (termed **cline**), geographic (termed **variety**) —*see* **adaptation, cline, ecological niche, geographic race, geographic variation, physiological character**

ectendomycorrhiza a **mycorrhiza** combining the features of an **ectomycorrhiza** and an **endomycorrhiza** —*synonym* ectendotrophic mycorrhiza —*see* **ectomycorrhiza, endomycorrhiza**

ectomycorrhiza *plural* **ectomycorrhizae** a **mycorrhiza** in which the fungal hyphae penetrate between cells of the epidermis and **cortex** of primary plant roots forming a **Hartig net** and a closely woven envelope (mantle) covering the root apex —*synonym* ectotrophic mycorrhiza —*see* **endomycorrhiza, ectendomycorrhiza**

ectoparasite an external **parasite** feeding from outside the host, e.g., a flea —*see* **endoparasite**

edaphic related to or caused by particular soil conditions

eddy a portion of fluid within the fluid mass that has a certain integrity and life history of its own —*note* the motion of the bulk fluid is the net result of the motion of the eddies

eddy flux 1. the rate of transport (or flux) of fluid properties such as momentum, mass, heat, or suspended matter by means of eddies in a turbulent motion 2. the rate of turbulent exchange

ED$_{50}$ —*see* **median effective dose**

edge the more or less well-defined boundary between two or more elements of the environment, e.g., a field adjacent to a woodland or the boundary of different silvicultural treatments

edge effect the modified environmental conditions or habitat along the margins (edges) of forest stands or patches

edge firing —*see* **firing technique**

edge match *GIS* an editing procedure to ensure that all features that cross adjacent map sheets have the same edge locations —*note* links connect the locations in one **geographic data set** to matching locations in the adjacent data set —*see* **gap**

edger —*see* **saw**

edge tree a tree on the edge of a crop, **stand,** or clump and therefore growing under conditions of light and exposure different from those prevailing within the crop or stand

edit *computers* to correct errors within, or modify, a computer file, a geographic data set, or a tabular file containing attribute data

effective age the period since a tree was released —*see* **age, age class, cohort**

effective area the central part of an **aerial photograph** delimited by the bisectors of overlap with adjacent photographs —*note* on a vertical photograph, all **images** within the effective area have less displacement than their corresponding image points on adjacent photographs that constitute a series within a **flight line**

effective population size a mathematical adjustment of the number of individuals in a **population** based on the distribution of reproductive success —*note* effective population size is used to calculate, the effect of **genetic drift** or rate of **inbreeding**, etc.

efficient *biometrics* 1. an estimator that has a mean square error smaller than any other estimator of the same population parameter 2. marked by an **experimental design** that secures a certain degree of **precision,** one design being deemed more efficient than another if it secures greater precision or the same precision at less cost

effluent 1. solid, liquid, or gaseous wastes that enter the environment as a by-product of human-oriented processes 2. the discharge or outflow of water from ground or subsurface storage

E$_H$ —*see* **redox potential**

E horizon —*see* **horizon**

EIS —*see* **environmental impact statement**

elapsed time *fire* the total time required to complete any step(s) in **fire suppression**—*note* elapsed time is generally divided chronologically into discovery, report, getaway, travel, attack, control, mop-up, and patrol times —*see* **speed of attack;** kinds of elapsed time are as follows:

—**attack time** the elapsed time from the end of report time to the first organized attack, including getaway time and travel time —*synonym* response time

—**control time** the elapsed time from the first work on a fire until holding the control line is assured — *note* control time is sometimes measured only from the time of containing a fire

—**discovery time** the elapsed time from the start of a fire (known or estimated) until the first discovery that results in fire suppression action

—**getaway time** the elapsed time from receipt of notification by the personnel charged with initiating fire suppression to the departure of the first attack unit

—**mop-up time** the elapsed time from control of a fire until organized mop-up is complete

—**patrol time** the elapsed time from completion of original mop-up until the end of patrol activity

—**report time** the elapsed time from fire discovery until the first personnel charged with initiating fire suppression are notified of its existence and location

—**travel time** the elapsed time from departure of the initial attack crew until they arrive at and begin work on the fire

elasticity 1. *economics* a measure of the percentage change in one variable brought about by a 1 percent change in some other variable —*note* the concept of elasticity is often used to describe how the quantity of a good demanded responds to a change in its price, e.g., an elasticity of –2 means that a 1 percent increase in price causes a 2 percent decline in the quantity demanded; the price elasticity of supply is defined in an analogous way **2.** *utilization* the capacity of bodies to return to their original shape, dimensions, or position on the removal of a deforming force —*see* **modulus of elasticity, resilience**

elastic limit the **stress** value beyond which a stressed body will not return to its original shape or dimensions when the deforming force is removed

electromagnetic radiation energy propagated through space or through material media in the form of an advancing disturbance in electric and magnetic fields existing in space or in the media — *synonym* electromagnetic energy, radiation

electromagnetic spectrum the ordered array of known electromagnetic radiation extending from the shortest cosmic rays to the longest radio waves and including gamma rays, X-rays, ultraviolet radiation, visible light, infrared radiation, microwaves, and all other wavelengths of radio energy

electrophoresis a technique to separate proteins and other large molecules based on their size, configuration, or electrical charge

elemental chlorine-free pulp —*see* **pulp**

elfin forest a stunted **woodland** at high elevations in warm, moist areas with trees and **forest** floor generally covered with lichens or mosses (**bryophytes**) and other primitive plants —*synonym* elfin woodland —*see* **krummholz**

elite a tree, **stand,** or group of **genotypes** verified by appropriate testing as being genetically **superior** or desirable for a specified environment and propagation system —*note* the superiority of cross-bred parents is determined by **progeny test**s and that of clones by clonal tests —*see* **certify, clonal test, plus, plus tree**

elongation zone the portion of a new root where elongation occurs through cell wall loosening and expansion —*see* **quiescent center**

eluvial horizon a soil **horizon** that has been formed by the process of **eluviation**

eluviation the removal of soil material in suspension (or in solution) from a layer or layers of a soil —*see* **leaching**

emasculation the removal of immature male structures to prevent **self-pollination** or unwanted cross-pollination —*see* **bisexual, cross-pollination**

embryogenesis a process by which an embryo initiates and develops from a **zygote** or asexually from a **somatic cell** or group of cells

emergence 1. *plants* the appearance of a developing aerial part of a plant, particularly of a germinant, above the surface of the substrate **2.** *insects* the act of an adult insect leaving the pupal case or last **nymph**al skin —*see* **eclosion 3.** *insects* the act of leaving the **host** shortly after true emergence **4.** the initiation of activity upon release from dormancy, especially after **hibernation**

emergence period the time interval between the appearance of the first and last adults or **larva**e of an insect species during a seasonal cycle

emergent —*see* **crown class**

emissivity the ratio of the emittance of electromagnetic radiation from a given surface at a specified wavelength and emitting temperature to the emittance of an ideal black body at the same wavelength and temperature

empirical yield table —*see* **yield table**

emulsifier a chemical that allows another substance to form an **emulsion** or to stabilize in water —*note* an emulsifier is commonly added to oil-based pesticides to allow them to mix with water —*see* **surfactant**

emulsion a colloidal suspension of one liquid in another —*note* e.g., oil in water

encapsulation *computers* a technique in which data are packaged with corresponding procedures —*note* in object-oriented technology, the mechanism for encapsulation is the object

enclave a small, often relic **community** of one kind of plant in an opening of a larger plant community

enclosure a fenced area, generally of limited extent, within which livestock or wild animals may be held for a specific purpose —*synonym* holding paddock, corral —*see* **exclosure**

endangered species any species of plant or animal defined through the Endangered Species Act of 1976 as being in danger of extinction throughout all or a significant portion of its range, and published in the Federal Register —*see* **candidate species, priority animal taxa, recovery, sensitive species, threatened species**

endemic 1. indigenous to (native) or characteristic of a particular restricted geographical area —*antonym* exotic **2.** a disease constantly infecting a few plants throughout an area **3.** a population of potentially injurious plants, animals, or **virus**es that are at low levels —*see* **epidemic**

endodermis the layer of primary tissue that surrounds the vascular tissue of stems and roots and contains the **casparian strip**

endogenous 1. growing from or on the inside **2.** intrinsic, caused by internal factors —*see* **exogenous**

endomycorrhiza *plural* **endomycorrhizae** a vesicular, arbuscular **mycorrhiza** in which the fungal **hypha**e are intracellular in the root cortex, often producing vesicles and specialized branched **haustoria** (arbuscules) in the cortex tissue —*synonym* endotrophic mycorrhiza, vesicular-arbuscular mycorrhiza —*see* **ectendomycorrhiza, ectomycorrhiza**

endoparasite a **parasite** that enters or is oviposited in **host** tissue and feeds from within, e.g., a tapeworm —*see* **ectoparasite**

endophyte a plant, e.g., **dwarf mistletoe,** living within another plant, usually as a **parasite** —*see* **haustorium, infection, systemic infection**

endosperm the triploid tissue in the seeds of some angiosperms that furnishes food for the embryo —*note 1.* the hereditary characters of an endosperm may be determined independently from those of the embryo —*note 2.* the analogous tissue to an endosperm in conifers is **haploid** female tissue and is referred to as the megagametophyte —*see* **double fertilization, gamete, megagametophyte, polyploid, xenia**

energy plantation —*see* **plantation**

engine *fire* any ground vehicle providing specified levels of pumping, water, and hose capacity —*see* **ground tanker** —*note* an engine is an **ICS** term

engine company *fire* any ground vehicle providing specified levels of pumping, water, hose capacity, and personnel —*note* engine company is an **ICS** term

engineered wood composite a product made from wood elements that have been glued together to make a different, more useful, or more economical product than solid sawn wood —*see* **hollow-core construction;** kinds of engineered wood composites include the following:

—**finger joint** a joint made by connecting short pieces of wood by machining and gluing fingerlike joints at the ends of each piece —*note* the process can produce boards of any length

—**flakeboard** —*see* **particle board**

—**glulam** glue-laminated timber consisting of layers of lumber glued together to form larger, longer, and stronger structural elements than can be obtained with solid sawn lumber —*note* glulam is commonly used for beams or arches

—**hardboard** a medium- to high-density panel made from wood fibers that are heated and compressed and in which **lignin** is one of the materials used to bond fibers together —*synonym* Masonite™ —*note* the fibers are obtained by defibrating wood chips by the "explosion" caused by the sudden release of the high steam pressure to which they have been subjected

—**insulation board** a low-density panel similar in manufacture to hardboard except that hot-pressing is not used and ligneous bonding of fibers is not achieved

—**laminated veneer lumber** a panel made by gluing layers of dry veneer having the grain direction of all layers oriented in the same direction

—**medium-density fiberboard (MDF)** a dry-formed panel product manufactured from wood fibers combined with a synthetic resin or other suit-

engineered wood composite *continued*

able binder and compressed to a density from 31 to 50 lb/ft^3 (496 to 800 kg/m^3) in a hot press

—**oriented-strand board (OSB)** a panel made by gluing, heating, and compressing three to five layers of thin flakes or strands of wood that are oriented at right angles to each other, the center layer of which may have strands or flakes oriented randomly —*note 1.* this arrangement increases panel stiffness and strength —*note 2.* oriented-strand board is used structurally

—**particle board** a panel made from sliced or flaked chips and sometimes sawdust that is glued, heated, and compressed *syn* flakeboard —*note* particle board is used nonstructurally, mainly for sheathing

—**plywood** a panel made by gluing layers of veneer together such that the grain of alternate veneers is perpendicular —*note* plywood is composed typically of three, four, or five veneers (plies) —*see* **peeler**

engraver beetle a **bark beetle** of the genera *Scolytus* and *Ips* whose adults and **larvae** scar the outer surface of the xylem of the **host** when constructing galleries

enrichment planting the improvement of the percentage of desirable species or genotypes or increasing biodiversity in a forest by **interplanting** —*synonym* reinforcement planting —*see* **improvement planting, refilling**

enterprise GIS a large computer system connected through networks containing large amounts of centrally stored data —*note 1.* the computer system may be one or many, perhaps using different types of computers, with the data being used throughout the organization or enterprise —*note 2.* **distributed processing** occurs within an enterprise GIS

entomophagous pertaining to organisms that feed on insects —*see* **insectivorous**

entomophilous pertaining to plants pollinated by insects

entomophily pollination by insects —*see* **anemophily, ornithophily**

entrainment *meteorology* the mixing of environmental air into a preexisting organized air current so that the environmental air becomes part of the current —*antonym* detrainment

entrance fee *recreation* a charge to enter a **recreation** site

entrepreneur a person who takes the initiative in combining land, labor, and capital, the three fundamental factors of production, to produce a good or service —*note 1.* the entrepreneur is the driving force and catalyst behind production, the agent who combines the resources in what is hoped will be a profitable venture, and the person who makes both the short-term tactical decisions about the business and the long-term strategic decisions that set the course of the firm —*note 2.* entrepreneurs introduce new products, new techniques, or even new forms of business while **risk**ing their time, effort, personal capital, business reputation, and invested funds of business associates or stockholders

entry condition *economics* a characteristic of an industry that determines how difficult it is for a new firm to begin production, e.g., obtaining wastewater discharge permits for a new paper mill —*note* in perfectly competitive markets, entry is assumed to be costless, while in a monopolistic market, entry conditions are expensive

enumeration —*see* **forest inventory**

environment 1. *ecology* the sum of all external conditions affecting the life, development, and survival of an organism —*see* **variation** 2. *GIS* a set of parameters defining various display, editing, and data manipulation conditions that remain active during a session until explicitly changed by the user

environmental and amenity value a component of natural and cultural heritage that has worth or utility —*note* in an economic framework, environmental and amenity values may include user values, as well as nonuse values such as existence values, bequest values, and option values —*see* **nonuse**

environmental assessment (EA) a concise, public document containing a federal agency's analysis of the significance of potential environmental consequences —*note 1.* the environmental assessment need not contain the level of analysis contained in an **environmental impact statement** —*note 2.* an environmental assessment is used to determine whether an environmental impact statement" is needed or a "finding of no significant impact" is warranted —*note 3.* an EA is one of four classes of National Environmental Policy Act of 1969 documentation, the other three being **environmental impact statement, conformance determination record,** and **categorical exclusion**

environmental impact the positive or negative effect of any action upon a given area or resource

environmental impact statement (EIS) a detailed statement of a federal project's environmental consequences, including adverse environmental effects that cannot be avoided, alternatives to the proposed action, the relationship between local short-term uses and long-term productivity, and any irreversible or irretrievable commitment of resources —*note 1.* an EIS is one of four classes of National Environmental Policy Act of 1969 documentation, the other three being **environmental assessment,**

categorical exclusion, and conformance determination record —*note 2.* only the EIS has a statutory basis —*note 3.* a programmatic environmental impact statement is the document disclosing the environmental consequences of a program or plan that guides or prescribes the use of resources, allocates resources, or establishes rules and policies, in contrast to disclosure of the environmental consequences of a site-specific project —*see* **finding of no significant impact, lead agency, notice of intent, tiering**

environmental lapse rate —*see* **lapse rate**

environmental quality incentives program (EQIP) an environmental cost-share program of the US Department of Agriculture administered by the Natural Resources Conservation Service and the Farm Service Agency —*note* the program provides funding to private landowners for a variety of **conservation** practices, including **forestry,** that address specific local conservation issues

environmental stress 1. the impact to the health and condition of a forest by the excessive effects of one or more influencing factors **2.** *urban forestry* the impact to the health and condition of urban and community trees due to increased **heat island** effect, **soil compaction,** construction damage, and air pollution

environmental toxicology the study of the movement of toxic compounds through **ecosystems** and their impacts

enzyme a protein molecule produced by living cells —*note* enzymes act as catalysts in speeding up highly specific chemical reactions in biological processes

EOS —*see* **earth observing system** or **program**

ephemeral short-lived or transitory

ephemeral stream a stream or portion of a stream that flows only in direct response to **precipitation,** receiving little or no water from springs and no long continued supply from snow or other sources, and whose channel is at all times above the water table —*see* **intermittent stream**

epicenter the geographic location in which a **pest** outbreak originates or is first detected —*see* **infection center**

epicormic branch 1. a shoot arising spontaneously from an **adventitious** or dormant bud on the stem or branch of a woody plant often following exposure to increased light levels or fire —*synonym* epicormic shoots, epicormic sprouts, water sprouts **2.** *dwarf mistletoe* a branch arising from a dormant bud in a **witches' broom** —*see* **coppice**

epicotyl the **stem** portion of the **plumule** in seedlings —*see* **hypocotyl**

epicuticular wax a surface leaf wax —*note* such a wax is important in controlling **desiccation,** in absorption of certain wavelengths of light, and as an insect and disease barrier —*see* **cuticle**

epidemic 1. *entomology* pertaining to populations of plants, animals, and **virus**es that build up, often rapidly, to unusually and generally injuriously high levels —*synonym* **outbreak** —*note* many insect and other animal populations cycle (periodically or irregularly) between **endemic** and epidemic levels —*see* **epizootic 2.** *pathology* a disease sporadically infecting a large number of hosts in an area and causing considerable loss **3.** *pathology* the quantitative progress of disease regardless of the initial or final amount, or of the rapidity of change —*see* **infestation, pandemic, population dynamics**

epidemiology the ecology of disease and the practical application of ecological relationships in disease management —*synonym* epiphytology —*see* **etiology**

epidermis the outermost layer of cells on the primary plant body —*note* the epidermis often has strongly thickened and **cutin**ized outer walls —*see* **cuticle, root hair**

epigenetic pertaining to interactions among developmental processes above the level of primary **gene** action —*note* epigenetic variation does not follow the rules of Mendelian inheritance, is often the result of changed gene expression, and may be reversible —*see* **Mendel's principles**

epilimnion the upper water layer extending from the surface to the thermocline in a stratified body of water —*note 1.* the epilimnion is less dense than the lower waters and is wind circulated and essentially homothermous —*note 2.* the epilimnion is more or less uniformly warm in the summer

epinasty the more rapid growth, particularly elongation, of the upper side of a plant organ causing the plant to curl or bend downward

epipedon a diagnostic surface **horizon** that includes the upper part of the soil that is darkened by organic matter, or the upper eluvial horizons, or both

epiphyllous pertaining to an organism growing on living leaves —*see* **corticolous**

epiphyte a plant growing on but not nourished by another plant —*see* **hemiphyte, parasite**

epistasis an inter**locus** genetic interaction in which the expression of combinations of specific **genes** from different loci is not accurately predicted by a simple linear combination of their average effects —*see* **allele, dominance**

epizootic 1. living on animals from the outside or on their surface, i.e., ectoparasitic or commensal **2.** of a population of animals that builds up to abnormal levels —*see* **epidemic**

EQIP —*see* **environmental quality incentives program**

equilibrium 1. *ecology* a state in which all populations in a community remain of constant size 2. *ecology* a state in which all abiotic conditions are stable 3. *economics* a situation in which supply and demand are in balance —*note* at an equilibrium price, the quantity demanded by purchasers is exactly equal to the aggregate quantity supplied by producers

equitability a measure of relative species distribution calculated as a diversity index

eradicant a pesticide, particularly a fungicide, used to eliminate a pathogen from its **host** or environment, usually by killing the attacking organism at its source before it can reach a host

eremophyte a plant of the desert or the steppe — *synonym* **psammophyte, xerophyte**

erode to wear away material by wind, water, or glacial ice

erodible pertaining to the susceptibility of a soil to **erosion**

erosion 1. the wearing away of the land surface by rain, running water, wind, ice, gravity, or other natural or anthropogenic agents, including such processes as gravitational **creep** and tillage 2. the detachment and movement of soil or rock fragments by water, wind, ice, or gravity; kinds of erosion include the following:

—**accelerated erosion** erosion much more rapid than normal, natural, or geologic erosion, primarily as a result of the influence of human activities or, in some cases, of other animals or natural catastrophes that expose bare surfaces, e.g., fires

—**geologic erosion** the normal or natural erosion caused by geologic processes acting over long geologic periods and resulting in the wearing away of mountains, the building up of floodplains, coastal plains, etc. —*also* natural erosion

—**gully erosion** the removal of soil by water running in narrow channels, which may be eroded to depths ranging from 1 to 2 ft (0.30 to 0.61 m) to as much as 75 to 100 ft (22.86 to 30.48 m)

—**rill erosion** the removal of soil by numerous small channels only several inches deep —*note* rills occur mainly on recently cultivated soils or recent cuts and fills

—**sheet erosion** the movement of a thin, fairly homogeneous layer of soil material by surface runoff water —*note* sheet erosion may be imperceptible, particularly when caused by wind, or else evidenced by numerous fine **rills**

erosion *continued*

—**slip erosion** a sliding downhill of the mantle rock —*note* the large-scale, spectacular form of slip erosion is a **landslide**

—**splash erosion** the splattering of small soil particles caused by the impact of raindrops on wet soils —*note* the loosened and spattered particles may or may not be subsequently removed by surface runoff

—**streambank erosion** the scouring of material and the cutting of channel banks by running water

—**streambed erosion** the scouring of material and cutting of channel beds by running water

erosion pavement a layer of coarse fragments, such as **sand** or gravel, remaining on the surface of the ground after the removal of fine particles by **erosion**

erosive pertaining to the action of wind or water having sufficient velocity to cause **erosion** —*see* **erodible**

ERS —*see* **earth resources satellite**

escape 1. *ecology* an exotic plant or animal later found in the wild 2. *genetics* an individual that appears **pest**-resistant because it was never attacked 3. *genetics* an introduced (nonnative) plant that has the ability to reproduce successfully —*see* **nonnative, resistance**

escaped fire a fire that has exceeded initial attack capabilities —*see* **extended attack situation**

escaped fire situation analysis (EFSA) a decision-making process that evaluates alternative suppression strategies against selected environmental, social, political, and economic criteria —*note* EFSA provides a record of decisions —*see* **wildland fire situation analysis**

escarpment a long, precipitous, clifflike ridge (above or below ground) commonly formed by faulting or fracturing

esker a long, narrow, sinuous, steep-sided ridge composed of irregularly stratified **sand** and gravel that was deposited by a subglacial or supraglacial stream flowing between ice walls, or in an ice tunnel of a retreating glacier, and was left behind when the ice melted —*note* eskers range in length from < 1km to > 160 km (< 0.6 to > 99.4 mi), and in height from 3 to 30 m (9.8 to 98.4 ft)

essential oil a volatile substance found in different parts of many plants, including trees, and generally consisting of mixtures of hydrocarbons (i.e., terpenes), alcohols, esters, aldehydes, and ketones (e.g., camphor) but sometimes homogeneous —*note* 1. essential oils are in part responsible for the odor of flowers, leaves, and wood, from which they can be obtained by extraction or steam distillation —*note 2.* some forest trees yield essential oils that are, or have been, important commercially, e.g., camphor, cinnamon, eucalyptus, sandalwood —*see* **natural resin, pine oil, rosin, tung oil**

established stand a **reforestation** unit of suitable trees that are past the time when considerable juvenile mortality occurs from frost, drought, weeds, or browsing —*note* the unit may still need treatments to control **stand** composition and structure, to reduce likelihood of damage from fire, insects, or disease, and to enhance growth

establishment —*see* **stand establishment**

establishment cut —*see* **regeneration method (shelterwood)**

establishment period the time between the initiation of a new **stand** or age class and its establishment

estivate *also* **aestivate** to enter a dormant state during summer

estuarine zone an environmental system consisting of an **estuary** and those transitional areas that are consistently influenced or affected by water from an estuary, such as salt marshes, coastal and intertidal areas, bays, harbors, lagoons, inshore waters, and channels —*see* **lagoon**

estuary 1. the portion of a coastal stream influenced by the tide of the body of water into which it flows **2.** a bay at the mouth of a river where the tide meets the river current **3.** an area where fresh and marine waters mix

etiolation the paleness or yellowness in a plant due to nondevelopment of chlorophyll caused by inadequate light —*note* etiolation is typified by long, attenuated stems having insufficient supporting tissue and small yellowish or whitish leaves —*see* **chlorosis**

etiology 1. the study of the causes of diseases **2.** the study of causal relationships —*see* **epidemiology**

eugenic tending to improve the genetic qualities of future generations —*note* the term is applied especially to human-caused events or activities such as reserving the best **phenotype**s for seed trees —*see* **dysgenic, progenic, roguing**

euphotic zone the lighted region of a body of water that extends vertically from the surface to the depth at which light is insufficient to maintain light-requiring biological processes

eutrophic a highly productive **habitat** rich in nutrients and organic materials —*see* **eutrophication**

eutrophication the process by which a body of often shallow water becomes either naturally or by pollution rich in dissolved nutrients, especially nitrates and phosphates, with a seasonal deficiency in dissolved oxygen —*note* eutrophication leads to

increased production of organic matter and is the natural process of maturing (aging) of a lake

evaporation pond a pond into which water is discharged and then allowed to evaporate in order to recover materials suspended or dissolved in the water —*note* an evaporation pan is a dish used in the measurement of evaporation of water in the atmosphere

evapotranspiration the conversion of water, whether surface water, soil moisture (both by evaporation), or within plants (by **transpiration**) into water vapor that is released to the atmosphere —*note* potential evapotranspiration can be estimated from simplified heat energy considerations of readily measured meteorological phenomena; actual evapotranspiration may be the result of various factors, e.g., restricted water supplies or plant physiological processes modifying that potential

even-aged stand a stand of trees composed of a single age class in which the range of tree ages is usually ± 20 percent of rotation —*see* **stand**

evenflow yield a flow of goods or services from a **forest** that remains approximately constant in successive periods —*note* the sequential flow pattern specifying the percent increase or decrease in successive periods is $H_j+1 \le (1+\beta) H_j$ where H = level of **yield**, j = period (year), and β = percentage increase in yield from the subsequent period (ranging between 0 and 1) —*see* **nondeclining yield**

evenness *ecology* the even distribution of individuals among **species** —*note* maximum evenness is said to occur when species are spaced equally among species —*see* **species richness**

evolution the change in **gene** frequencies in natural **population**s of a **species** over time —*note* the causative processes include **mutation, genetic drift, migration,** and **natural selection** —*see* **adaptation, gene frequency, mutation rate, phylogeny, selection**

exclosure a fenced area, generally of limited extent, enclosing vegetation and keeping out livestock or wildlife —*see* **enclosure**

exclusive jurisdiction *recreation* a jurisdiction where federal park law enforcement officers have total authority —*note* state laws are not applicable and cannot be enforced by state law enforcement officers within the boundary of the **recreation** site

excurrent crown the conical crown form resulting when terminal growth exceeds branch lateral growth —*note* excurrent crowns are typical of many northern conifers and a few deciduous trees such as yellow poplar, sweetgum, and white ash —*see* **decurrent crown**

exempt livestock grazing animals permitted to graze on federal (public) land free of charge —*note* the term is usually confined to **livestock** actually used for domestic purposes, e.g., saddle horses, milk cows —*see* **grazing fee**

exogenous 1. growing from or on the outside **2.** extrinsic, originating from or due to external causes —*see* **endogenous**

exotic a plant or species introduced from another country or geographic region outside its natural range —*note* an exotic can become naturalized —*see* **escape, naturalize, nonnative**

expansion path the locus of those cost-minimizing input combinations (e.g., of land, labor, and capital) that will be chosen at different levels of **output** when the prices of inputs are held constant

expectation *biometrics* the mean value of a function of random variables obtained by repeated sampling from a **population**

experimental design a method of arranging sampling or experimental units to minimize the effect of variation caused by factors not controlled in the experiment, and to make it possible to estimate the magnitude of such effects in relation to those due to variations in treatments, selection of treatments, or assignment of treatments to experimental units —*synonym* design

experimental error the variation among experimental plots or other experimental units due to causes other than the treatments that have been applied —*note 1.* experimental error may refer to a **variance** or a **standard error** —*note 2.* experimental error does not imply a mistake but instead indicates that some variation is essentially random or cannot be controlled

experimental plot 1. an area of ground laid out to determine treatment effects **2.** the major area or unit of an established experimental study requiring examination, often divided into subplots —*synonym* trial plot, **sample plot** —*see* **experimental unit**

experimental unit the entity (e.g., plot, tree, test tube) to which an experimental treatment is (usually randomly) applied in an experimental design —*note* experimental units are commonly selected to be as homogeneous as possible —*see* **experimental plot, sample plot, sampling unit**

expert system 1. a program that expresses a domain of human expertise as a set of rules **2.** reasoning about new problems by executing those rules —*note* expert systems are used, e.g., to identify diseases, locate mineral deposits, define **habitat type**s, configure hardware systems, guide conversion choices at mills, select stock portfolios

explant an organ, tissue, or other plant part excised from a donor plant that is used to initiate an *in vitro* culture

exploitation cutting —*see* **high grading**

ex situ off the site; away from the natural **habitat** —*see* **in situ**

extended attack situation *fire* a situation in which a fire cannot be controlled by the **initial attack** crew within a reasonable period of time —*note* in an extended attack situation, the fire usually can be controlled by additional resources within 24 hours after suppression begins —*see* **escaped fire**

extended rotation a rotation longer than necessary to grow timber crops to financial maturity or size and generally used to provide habitat or nontimber values

extensive forestry the practice of **forestry** on a basis of low operating and investment costs per acre —*see* **intensive forestry**

extent *GIS* the minimum and maximum x and y coordinates for a set of geographic **feature**s

externality a cost (typically) or benefit of a business decision that does not enter into the financial accounting of the firm, organization, industry, or government but which is borne by others or society at large, e.g., water pollution by a firm creates an externality for the municipality downstream that must remove the pollutants during potable water treatment —*note 1.* externalities alter the optimal output level because they are not included in either the marginal cost or long-run average cost curves of the unit creating them —*note 2.* internalizing the externality, i.e., forcing the unit creating the externality to bear the true costs, has been a priority of public policy on pollution and is based on nuisance aspects of common law related to private property ownership

external yarding distance the distance from the landing to the farthest reachable point within the cutting boundary

extinction *ecology* the global death of the last surviving individual of a species, group, or gene

extinction coefficient the degree of light attenuation in water; the availability of light with increasing depth as a negative exponential

extirpation 1. local extinction of a species from an area **2.** loss of some but not all **population**s of a species

extra burning period any 24-hour period following the termination of the first burning period for any specific fire that is neither contained nor controlled

extraction 1. *timber* the primary transport of trees or logs, as in **yard**ing, **skid**ding or **forward**ing —*synonym* logging **2.** the pulling out by force, e.g., stump extraction **3.** the removal of substances by chemical or physical processes, e.g., chemical extraction

extra-period fire a fire not contained by 10 AM of the day following its discovery

extreme fire behavior —*see* **fire behavior**

extrinsic resource any resource of human origin, especially in contrast to resources of natural origin —*note* often used in recreational planning —*antonym* intrinsic resource

F

face 1. the side of a hill or mountain being logged **2.** one side of a tree, log, or **cant 3.** the wedge-shaped notch of wood removed from a tree's base during felling **4.** *sawmilling* the flat side or cut side of a piece of lumber **5.** *grading* the surface on which the grade or quality is mainly judged in trees, logs, square-cut timber, veneer, coreboard, or panels undercut **6.** *turpentining or resin tapping* the roughly vertical or longitudinal strip on a bole that is cleared of outer bark, initially cut and regularly chipped in a smooth or herringbone manner to yield oleoresin, often referred to as a **catface**

face cord a stack of wood tha measures 4×8 ft × some piece length less than 4 ft (1.2×2.4 m × some piece length less than 1.2 m) —*note* the term is often used for firewood —*see* **cord**

face mark a mark to denote the better face of a board or plank

face measure the area of one **face** of a piece of timber —*note* face measure is generally given in square feet

factor an element that affects the results of an observation or experiment —*note 1.* the term is used particularly to describe a set of related treatments in an experiment; each treatment of the set is a different state or level of the factor, e.g., different varieties of the same plant species, different levels of application of a fertilizer, different methods of cultivation —*note 2.* the randomization of an **experimental design** is undertaken to separate the effect of these controlled factors from the effects of the uncontrolled factors that result in **experimental error**

factorial experiment an experiment in which all levels of two or more treatments or factors are applied singly and in combinations so that both the main effects of the treatments and the interaction of the treatments can be observed

factorial mating a mating scheme in which m males are each crossed to the same n females is an $m \times n$ factorial —*note* e.g., if two trees designated male are crossed to each of three designated females, that is a 2×3 factorial with six total crosses

facultative a species with the capacity to live under different environmental conditions —*note 1.* when the term is used in reference to species occurrence in a **wetland** or upland **habitat,** the species is most likely (67 to 99 percent frequency) found in a **wetland** and called a facultative wetland species; if the species is most likely (67 to 99 percent frequency) found in an upland, it is called a facultative upland species; if the species is sometimes found in a wetland or upland (34 to 66 percent frequency), it is called a facultative species —*note 2.* facultative parasites can function as either parasites or saprophytes —*note 3.* facultative anaerobes can function in aerobic or **anaerobic** conditions —*see* **obligate**

facultative parasite 1. a **parasite** capable of existing independently of a **host** or under a variety of modes of life **2.** *pathology* organisms that usually live as parasites but under certain conditions are capable of saprophytic growth —*see* **obligate parasite**

fairlead *harvesting* a device containing sheaves or rollers to permit the cable to be fed from a range of directions without binding

fall block *harvesting* a block in tight-skyline systems that can be lowered to pick up loads on the ground and then raised for hauling them to the landing —*note* the block is long and narrow, with the sheave(s) at the top, and balanced so that most of the weight is at the bottom

faller one who fells trees, i.e., cuts them down —*synonym* feller

falling wedge *harvesting* a metal or plastic wedge driven into the backcut to cause a tree to fall in the desired direction —*synonym* felling wedge

false color the use of one color to represent another color or radiation which humans cannot see, e.g., the use of red to represent infrared light in color infrared film —*note* false color is also used in **digital image processing** to enhance the visualization of specific features of interest

false heart wood discolored by natural causes, such as fungus, frost, or abnormal conditions of growth, so that it stimulates **heartwood** —*note* false heart is often markedly irregular in shape as seen on a cross-section of the log

false ring a second or later growth ring of **latewood**-type cells in wood or a tree stem, formed within one growing season and caused by interrupted growth due to drought, late frosts, defoliation, etc. —*see* **discontinuous ring**

family *genetics* a group of individuals directly related by descent from at least one common ancestor —*see* **stability**

family selection the process of choosing **progeny** families based on their mean performance —*note* in addition, the best individuals are usually selected from the best families (**combined selection**) —*see* **combined selection, individual selection**

farm-field test a test done at close spacing under near-ideal conditions, usually for the purpose of early selection or **culling**

farm forestry the techniques of forestry as applied to planting, growing, managing, and using farm woodlands —*see* **agroforestry, forest farming**

farm woodland the wooded portion of a farm or ranch, or the wooded land operated in connection with a farm or ranch —*synonym* farm woodlot

FAS 1. *lumber grading* an acronym for "firsts and seconds" in lumber or log grades compared with grade 3, utility, or other lesser grades **2.** *commerce* an acronym for "free alongside ship," indicating that the price quoted by the seller includes delivery of the goods on the quay within reach of the ship's loading tackle —*see* **FOB**

fasciation a malformation of organs, generally stems, characterized by the coalescent development of a row of linked growing points giving rise to a flattened, ribbonlike structure —*note 1.* fasciation is rare and of largely uncertain origin and more common on conifers than hardwoods —*note 2.* fasciation is not always a pathologic abnormality

fasciculation a broomlike growth of densely clustered branches —*note* fasciculation is often referred to as **witches' broom**

fatigue the diminution of strength in solid bodies that results from subjecting them to repeated cycles of loading

fatwood coniferous wood having an abnormally high content of resin and therefore easily set alight —*synonym* lightwood —*see* **naval stores**

fault a fracture or fracture zone of the earth with displacement along one side with respect to the other

favorable grade the gradient of road or trail that slopes downward in the direction of travel

feasibility the relative advantage of managing or improving a unit considering its capability and suitability for a specific use under the existing or projected socioeconomic climate

feasible region the set of all possible **feasible solutions** to a mathematical **programming** problem

feasible solution a set of values for **decision variables** that satisfy all **constraints** in a mathematical **programming** problem

feature *GIS* a representation of a geographic entity, such as a point, line, or polygon

feature class *GIS* **1.** the type of feature represented in a **geographic data set** —*note* this includes **arcs, nodes,** label **points, polygons, tics, annotation,** links, boundaries, **routes,** and sections **2.** the type of representation for a map feature —*note 1.* a feature class is often called an object, an entity, or a geographic phenomenon; when referring to map data, it includes points, lines, areas, and surfaces —*note 2.* one or more features are used to **model** map features, e.g., **arcs** and nodes can be used to model linear features such as street centerlines

fecundity the number of eggs, seeds, or offspring in the first stage of the life cycle produced by an individual —*see* **fitness**

feed *range management* **1.** any noninjurious, edible material having nutritive value when ingested —*synonym* fodder **2.** the act of providing feed to animals —*note* this generally implies unharvested feed, i.e., *in situ* edible herbage and other **range** plants —*see* **forage, range plant**

feel for fire —*see* **fire suppression**

feller —*see* **faller**

feller-buncher *harvesting* a harvesting machine that cuts a tree with a **shear** or saw and carries one or more cut trees in its hydraulically operated arms as it moves to cut the next tree —*note* a feller-buncher deposits small piles of cut trees on the ground to be picked up and transported by a grapple **skidder,** clam-bunk skidder, tree-length forwarder, or cable yarder but not by a regular **forwarder**

felling the cutting down of trees —*synonym* cutting, falling

felling head an attachment to a **tractor,** designed to fell standing trees

fen a **peat**-accumulating **wetland** that receives some drainage from surrounding mineral soils and usually supports marshlike vegetation including sedges, rushes, shrubs, and trees —*note* fens are less acidic than bogs, and derive most of their water from groundwater rich in calcium and magnesium

fertilization **1.** the union of the **nucleus** and other cellular constituents of a male **gamete** (pollen or sperm) with those of a female gamete (ovum or egg) to form a **zygote** from which may develop a new plant —*note* in some **species**, fertilization may occur months after **pollination** —*see* **double fertilization, megagametophyte, parthenogenesis, receptivity** **2.** the addition of nutrient elements to increase growth rate or overcome a nutrient deficiency in the soil

fiber —*see* **cells (wood)**

fiber product a product derived from wood and bark, e.g., composition board, and wood chips

fiber saturation point **(FSP)** the point at which all the liquid water has been removed from the cell but the cell wall is still saturated

fiddleback the figure produced by a type of fine wavy grain found in, e.g., species of *Acer,* which are traditionally used for the backs of violins —*see* **bird's-eye**

fiducial marks index marks rigidly connected with the camera lens through the camera that form **images** on the negative —*note* the marks are arranged so that the intersection of lines drawn between opposite fiducial marks defines the **principal point** of a photograph

field capacity, *in situ* the content of water, on a mass or volume basis, remaining in a soil two or three days after having been wetted (saturated) with water and after free (gravitational) drainage is negligible —*synonym* field water capacity

field nursery a facility, generally not permanent, established in or near a planting site rather than near an administrative or executive headquarters —*see* **nursery**

fifth wheel a weight-bearing swivel mounted over the driving axle(s) of a truck to attach a trailer

file *computers* a single set of related information in a computer that can be accessed by a unique name —*note 1.* examples include a text file created with a text editor, a data file, a DLG file —*note 2.* files are the logical units managed on disk by the computer's operating system; they may be stored on tapes or disks

film format the physical size of an analog **image** —*note 1.* small format is a 35 mm film negative; large format is a 9×18 in (22.8×45.7 cm) frame of film —*note 2.* the term can also refer to the general characteristics of a digital image data set

filter strip a strip or area of vegetation for removing sediment, organic material, organisms, nutrients, and chemicals from runoff or wastewater

final crop that portion of the growing stock (to be) kept until final commercial harvest

final cutting the removal of the remaining crop trees in an **even-aged stand**

final yield the products obtained from the final crop (final cutting)

finance chief —*see* **large fire organization**

finance section chief —*see* **incident command system**

financial maturity the **rotation** at which the current value growth rate of the **stand** equals the alternative rate of return —*see* **soil rent(al)**

finding of no significant impact **(FONSI)** a public document that briefly presents the reasons why an action will not have a significant impact on the human environment and, therefore, will not require the preparation of an **environmental impact statement**

fine fuel —*see* **fuel type**

fine material wood residue not suitable for chipping, such as planer shavings and sawdust —*see* **coarse material**

fine root a small and usually nonwoody root generally less than 2 mm (0.08 in) in diameter

finger —*see* **forest fire**

finger joint —*see* **engineered wood composite**

FIP —*see* **forestry incentives program**

fire analysis a review of **fire management** actions taken on a specific fire, group of fires, or fire season to determine effective and ineffective actions and recommend or prescribe ways and means of doing a more efficient job

fire behavior the manner in which a fire reacts to fuel, weather, and topography; kinds of fire behavior include the following:

—**backing fire** a fire spreading, or ignited to spread, into (against) the wind, in the absence of wind, or downslope

—**blowup** a sudden increase in fire intensity sufficient to preclude immediate control or to upset existing suppression plans, often accompanied by violent convection

—**conflagration** a raging, destructive fire —*note* often used to distinguish a raging fire with a moving front from a **fire storm**

—**creeping fire** a fire spreading slowly over the ground, generally with a low flame

—**crown fire** a fire that spreads across the tops of trees or shrubs more or less independently of a surface fire —*note* crown fires are sometimes classed as running (independent or active) or dependent (passive) to distinguish the degree of independence from the surface fire

—**extreme fire behavior** a level of fire characteristics that ordinarily preclude methods of direct control, usually involving high rate of spread, prolific **crown fire**s or spotting, presence of fire whirlwinds, or a strong **convection column** —*note* extreme fire behavior is difficult to predict because such fires behave erratically, sometimes dangerously

—**fire whirlwind** a spinning, tornadolike vortex of ascending hot air, flame, smoke, and debris —*note* a fire whirlwind is one of the most destructive fire phenomena and can have the strength of a tornado

—**flareup** any sudden acceleration in the rate of spread or intensity of a fire or part of a fire that is of relatively short duration and does not radically change existing control plans

—**mass fire** a fire resulting from many simultaneous ignitions and generating a high level of energy output

—**running fire** a rapidly advancing surface fire with a well-defined head and with a marked increase in **fireline** intensity and rate of spread

—**smoldering fire** a fire burning without flame and barely spreading

—**spot fire** a fire ignited beyond the zone of direct ignition from the main fire, caused by windborne sparks or embers

fire behavior *continued*

—**underburn** a fire that consumes surface fuels but not trees and **shrub**s

fire boss —*see* **large fire organization**

firebrand any burning material that could start another fire, e.g., leaves, pinecones, glowing charcoal, and sparks

firebreak any natural or constructed discontinuity in potential fuels that segregates, stops, and controls the spread of fire or provides a **control line** from which to control a fire —*see* **barrier, control line, fuelbreak, scratch line**

fire cache —*see* **fire tool cache**

fire camp a location equipped to provide service and support for **fire fighters** and equipment being used for **fire suppression** —*note* fire camp is an **LFO** term —*synonym* base camp —*see* **incident base, spike camp**

fire climax a community maintained by regular fires and therefore differing from any other **climax** community —*see* **pyrophyte**

fire danger the sum of constant danger and variable danger factors affecting the inception, spread, resistance to control, and subsequent **fire damage** —*note* fire danger is often expressed as an index —*see* **fire hazard**

fire danger rating a **fire management** system that integrates the effects of selected **fire danger** factors into one or more qualitative or numerical indices of current fire protection needs

fire dependent requiring one or more fires of varying frequency, timing, severity, and size in order to achieve optimal conditions for population survival or growth

fire detection the act or system of discovering and locating fires —*synonym* detection

fire discovery —*see* **fire suppression**

fire district a rural or suburban fire organization, usually tax supported, that maintains fire companies and apparatus —*synonym* fire protection district

fire edge —*see* **forest fire**

fire effect the physical, biological, and ecological impact of fire on the environment

fire fighter a person whose principal function is **fire suppression** —*synonym (obsolete)* fireman —*see* **smoke jumper, fire guard**

firefinder a modified **alidade** used by lookouts to determine the horizontal bearing and sometimes the vertical angle of a fire from a lookout

firefinder map a map that is generally mounted on

a wood or metal base and that has an **azimuth** circle at the center of which a **firefinder** is pivoted

fire-flood cycle the greatly increased rate of water runoff and soil movement from steep slopes that may follow removal of the vegetative **cover** by burning

fire guard a fire fighter, lookout, patrol, prevention guard, or other person directly employed for prevention or detection and suppression of fires —*see* **fire warden**

fire hazard the ease of ignition and resistance to control of the fuel complex —*note* the fire hazard is determined by the volume, type condition, arrangement, and location of fuels —*synonym* hazard —*see* **fire danger, fire risk**

fire intensity the rate of heat release for an entire fire at a specific point in time

fire lane a cleared path wide enough to permit single-lane vehicular access in a remote area

fireline 1. any strip of land cleared or treated to control a fire's spread 2. that portion of a **control line** from which flammable materials have been removed by scraping or digging to mineral soil —*see* **black line, scratch line**

fireline intensity the rate of heat release per unit length of **fireline,** usually expressed in KW/m or BTU/ft-sec —*note* fireline intensity is defined as HWR where H is the heat of combustion, W is the weight of fuel consumed by flaming front per unit area, and R is the lineal **rate of spread**

fire management all activities required for the protection of burnable **wildland** values from fire and the use of fire to meet land management **goals** and **objectives**

fire pack a one-person unit of fire tools, equipment, and supplies prepared in advance for carrying on the back

fire plow a heavy-duty share or disc plow designed to be pulled by a horse or tractor to construct **firebreaks** and **firelines**

fire prevention all activities that minimize the incidence of wildfires —*see* **fire suppression**

fire progress map a map on which the location of the fire perimeter, deployment of suppression forces, and progress of suppression of large fires are tracked —*synonym* fire status map

fireproof to remove or treat fuel with **fire retardant** to reduce the danger of fires igniting or spreading —*note* protection from fireproofing is relative and not absolute

fire rake —*see* **hand tool**

fire regime the characteristic frequency, extent, in-

tensity, severity, and seasonality of fires within an ecosystem

fire-resistant tree a species with morphological characteristics that give it a lower probability of being injured or killed by fire —*note* the characteristics of a fire-resistant tree include a thick platy or corky bark and buds protected by long needles —*antonym* fire-sensitive tree

fire retardant any substance except plain water that, by chemical or physical action, reduces flammability of fuels or slows their **combustion** rate —*note* a fire retardant is often a **slurry** applied aerially or from the ground during a **fire-suppression** operation —*synonym* retardant —*see* **foam, long-term fire retardant, short-term fire retardant, viscous water, wetting agent**

fire risk 1. the chance that a fire may start as affected by the nature and incidence of causative agents 2. an element of the **fire danger** in any area —*see* **fire hazard** 3. any causative agent

fire scar 1. a healing or healed injury or wound on a woody plant caused or accentuated by one or more fires —*note* a fire scar can be used to estimate fire history in the area 2. the mark left by a fire on the landscape

fire season the period(s) of the year when fires are likely to occur, spread, and damage **wildland** values sufficient to warrant organized **fire suppression**

fire seasonality the distribution of fires within a year

fire severity the degree to which a site has been altered or disrupted by fire; a product of **fire intensity,** fuel consumption, and residence time —*synonym* severity —*see* **light burn, moderate burn, severe burn**

fire shelter a personal protection item carried by **fire fighters** which, when deployed, unfolds to form a pup-tent-like shelter of heat-reflective materials —*note* a fire shelter is designed to provide a last resort after a fire fighter has become trapped by fire; the current model weighs 2.8 lb (1.3 kg) and can be deployed in 20 to 25 seconds —*synonym* **forest** fire shelter

fire shovel —*see* **hand tool**

fire simulator a training device that imposes simulated fire and smoke on a projected landscape scene, for the purpose of instructing fire suppression personnel in fire situations and **fire suppression** techniques —*note* a fire simulator is generally an integrated set of several types of projectors and a large screen

fire storm violent **convection** caused by a large continuous area of intense fire, often characterized by destructively violent surface indrafts, a towering

convection column, long-distance spotting, and sometimes by tornadolike vortices —*see* **fire behavior**

fire suppression all work and activities connected with fire-extinguishing operations, beginning with discovery and continuing until the fire is completely extinguished —*synonym* fire control, suppression —*see* **fire presuppression, fire prevention;** kinds of fire suppression include the following:

—**bump-up method** a progressive method of **fireline** construction on a **wildfire** without changing relative positions in the line, whereby work is begun with a suitable space between workers; whenever one worker overtakes another, all those ahead move one space forward and resume work on the uncompleted part of the line; the last worker does not move ahead until work is completed in his or her space; forward progress of the crew is coordinated by a crew boss

—**cold trailing** a method of controlling a partly dead **fire edge** by careful inspection and feeling with the hand to detect any fire and extinguishing it by digging out every live spot and trenching any live edge

—**coyote tactics** a progressive line-construction duty involving self-sufficient crews who build fireline until the end of their work period, remain at or near the point while off duty, and at the beginning of the next period resume building fireline where they left off

—**direct attack** any treatment of burning fuel at the active edge of a fire in an effort to control, it usually involving wetting, smothering, and physical separation of burning from nonburning **wildland** fuel —*synonym* direct fire suppression

—**feel for fire** to examine burned material after a fire is apparently out by feeling with the bare hands to find live embers

—**fire discovery** a determination that a fire exists —*synonym* discovery

—**flank** to work along the **flank**s of a fire, whether simultaneously or successively, from a less active or anchor point toward the head of the fire in order to contain it

—**hot-spot** to reduce or stop the spread of fire at points of particularly rapid rate of spread or special threat —*note* hot-spotting is generally the initial step in prompt control, with emphasis on first priorities

—**indirect attack** a method of fire suppression in which the control line is located a considerable distance from the active edge of a fire, often using natural or constructed **firebreak**s or fuelbreaks and favorable breaks in topography, and intervening

fire suppression *continued*

wildland fuel is burned out or (occasionally) the main fire is allowed to burn to the **control line** —*note* indirect attack is generally used for fires with a rapid rate of spread or high intensity —*synonym* indirect fire suppression, indirect method

—**initial attack** 1. the first action taken to suppress a fire via ground or air 2. suppression efforts taken by resources that are initially committed —*note* initial attack is an **ICS** term

—**leapfrog method** a method of managing personnel on fire suppression whereby each worker is assigned a task, e.g., clearing or digging on a section of the **control line,** and having completed that task, passes other workers in moving to a new assignment —*synonym (obsolete)* man-passing-man

—**mop-up** the extinguishing or removal of burning material near **control line**s, felling of **snag**s, and trenching of logs to prevent rolling after an area has burned, to make it safe or to reduce residual smoke

—**one-lick method** a progressive system of building a **fireline** on a **wildfire** without changing relative positions in the line, whereby each worker does one to several licks (strokes) with a given tool and then moves forward a specified distance to make room for the worker behind —*synonym* progressive method of line construction

—**parallel attack** a method of fire suppression in which a **fireline** is constructed approximately parallel to, and just far enough from, the **fire edge** to enable workers and equipment to work effectively, though the fireline may be shortened by cutting across unburned **fingers** —*note* in this method, the intervening strip of unburned **wildland** fuel is normally burned out as the control line proceeds but may be allowed to burn out unassisted if it causes no delay or threat to the fireline

—**tie-in** the act of connecting a **control line** to another line or an intended **firebreak**

fire swatter —*see* **hand tool**

fire tool cache a supply of fire tools and equipment assembled in planned quantities or standard units at a strategic point for exclusive use in **fire suppression** —*synonym* fire cache

fire triangle an instructional aid in which the sides of a triangle are used to represent the three factors (oxygen, heat, and fuel) necessary for combustion and flame production —*note* removal of any of the three factors in the fire triangle prevents burning

fire warden the officer in charge of fire protection in a specific area —*see* **fire guard**

fire weather forecast to predict any special or adverse weather conditions that present a high probability of extreme **fire behavior**; there are three kinds of fire weather forecasts:

—**red flag cancellation** the notification that a red flag watch or red flag warning has been canceled

—**red flag warning** the notification that an adverse weather pattern continues to develop and that adverse conditions are expected within 24 hours —*note* red flag warning is the stage 2 alert

—**red flag watch** the notification, usually 24 to 72 hours ahead of the event, that current and developing meteorological conditions may evolve into dangerous fire weather —*note* red flag watch is the stage 1 alert

fire whirlwind —*see* **fire behavior**

firing technique a method of differentiating between ground and aerial ignition, between line and point source ignition, or of reflecting the type of fire resulting from one or more ignitions —*see* **ignition pattern**

fish habitat the aquatic environment and the immediately surrounding terrestrial environment that afford the necessary biological, chemical, and physical support systems required by fish species during various life history stages

fish ladder an inclined waterway, commonly an artificial channel or stepped pools, to permit migrating fish to pass over or around a dam or waterfall

fitness *ecology, genetics* **1.** the relative competitive ability of a **genotype** (survivorship × **fecundity**) expressed as the average number of surviving progeny (relative reproductive success) of the genotype compared with the average number of surviving progeny of the competing genotypes **2.** the resulting composite in an individual of all **trait**s selected by **natural selection** —*see* **fecundity**

fixed cost a cost that must be paid to engage in a business, such as property taxes and insurance —*note* fixed costs are, in many respects, irrelevant to the theory of short-run price determination

flagging colored plastic or paper ribbon attached to trees, bushes, or stakes to mark boundaries or to make stakes and other objects visible

flakeboard —*see* **engineered wood composite**

flame-resistant clothing —*see* **personal protective equipment**

flame thrower a device for throwing a stream of flaming liquid —*note* a flame thrower is used to facilitate rapid burning in suppression firing or in **prescribed burn** —*see* **drip torch, ignition tool**

flammability the relative ease with which a substance ignites and sustains **combustion**

flank —*see* **fire suppression**

flareup —*see* **fire behavior**

flashboard a plank generally held horizontally in vertical slots on the crest of a dam or check structure to control the upstream water level

flat an area of shallow water that is periodically exposed or has almost constant elevation —*note* if the shallow area is not vegetated it is sometimes termed a shoal —*see* **marsh**

flat file *computers* a structure for storing data in a computer system in which each record in the file has the same data columns or fields —*note* usually, one field is designated as a key that is used by computer programs for locating a particular record or set of records or for sorting the entire file in a particular order

flatheaded borer a member of genera of the family Buprestidae (Coleoptera) whose **larvae** tunnel in the bark and wood of living, generally damaged or dying trees, or of recently felled trees and logs —*note* the larvae of flatheaded borers are recognizable mainly by their flattened thoracic segments —*synonym* flathead borer, flathead beetle —*see* **roundheaded borer**

flat-sawn pertaining to a sawn board in which the growth rings meet the **face** and back sides at angles less than 45° —*see* **quarter-sawn, radially sawn**

F layer —*see* **horizon**

flight altitude the vertical distance above a given datum of an aircraft in flight or during a specified portion of a flight —*note* in **aerial photograph**y, the datum is either the mean ground level of the area being photographed or mean sea level

flight limit the maximum distance a bird can travel during one continuous flight

flight line a line drawn on a map or chart to represent the actual course or route taken by an aircraft

flight strip a succession of overlapping **aerial photograph**s taken along a single **flight line**

FLIR —*see* **forward-looking infrared**

flitch 1. a large piece from the side of a log (i.e., clear of the **pith**), which is sawn or hewn on two or more sides, **wane**y, bevel-edged or square-edged, and intended for further conversion —*see* **cant 2.** a package of sheets of **veneer** laid together in the sequence of their cutting

flocculation the coagulation of colloidal soil particles due to the ions in solution —*note* in most soils, the **clay**s and humic substances remain flocculated because of the presence of doubly and triply charged cations

flood any water flow that exceeds the bank capacity (greater than bank discharge) of a stream or channel and flows out onto the floodplain —*see* **annual flood, flow, high water line**

flood peak the highest value of the stage or discharge attained by a **flood,** i.e., peak stage or peak discharge

floodplain the level or nearly level land with alluvial soils on either or both sides of a stream or river that is subject to overflow flooding during periods of high water level —*note* an active floodplain commonly has newly deposited fluvial sediments, recently rafted debris suspended on trees or vegetation, or recent scarring of trees by material moved by floodwaters

flood routing a procedure whereby the time and magnitude of a **flood** wave (crest of flood water) at a point on a flooding stream is determined from known or assumed data at upstream points

flood stage 1. the elevation, measured from some datum, at which the level or flow of a natural body of water exceeds its normal or natural banks 2. the maximum elevation of water attained, measured from some datum, during a **flood**

flow 1. the movement of a stream of water or other mobile substances from place to place 2. the movement of water, and the moving water itself; the volume of water passing a given point per unit of time —*see* **discharge** —*note 1.* base flow is the portion of stream discharge that is derived from natural storage —*note 2.* subsurface flow is that portion of the groundwater moving horizontally through and below the stream bed —*note 3.* surface flow is that part of water in a channel flowing on the surface of the substrate —*see* **flood**

flower the reproductive organ (a modified shoot) of **Angiospermae** characterized by **pistil**s or **stamen**s and generally also sepals and petals (perianth) —*note* the so-called flowers of conifers are the male and female strobili before and during pollination —*see* **bract, carpel, conelet, fruit, ovule, stigma, strobilus**

flower induction the stimulation of the onset of flowering or the number of **flower**s

flume *hydrology* 1. an open conduit on a prepared grade, trestle, or bridge for the purpose of carrying water, (*obsolete* logs, or lumber) across creeks, gullies, ravines, or other obstructions 2. an entire canal that is elevated above natural ground for its entire length 3. a calibrated device used to measure the flow of water in an open conduit

flush a site around a streamlet or spring that is kept wet or moist (flushed) by moving water

flute a longitudinal groove that may develop on a tree stem, often between the ribs of buttresses or in a convoluted tree bole, especially along swollen bases

fluvial 1. of or pertaining to rivers 2. growing or living in streams or ponds 3. produced by river or stream action, as a fluvial plain

foam a stream of air bubbles surrounded by a tenacious film of water and a foaming agent capable of smothering fires, created by introducing compounds into a stream of water by special nozzles or proportioning devices —*see* **fire retardant**

foaming agent a chemical that causes a **pesticide** formulation to produce a thick foam —*note* foaming agents are useful in reducing **drift**

FOB an acronym for free on board, indicating that the price quoted includes loading the goods on or in the specified carrier

focal length the distance measured along the optical axis from the optical center (rear nodal point) of the lens to the plane of critical focus

fodder tree a tree or shrub species used to provide food for domestic animals —*note* the plant parts eaten may include leaves, stems, **fruit,** pods, **flower**s, **pollen,** or nectar

foehn *also* **föhn** a warm, dry, strong wind that flows down into valleys when stable, high-pressure air is forced across and then down the lee slopes of a mountain range —*note 1.* the descending air of a foehn is warmed and dried due to adiabatic compression producing critical fire weather conditions —*note 2.* a foehn may be locally called Santa Ana wind, devil (diablo) wind, north wind, east wind, Mono wind, and sirocco —*see* **canyon wind, mountain and valley winds**

fog 1. a visible aggregate of minute water droplets suspended in the atmosphere near the earth's surface —*note* according to international definition, fog reduces visibility below 1 k (0.62 mi) —*see* **radiation fog** 2. *fire* a jet of fine water spray discharged by spray nozzles used to extinguish fires —*note 1.* fog is generally considered most efficient at nozzle pressures of about 100 psi (690 kPa) —*note 2.* high-pressure fog is delivered through gun-type nozzles attached to small hoses supplied by pumps discharging at pressures greater than 250 psi (1,724 kPa), which is the normal maximum pressure for standard ground tankers

F_1 the first generation of a **cross** —*note* if each parent is true breeding (**homozygous**), the F_1 individuals are expected to be genetically identical —*see* **cross-pollination, F_2, heterozygous**

FONSI —*see* **finding of no significant impact**

font *computers* a logical set of related patterns representing text characters or point symbology —*note* a font pattern, e.g., A,B,C, is the basic building block for markers and text symbols; after the desired patterns are placed in fonts, any desired symbol can be built

food patch a natural, sown, or planted area with grains, berry-bearing bushes, etc., supplying food for wildlife —*synonym* food plot —*see* **bait, covert**

food web the interlocking pattern of feeding relationships in a community

FOPS falling objects protection, such as a device to protect an operator added to equipment working in the woods

forage 1. browse and herbage that is available either naturally or produced seasonally or annually (forage crop) on a given area or **range** that can provide food for grazing animals or be harvested for feeding **2.** to search for or consume forage —*see* **feed, grazing season, range plant**

forb any broad-leafed, herbaceous plant other than those in the Poaceae (Gramineae), Cyperaceae, and Juncaceae families —*see* **grass, herb**

foreign key *computers* the **column** of data used to **relate** one file to another in **relational database management system (RDBMS)** terms

forest an **ecosystem** characterized by a more or less dense and extensive tree **cover,** often consisting of **stand**s varying in characteristics such as species composition, structure, age class, and associated processes, and commonly including meadows, streams, fish, and wildlife —*note* forests include special kinds such as **industrial forests, nonindustrial private forests, plantations,** public forests, **protection forests,** and urban forests, as well as parks and **wilderness** —*see* **forester, forestry, old-growth forest, second-growth forest, urban forestry, virgin forest**

forest concession 1. a temporary (or terminable) and defined facility involving the use of a **forest** or its produce, sanctioned by the owner of a forest to individuals or communities —*synonym* forest privilege **2.** a contract, license, or permit granted to a firm or a person to extract and market timber (timber concession) or other produce commercially from a defined area of the forest within a given period —*note* a timber concession may specify the number, type, and size of tree that may be harvested

forest cover 1. all trees and other plants occupying the ground in a **forest,** including any **ground cover 2.** all woody growth occupying the ground in a forest as distinct from the ground cover **3.** a category of forest site, including all the interchangeable phases of vegetation that it supports, defined mainly by the general nature of the ground cover

forest cover type —*see* **forest type**

forest decline the loss in **stand** or **forest health** and vigor attributed to air pollution —*note* various

names have been given to this phenomenon, including forest death (Waldsterben) and forest damage (Waldschaden)

forest entomology that branch of **forestry** concerned with the interrelationships between insects and trees —*see* **integrated pest management**

forester a professional engaged in the science and profession of **forestry** —*note* foresters are commonly credentialed by states or other certifying bodies, e.g., the Society of American Foresters, and may be licensed, certified, or registered indicating specific education and abilities; the requirements for credentialling differ and usually include earning a baccalaureate degree in forestry, sometimes equivalent experience, and usually passing a comprehensive examination —*see* **accreditation, forest, forest technology recognition**

forest farming the intentional culture of specialty crops such as mushrooms and ginseng grown within a **forest** environment —*synonym* **nontimber forest products,** specialty crop systems —*see* **agroforestry, farm forestry**

forest finance the application of principles of valuation, accounting, and investment analysis to the practice of **forestry** —*note* **forest** finance includes forest taxation, forest insurance, and forest credit —*see* **forest valuation**

forest fire an uncontrolled fire on lands covered wholly or in part by timber, brush, grass, grain, or other flammable vegetation —*see* **brush fire, grass fire, natural fire, wildfire, wildland fire situation analysis** —*note* forest fires are defined as follows for legal purposes:

—**crown fire** a fire that advances across the tops of trees or shrubs more or less independently of the **surface fire** —*note* a crown fire is sometimes classed as running (independent or active) or dependent (passive) to distinguish its degree of independence from the surface fire

—**finger** a long, narrow extension of a fire projecting from the main body

—**fire edge** any part of the boundary of a fire at a specified moment

—**flank** that part of a fire's perimeter that is roughly parallel to the main direction of spread

—**ground fire** a fire that burns the organic material in the soil layer, such as peat or duff —*synonym* muck fire, organic soil fire, peat fire —*see* **surface fire**

—**head** that portion of a fire edge with the greatest rate of spread —*note* the head of a fire is generally leeward or upslope

—**rear 1.** the portion of a fire spreading directly into the wind or down slope **2.** the portion of a **fire**

forest fire *continued*

edge opposite the **head** —*synonym* heel **3.** the slowest spreading portion of a fire edge

—**surface fire** a fire that burns only surface fuels such as litter, loose debris, and small vegetation —*see* **ground fire**

forest floor the accumulated organic matter at the soil surface, including **litter** and unincorporated **humus** —*note* using US and Canadian soil terminologies, the floor includes the L and F soil layers and therefore excludes the H, Oa, humus layers, and **coarse woody debris** larger than 10 cm (3.9 in) in diameter and 1 m (3.3 ft) in length —*see* **coarse woody debris**

forest fragmentation —*see* **checkerboard ownership, fragmentation**

forest genetics the study of heredity in trees —*see* **genetics**

forest health the perceived condition of a **forest** derived from concerns about such factors as its age, structure, composition, function, vigor, presence of unusual levels of insects or disease, and **resilience** to disturbance —*note* perception and interpretation of forest health are influenced by individual and cultural viewpoints, land management **objective**s, spatial and temporal scales, the relative health of the **stand**s that comprise the **forest**, and the appearance of the forest at a point in time

forest influences all the modifying effects of **forest** cover on the environment, particularly on water supplies, soil, and microclimate

forest integrity a judgment of the composition, dynamics, function, and structural attributes of a **forest**

forest inventory 1. a set of **objective** sampling methods designed to quantify the spatial distribution, composition, and rates of change of **forest** parameters within specified levels of precision for the purposes of management **2.** the listing (enumeration) of data from such a survey —*synonym* **cruise, forest survey** —*note* inventories may be made of all forest resources including trees and other vegetation, fish, insects, and wildlife, as well as street trees and urban forest trees —*see* **dynamic sampling, point sampling**

forest land *federal land management* land at least 10 percent stocked by forest trees of any size, including land that formerly had such tree cover and that will be naturally or artificially regenerated —*note 1.* forest land includes (a) transition zones, such as areas between forested and nonforested lands that are at least 10 percent stocked with forest trees, and forest areas adjacent to urban and built-up lands, (b) piñon-juniper and chaparral areas —*note 2.* the minimum area for classification of forest land is 1

acre (0.4 ha); roadside, streamside, and shelterbelt strips of trees must have a crown width of at least 120 ft (36.6 m); unimproved roads and trails, streams, and clearings in forest areas are classified as forest if less than 120 ft (36.6 m) wide

forest land class a classification of an area based on its capability of producing industrial wood (i.e., all commercial roundwood products except fuelwood), its legal status concerning timber utilization, and its proximity to urban and rural development

forest management the practical application of biological, physical, quantitative, managerial, economic, social, and policy principles to the regeneration, management, utilization, and **conservation** of **forest**s to meet specified **goal**s and **objective**s while maintaining the productivity of the forest —*note* forest management includes management for aesthetics, fish, recreation, urban values, water, **wilderness**, wildlife, wood products, and other forest resource values —*see* **biological legacy, ecosystem management, forest regulation, forestry, operations research, sustainable forest management, sustained yield**

forest management unit —*see* **compartment**

forest outlier an area of **forest** separated from the main occurrence of its type generally because of some local variation in ecological conditions or past **migration** of vegetation associated with major climatic changes —*note* in tropical Africa, the term typically describes an isolated area of high forest surrounded by savanna, almost always associated with a stream and increased soil moisture

forest pathology the branch of **forestry** concerned with diseases and disorders of forest trees, individually and collectively

forest plan *federal land management* a document that guides all natural resource management and establishes management standards and guidelines for a national forest, and that embodies the provisions of the National Forest Management Act of 1976

forest planning —*see* **land management planning**

forest protection the branch of **forestry** concerned with the prevention and control of damage to forests arising from the action of humans and livestock (particularly unauthorized fire, grazing and browsing, felling, fumes and smoke), **pest**s, and pathogens, and also from storm, frost, and other climatic agents

forest regulation 1. the technical (in contrast to the administrative and business) aspects of controlling **stocking**, harvests, growth, and **yield**s to meet management **objective**s including **sustained yield 2.** the control of private **forest management** by ex-

forest regulation *continued*

ercise of public authority **3.** a legal enactment or ordinance affecting forests —*see* **operations research**; kinds of forest regulation include the following:

—**area regulation** an indirect method of controlling (and roughly determining) the amount of forest produce to be harvested, annually or periodically, on the basis of stocked area —*synonym* area control

—**area/volume regulation** an indirect method of controlling annual or periodic harvest based on both growing stock and stocked area —*synonym* area/volume control

—**basal area regulation** a method of controlling and determining the amount of timber to be cut annually or periodically from a forest according to its basal area relative to that of the growing stock and its increment —*synonym* basal area control

—**volume regulation** a direct method of controlling and determining the amount of timber to be cut annually or periodically by calculations based on **growing stock** volume and increment, disregarding area —*synonym* volume control

forest rent(al) the average annual net income per unit area from a **forest** of a given age —*see* **soil rent(al)**

forestry the profession embracing the science, art, and practice of creating, managing, using, and conserving **forest**s and associated resources for human benefit and in a sustainable manner to meet desired **goals**, **needs**, and values —*note* the broad field of forestry consists of those biological, quantitative, managerial, and social sciences that are applied to **forest management** and **conservation**; it includes specialized fields such as agroforestry, urban forestry, industrial forestry, nonindustrial forestry, and **wilderness** and recreation forestry —*see* **agroforestry, forester**

forestry incentives program (FIP) a program of the USDA, jointly administered by the Natural Resources Conservation Service and the Forest Service, to provide cost-share funding to private landowners to practice **forestry** on highly productive sites for the purpose of timber production

forest reserve an area designated under a forest act or ordinance in which timber production is allowed but not conversion to agriculture or other nonforest uses —*note* the term is used in Commonwealth countries; alternative terms are demarcated forest and permanent state forest —*see* **national forest**

forest stewardship the management of **forest**s for all goods, benefits, and values that can be sustained for present and future generations

forest stewardship program a program administered by the USDA Forest Service that provides funding to state **forestry** agencies for the purpose of assisting nonindustrial private **forest** owners in the development of Forest Stewardship Plans

forest survey a procedure to determine, on a given area, data such as soil conditions and topography, together with the extent, condition, composition, and constitution of the **forest**, for such purposes as purchase, management, or as a basis for forest policies and programs —*synonym* **cruise**, forest **inventory**

forest technology recognition a peer-review program, first established by the Society of American Foresters in 1982, that evaluates and certifies that specific US associate degree educational curricula meet standards established by the profession as essential to those who practice **forest** technology —*see* **accreditation, certify, forester**

forest tree breeding the application of knowledge of genetics to developing improved trees —*see* **breeding arboretum, controlled pollination, forest tree improvement, mass selection, mating design**

forest tree improvement the practice of tree breeding in combination with cultural practices —*synonym* **forest tree breeding** —*see* **genetics, improved**

forest type a category of **forest** usually defined by its vegetation, particularly its dominant vegetation as based on percentage **cover** of trees, e.g., sprucefir, longleaf-slash pine, Douglas-fir —*synonym* forest cover type —*see* **stand type**

forest valuation the branch of **forestry** concerned with evaluating **forest** estates and their components —*see* **forest finance, appraisal**

forest village *international forestry* a village community established in or proximate to a reserved or protected **forest**

forest wind a light breeze that blows from **forest**s toward open country on calm, clear nights

form 1. *ecology* a sporadic variant distinguished by a single or very few correlated characters, without a distinct distribution area, e.g., flower color, the variations from type being less, and considered of less importance, than those shown by varieties —*note* they may be **phenotypes** or **genotypes 2.** *ecology* the category subordinate in rank to that of **variety** within the hierarchy of plants **3.** *biometrics* the degree and mode of **taper** of a tree or log —*synonym* stem form, stem taper, tree form

format *computers* the pattern into which data are systematically arranged for use on a computer

formation *ecology* **1.** a major unit of vegetation

comprising all plant communities that resemble each other in appearance and in major features of the environment, e.g., tropical **rainforest,** reed swamp —*see* **association** 2. a level in a classification based on ecological groupings of vegetation units that have broadly defined environmental and physiognomic factors in common —*note* this level is subject to revision as vegetation **alliance**s and community associations are organized under the upper levels of the hierarchy

form class 1. any of the intervals into which a numerical expression of the taper (of a tree stem or log) may be divided for classification or use, i.e., commonly a range of form factors, form quotients, or form-point heights 2. the actual trees or logs falling into such an interval 3. historically, Girard form class, a form quotient computed as the ratio between stem diameter inside bark at the top of the first log divided by **DBH** multiplied by 100

form factor the ratio of actual tree volume to that of some geometric solid, e.g., a cylinder having a diameter equal to **DBH** and height equal to total or merchantable tree height

form height the product of tree height (H) and form factor (F), and hence also (since volume = BA × H × F) expressing the ratio of tree volume to **basal area** (BA), i.e., volume per unit basal area

form quotient the ratio of an upper-stem diameter on a tree to **DBH** —*note 1.* form quotient is used as an independent variable with DBH and height to predict the volume of a tree stem —*note 2.* normal form quotient is the ratio of diameter at half tree height over DBH, and absolute form quotient (used for short trees) is the ratio of diameter at half tree height above breast height over DBH

formulation the precise way in which a chemical compound or mixture is prepared for practical use —*note* the formulation of a **pesticide** specifies the type, form, and proportion of any constituent such as an **adjuvant** or **stabilizer** that is added to the **active ingredient**

FORPLAN a **linear programming** system used for developing and analyzing forest planning alternatives

forward to haul a log from the stump to a collection point by a **forwarder** —*see* **skid, yard**

forwarder *harvesting* a self-propelled machine, usually self-loading, that transports trees or logs by carrying them completely off the ground

forward-looking infrared (FLIR) a hand-held or aircraft-mounted device designed to detect heat differentials and display their images on a video screen —*note* FLIRs have thermal resolution similar to infrared (IR) line scanners, but their spatial resolution is substantially less; they are commonly used to detect **hot spots** and **flareups** obscured by

smoke, evaluate the effectiveness of firing operations, or detect areas needing **mop-up**

4GL —*see* **fourth-generation language**

Fourier analysis a method of dissociating time series or spatial data into sets of sine and cosine waves

fourth-generation language (4GL) a type of computer language that accepts system requirements as input and generates a program to meet those requirements as output —*note* 4GL is useful primarily for well-understood procedures such as the generation of menus, forms, and reports

foxtail an abnormal elongation of the terminal without the development of side branches —*note* foxtails occur in conifers, particularly pines, and may develop for several sequential years —*see* **multinodal, uninodal**

fractal an object having a fractional dimension, i.e., having variation that is self-similar at all scales in which the final level of detail can never be reached by increasing the scale at which observations are made

fragile area *recreation* an identifiable area where the **ecosystem** is sensitive and vulnerable and could be destroyed, severely altered, or irreversibly changed by human acts

fragipan a natural subsurface **horizon** with very low organic matter, high **bulk density,** or high mechanical strength relative to overlying and underlying horizons that typically has **redoximorphic feature**s, is slowly or very slowly permeable to water, is considered root restricting, and usually has few to many bleached, roughly vertical planes which are faces of coarse or very coarse polyhedrons or prisms —*note* a fragipan has hard or very hard consistence (seemingly cemented) when dry but shows a moderate to weak brittleness when moist

fragmentation the process by which a landscape is broken into small islands of **forest** within a mosaic of other forms of land use or ownership —*note* e.g., islands of a particular age class (e.g., old growth) that remain within areas of younger-aged forest —*note* fragmentation is a concern because of the effect of noncontiguous forest **cover** on **connectivity** and the movement and dispersal of animals in the landscape —*see* **checkerboard ownership**

frass the waste product of insect feeding —*note* frass of herbivorous insects is composed of plant fragments and insect excrement; frass of wood-eating insects is termed bore dust

fraying abrasion of the bark and wood of stems by deer —*note* fraying occurs, for example, when deer rub the velvet off their maturing antlers or demarcate their breeding areas

free-burning pertaining to a fire or part of a fire that has not been slowed by natural barriers, **precipitation,** or control measures

free drop *fire* cargo not attached to a parachute that is dropped intentionally from an aircraft in flight

free feeding a type of insect feeding that occurs on part or all of a leaf or needle except on the largest leaf veins

free thinning —*see* **thinning**

free-to-grow a seedling or small tree free from direct competition from other trees, **shrubs,** grasses, or herbaceous plants

frequency 1. *biometrics* the number of occurrences of a given type of event or the number of members of a population falling into a specified class **2.** *biometrics* the number of plots, counts, or intervals in which an object (e.g., species) is detected —*see* **incidence, population density, severity 3.** *ecology* the number of individuals in a **community 4.** *ecology* the proportion of samples in which a species occurs —*see* **constancy 5.** *range management* the ratio between the number of sample units that contain a species and the total number of sample units —*see* **density**

frequency distribution a graphical, tabular, or mathematical representation of the manner in which the occurrences of a **continuous** or **discrete, random variable** are distributed over the range of its possible values

friction velocity the reference wind velocity defined by the relation $\tau = (\upsilon^*/\rho)$, where τ is the Reynolds stress, ρ the density, and υ^* the friction velocity

frill girdling —*see* **girdle**

front *meteorology* the interface or transition zone between two air masses of different density

front-end loader *harvesting* a wheeled or tractor loader, with forks, lifts, or grapples attached to lifting arms at the front end

frost-free season the period between the last injurious frost in the spring and the first injurious frost in the autumn

frost heave the upward displacement of normal soil levels or of road courses as a result of expansion due to ice formation in frozen soil —*note* in nurseries and **plantations,** it may cause the partial or total extrusion of seedlings or other small plants

fructification 1. the formation of a fungal fruiting body **2.** the fungal fruiting body itself —*see* **sporophore**

fruit the seed-bearing organ of a flowering plant; a ripened ovary —*see* **flower, strobilus**

FSP —*see* **fiber saturation point**

F_2 the second generation, produced by intercrossing or **self**ing the **F_1** individuals —*note* the individuals within an F_2 generation characteristically vary greatly —*see* **cross-pollination, F_1, heterozygous, hybrid, self-pollination**

fuelbreak a generally wide (60 to 1,000 ft or 18 to 305 m) strip of land on which native vegetation has been permanently modified so that a fire burning into it can be more readily controlled —*note* some fuelbreaks contain **firelines** that can be quickly widened with hand tools or by burning —*see* **barrier, control line, scratch line**

fuel characteristics the properties that describe **wildland** fuel include the following:

—**chemistry** the makeup of wildland fuels —*note* fuel chemistry consists of cellulose, hemicellulose, lignin, and nonstructural components; extractives (volatiles), which tend to increase flammability; and mineral ash, which tends to decrease flammability

—**compaction** the ratio of space occupied by fuel particles in a given volume of space —*synonym* packing ratio (β)

—**continuity** the degree or extent of continuous or uninterrupted distribution of fuel particles, horizontally or vertically, which allow fire to spread

—**load** the oven-dry weight of fuel per unit area —*note* load is often described by size or **timelag** class, and as live or dead, herbaceous or woody

—**moisture content** the amount of water in a fuel per oven-dry weight —*note* moisture content is usually expressed in percent

—**size** the size of individual fuel particles —*note* size is usually expressed as a **timelag** size class or as the surface area to volume ratio (σ)

fuel chemistry —*see* **fuel characteristics**

fuel compaction —*see* **fuel characteristics**

fuel continuity —*see* **fuel characteristics**

fuel load —*see* **fuel characteristics**

fuel management the act or practice of controlling flammability and reducing resistance to control of wildland **fuels** through mechanical, chemical, biological, or manual means, or by fire in support of land management **objectives**

fuel moisture content —*see* **fuel characteristics**

fuel moisture indicator stick a specially manufactured stick or set of sticks of known dry weight continuously exposed to the weather and periodically weighed to determine changes in moisture content —*note* the sticks indicate the relative flammability of dead **wildland** fuels that roughly correspond to 10-hour **timelag** fuels

fuel size —*see* **fuel characteristics**

fuel treatment any manipulation or removal of **wildland** fuels to reduce the likelihood of ignition or to lessen potential damage and resistance to control, e.g., lopping, chipping, crushing, piling, and burning —*synonym* fuel modification, hazard reduction —*see* **fuel management**

fuel type an identifiable association of **wildland** fuel elements of distinctive species, form, size, arrangement, or other characteristics that will cause a predictable rate of spread or resistance to control under specified weather conditions; kinds of fuel include the following:

—**activity fuel** the combustible material resulting from or altered by forestry practices such as timber harvest or **thinning,** as opposed to naturally created fuels

—**aerial fuel** the standing and supported live and dead combustibles not in direct contact with the ground and consisting mainly of shrub and tree crowns, stems, foliage, branches, and vines

—**fine fuel** fast-drying dead combustible material, generally characterized by a comparatively high surface area-to-volume ratio and diameters of less than 0.25 in (0.64 cm), that is consumed rapidly by fire when dry, e.g., grass, leaves, and needles —*note* fine fuels have a **timelag** of one hour or less —*synonym* flash fuels, light fuels

—**ground fuel** combustible material below the **surface fuel** layer such as peat, duff, and roots

—**heavy fuel** combustible material of large diameter, usually > 3 in (7.6 cm), that ignites and burns more slowly than fine fuels, e.g., **snags,** logs, large branchwood, and peat—*synonym* coarse fuel —*see* **black line**

—**ladder fuel** combustible material that provides vertical continuity between vegetation strata and allows fire to climb into the crowns of trees or **shrubs** with relative ease —*note* ladder fuels help initiate and ensure the continuation of a **crown fire** —*synonym* fuel ladder

—**natural fuel** combustible material resulting from natural processes and not directly generated or altered by land management practices

—**surface fuel** the loose surface litter on the soil surface, e.g., fallen leaves or needles, twigs, bark, cones, branches, grasses, shrub and tree reproduction, downed logs, stumps, seedlings, and **forbs** interspersed with or partially replacing the litter

fuel type classification the division of **wildland** areas into **fire hazard** classes

fuelwood wood used for conversion to some form of energy, e.g., in residential use or in cogeneration plants

full-log suspension the lifting of an entire log above the ground during **yard**ing operations

full-sib progeny the offspring resulting from a cross of a single pair of parents —*see* **half-sib progeny, sib, specific combining ability**

full-tree harvesting cutting and removing an entire upper portion of a tree consisting of trunk, branches, and leaves or needles —*synonym* whole-tree harvesting

fulvic acid soil organic matter that is soluble in both alkali and dilute acid —*note* fulvic acid remains in solution after removal of **humic acid** by acidification

functional response a behavioral response of **parasites** or **predators** in which attacks on a particular **host** or prey species increase with increasing density of the **host** or prey species

fungicide a chemical or substance that kills, destroys, or inhibits the growth of fungi or their spores —*see* **fungistatic, phytocide**

Fungi Imperfecti a major group of fungi, many of which have no known sexual, i.e., perfect, stage

fungistat a fungal **protectant**

fungistatic 1. relating to a state in which a fungus is living but not growing 2. a contact chemical action that inhibits the growth of fungi or the germination of fungal **spores** without killing them

fungus *plural* **fungi** a nonvascular plant lacking chlorophyll (and therefore does not photosynthesize), having cell walls with both cellulose and chitin, having a vegetative body called a **thallus** composed of hyphae, and reproducing by **spores** —*note* fungi are usually nonmobile, filamentous, and multicellular; they include molds, mildews, yeasts, mushrooms, and puffballs

fungus mat a dense, leathery mass of fungus **mycelium,** often formed in decayed wood by certain wood-rotting fungi —*synonym* fungal mat —*see* **mycelial form**

furnish the mixture of fiber, water, and all other materials such as fillers and dyes, from which reconstituted wood products are made —*note* the composition and character of the furnish will determine the kind of product made

furniture beetle a member of the genus *Anobium*, particularly *A. punctatum,* whose **larvae** tunnel in seasoned softwood and hardwood timber (not just furniture), mainly in the sapwood

fusiform ray —*see* **cells (wood)**

fusiform rust a disease caused by *Cronartium quer-cuum* that forms spindle-shaped **gall**s on the main stem and branches of two- and three-needled pines —*note 1.* fusiform rust is common in the South —*note 2.* the pathogen is a **macrocyclic, heteroe-cious** rust with *Pinus* and *Quercus* **hosts**

future value 1. the value at some future time of a cost or a benefit or a series of costs or benefits 2. the value of compounded costs or benefits at the end of an investment period —*antonym* net present value

G

gabion a wire basket (**crib**) filled with clean rocks used as a retaining structure to stabilize a soil slope or riverbank or to provide support for a bridge —*see* **riprap**

gall a pronounced swelling or abnormal growth, usually localized, of greatly modified tissue struc-ture arising on plants in response to irritation by a foreign organism, commonly an insect or pathogen

gall adelgid an **adelgid** of the genera *Adelges* or *Pineus* whose feeding frequently causes deforma-tion of the **host** tissues, e.g., conelike swellings or **gall**s on the twigs of spruces and true firs, and also twig dieback and defoliation —*note* examples of gall adelgids include the Cooley spruce gall adel-gid *(Adelges cooleyi)*, the eastern spruce gall adel-gid *(A. abietis)*, and the balsam **woolly adelgid** *(A. piceae)* —*see* **aphid**

gallery —*see* **insect hole**

gall midge a small fly of the family Cecidomyidae whose pink or yellowish **larvae** (**maggots**) cause many kinds of small **gall**s on plants, generally on leaves, roots, cones (cone midges), seeds, or twigs —*note* some gall midges give rise to pockets of resin in the bark of conifers (**pitch midges**), e.g., maple **leaf spot** gall midge, balsam gall midge, and birch midge

gall rust a **rust** disease that produces conspicuous, perennial, globose **gall**s on the stems of hard pines —*note 1.* eastern **gall rust** (also called pine-oak gall rust) is caused by *Cronartium quercuum* which is closely related to **fusiform rust** and is **heteroe-cious** on jack pine *(Pinus banksiana)*, oak *(Quer-cus)*, and chinquapin *(Castanopsis)* **host**s —*note 2.* western gall rust (also called pine-pine gall rust) is caused by *Entocronartium harkenssii*, which is **au-toecious** on hard pines, including jack pine

gall wasp an insect in the family Cynipidae (cynipid wasps) or Eurytomidae (eurytomids), whose **lar-vae** cause many kinds of **gall**s on trees, particularly oaks —*note 1.* e.g., the oak apple galls, gouty oak galls, and horned oak galls are caused by cynipid wasps; Euura sawflies in the family Tenthredinidae also produce galls on willow —*note 2.* true wasps are in the family Vespidae

game animals habitually hunted for food, particular products or trophies, or sport —*note* larger ani-mals, mainly ungulates, large carnivores (including such fish as tarpon and sharks), and bears are termed big game; smaller animals are called small game

gametangium *plural* **gametangia** a structure con-taining **gamete**s or nuclei that fuse and produce sexual **spore**s —*see* **zygospore**

gamete a male or female reproductive cell, typically the product of **meiosis**, capable of uniting in the process of **fertilization** with one of the opposite sex —*see* **chromosome number, diploid, endosperm, gametangium, haploid, homologous chromosomes, microspores, somatic cell, zygote**

gametophyte the haploid (*n*) **gamete**-producing phase or generation in organisms such as trees that alternate **haploid** (*n*) and **diploid** (*2n*) phases or generations

gamma diversity landscape-level or regional diversity

gang saw —*see* **saw**

gap **1.** *GIS* the distance between two objects that should be connected —*note* gaps often occur during digitizing or edge-matching processes —*see* **digitize, edge match 2.** *ecology* the space occurring in forest **stands** due to individual or group tree **mortality** or **blowdown**

gap dynamics the change in space and time in the pattern, frequency, size, and **succession**al processes of **forest** canopy gaps caused by the fall or death of one or more canopy trees

gar(r)ique low, generally open **scrub**, representing the remains of Mediterranean **sclerophyllous** woodland or **maquis** (but neither as tall nor as dense as the latter), found particularly in the south of France

gate delimber a metal gate chained between two trees that delimbs trees that are backed through the gate with a **grapple skidder** —*see* **delimber**

gauge *also* **gage** **1.** a device for measuring **precipitation,** water level, discharge, velocity, pressure, temperature, etc. **2.** a standard of measure, as of wire or metal thickness

Gaussian distribution —*see* **normal distribution**

GCA —*see* **general combining ability**

gelatinous fiber —*see* **cells (wood)**

gene the smallest transmissible unit of genetic material (basic unit of heredity) consistently associated with a single primary genetic effect —*note* genes are ultramicroscopic and act as if linearly arranged at fixed places (loci) on a **chromosome** transmitted in the **gamete**s from parent to offspring, governing the transmission and development of a hereditary character —*see* **allele, character, cytoplasm, genotype, germplasm, locus, mutation**

gene flow the consequence of cross-fertilization between members of a **species** that results in the spread of **alleles** across and between populations —*see* **migration**

gene frequency the frequency of occurrence of a particular **allele** in a **population** —*see* **evolution, Hardy-Weinberg model, migration**

general combining ability (GCA) the relative ability of a individual to transmit genetic superiority to its offspring when crossed with other individuals —*note 1.* the general combining ability of a parent signifies the average performance of its progenies in various **cross**es, compared with progenies of other parents in the same test —*note 2.* the breeding value of a parent is twice its GCA —*see* **additive genetic variation, breeding value, combining ability, progeny, specific combining ability**

general fire headquarters (GHQ) —*see* **large fire organization**

generalize *GIS* **1.** to reduce the number of points, or **vertices,** used to represent a line **2.** to increase the **cell** size and **resample** data in a **raster** format GIS

generalized linear models a class of statistical models that share properties such as linearity and a common method for computing parameter estimates —*note* **linear regression** and **analysis of variance** are special cases of generalized linear models

general staff —*see* **incident command system**

genetic architecture **1.** the distribution of genetic variation in a **species** or other **taxon,** usually described hierarchically as variation at the regional, local, **family** and individual levels **2.** relating to proportions of **additive** and **nonadditive variation** in a **population**

genetic correlation a measure of the degree of genetic relationship between two **characters,** e.g., the correlation between **general combining ability** values —*note* genetic correlation is not to be confused with the correlation between **phenotype**s —*see* **linkage**

genetic diversity the genetic variability within a population or a species, usually assessed at three levels: (a) within breeding populations, (b) between breeding populations, and (c) within species

genetic drift a change in **gene frequency** and **population** characteristics due to chance rather than **selection,** and usually more prevalent in small populations

genetic engineering the directed genetic modification of an individual organism to have a new heritable **trait** by splicing a specific **gene** into the individual's genomic **DNA** sequence

genetic entry the unit of a test or **selection,** i.e., individual, **clone, family, provenance,** or **species**

genetic gain the average improvement in a **progeny** (clonal) **population** over the mean of the parental population, resulting from **selection** in the parental population —*note* the amount of gain depends on **selection intensity**, parental variation, and **heritability**

genetic load the number of recessive, deleterious, or lethal **gene**s in a **population**

genetic replication 1. the copying or transmission of **DNA 2.** a tool of **genetic test**ing in which genetic entries are replicated across environments —*see* **gene, genetic test**

genetics the basic science dealing with causes of resemblances and differences among organisms related by descent —*note* genetics takes into account the effects of **gene**s and the environment —*see* **clonal replication, forest tree breeding, forest tree improvement**

genetic test a planting established for evaluating known genetic entities for one or more purposes —*see* **genetic replication, progeny test, roguing**

genetic transformation the incorporation of **DNA** from a donor into a recipient host's DNA —*see* **chimera, transgenic**

genetic tree improvement —*see* **forest tree improvement**

genome a complete **haploid** set of **chromosomes** as found in a **gamete**

genotype 1. an individual's hereditary (genetic) constitution —*note* the genotype interacts with the environment to produce the **phenotype 2.** individual(s) characterized by a certain genetic constitution —*see* **gene, geographic variation, heritability, hybrid, trait**

genotype-environment (G × E) interaction the change in relative rank or extent of differences in a particular **trait** among **species** or individuals when grown in different environments —*see* **progeny test**

geocode *GIS* to identify a location as one or more x,y coordinates from another location description such as an address —*note* an address for a lumberyard can be matched against a **TIGER** street network to locate the lumberyard

geographic data *GIS* the composite locations and descriptions of entities

geographic database *GIS* efficiently stored and organized spatial data and possibly related descriptive data

geographic data set *GIS* a collective term for all geographically located data structured in **raster, arc-node, polygon, triangulated irregular network (TIN),** and other formats —*synonym* geodataset —*see* **arc-node topology, topology**

geographic information retrieval and analysis (GIRAS) a data file in either analog or digital form from the US Geological Survey, containing information for areas in the continental United States, including attributes for land use, land cover, political units, hydrologic units, census and county subdivisions, and federal and state landownerships

geographic information system (GIS) an organized collection of computer hardware, software, geographic and descriptive data, personnel, knowledge, and procedures designed to efficiently capture, store, update, manipulate, analyze, report, and display the forms of geographically referenced information and descriptive information —*note 1.* a central component of information storage is the necessity for topology to be maintained and coordinated by the software; otherwise, certain complex spatial operations are not possible or would be very difficult, time-consuming, or impractical —*note 2.* the major components of a GIS are the user interface, database management, data entry, product generation, and spatial data manipulation and analysis, which may be centralized or distributed across a network

geographic object *GIS* a user-defined geographic phenomenon that can be **model**ed or represented using **geographic data set**s, e.g., roads, power lines, inventory sample sites, accident locations, ownership lines, and inholding parcels

geographic race a **race** native to a geographic area —*see* **ecotype, geographic variation, local seed source, provenance, seed source, seed zone**

geographic resource analysis support system (GRASS) 1. a public-domain **raster** GIS modeling product of the US Army Corps of Engineer Construction Engineering Research Laboratory (CERL) **2.** a **raster** data format that can be used as an exchange format between two GISs

geographic variation the phenotypic differences among plants growing in different portions of a **species**' range —*note* if the phenotypic differences are more genetic than environmental, the variation is usually specified as racial, ecotypic, or clinal —*see* **cline, ecotype, genotype, geographic race, phenotype**

geological erosion —*see* **erosion**

geometric correction an **image**-processing procedure that corrects spatial distortions in **digital images** or removes sensor-, platform-, or scene-induced geometric errors to make an **aerial photograph** or digital image conform to a specific map projection

geometric mean a measure of central tendency calculated as the nth root of the product of n values, e.g., in obtaining a single diameter measurement (d) for an elliptical stem having two diameters (d_1 and d_2), $d = \sqrt{(d_1 \times d_2)}$ —*see* **arithmetic mean, mode**

geophyte a perennial, herbaceous land plant having tubers, bulbs, or rhizomes, etc., that lie below the ground surface and are capable of becoming dormant and thus surviving unfavorable seasons —*note* a geophyte is one of the cryptophytic lifeforms of Raunkiaer —*see* **cryptophyte, life-form**

georeference *GIS* a means of establishing the relationship between coordinates on a paper map or manuscript, or between the pixel coordinates of a digital image, and known real-world coordinates

georelational model *GIS* a geographic data **model** that represents both spatial features and their related descriptive data —*note* **RDBMS** tables store descriptive data, which are associated, or related, to features by the feature identification process (ID)

geotropism the response of plant organisms in either growth or position to the pull of gravity —*note* geotropism is positive when the response is toward the earth's center of gravity (e.g., the initial growth of most roots) and negative when away from it (e.g., the initial growth of most **stem**s) —*see* **chemotropism, hydrotropism, phototropism**

germ cell a **haploid** (*n*) cell —*synonym* reproductive cell —*see* **gamete, somatic cell, vegetative cell**

germinant a seed in the process of **germination**

germination **1.** *phenology* the beginning of growth of a mature, generally dormant seed, spore, or pollen grain —*note* germination is generally characterized by rupture of the seed coat, or of the spore or pollen grain wall, and the emergence of a **radicle, plumule,** thallus, or hypha **2.** *propagation* the development of a seedling from a seed, i.e., the realization of **viability**

germinative capacity **1.** the percent of seeds, spores, or pollen grains in a given sample that actually germinate irrespective of time —*note* the effective germination capacity excludes **cull** seedlings and is therefore a lower measure than total germinative capacity **2.** the percent of seeds germinating within twice the period of **germinative energy** **3.** the number of seeds that germinate in a germinator, plus the number of sound seeds remaining at the end of the test, expressed as a percent of the total sample —*note* in any batch of seeds the percent that is pure, i.e., of the species required, multiplied by the germination capacity, gives the proportion of pure live seed —*see* **seed purity, seed quality, viability**

germinative energy **1.** the percent of seeds, spores or pollen grains in a given sample germinating within a given period (the energy period), e.g., seven, 14, or 18 days, under optimum or stated conditions **2.** the percent of seeds, spores, or pollen grains in a given sample that have germinated up to the time of peak germination, gener-

ally taken as the highest number of germinations in a 24-hour period —*note* germinative energy is a measure of the rate of germination —*see* **germinative capacity, seed purity, seed quality, viability**

germ line the sequence of cells from **zygote** to functional **germ cell** whose cell descendants eventually undergo **meiosis** and produce **gamete**s

germplasm **1.** within an individual or group, the collective hereditary materials that are the physical basis for inheritance; the hereditary stream **2.** the **genotype,** with particular reference to its transmission to the next generation —*see* **gene, heredity, reproductive material**

germ tube *pathology* the first **mycelium** or hypha emerging from a germinating **spore** or other resting structure —*see* **pollen tube**

getaway time —*see* **elapsed time**

gilgai the microrelief of small basins and knolls or valleys and ridges on a soil surface, produced by expansion and contraction during wetting and drying (usually in regions with distinct, seasonal, **precipitation** patterns) of clayey soils that contain **smectite**

gill *in fungi* the lamellae or bladelike (lamellate) **spore**-bearing structure on the underside of the fruiting body (mushroom cap) on which the hymenium is borne

GIRAS —*see* **geographic information retrieval and analysis**

girdle to make more or less continuous incisions around a living stem, through at least both bark and cambium, generally with the object of killing the tree; kinds of girdling include the following:

—**chemical girdling** making a girdle and further, using an herbicide to kill the tree

—**frill girdling** making a series of downward, more or less overlapping incisions, generally for the introduction of an herbicide

—**mechanical girdling** removing a broad band of bark, from several inches (cm) to several feet (m) wide, all round a living bole, with some sapwood or without, so as to kill (with or without the aid of an herbicide), or at least weaken the tree —*synonym* band girdling

GIS —*see* **geographic information system**

glacial drift all mineral material transported by a glacier and deposited directly by or from the ice, or by running water emanating from a glacier —*note* glacial drift includes unstratified material (**till**) that forms **moraine**s, and stratified **glaciofluvial deposit**s that form outwash plains, **esker**s, **kame**s, **varve**s, and **glaciolacustrine sediment**s

glaciofluvial deposit material moved by glaciers and subsequently sorted and deposited by streams flowing from the melting ice —*see* **glacial drift**

glaciolacustrine sediment material ranging from sand to clay derived from glaciers and deposited in glacial lakes by water originating from the melting ice —*see* **glacial drift**

glade an open space in a **forest**

gleyed a soil condition resulting from prolonged soil saturation, which is manifested by the presence of bluish or greenish colors through the soil mass or in mottles (spots or streaks) among the colors —*note* gleying occurs under reducing conditions, by which iron is reduced predominantly to the ferrous state

global positioning system (GPS) a commonly hand-held, satellite-based navigational device that records x,y,z coordinates and other data allowing users to determine their location on the surface of the earth (usually within meters) —*note* GPS signals are obtained from satellites orbiting the earth such as NAVSTAR (NAVigation System with Time And Ranging), a network of 24 radiotransmitting satellites and ground stations developed by the US Department of Defense

glowing combustion phase the stage of burning in which the oxidation of solid fuel is accompanied by incandescence —*note* in the glowing phase, all volatile materials have already been driven off and there is no visible smoke; this phase follows the smoldering combustion phase and continues until the temperature drops below the combustion threshold value, or until only noncombustible ash remains

glulam —*see* **engineered wood composite**

goal the end state, aspiration, or purpose that reflects what a decision maker hopes to achieve —*note 1.* a goal is normally expressed in broad, general terms (without specific target dates or quantities) or specifically stated in the context of goal criteria (e.g., increase by 100 percent the number of tule elk on a refuge) —*note 2.* goal statements form the principal basis from which **objectives** are developed

goal programming —*see* **programming**

going fire any **wildfire** on which suppression action has not reached an extensive **mop-up** stage —*synonym* active fire

goods and services the various **outputs** and benefits, including on-site uses, produced from **forest** and **range**land resources

GPS —*see* **global positioning system**

gradation 1. the whole rise and fall of a population, e.g., of a biotype or an organism 2. the buildup of an epidemic

grade 1. *engineering* the rise or fall of a ground surface or of the line of a road, ditch, or other linear construction, expressed as one unit vertical to so many units horizontal (e.g., 1/20 or one in 20) or as a percent or degrees of slope —*synonym* gradient —*note* the slope at right angles to the line of a linear construction is termed the side grade 2. *engineering* the proportion and distribution of coarse, medium, and fine soil particles in relation to structural use 3. *utilization* an established quality or use classification of lumber, trees, or other forest products

graded stream a stream in which, over a period of years, the slope adjusts naturally so that it provides, with available discharge and with prevailing channel characteristics, just the velocity required for transportation of the load (of sediment) supplied from the drainage basin

gradient analysis the analysis of species composition along a gradient of environmental conditions

gradient wind any horizontal wind velocity tangent to the contour line of a constant pressure surface (or to the isobar of a geopotential surface) at the point in question

grading the classification of logs, stems, lumber, or seedlings according to quality, value, potential use, or function —*see* **scale**

grading rules descriptions of various grades of timber or logs and how these grades are to be determined —*note* grading rules for logs, cants, and other sawn timber have been drawn up for many of the world's timber-exporting centers, and for internal trade, in order to establish assortments that best meet buyers' **needs**

graduated circle *GIS* a circular symbol whose area, or some other dimension, represents a quantity

graft to place a portion (the **scion**) of one plant in close cambial contact with the cambium of another plant or another part of the same plant (generally a **rootstock**), with the object of securing vegetative union between the two, the scion being detached from its parent plant either before or after the operation —*note 1.* both the site of union and the composite individual are termed grafts —*note 2.* the genotype, but not necessarily the **phenotype** of the rootstock and the scion, remains unchanged after grafting —*note 3.* vegetative union occurring naturally is termed a natural graft, most commonly between roots (root graft) —*see* **bud, clone, stock, vegetative propagation**

graft incompatibility the inability of the **rootstock** and **scion** to form or maintain a union, resulting in loss of desired growth or death —*see* **incompatibility**

grain 1. the direction of most wood fibers relative to the long axis (or pith) of a stem —*see* **spiral grain**

2. the relative size of pores in a cross-section of wood, e.g., coarse- or fine-grained, open or closed grain

grain tolerance *GIS* a parameter controlling the distance between vertices on curves —*note 1.* grain tolerance restricts the number of vertices and the distance between them on **arcs** representing curves; the smaller the grain tolerance, the closer the vertices can be —*note 2.* grain tolerance differs from density tolerance, which has no effect on shape —*see* **vertex**

graphical user interface (GUI) a graphical method used to control how a user interacts with a computer to perform various tasks —*note 1.* instead of issuing commands at a prompt, the user is presented with a dashboard of graphical buttons and other functions in the form of icons and objects on the display screen; the user interacts with the system using a mouse to press an icon button to perform the function —*note 2.* other GUI tools are more dynamic, and can involve moving an object on the screen to invoke a function, e.g., a slider bar is moved back and forth to determine a value associated with a parameter of a particular operation, such as setting the scale of a map

graphics display terminal a computer terminal used to view and manipulate spatial information —*note* can also be used for graphic input (e.g., during feature selection), digitizing, editing, etc. —*see* **digitize**

graphics page the area on a graphics display device reserved for map display, or the plotter page area —*note* page units are typically in centimeters or inches instead of real-world coordinates such as meters or feet

grapple *harvesting* hinged jaws or arms capable of being opened and closed and used to grip logs or trees during **skid**ding or loading

grapple skidder *harvesting* a skidder fitted with a **grapple** for **skid**ding logs

GRASS —*see* **geographic resource analysis support system**

grass a member of the family *Poaceae* (Gramineae) —*see* **forb, herb**

grass fire a fire in which the predominant fuel is grass or grasslike —*see* **brush fire, forest fire**

grassland land on which the vegetation is dominated by grasses, grasslike plants, or **forb**s —*see* **herbland, pasture, range**

grasslike plant a plant of the Cyperaceae or Juncaceae families which vegetatively resembles a true grass of the Gramineae family

graticule 1. *surveying* a network (**grid**) of intersecting parallels and **meridian**s (or lines of latitude and longitude) on a map —*note* the lines may be straight or curved, depending on the type of map projection employed **2.** *optical systems* a scale or a set of intersecting lines to facilitate the measurement of angles and distances

gravitational water water which moves into, through, or out of the soil under the influence of gravity

gravity wind a wind (or component thereof) directed down the slope of an incline and caused by greater air density near the slope than at the same levels some distance horizontally from the slope

grazing the eating of any kind of standing vegetation by animals —*see* **browse**

grazing allotment a specific **range** area to which certain **livestock** of a permit holder (**permittee**) are assigned —*synonym* range allotment

grazing fee a charge, usually on a monthly basis, for grazing use by a given kind of animal —*synonym* grazing rent —*see* **exempt stock, permit holder**

grazing management the manipulation of grazing and browsing animals to accomplish a desired result —*see* **deferred grazing**

grazing method a defined procedure or technique of **grazing management** designed to achieve a specific objective(s) —*note* one or more grazing methods can be utilized within a **grazing system**

grazing period the length of time that animals are allowed to graze on a specific area

grazing preference 1. selection of certain plants, or plant parts, over others by grazing animals —*see* **browsing preference, palatability 2.** *in the administration of public lands* a basis on which permits and licenses are issued for grazing use

grazing season 1. *on public lands* an established period for which grazing permits are issued —*note* a season may be established on private land in a grazing management plan **2.** the time when animals are allowed to utilize a certain area —*see* **grazing period, periodic grazing**

grazing system a specialization of **grazing management** that defines the periods of grazing and nongrazing —*note* although descriptive common names may be used, the first usage of a grazing system name is customarily followed by a description that includes number of pastures (or units) number of herds, length of grazing periods, and length of nongrazing periods for any given unit in the system, followed by an abbreviation of the unit of time used —*see* **deferred grazing, deferred rotation, forage, grazing method, rest-rotation, rotation(al) grazing, short-duration grazing**

greenbelt a parklike strip of unoccupied land with

little or no development, usually surrounding or partially surrounding urban areas

green-chain tally a lumber tally, made at the mill, of material in green condition —*synonym* mill tally

green-chain tally board foot a board foot of lumber as it comes out rough and unseasoned from the sawmill —*note* this measure is used to construct **mill tally** log rules

greenhouse effect the warming effect exerted by the atmosphere upon the earth because the atmosphere (mainly its water vapor and carbon dioxide) absorbs radiant energy from the earth and re-emits infrared radiation or heat —*note* the atmosphere traps heat similar to glass in a greenhouse

green manure green or mature (but not composted) plant material incorporated into the soil to ameliorate soil condition —*see* **cover crop**

green tree retention —*see* **reserve tree**

grid *GIS* one of many data structures used to represent map features; a **raster**-based data structure composed of **cell**s of equal size arranged in columns and rows —*note* the value of each cell, or group of cells, represents the value of the feature —*synonym* raster —*see* **graticule, grid cell**

grid cell *GIS* a discretely uniform unit that represents a portion of the earth, such as a square meter or square mile —*note* each grid **cell** has a value that corresponds to the feature or characteristic at that site, such as a soil type, census tract, or vegetation class

gross primary production the total assimilation of energy and nutrients by an organism or a plant community per unit of time —*see* **net primary production**

gross scale measurement of log content in log-scale board feet or cubic feet without deduction for defects —*synonym* full scale, gross volume

gross yarding the removal of all woody material of specified size from a logging unit to a landing

ground control the use of **control point**s that are identifiable on **aerial photograph**s to provide the scale (horizontal control) and height data (vertical control) necessary for mapping from such photographs

ground cover the herbaceous plants (including grasses and ferns) and the lowest **shrub**s occupying an area —*note* **bryophyte**s and lower forms of vegetation may be distinguished as the ground layer (ground flora) —*see* **forest cover, vegetation cover**

ground distance the measured distance between two points on the ground, used with either map or photo distance to compute map or photo scale

ground fire —*see* **forest fire**

ground fog a fog that hides less than 0.6 of the sky and does not extend to the base of any clouds that may lie above it

ground fuel —*see* **fuel type**

ground-lead logging a **cable-yarding** method in which the **main line** lead **block** is hung on a stump and no lift is provided by the yarder

ground level *of a standing tree or its stump* a conventional point for specifying and standardizing the base of the ground —*note* on slopes it may be set at the highest point where the ground touches the stem, or the mean of the highest and lowest points (mean ground level)

ground pressure the weight of a vehicle, under specific conditions, that is transmitted to the ground —*note* ground pressure is computed as the weight per unit area of contact between the ground and the wheels or tracks in the static condition

ground skidding pulling logs along the ground without using an **arch** or **fairlead** to raise the forward ends

ground tanker a vehicle equipped with tank, pump, and necessary tools and equipment for spraying water or chemicals on wildfires —*synonym* engine, fire truck, pumper, tanker

groundwater the subsurface water in both **phreatic** (saturated) and **vadose** (unsaturated) zone water at a pressure equal to or greater than atmospheric that is free to move under the influence of gravity —*note* groundwater is recharged by infiltration and enters streams through seepage and springs —*see* **perched groundwater, phreatic**

groundwater budget the summation of the movement of water into and out of a ground water reservoir during a specified time

groundwater discharge the flow of water from the groundwater reservoir onto the earth's surface

groundwater recharge the flow of water from the earth's surface into the groundwater reservoir

groundwood pulp —*see* **pulp (mechanical)**

group *silviculture* a unit of harvest or regeneration in group selection —*note 1.* the minimum size of a group depends primarily on (a) the creation of microclimate conducive to establishment of desired regeneration of particular tolerance, and (b) the area needed for safe felling and **yard**ing of harvested trees —*note 2.* group size is often expressed as a function of surrounding tree height; its boundary may be defined as at the drip-line of edge trees —*see* **group selection, incident command system, patch, regeneration method**

group selection —*see* **regeneration method**

growing space 1. the physical area available to and utilized by a tree **2.** that portion of the resources of the site (light, water, nutrients, etc.) available to and utilized by a tree —*note* growing space is not usually directly measurable but often represented from crown projection or leaf area or as an area allocation obtained using various mathematical techniques

growing stock all the trees growing in a **forest** or in a specified part of it, usually commercial species, meeting specified standards of size, quality, and vigor, and generally expressed in terms of number or volume

growth-and-yield model —*see* **yield table**

growth form the characteristic general appearance, i.e., shape, posture, and mode of growth, rather than size or color, of an organism —*note* with plants, growth form is preferably termed the (growth) habit, e.g., pyramidal and erect, bushy and procumbent —*see* **life-form**

growth regulator an organic substance, usually a **hormone**, effective in minute amounts for controlling or modifying growth processes of (usually) plants or insects —*note 1.* insect growth regulators typically control such processes as molting and maturation from one **stage** to the next; plant growth regulators typically control cell enlargement, elongation, division, and activation —*note 2.* synthetic and natural growth regulators are often used as **pesticides**

growth ring the cumulative layers of cells produced during a single growing season and characteristically containing **earlywood** and **latewood** cells of differing morphology —*synonym* annual ring —*note* growth rings commonly occur annually in trees grown in temperate regions having distinct growing seasons and a period of dormancy; in tropical regions having more than one active growth in one year, there is no clear demarcation indicating the beginning or the end of successive growth increments —*see* **discontinuous ring, false ring**

growth stress the forces that develop within a tree as it grows, especially in rapidly growing hardwoods —*note* growth stresses may be suddenly released on felling or sawing, resulting in shattering —*see* **shake**

grub 1. a thick-bodied **larva** with thoracic legs and well-developed head (scarabaeiform), usually sluggish —*note* a grub is the early stage of development of an insect with complete **metamorphosis,** particularly beetles **2.** to remove stumps or **shrubs** from the ground by hand or machine, typically prior to road building or regeneration —*see* **scalp, site preparation**

guard unit the geographic subdivision of a fire-protected area delimiting the initial attack boundaries of a single **fire guard** or fire crew

GUI —*see* **graphical user interface**

gully a channel or miniature valley cut by concentrated runoff, through which water commonly flows only during and immediately after heavy rains or during the melting of snow —*note 1.* gullies may be branching or linear, long, narrow, and of uniform width —*note 2.* the distinction between gully and rill is one of depth: a gully is sufficiently deep that it would not be obliterated by normal tillage operations; a rill is of lesser depth and would be smoothed by ordinary farm tillage

gully erosion —*see* **erosion**

gun-hour —*see* **hunter day**

Gymnospermae the group of vascular flowering plants that produce seeds not enclosed in an ovary (naked seeds) —*note 1.* an important division is Coniferophyta, which contains most conifers and their allies; other important divisions are Ginkgophyta and Cycadophyta —*note 2.* the pollen- and ovule-bearing structures of gymnosperms are strobili but are often called flowers for convenience —*synonym* **gymnosperm**s —*see* **Angiospermae, strobilus**

Gymnosporangium **rust** a disease caused by **species** of the genus *Gymnosporangium* and a few species in the closely related genera *Roestelia* and *Uredo* having telial **hosts** in the Cupressaceae and aecial hosts usually in the Rosaceae —*note Gymnosporangium* rust causes economic damage to pomaceous crops and to ornamental cedars and junipers —*synonym* **stem rust** —*see* **aecium**

gyn-, gyno- *prefix* female —*see* **andr-, andro-**

gynoecium all the female parts of a **flower**

gyppo *also* **gypo 1.** an independent logger who runs a small-scale logging operation **2.** a small, independent sawmill or other wood-related operation **3.** a person paid on a piecework basis, such as a gyppo car loader or a gyppo trucker

H

habitat 1. a unit area of environment **2.** the place, natural or otherwise, (including climate, food, **cover**, and water) where an animal, plant, or **population** naturally or normally lives and develops —*see* **home range, natural range, range, site**

habitat conservation area (HCA) a contiguous block of habitat to be managed and conserved for breeding pairs, connectivity, and distribution of spotted owls —*note* the application of habitat conservation areas may vary thoughout the owl's range according to local conditions

habitat conservation plan (HCP) an agreement between the Secretary of the Interior and either a private entity or a state, specifying the conservation measures that will be implemented in exchange for a permit that would allow **taking** of a threatened or endangered species —*see* **threatened species**

habitat diversity the number of different types of habitat within a given area

habitat fragmentation —*see* **fragmentation**

habitat quality the overall rating of the quality or quantity of plant or animal habitat —*synonym* suitability index

habitat type 1. *ecology* a land or aquatic unit consisting of an aggregation of **habitat**s having equivalent structure, function, and responses to disturbance **2.** *ecology, silviculture* an aggregation of units of land capable of producing similar plant communities at **climax** —*synonym* **potential vegetation** —*note* habitat typing is used in some regions of the west for site classification

half-and-half rule a rule that averages the **stand** output or condition over a planning period that experiences a discontinuity, such as harvest, at the midpoint

half-sib progeny the offspring resulting from a cross of one parent with more than one other parent —*see* **dominance genetic variation, full-sib progeny, sib**

half-track *harvesting* a vehicle supported on endless articulated tracks and steered by wheels

halophyte a plant that is more or less restricted to saline soil or to sites that are influenced by salt water —*see* **helophyte**

hand tool *firefighting* a **fire suppression** tool primarily designed and used by **fire fighters** to construct **firelines** on a **forest** fire; kinds of hand tool include the following:

—**brush hook** a heavy cutting tool with a wide blade, generally curved to protect the blade from being dulled by rocks, designed primarily to cut brush at the base of the stem and used in much the same way as an ax

hand tool *continued*

—**double-bit(ted) ax** an ax having a head with two cutting edges

—**fire rake** a long-handled combination rake and cutting tool having a blade with a single row of three or four sharpened teeth —*note* a fire rake is sometimes made by fastening mowing machine cutter teeth to a piece of angle iron —*synonym* council tool, rich tool

—**fire shovel** a shovel with a tapered blade with both edges sharpened for scraping, digging, grubbing, and cutting

—**fire swatter** a **fire suppression** tool used in direct attack for beating out flames along a **fire edge** —*note* a fire swatter may be improvised and consist merely of a green pine bough or wet sacking, or be a manufactured tool, e.g., a flap of belting fabric fastened to a long handle —*synonym* swatter, fire broom

—**mattock** a hand tool with a narrow hoeing surface at one end of the blade and a pick or cutting blade at the other end, used for digging and grubbing

—**mccleod** a combination hoe or cutting tool and rake, with or without removable blades

—**pulaski** a combination chopping and trenching tool that combines a single-bitted ax blade with a narrow trenching blade resembling an adz hoe fitted to a straight handle

—**rich tool** —*see* **fire rake**

haploid having one complete set of **chromosomes** per cell —*note* these are the *n* chromosomes normally in sex cells compared with the *2n* in vegetative cells —*see* **chromosome number, diploid, gamete, meiosis, polyploid**

hardboard —*see* **engineered wood composite**

hardening off 1. the natural process of adaptation by plants to cold, drought, etc. **2.** preparing seedlings or rooted cuttings in a nursery for transplanting or planting out, by gradually reducing watering, shade, or shelter and thus inducing changes in the leading shoot that render it more tolerant of desiccation, cold, etc. —*see* **acclimation**

hardness a property of wood that enables it to resist indentation, generally measured by the loading, applied at a standard rate, that is required to imbed a 0.444-in- (1.28 cm) diameter steel ball to a depth equal to its radius

hardpan a soil layer with physical characteristics that limit root penetration and restrict water movement

hard seed seed having coats (i.e., testas) more or less impermeable to water —*note* hard seed often requires scarification by heat, chemicals, or mechanical action for germination

hard snag —*see* **snag**

hardware *computers* components of a computer system, such as the central processing unit (CPU), terminals, plotters, **digitizer**s, or printers

hardwood trees belonging to the botanical group **Angiospermae** 2. the **xylem** of Angiospermae —*note* hardwood shows extreme variation in vertical and horizontal (radial) systems of elements but, with few exceptions, is composed of **vessels** and **rays** —*note* the wood of hardwoods may be either physically hard (high specific gravity) or soft (low specific gravity) —*see* **softwood, lumber**

Hardy-Weinberg model a **mathematical model** of the theoretical relationship maintained from generation to generation between **gene** frequencies and **genotype** frequencies in a large **random mating** population in the absence of **mutation, migration,** and **selection** —*see* **gene frequency**

Hartig net the network of intercellular fungus hyphae in the root **cortex** of an **ectomyccorrhiza**

harvest cutting an intermediate or final cutting that extracts salable trees

harvester a machine that falls trees and performs processing functions at the stump —*see* **processor**

harvesting the **felling, skid**ding, on-site processing, and loading of trees or logs onto trucks —*synonym* **logging**

harvesting method a procedure by which a **stand** is logged; emphasis is on meeting logging requirements while concurrently attaining silvicultural **objective**s —*synonym* cutting method —*see* **regeneration method, variable retention harvest system**

harvest scheduling a process for allocating cutting and other silvicultural treatments over a **forest** with emphasis on which treatments to apply and where and when to apply them

haulback block *harvesting* a **block** used to guide the **haulback line**

haulback line *harvesting* a wire rope used in cable logging to haul the main line with **carriage, butt rigging,** or **choker**s back to the point where the logs are to be attached

haustorium *plural* **haustoria** 1. *botany* in (semi)parasitic higher plants, a modified root or shoot serving both to attach the parasite to its host and to obtain nourishment from it 2. *in fungi* a specialized branch of a fungal hypha that absorbs food for the rest of the fungal colony, often by penetrating the living **host** cell but not the plasma membrane —*note* haustorium is the old name for the dwarf **mistletoe**'s endophytic system —*see* **endophyte, holdfast, hyphal hole, powdery mildew, sinker root**

hazard 1. *entomology* the degree of vulnerability of a **stand** to a particular **pest** given that the insect is present —*see* **risk, susceptibility, uncertainty** 2. *fire* —*see* **fire hazard**

hazardous material anything that poses a substantial present or potential hazard to human health or the environment when improperly treated, stored, transported, disposed of, or otherwise managed

hazard-rating system *entomology, pathology* a ranking of trees or forest **stand**s according to the probability of damage or impact from one or more insects or diseases

hazard tree inspection *urban forestry* close observation of trees that have been identified as a potential **risk,** for failure that would cause injury to a person or damage to property

HCA —*see* **habitat conservation area**

HCP —*see* **habitat conservation plan**

head *hydrology* 1. the height of water above any plane of reference 2. the kinetic or potential energy possessed by each unit weight of a liquid, expressed as the vertical height through which a unit weight would have to fall to release the average energy possessed —*note* head is used in various compound terms, such as pressure head, velocity head, and lost head 3. the internal pressure expressed in ft or lb/in^2 (m or g/cm^2) of an enclosed conduit 4. *fire* —*see* **forest fire**

head saw —*see* **saw**

head tree (head spar) *harvesting* a spar tree or portable **spar (tower)** at the landing of a **skyline** logging operation

headwater 1. the source of a stream 2. the water upstream from a structure or point on a stream 3. the upper tributaries of a drainage basin

heart decay decomposition of the central stemwood of living trees, not necessarily limited to true **heartwood** —*note 1.* heart decay is caused by numerous **species** of fungi and is the most damaging of all types of tree diseases —*note 2.* some heart decays also cause root decay —*synonym* heart rot —*see* **decay, conk**

heartwood the inner, nonliving part of a tree stem that is altered to a protective state as a result of normal, genetically controlled aging processes as cells die, and that provides mechanical support —*note 1.* heartwood cells have no living contents and no active or dynamic transport processes —*note 2.* extractives are often deposited in heartwood and these generally impart a color that is darker than the **sapwood** —*see* **false heart**

heath 1. an open, uncultivated tract of land with a sandy or gravely soil supporting low vegetation (typically coarse grasses and Ericaceae) and occasionally scattered tree growth, particularly pine —*note* a heath is considerably drier than a **moor 2.** the vegetation developing on poor, usually acid, sandy, or gravely soils in lowlands and dominated by heathers (*Calluna* sp. and *Erica* sp.)

heating degree-day a form of **degree-day** used as an indication of fuel consumption —*note* in US usage, one heating degree-day is given for each degree that the daily mean temperature departs below the base of 65°F or 19°C

heat island the phenomenon that cities are 5 to 9°F (2.8 to 5.0°C) warmer than the rural areas that surround them because of their heat-absorbing concrete and black asphalt infrastructure —*synonym* oasis effect —*see* **island**

heat probe an apparatus used to detect heat —*note* a heat probe is used during **mop-up** of fires to determine areas needing further suppression activity —*synonym* heat scanner —*see* **forward-looking infrared (FLIR), infrared imagery**

heavy fuel —*see* **fuel type**

hedge 1. *genetics* to repeatedly clip an **ortet** or some of its **ramet**s to produce a low-hedged plant to slow or halt **maturation** of the plant and to control its size and shape for efficient collection of **cuttings 2.** *wildlife* to graze or browse vegetation to the extent that it appears artificially clipped or pruned —*synonym* close cropped

hedge orchard an orchard of **hedge**d plants that produces cuttings or other tissue for vegetative propagation

hedgerow a closely planted line of **shrub**s or small trees, often forming a boundary or fence

heel boom *harvesting* a loading boom that uses tongs or a grapple to heel or force one end of a log against the underside of the boom to control and carry it

heeling in placing small bundles of **bare-root seedling**s in a shallow trench or hole and covering the roots or rooting portions with soil as a temporary storage technique prior to transplanting or outplanting —*see* **trench planting**

height class 1. any of the intervals into which a range of tree or plant heights may be divided **2.** the actual trees or plants falling into such an interval

height:diameter ratio the ratio of tree height to **diameter at breast height**, which provides a measure of tree taper and, indirectly, of past **stand** management, density, and stand stability

held line a **fireline** that still contains the fire when **mop-up** is completed —*note* a held line excludes lost lines, natural barriers not suppression fired, and unused secondary lines —*synonym* hold line

helibase a location within the general **incident** area for parking, fueling, maintenance, and loading of helicopters —*note* helibase is an **ICS** term —*see* **heliport, helispot**

helijumper a **fire fighter** trained and equipped to jump from a helicopter to fight fire in areas where helicopters cannot land —*see* **smoke jumper**

heliport a permanent or semipermanent landing location for helicopters that is accessible by road and where fuel, service, and supply can be made available —*see* **helibase, helispot**

helispot a temporary landing location for helicopters, normally constructed on or near the **fireline** for access of personnel and supplies, generally without auxiliary facilities and often without road access —*see* **helibase, heliport**

helitack 1. the use of helicopters to transport crews, equipment, and fire retardants or suppressants to the **fireline** during initial and later stages of a fire **2.** the crew that performs helicopter management and attack activities —*see* **air attack**

helitank a specially designed fabric or metal tank fitted closely to the bottom of a helicopter and used for transporting and dropping suppressants or **fire retardant**s —*synonym* helibucket

helitanker a helicopter equipped with a **helitank** or helibucket

helitorch —*see* **ignition tool**

helophyte a **cryptophyte** that mainly or exclusively grows in soil or mud saturated with water —*note 1.* the overwintering buds commonly lie in the mud —*note 2.* helophytes do not include all the plants ordinarily known as marsh plants —*see* **halophyte, life-form**

hemicellulose —*see* **cells (wood)**

hemicryptophyte a land plant whose shoots die back to ground level at the beginning of the unfavorable season, leaving the perennating resting buds at the soil surface —*see* **cryptophyte, life-form**

hemimetabolous an insect life cycle characterized by incomplete **metamorphosis**

hemiphyte a plant that begins life as an **epiphyte** but later sends roots into the soil —*see* **epiphyte, parasite**

herb a nonwoody, vascular plant such as a grass, a grasslike plant, a fern, or a forb —*see* **herbaceous** —*note* herbs are collectively termed herbage —*see* **grass**

herbaceous a class of vegetation dominated by nonwoody plants known as **herb**s (graminoids, **forb**s, and ferns) —*note 1.* herbs generally form at least 25 percent **cover**; trees, **shrub**s and dwarf shrubs generally have less than 25 percent cover —*note 2.* in rare cases, herbaceous cover exceeds the combined cover of trees, shrubs, dwarf shrubs, and nonvascular plants and is less than 25 percent cover —*note 3.* height classes for the graminoids are short (< 0.5 m or 1.6 ft), medium-tall (0.5 to 1 m, or 1.6 to 3.3 ft) and tall (> 1 m or 3.3 ft); height classes for the forbs are low (< 1 m or 3.3 ft) and tall (> 1 m or 3.3 ft) —*note 4.* for both graminoids and forbs, the height classes are measured when the inflorescences are fully developed

herbicide a **pesticide** used for killing or controlling the growth of plants

herbivore an animal that consumes living plant material —*synonym* phytophage —*see* **carnivore, scavenger**

herbland land on which herbaceous **species** dominate the vegetation —*see* **grassland, range**

herder a person who tends **livestock** on a **range** —*note* the term is usually applied to the person herding a band of sheep or goats

heredity the sum of qualities and potentialities of an individual that are derived from the genetic characteristics of its parent —*see* **germplasm**

heritability the proportion of variability of a character due to **heredity**, the remainder being due to environment —*note 1.* high heritability indicates that an individual **phenotype** is indicative of its **genotype** —*note 2.* if calculated from parent-**progeny** data, heritability estimates the degree of resemblance between parent and progeny —*see* **breeding value, broad-sense heritability, clonal test, genetic gain, genotype, narrow sense heritability**

heteroecious a type of life cycle found in **rust fungi** with **stages** on alternate unrelated **host** species, in contrast to **autoecious** —*note* heteroecious rusts include **fusiform rust** and white pine blister rust

heterogeneity 1. *biometrics* the state of being not identical in some or all parameters in one or more samples or **populations**, e.g., heterogeneity of **variance** —*see* **homogeneity 2.** variation in the environment over space and time

heterogeneous exhibiting dissimilarity among members of a group —*note* the term is not to be confused with **heterozygous** —*see* **homogeneous**

heterosis a characteristic exhibited when the mean **hybrid phenotype** exceeds the range of the parents —*note 1.* statistically, heterosis is the increase in a **trait** over the mean value for that trait in the parents —*note 2.* heterosis is usually applied to traits such as size or general vigor —*see* **F₁, heterozygous, hybrid, inbred line, inbreeding, phenotype, transgressive segregation** —*synonym* hybrid vigor

heterotrophic pertaining to organisms that are consumers and dependent on other organisms for their source of energy (food) —*see* **autotrophic**

heterozygosity the state of being **heterozygous**, i.e., the two **alleles** at a **locus** are not identical, such as Aa —*see* **homozygosity**

heterozygote a plant (tree) that is **heterozygous** at a particular gene locus

heterozygous 1. having one or more sets of unlike **alleles** —*note* an Aa cell or plant is heterozygous whereas the AA and aa **genotypes** are **homozygous 2.** pertaining to differences in the arrangement of **genes** on **chromosomes** —*note* a heterozygous tree is called a **heterozygote** —*see* **character, dominance, F₁, F₂, heterosis, hybrid, overdominance**

heuristics a rule-based procedure for quickly finding a solution to a problem —*note* heuristic techniques are used to find initial **feasible solutions** for the transportation **simplex method** as well as in other applications; heuristics generally do not produce **optimal solutions**, although some have been demonstrated to be nearly so

hexaploid a plant containing six sets ($6n$) of **chromosomes** —*see* **chromosome number, polyploid**

hibernation a state in which certain species of animals pass the winter or cold season in a dormant condition with greatly reduced metabolic activity —*see* **dormancy**

hidden fire scar a **fire scar** in a tree resulting from fire injury to the cambium without destruction of the overlying bark and therefore not readily discernible

hierarchic data model a type of data storage that links data in a treelike fashion, similar to the concept of family lines, where data relations can be traced through particular arms of the hierarchy —*note* these data are dependent on the data structure

hierarchy 1. information that has order and priority **2.** a sequence of sets composed of smaller subsets

high *meteorology* an area of high pressure, i.e., a maximum of atmospheric pressure in two dimensions (closed **isobars**) in the synoptic surface chart, or a maximum of height (closed contours) in the constant-pressure chart —*see* **synoptic chart**

high drop an **air tanker** drop made from a higher than normal altitude above the vegetative canopy —*note* a high drop is usually ordered for tactical or safety reasons

high forest a stand of trees, generally of seedling origin, that normally develop a high, closed canopy—*see* **low forest**

high forest method a treatment designed to produce

stands originating from seed —*note* methods include even-aged (clearcutting, seed-tree, and shelterwood) and uneven-aged (selection) treatments —*see* **regeneration method**

high grading the removal of the most commercially valuable trees (high-grade trees), often leaving a residual **stand** composed of trees of poor condition or **species** composition —*note* high grading may have both genetic implications (i.e., **dysgenic** effects) and long-term economic or stand health implications —*see* **overcut**

highlead logging a cable logging system in which logs or trees are yarded by means of a **wire rope** passing through a **block** at the top of the **head spar** or **tower** —*see* **cable yarding, skyline**

high moor a type of **bog** in which both the vegetation and the peat have low nutrient status, the vegetation having developed either on basin sites receiving runoff water poor in minerals and N (as from coarse or siliceous soils) or in sites in a cool humid climate (as in higher latitudes) where heavy **precipitation** has leached most of the nutrients from the soil and caused waterlogging for much of the year, creating a blanket bog or blanket peat —*note 1.* *Sphagnum* sp. and ericaceous shrubs are typical of high moor vegetation in the northern temperate zone —*note 2.* a raised bog is a special form of high moor in which the peat accumulation in the center is greater than at its edges; the central portion is thus raised above the natural groundwater level, becomes solely dependent for moisture on **precipitation,** and is therefore exceedingly low in plant nutrients —*see* **low moor**

high water line the point of a maximum water level of a body of water during **flood** conditions

histic epipedon a thin organic soil **horizon** that is saturated with water at some period of the year unless it is artificially drained, and that is at or near the surface of mineral soil

histogram a graphical representation of a univariate **frequency distribution** in which the rectangles proportional in area to the class frequencies are erected on sections of the horizontal axis, the width of each section representing the corresponding class interval of the **random variable**

historical climate a climate of the historical period, which may be taken as the past 7,000 years

H layer —*see* **horizon**

hoedad a hoelike tool with an elongated blade, used for planting trees —*see* **dibble**

hog a machine used to convert waste wood into chips for use as fuel or other purposes

holdfast a dislike swelling in **dwarf mistletoe,** at the distal end of the **radicle,** through which **infection** of the **host** takes place —*note* the holdfast was

formerly referred to as the haustorial disk —*see* **haustorium**

holdover fire a fire that remains dormant for a considerable time after it starts —*synonym* hangover fire, sleeper fire —*see* **overwintering fire**

hollow a small depression on a level surface —*synonym* pit

hollow-core construction a panel construction with facings of plywood, hardboard, or similar material bonded to a framed core of wood lattice, paperboard rings, etc., which support the facings at suitable intervals —*see* **engineered wood composites**

holocellulose —*see* **cells (wood)**

holometabolous an insect life cycle characterized by complete **metamorphosis**

home garden the intimate association of multipurpose trees and shrubs with annual and perennial crops and, invariably, livestock within the compounds of individual houses, the whole crop-tree-animal unit being managed by family labor —*synonym* forest garden

home range the area covered by the normal annual mobility of a wildlife species —*see* **habitat, natural range**

homoclimes places having similar climates and therefore similar **climagrams**

homogeneity *of one or more samples or **populations*** the state of being identical in some or all parameters, e.g., homogeneity of **variance** —*see* **heterogeneity**

homogeneous exhibiting similarity among members of a group —*note* the term is not to be confused with **homozygous** —*see* **heterogeneous**

homologous chromosomes pairs of **chromosomes** that are similar in size, shape, genetic content, and arrangement and are present in all **diploid** cells of an organism —*note* homologous chromosomes pair physically at **meiosis** —*see* **allele, gamete, linkage**

homozygosity the state of being **homozygous**, i.e., both **alleles** at a **locus** are identical, e.g., aa or AA —*see* **heterozygosity**

homozygous having one or more sets of like **alleles**, e.g., both dominant (AA) or both **recessive** (aa) —*note* the homozygote breeds true when mated with the same **genotype** —*see* **heterozygous, inbred line, overdominance**

honeycombing fissures in the interior of a piece of lumber generally caused by drying stress resulting from **case-hardening** —*synonym* collapse check, honeycomb check, internal check

honeycomb rot —*see* **pocket rot**

honeycomb wood boring the construction of irregular, interconnecting galleries in the **heartwood** or other dead parts of trees by **termite**s and **carpenter ant**s

honeydew a sticky liquid sugar derived from plant sap excreted by **scale**s, **aphid**s, and some other insects —*note* a black **sooty mold** often grows on honeydew

honey fungus —*see* **Armillaria root disease** —*synonym* honey mushroom

horizon, soil a layer of soil approximately parallel to the land surface and differing from adjacent genetically related layers in physical, chemical, and biological properties or characteristics such as color, **structure**, texture, consistency, kinds and number of organisms present, degree of acidity or alkalinity; kinds of soil horizon include the following:

—**albic horizon** a mineral soil horizon from which **clay** and free iron oxides have been removed, or in which the oxides have been segregated to the extent that the color of the horizon is determined primarily by the color of the primary **sand** and **silt** particles, rather than by coatings on these particles

—**argillic horizon** a mineral soil horizon that is characterized by the illuvial accumulation of phyllosilicate clays —*see* **illuviation**

—**cambic horizon** a mineral soil **horizon** that has a texture of **loam**y, very fine **sand** or finer, has soil **structure**, contains some weatherable minerals, and is characterized by the alteration or removal of mineral material as indicated by mottling or gray colors, stronger **chroma**s or redder hues than in underlying horizons, or the removal of carbonates

—**illuvial horizon** a soil layer or horizon in which material carried from an overlying layer has been precipitated from solution or deposited from suspension; the layer of accumulation

—**A horizon** a mineral horizon that formed at the surface or below an **O horizon,** obliterating all or much of the original rock structure and (a) characterized by an accumulation of humified organic matter intimately mixed with the mineral fraction and not dominated by properties characteristic of **E** or **B horizon**s, or (b) with properties resulting from cultivation, pasturing, or similar kinds of disturbance

—**B horizon** a soil horizon that formed below an A, E, or O **horizon,** dominated by obliteration of all or much of the original rock structure and showing one or more of the following: (a) illuvial concentration of silicate clay, iron, aluminum, humus, carbonates, gypsum, or silica, alone or in combination; (b) evidence of removal of carbonates; (c) residual concentration of **sesquioxide**s; (d) coatings of sequioxides that make the horizon conspicuously lower in value, higher in chroma, or redder

horizon, soil *continued*

in hue than the overlying or underlying horizons without apparent **illuviation** of iron; (e) alteration that forms silicate clay or liberates oxides, or both, that forms granular, blocky, or prismatic **structure** if volume changes accompany changes in moisture content; or (f) brittleness

—**C horizon** a horizon or layer, excluding hard bedrock, that is little affected by pedogenic processes and lacks properties of O, A, E, or B horizons —*note* the material of C horizons may be either like or unlike that from which the **solum** presumably formed

—**E horizon** a mineral soil horizon in which the main feature is loss of silicate clay, iron, aluminum, or some combination of these, leaving a concentration of **sand** and **silt** particles of quartz or other resistant materials

—**F layer** the fragmentation layer in the forest floor, immediately below the **litter** layer, composed of fragmented, partially decomposed organic materials that are sufficiently well preserved to permit identification as to origin —*note* the term is no longer used in the US system of soil taxonomy —*see* **Oa horizon**

—**H layer** the **humus** layer of the forest floor, consisting largely of well-decomposed, amorphous organic matter —*note* the term is no longer used in the US system of soil taxonomy —*see* **Oe horizon**

—**L layer** the litter layer of the forest floor, consisting of unaltered dead remains of plants and animals —*note* the term is no longer used in the US system of soil taxonomy —*see* **Oi horizon**

—**O horizon** a soil layer dominated by organic materials occurring at the surface of the soil

—**Oa horizon** an organic soil horizon composed of highly decomposed organic material where rubbed fiber content averages < 1/6 of the volume —*see* **H layer**

—**Oe horizon** an organic soil horizon composed of organic material of intermediate decomposition in which rubbed fiber content is 1/6 to 2/5 of the volume —*see* **F layer**

—**Oi horizon** an organic soil horizon composed of slightly decomposed organic material in which rubbed fiber content is more than about 2/5 of the volume —*see* **L layer**

hormone 1. *animal (insect) hormone* a chemical substance formed in the endocrine system that is secreted internally into the body fluids and that influences or activates specifically receptive organs or physiological processes **2.** *plant hormone* an organic plant compound such as auxin or gibberellin that in minute (trace) quantities, remote from where it is formed, controls growth and differentiation of plant tissue —*see* **growth regulator, pheromone, semiochemical**

horntail 1. a large (25 mm, or 0.98 in, or greater) insect in the family Siricidae and with both sexes having a hornlike process at the end of the abdomen —*note* horntails have thick waists; wasps (Vespidae), bees (Apidae), and ants (Formicidae) have narrow waists —*synonym* woodwasp **2.** a short spine on the last body segment of Siricid larvae, for which they are named

hose lay the arrangement of connected lengths of fire hose and accessories on the ground, beginning at the first pumping unit and ending at the point of water delivery —*note* a simple (single) hose lay has no laterals; a progressive hose lay has one or more double shutoff (gated) Y-shaped connectors (wyes) inserted in the main line, permitting lateral lines to be run to the fire edge, thus providing continuous application of water during extension of the lay

host an organism on or within which another organism develops and obtains all or part of its food

host specificity the degree to which an organism is restricted to a particular type of **host**

hot logging a logging operation in which the logs are not decked and stored but loaded onto a truck as soon as they are **skid**ded to a landing

hotshot crew an intensively trained fire crew used primarily in hand line construction

hot spot a particularly active part of a fire

hot-spot —*see* **fire suppression**

hour protocol *fire* the maximum allowable time, usually from time of origin to initial attack, beyond which, if **fire suppression** has not begun, the burned area will likely exceed an acceptable maximum for a specified unit or cover type

hue a measure of the chromatic composition of light that reaches the eye —*note* hue is one of the three variables of color used in describing soils —*see* **chroma, value, Munsell color system**

human-caused fire a fire caused directly or indirectly by person(s)

humic acid the dark organic material that can be extracted from soil with dilute alkali and other reagents and that is precipitated by acidification to pH 1 to 2 —*see* **soil reaction**

humic substance a yellow or black organic substance of relatively high molecular weight formed by secondary synthesis reactions in soils —*note* humic substance generally refers to the colored material or its fraction obtained on the basis of solubility characteristics

humin the fraction of the soil organic matter that cannot be extracted from soil with dilute alkali

hummock a small, mounded rise of organic matter and vegetation on a level surface —*synonym* mound

humus black or brown organic material of complex composition which is the end-product of microbial breakdown of plant and animal residues at the soil surface —*synonym* soil organic matter

humus layers 1. the group of organic and organic-enriched mineral horizons at the soil surface **2.** a group of soil horizons located at or near the surface of a **pedon**, which have formed from organic residues either separate from or intermixed with mineral materials

hunter day a measure of the hunting pressure or opportunity on an area expressed in the number of hunters the area can support in one day —*note 1.* a day is an undefined period of time —*note 2.* the term hunter day has mostly replaced an earlier term, gun-hour, which represents the equivalent of one hour of hunting by one hunter

hunter kill the number of game animals removed from a population by hunting and generally assessed annually —*synonym* kill, bag, exploitation

hunting pressure the intensity of hunting as measured by **hunter day**s, gun hours, or other units on a given area —*note* hunting pressure is generally considered in relation to its effect on the game population —*synonym* shooting incidence —*see* **population pressure**

hybrid the **progeny** of genetically different parents —*note* the term is applied to the progeny from matings within **species** (intraspecific) or to those between species (interspecific) —*see* **allele, cross-pollination, F_1, F_2, genotype, heterosis, heterozygous, species hybrid**

hybrid index a numerical rating used to denote the probable contribution of two parental **race**s or **species** to individuals in a **population**

hybridization 1. *interspecific hybridization* a cross between **species 2.** *intraspecific hybridization* a cross between **population**s within a species or between individuals of contrasting **genotype**s within a population **3.** *introgressive hybridization* the moving of **gene**s from one species or **population** to another by repeated backcrosses —*see* **backcross, hybrid swarm, introgression**

hybrid swarm a population consisting of **hybrid**s and various types of **backcross**es between two or more intercrossing **sympatric** species —*note* the population may include one or more of the parent **species,** or these may be replaced by the backcrosses —*see* **ecological niche, introgression**

hybrid vigor —*see* **heterosis, F_1, hybrid**

hydraulic budget a compilation of the total water inputs and outputs to and from a lake or watershed

hydraulic conductivity —*see* **permeability**

hydraulic gradient **1.** the slope of the water **2.** the drop in pressure head per length in the direction of stream flow

hydraulic head the height of the free surface of a body of water above a given point beneath the surface, or the height of the water level at an upstream point compared with the height of the water surface at a given location downstream

hydraulic radius the flow area of any conduit, open or closed, divided by its wetted perimeter —*note* hydraulic radius is the r in **Manning's formula**

hydric soil a soil that is wet long enough to periodically produce **anaerobic** conditions, thereby influencing the growth of plants

hydrograph a graph showing for a given point on a stream the **discharge,** stage, velocity, or other property of water with respect to time

hydrologic balance the relationship between the quality and quantity of water inflow, water outflow, and water storage in a hydrologic unit such as a drainage basin, aquifer, soil zone, lake, or reservoir —*note* hydraulic balance encompasses the dynamic relationships among **precipitation,** runoff, evaporation, and changes in ground and surface water storage

hydrologic cycle the process of evaporation, **transpiration**, vertical and horizontal transport of vapor, condensation, **precipitation, interception,** runoff, **infiltration,** percolation, storage, the flow of water from continents to oceans, and return — *note* the hydrologic cycle is a major factor in determining climate through its influence on surface vegetation, clouds, snow and ice, and soil moisture

hydrologic model a mathematical formulation that simulates hydrologic phenomena considered as processes or as systems

hydrologic obliteration —*see* **decommission**

hydrolysis the conversion, by reaction with water, of a complex substance into two or more smaller molecules —*note* hydrolysis is often promoted by small (catalytic) amounts of acids, alkalais, or enzymes, e.g., in conversion of **cellulose** into glucose, xylan into xylose, and esters into alcohols and acids

hydromorphic soil a suborder of **intrazonal soil**s, consisting of seven great soil groups, all formed under conditions of poor drainage in marshes, swamps, seepage areas, or flats —*note* the term is not used in the current US system of soil taxonomy —*see* **soil order**

hydrophilic having a strong affinity for water molecules

hydrophobic having little or no affinity for water molecules —*note* hydrophobic substances have more affinity for other hydrophobic substances than for water

hydrophyte **1.** a plant that has evolved with adaptations to live in aquatic or very wet **habitat**s, e.g., a cattail, water lily, or water tupelo **2.** a **cryptophyte** whose vegetative shoots remain submerged in the mud during the unfavorable season, only the flowers and inflorescences rising above the surface —*note* hydrophyte is one of Raunkiaer's **life-form**s

hydrosere —*see* **succession**

hydrotropism the response of a plant organ in growth or position to a gradient in water potential —*see* **chemotropism, geotropism, phototropism**

hygric **1.** of sites or **habitat**s, characterized by decidedly moist or humid conditions **2.** of plant **species**, tolerating or well adapted to humid conditions

hygrophyte a plant that is more or less restricted to moist sites but not considered an aquatic plant

hyperparasite an organism that is a **parasite** of, or in, another plant —*see* **hyperparasitization**

hyperparasitization **parasitization** of a **parasite**, i.e., by a **hyperparasite** —*note* an example is a fungus parasitizing a **dwarf mistletoe** —*synonym* secondary **parasitization** —*see* **multiparasitism, primary parasite, superparasitization**

hyperplasia pathologic overgrowth due to an abnormal increase in the number of cells

hyperspectral scanner an imaging system designed to collect spectral reflectance data and consisting of many narrow wave **band**s —*note 1.* this scanner is generally designed to collect data in the visible through midreflective infrared portions of the electromagnetic spectrum —*note 2.* a hyperspectral scanner differs from **multispectral scanner** data which contain fewer, broader bands

hypertrophy pathologic overgrowth due to abnormal cell enlargement —*note* the term is used usually in reference to the cortical tissues on the underside of a leaf or fruit

hypha *plural* **hyphae** one of the filamentous elements of microscopic size that form the **thallus** of a fungus —*see* **mycelium**

hyphal hole a small breach in a cell wall created by dissolving action of an advancing **hypha** of, for example, a wood-inhabiting fungus —*synonym* bore hole —*see* **haustorium**

hypocotyl that part of the axis of a developed seedling embryo immediately below the **cotyledons** —*see* **epicotyl, plumule, radicle**

hypolimnion the bottom layer of a stratified lake

that is isolated from the atmosphere and more or less cold in the summer —*see* **aphytal, profundal**

hypoplasia pathologic undergrowth of a part of a plant

hyporheic zone the area under a stream channel or floodplain that contributes water to the stream

hypsometer any instrument for measuring the heights of standing trees or their stems from observations taken at some distance from them —*see* **clinometer**

I

IBI —*see* **index of biotic integrity**

ICS —*see* **incident command system**

ideoblast a cell differing markedly in form and contents from other constituents of the same tissue —*note* ideoblasts in wood include crystaliferous cells, oil cells, and mucilage cells

ideotype an idealized multitrait characterization, e.g., a crown that is long, narrow, and dense with high branch angles

IFOV —*see* **instantaneous field of view**

IGES —*see* **initial graphics exchange specification**

ignition pattern the manner in which fire is ignited as part of suppression efforts or a **prescribed burn** —*note 1.* the distance between ignition lines or points and the sequence of igniting them is determined by weather, fuel, topography, firing technique, other factors that influence **fire behavior** and **fire effects,** and management **objectives** —*note 2.* basic ignition patterns include the following:

—**area ignition** lighting several individual fires throughout an area to be burned, either simultaneously or in rapid succession, and spaced so that they soon interact to produce a hot, fast-spreading fire throughout the area —*synonym* simultaneous ignition

—**back firing** lighting a fire at the uphill or downwind edge of the unit and allowing it to spread downhill or into the wind —*note 1.* in fire suppression, a backfire is intended to strengthen fire suppression action on wildfires —*note 2.* in **prescribed burn**ing, a backfire is intended to control fire movement in relation to wind or slope —*see* **fire behavior**

—**center firing** lighting a fire in one (edge firing) or more concentric rings to increase indraft and fireline intensity —*synonym* ring firing

—**chevron firing** lighting a fire by burners proceeding simultaneously downhill from the apex at a ridge point —*note* chevron firing is a special case of flank firing

—**flank firing** lighting a fire by burners progressing simultaneously into the wind or downhill, so that the fire spreads at a right angle to the wind or across the slope

—**head firing** lighting a fire at the upwind or downhill edge of a unit, so that the fire spreads rapidly with the wind or uphill

—**spot head firing** lighting a fire in spots in lines across the unit, beginning near the downwind or uphill end of the unit and then in successive lines

ignition pattern *continued*

progressively farther into the wind or downhill

—strip head firing lighting a fire in lines across the unit, beginning near the downwind or uphill end of the unit and then in successive lines progressively farther into the wind or downhill

ignition tool a device used to ignite a prescribed fire —*note* in addition to the tools listed below, ignition tools include fusees (flares), primacord, and jelly gasoline; kinds of ignition tool include the following:

—aerial ignition device (AID) an incendiary apparatus designed to ignite **wildland** fuels from an aircraft —*see* **aerial torch**

—drip torch a hand-held apparatus for igniting **prescribed fires**, backfires, or burnout areas by dripping flaming liquid fuel at an adjustable rate on the materials to be burned —*note* a drip torch consists of a fuel fount, burner arm, and igniter; fuel used is generally a mixture of 65 to 80 percent diesel and 20 to 35 percent gasoline —*see* **flame thrower, helitorch**

—helitorch an aerial ignition device slung from or mounted on a helicopter that dispenses ignited globs of gelled gasoline —*synonym* flying **drip torch, aerial torch** —*note* helitorch is an **ICS** term

—ping-pong ball system a mechanized method of dispensing delayed **aerial ignition devices** (DAIDs) at a selected rate —*note 1.* the DAIDs are 1.25-in (3.2-cm) diameter polystyrene balls containing potassium permanganate; the balls are fed into a dispenser, generally mounted in a helicopter, where they are injected with a water-glycol solution and then dropped through a chute leading out of the helicopter; the chemicals react thermally and ignite in 25 to 30 sec —*note 2.* the space between ignition points on the ground is primarily a function of helicopter speed, the gear ratio of the dispenser, and the number of chutes used (up to four)

illite a clay mineral of the 2:1 layer silicate type with sufficient interlayer K to give it a nonexpanding nature and a low permanent charge —*synonym* clay mica

illuvial horizon —*see* **horizon, soil**

illuviation the process of deposition of soil material removed from one **horizon** to another in the soil, usually from an upper to a lower horizon in the soil profile —*see* **horizon, argillic, spodic horizon**

image *GIS* a graphic representation or description of an object, typically produced by an optical or electronic device —*note 1.* an image consists of remotely sensed data such as satellite data, scanned data, and photographs —*see* **remote sensing** —*note 2.* an image is stored as a **raster** data set of binary or integer values that represent the intensity

of reflected light, heat, or another range of values on the electromagnetic spectrum —*note 3.* remotely sensed images are photographic or digital representations of the earth

image catalog *GIS* an organized set of spatially referenced, possibly overlapping, images that can be accessed as one logical image

image classification the process of assigning individual **pixels** of a multispectral **image** to categories, generally on the basis of spectral reflectance characteristics

image compression the process of reducing the number of **bits** constituting a **digital image,** removing redundancies in the digital data to the least number required to display the **image**

image footprint the total ground coverage recorded by a remotely sensed **image** —*see* **remote sensing**

imago *plural* **imagoes** or **imagines** the adult **stage** of an insect

immature indistinguishable from adults by external characters but of less than breeding age —*synonym* subadult —*see* **juvenile**

immunity the ultimate level of **resistance** to a pesticide —*see* **susceptibility**

impact 1. *assessment* a spatial or temporal change in the environment caused by human activity **2.** *entomology, pathology* the cumulative net effect of insect or disease populations on any or all forest resources —*note* an impact is sometimes limited to those effects that require a management action now or in the future

impedance *GIS* the amount of resistance (or cost) required to traverse a portion of a network such as a **line,** or through one **cell** in a **grid** —*note* resistance may be any number of factors defined by the user, such as travel distance, time, speed of travel times the length, slope, or cost

imperfect stage a phase in the life history of a fungus in which either only asexual **spores** are formed or no spores at all —*synonym* imperfect state

importance value *ecology* **1.** an index of the relative **abundance** of a **species** in a given community **2.** the sum of relative **density,** relative **frequency,** and relative **dominance** —*note* any one of these three parameters could also be considered an importance value

improved a nontechnical term often referring to (a) open-pollinated seed from selected trees —*see* **certify, open pollination** (b) seedlings, trees, etc., that have been genetically selected or bred to increase growth potential, disease resistance, or other desirable characteristics —*see* **forest tree breeding, forest tree improvement**

improvement cutting the removal of less desirable

trees of any species in a **stand** of **pole**s or larger trees, primarily to improve composition and quality —*see* **cleaning, liberation, weeding**

improvement planting any planting done to improve the value of a **stand**, not to establish a regular **plantation** —*see* **enrichment planting, refilling**

inbred line a **population** derived by **inbreeding** — *note* an inbred **line** is relatively pure genetically (**homozygous**) and hence true breeding —*see* **heterosis, homozygous, selection, self, self-pollination**

inbreeding the production of offspring by mating related organisms, often by **selfing** —*note* this procedure, especially if carried out for a number of generations, exposes undesirable **recessive character**s but is used with **selection** to fix desirable ones, i.e., to render them true-breeding —*see* **coancestry, heterosis, inbred line, inbreeding depression, self-pollination**

inbreeding coefficient a quantitative measure of **inbreeding**, F, generally ranging from 0.0 (the base population) to 1.0 (fully **homozygous**) —*note* a negative F value indicates **outcrossing** and greater **heterozygosity** than in the base **population**

inbreeding depression the reduction in vigor or fertility that often accompanies **inbreeding** of normally crossbred organisms, usually attributed to an accumulation of deleterious **recessive genes**

incendiary fire a **wildfire** willfully ignited by anyone to burn or spread to vegetation or property not owned or controlled by that person and without consent of the owner or the owner's agent —*synonym* arson fire

incidence 1. the number of occurrences of a phenomenon over time —*see* **frequency** 2. *pathology* the number of diseased units relative to the number of such units examined —*note* incidence is usually expressed as a percentage —*see* **severity**

incident *fire* an occurrence or event (including **wildfire**), either human-caused or a natural phenomenon, that requires action by emergency service personnel to prevent or minimize loss of life or damage to property or natural resources —*note* incident is an **ICS** term

incident action plan a document, initially prepared at the first planning meeting, containing general **fire suppression** objectives reflecting overall strategy for the incident and specific suppression and rescue action plans for the next operational period —*note* incident action plan is an **ICS** term

incidental take the **taking** of a threatened or **endangered species** that is incidental to, and not the purpose of, the carrying out of an otherwise lawful activity —*see* **threatened species**

incident base the location at which primary logistics functions are coordinated and administered —*note 1.* incident base is an **ICS** term —*note 2.* the incident **command** post may be in the same place as the incident base, but each incident is assigned its own incident base —*synonym* base —*see* **fire camp**

incident command system (ICS) *fire* the facilities, equipment, personnel, procedures, and communications operating within an organizational structure and responsible for managing assigned resources to accomplish stated **objectives** pertaining to a fire **incident** —*see* **national interagency incident management system** —*note* the following ICS terms are similar to and are replacing **large fire organization (LFO)** terms:

—**area command** an organization established to oversee the management of (a) multiple incidents, each if which is being handled by an incident management team (IMT) organization, or (b) a very large incident to which multiple IMTs are assigned —*note* area command sets overall strategy and priorities, allocates critical **resources** based on priorities, and ensures that incidents are properly managed, objectives are met, and strategies are followed

—**branch** the organizational level with functional or geographical responsibility for major segments of fire operations —*note* the branch level is between section and division or group

—**branch director** a person under the direction of the operations section chief who is responsible for implementing that portion of the incident action plan appropriate to the branch

—**command staff** an information officer, safety officer, and liaison officer who report directly to the incident commander

—**command team** a group of personnel, including at least an incident commander, section chiefs, situation status (SITSTAT) leader, resource status (RESTAT) leader, and communications unit leader, trained and available to command an incident using the incident command system

—**company** any piece of fire equipment with a full complement of personnel

—**division** a designated unit of a complex fire organized into two to four sectors for control, usually planned so that it can be personally and completely inspected by the division boss twice per shift —*note 1.* divisions are established when **resources** exceed the span of control of the operations section chief, and normally divide an incident into geographical areas of operation —*note 2.* the division level is between the strike team and the branch

—**division** or **group supervisor** a person responsible to the operations section chief or (when activated) the branch director, for implementing that

incident command system *continued*

portion of the incident action plan assigned to the division or group, allocating resources within the division or group, and reporting on the progress of control operations and the status of **resources**

—**finance section chief** a person responsible to the **incident commander** for all financial and cost-analysis aspects of the incident and for supervising members of the finance section

—**general staff** a group of incident management personnel consisting of finance section chief, incident commander, logistics section chief, operations section chief, and planning section chief

—**group** an organizational unit established to divide an incident into functional areas of operation and composed of **resources** assembled to perform a special function not within a single **division**

—**incident commander** an individual responsible for managing all incident operations —*synonym* fire boss in the **LFO** system

—**incident overhead** all supervisory positions described in the incident **command** system

—**logistics section chief** a person responsible to the incident commander for providing facilities, services, and material in support of an incident

—**manager** an individual within ICS organizational units assigned specific managerial responsibilities, e.g., staging area manager or camp manager

—**operations section chief** a person responsible to the **incident** commander for managing all operations directly applicable to an incident's primary mission

—**planning section chief** a person responsible to the incident commander for collecting, evaluating, disseminating, and using information about the development of an incident and the status of **resources;** supervising all members of the planning section; and finalizing the incident action plan

—**safety officer** a member of the **command** staff responsible to the incident commander for monitoring and assessing hazardous and unsafe conditions and developing measures for assessing personnel safety on an incident

—**section** an organizational unit having functional responsibility for primary segments of incident operations such as operations, planning, logistics, and finance —*note* the section level is between the branch and the incident commander

—**strike team** a specified combination of the same kind and type of **resources,** sharing communication and a leader

—**task force** any combination of **resources** that shares communication and a leader

—**unified command** an authority exercised by all agencies or individuals who have jurisdictional responsibility, and in some cases those who have functional responsibility at the incident, to contribute jointly to (a) determining overall **objectives** for the incident, and (b) selection of a strategy to achieve **objectives**

—**unit** the organizational element of an incident, having functional responsibility for a specific activity in the planning, logistics, or finance section

incident commander —*see* **incident command system**

incident overhead —*see* **incident command system**

incipient decay 1. early stages of **heart decay 2.** dwarf mistletoe **infection** in an early developmental **stage** in which external symptoms are not yet visible

included bark bark that has been covered by the growing together of adjacent, vertically growing stems or branches thus creating weakened attachments

inclusion one or more **polypedon**s or parts of polypedons within a delineation of a soil map unit —*note* an inclusion is too small to be delineated separately without creating excessive map or legend detail, occurs too erratically to be considered a component, or is not identified by practical mapping methods —*see* **pedon**

income and substitution effects two effects that occur jointly when the price of an item changes; an income effect is the change in consumer satisfaction that occurs when a price change for a particular item alters the income available to purchase other items; a substitution effect is the change in the quantity or mix of items purchased in response to the price change —*note* a substitution effect causes movement along an **indifference curve** (representing constant satisfaction) to a different mix of items, whereas an income effect shifts consumption to a different curve (representing a different satisfaction level) —*see* **output and substitution effects**

incompatibility a failure or partial failure in some process leading to fertilization —*note* e.g., the pollen tube growth may be deficient even though the egg and sperm cells are potentially functional —*see* **crossability, graft incompatibility, isolation, parthenocarpy, sterility**

incomplete block design an **experimental design** in which each **block** contains fewer than a complete **replication** of the treatments, necessitating a more elaborate analysis than is required for complete blocks

increaser plant species a plant **species** of the original or **climax** vegetation that increases in relative amount, at least for a time, under continued disturbance to the norm, e.g., heavy defoliation, fire, or drought —*see* **decreaser plant species**

increment 1. the increase in circumference (girth), diameter, basal area, height, volume, quality, or value of individual trees or crops **2.** the rate of increment, i.e., increase during a given period —*see* **accretion**

incremental planning planning done by sequential decisions as a project or system develops —*note* incremental planning is founded on the perceived need for negotiated solutions in which a more generally acceptable solution is derived at the local level without the need for centralized **decision making** or **comprehensive planning,** which may be slow to yield usable results —*synonym* disjointed incrementalism —*see* **strategic planning**

increment borer an auger-like instrument with a hollow bit and an extractor used to extract thin radial cylinders of wood (increment cores) from trees having annual growth rings, to determine increment or age —*note* in wood preservation, the borer measures the depth of penetration of the preservative

increment percent the growth (generally in volume or **basal area**) over a specified period, expressed as a percent of the amount at the beginning of the period

increment table a table of **mean annual increment**s prepared by dividing each volume entry in a **yield table** by the appropriate age

incubation *pathology* the period between **inoculation** and appearance of visible symptoms —*synonym* incubation period, latent period

indeterminate growth 1. growth whose structures complete development soon after they are initiated by a meristem **2.** structures whose growth is not fixed or limited, such as stems or roots —*see* **determinate growth**

index *computers* a specialized access table or structure within a database used by an **RDBMS** or **GIS** to speed searches for tabular or geographic data

index of biotic integrity (IBI) a measure of the extent to which water, **site quality,** or **forest** resource quality of an area deviates from that expected on relatively undisturbed sites of similar type —*see* **biological index**

Indian remote sensing satellite (IRS) India's dedicated earth resources satellite system, operated by the Indian Space Research Organization and the India National Remote Sensing Agency (NRSA) —*note* IRS sensors record 5-m (16.4 ft) panchromatic and 25-m (82.0 ft) multispectral data, the latter in three reflected **band**s

indicator plant (species) any plant (species) that, by its presence, frequency, or vigor, indicates any particular property of the site, particularly of the soil or aquatic areas

indifference curve a contour map of an individual's **utility function,** showing those alternative bundles of goods and services from which the individual derives equivalent levels of value —*note* usually an indifference curve considers only tradeoffs between two goods or services, although in reality tradeoffs are possible among the whole set of possible purchases

indigenous native to a specified area or region, not introduced —*see* **local seed source, nonnative**

indigenous land and territory the total environment of land, air, water, sea, sea-ice, flora, fauna, and other resources that **indigenous people** have traditionally owned, occupied, or used

indigenous people the living descendants of the people who inhabited the present territory wholly or partially at the time when persons of a different culture or ethnic origin arrived from other parts of the world —*see* **indigenous land and territory**

indirect attack —*see* **fire suppression**

indirect effects effects that are caused by an action and occur at a later time, or at another location, yet are reasonably foreseeable in the future —*see* **cumulative effects, direct effects**

individual assignment —*see* **fire suppression**

individual selection the process of choosing single plants based on their own merit as parents or **ortets** from a **family** or **population** —*synonym* phenotypic selection —*see* **combined selection, family selection, mass selection, phenotype**

individual tree selection —*see* **regeneration method**

industrial forest forest land owned by a company or individual operating a primary wood-using plant and managed primarily for wood products —*see* **nonindustrial forest**

industrial wood all commercial roundwood products except **fuelwood**

infection *pathology* **1.** the establishment of a food relationship between a microscopic organism, pathogen, or parasitic plant, and a **host 2.** the whole pathogenic organism or parasitic plant and associated host symptoms, e.g., a **limb rust** organism and associated **gall,** the aerial shoots and endophytic system of a **dwarf mistletoe** and associated host swelling —*see* **endophyte, infestation**

infection center a localized concentration of disease originating from one point of origin such as an infected stump —*see* **epicenter, root disease**

infection court the site of **infection** by a pathogen

infestation **1.** the attack by macroscopic organisms in considerable concentration —*note* examples are infestations of tree crowns by **budworm,** timber by **termites,** soil or other substrates by **nematodes** or weeds **2.** *pathology* the intermixing of one organism with another without establishing a food relationship —*see* **epidemic, infection**

infiltration *ecology, soils* the downward entry of water into the soil to the **groundwater** system

infiltration flux or **rate** the volume of water entering a specified cross-sectional area of soil per unit time (L t^{-1})

inflorescence **1.** the mode of development and arrangement of **flowers** on an axis **2.** flowering —*see* **peduncle, strobilus**

infrared (IR) imagery a photograph-like image created by optical-electronic equipment using the infrared wavelengths of the electromagnetic spectrum —*note 1. fire* IR imagery is used through dense smoke, haze, and vegetative canopy to (a) detect the incidence of wildfires in remote terrain, especially following lightning storms, (b) map the perimeters, hot spots, and spot fires of **going fires,** and (c) detect residual heat sources during mop-up; generally, the first two uses employ IR scanners in aircraft while the third uses hand-held IR scanners on the ground or in slow-flying helicopters —*note 2. fire* IR imagery is not cost effective through fog, rain, or other moisture —*synonym* heat probe, thermal imagery

infrared radiation the **electromagnetic radiation** that lies in the wavelength interval from about 0.8 μ to an indefinite upper boundary sometimes arbitrarily set at 1,000 μ (0.01 cm) —*see* **heat probe**

infrastructure the human improvements, such as roads, bridges, and water and sewer lines to natural settings, that permit a city, state, or region to function

infructescence the **fruit**ing stage of an inflorescence —*see* **peduncle**

ingrowth the volume, **basal area,** or number of those trees in a **stand** that were smaller than a prescribed minimum diameter or height limit at the beginning of any growth-determining period and that, during that period, attained the prescribed size

in-growth core a technique whereby a root-free mesh bag containing sieved mineral soil or other material is placed in the soil and removed at specific times to quantify root production and rate of decomposition

inhibition *fire* the process of extinguishing fire using an agent that interrupts the chemical reactions in the combustion process

inholding an area of land belonging to one landowner that occurs within a block of land belonging to another —*note* inholdings, such as small private parcels, often occur in federal or industrial forest land ownerships

initial attack **1.** *fire* a fire-suppression action in which the aggressiveness of the attack is made consistent with the safety of the fire fighters and the public and with the values to be protected **2.** *entomology* **primary host** selection and establishment of a focal point by **bark beetles** (termed pioneer beetles) for subsequent (secondary) attraction and aggregation by beetles in sufficient numbers to colonize a tree —*note* multiple attacks are necessary to overcome tree defenses; in many species, individuals of one sex initiate attacks —*see* **mass attack, primary host selection, secondary host selection**

initial graphics exchange specification (IGES) an interim standard format for exchanging graphics data among computer systems

inner gorge a stream reach bounded by steep valley walls that terminate upslope into a more gentle topography —*note* inner gorges are common in areas of rapid stream downcutting or uplift

inoculation *pathology* the arrival or deliberate introduction of a disease-producing organism into contact with the **host,** where **infection** may occur —*see* **inoculum, dispersal**

inoculum **spores** or any part of a pathogen that is able to initiate **infection** in a host —*see* **inoculation**

inoculum potential the total potential of a pathogen to cause **infection** —*note* the potential is related to both the quantity and the quality of **inoculum**

inorganic pesticide a pesticide without carbon in the molecular structure —*note* arsenic compounds are the only inorganic pesticides commonly used today —*see* **organic pesticide**

input *economics* the various factors of production, generally land, labor, and capital —*see* **output**

input-output analysis **1.** an analysis of the **outputs** of a system in relation to the inputs to the system **2.** a method of measuring and displaying the relationship of each sector of the economy to every other sector of the economy by means of a matrix table

insect a member of the class Insecta (phylum Arthropoda), characterized (as adults) by a body segmented into three distinct regions (head, **thorax,** abdomen), by a head with one pair of antennae, by a thorax with three (often nondistinct) segments each with a pair of legs, and usually one or two pairs of thoracic wings —*note* not all insects are winged: some (primitive) insects have never developed wings, some have vestigial wings, and some have evolved from winged ancestors into present wingless forms

insectary a place for rearing and keeping living insects —*note* a single-species population of insects of known origin in a laboratory insectary is often referred to as a laboratory culture, in contrast to a natural population or wild population —*synonym* insectarium **2.** *pest management* species that promote the welfare of **parasites** and **predators** of herbivorous **pests** by providing nectar, shelter, or alternative **hosts** —*note* if plants, the individuals are referred to as insectary plants

insect hole a bore hole, burrow, mine, passage, or tunnel in plant tissue, particularly wood or bark, made by an adult insect for mating, oviposition entry, emergence, or by a **larva** when feeding —*note 1.* the (mostly larval) tunnels of wood- and phloem-boring insects, sometimes packed with **frass**, are more commonly termed galleries and are generally made by wood borers, timber borers, shoot borers, **bark beetles**, or bark miners; bark beetles often form characteristic galleries that can be used in identification —*note 2.* if the insect takes wing more or less immediately after emergence, the hole is also called a flight hole —*synonym* emergence hole, gallery, mine, tunnel —*see* **pinhole, shothole**

insecticide a pesticide employed against insects

insectivorous an organism, especially a **predator,** that feed on insects —*see* **entomophagous**

in situ on site; within the natural **habitat** —*see* ***ex situ***

insolation solar radiation that has been received at the earth's surface

instance *GIS* an **object** that belongs to a particular **class** —*note* e.g., California is an instance of the class State

instantaneous field of view (IFOV) the narrow field of view designed into detectors, particularly scanning radiometer systems, so that while as much as 12° may be under scan, only that **electromagnetic radiation** from a very small area is being recorded at any one instant

instar 1. the form of an insect during a particular **stadium,** i.e., any post-egg **stage** initiated or terminated by **ecdysis** —*note* there are **larval, nymph**al, pupal, and adult instars **2.** any larval stadium —*note* instars are numbered consecutively, with the first instar being the period between larval hatching and the first ecdysis —*see* **life cycle**

insulation board —*see* **engineered wood composite**

intangible value a resource yield that is not directly quantifiable or cannot be valued by market mechanisms —*note* the net yields from intangible values extend beyond secondary benefits and include psychic and indirect monetary benefits to the users, such as aesthetic, scientific, educational, historic, or recreational aspects of the natural environment

integer a number without a decimal —*note* integer values can be less than, equal to, or greater than zero

integer linear programming —*see* **programming**

integrated control the control of **pests** which combines and integrates chemical methods with natural and biological control —*see* **pest management**

integrated forest protection the application of **integrated pest management** to **forest** situations with an emphasis on prevention

integrated pest management (IPM) the maintenance of destructive agents, including insects at tolerable levels, by the planned use of a variety of preventive, suppressive, or regulatory tactics and strategies that are ecologically and economically efficient and socially acceptable —*note 1.* it is implicit in IPM that the actions taken are fully integrated into total resource planning and management, including either the life span of the tree crop or the entire resource-planning horizon —*note 2.* IPM is an evolving concept that recognizes ecological, social, and economic values; early definitions were similar to that given for **integrated control** —*see* **forest entomology**

integrated resource(s) management the simultaneous consideration of ecological, physical, economic, and social aspects of lands, waters, and resources in developing and implementing **multiple-use, sustained-yield** management

integrated terrain unit mapping (ITUM) *GIS* the process of adjusting terrain unit boundaries to increase coincidence between the boundaries of interdependent terrain variables such as hydrography, geology, physiography, soils, and vegetation units —*note* when this is performed, one layer or unit of geographical or descriptive information often contains more than one central theme

intelligent infrastructure *computers* the result of automating infrastructure information management for spatially linked and networked facilities and land records systems, using modern computer image and graphics technology integrated with advanced **database management systems (DBMS)** —*note* intelligent infrastructure manages work processes that deal with design, construction, operation, and maintenance of infrastructure elements

intensive forestry the practice of **forestry** to obtain a high level of volume and quality of outturn per unit of area through the application of the best techniques of **silviculture** and management —*note* compared with extensive forestry, intensive forestry requires greater inputs of labor and capital in terms of quantity, quality, or frequency —*see* **extensive forestry**

interaction the extent to which the effect of one factor or treatment varies with changes in the strength, grade, or level of others in an experiment

interaction matrix a table with actions, conditions, resources, effects, etc., listed along two perpendicular axes developing a matrix in which each cell represents a relationship between the elements concerned —*note* the relationships in an interaction matrix may be either subjectively or objectively derived —*see* **matrix**

interarrival time the time between consecutive arrivals in a queueing problem, e.g., fire engines or air tankers arriving at a wildfire, log trucks arriving at a mill, or hikers arriving at a trailhead —*see* **queueing theory**

interception the deposition of rainfall, snowfall, or fog (**precipitation**) on vegetation —*note* intercepted precipitation may be redistributed as **throughfall** or **stemflow**, or evaporated or sublimated to the atmosphere or absorbed by the vegetation (generally thought to be negligible)

intercropping growing two or more crops as a mixture in the same field at the same time

interdisciplinary team a group of specialists assembled as a cohesive team with frequent interactions to solve a problem or perform a task —*note* interdisciplinary teams are assembled because commonly, no one scientific discipline is sufficiently broad to adequately analyze a problem or proposed action —*synonym* ID team —*see* **multidisciplinary team**

interface *computers* a hardware and software link that connects two computer systems, or a computer and its peripherals, for data communication

interflow that portion of rainfall that infiltrates the soil and moves laterally through the upper soil **horizon**s until intercepted by a stream channel, or until it returns to the surface at some point downslope from its point of **infiltration**

intermediate —*see* **crown class**

intermediate host the **host** that harbors the immature **stage**s or the asexual stages of a **parasite**

intermediate treatment any treatment or tending designed to enhance growth, quality, vigor, and composition of the **stand** after establishment or **regeneration** and prior to final harvest —*see* **stand improvement**

intermittent stream a stream, or portion of a stream, that does not flow year-round but only when it (a) receives base flow solely during wet periods, or (b) receives groundwater discharge or protracted contributions from melting snow or other erratic surface and shallow subsurface sources —*see* **ephemeral stream**

internal rate of return the discount rate that equates the various costs and benefits anticipated in future years

international log rule a formula **log rule** derived from the mathematical equation used to calculate the volume of a cylinder —*note 1.* the rule assumes $1/16$-in (0.16 cm) shrinkage for each inch (2.54 cm) of board thickness and a **taper** of 0.5-in (1.27 cm) for each 4-ft (1.2 m) log section —*note 2.* in one form it assumes a $1/8$-in (0.32) **kerf;** in a modified form, assuming a 0.25-in (0.64 cm) kerf, it is one of the official rules of the USDA Forest Service —*see* **Doyle rule, international $1/4$-inch rule, Scribner rule**

international $1/4$-inch rule a modification of the **international log rule** based on 4 ft (1.2 m) log sections; the formula is $V = (0.2D^2 - 0.71D)\ 0.905$, where V = board-foot volume and D = diameter inside bark at the small end in inches, that uses a $1/8$-in (0.32 cm) **kerf** —*note* probably the most accurate rule, it is used primarily with small-diameter logs —*see* **Doyle rule, log rule, Scribner rule**

interplanting setting young trees among existing **forest** growth, planted or natural

interpretation *recreation* an educational activity aimed at revealing meanings and relationships through the use of objects, first-hand experience, and illustrative media rather than through recitation of factual information to a passive audience

interseeding the dispersing of seed into an established vegetation **cover** —*note* inter**seeding** often involves sowing seeds into the center of narrow seedbed strips of variable spacing and prepared by mechanical or chemical methods —*see* **range reseeding**

interspecific occurring among members of different species —*see* **intraspecific**

interspecific hybrid a **hybrid** produced by crossing between members of different **species** —*see* **species hybrid**

intolerable loss *fire* a level of damage or loss greater than that which a given resource may sustain and still achieve targeted management production **goal**s

intolerant 1. a plant requiring sunlight and exposure for establishment and growth —*note* the term is usually applied to light, but may also refer to intolerance to flooding, salt, pollutants, etc. —*antonym* **tolerant 2.** pertaining to a plant having **intolerant** characteristics —*see* **stand establishment**

intraspecific occurring among members of a single species —*see* **interspecific**

intraspecific hybrid a **hybrid** produced by crossing between members of the same **species**

intrazonal soil *obsolete* **1.** one of the three orders in soil classification **2.** a soil with more or less well-developed characteristics that reflect the dominating influence of some local factor of relief, parent material, or age, over the normal effect of climate and vegetation —*note* this term is not used in the current US system of soil taxonomy; intrazonal soils include Brown Forest, Ground-Water Laterite, Rendzina, Solonchak, and Solonetz —*see* **soil order**

intrinsic rate of increase —*see* **biotic potential**

introduced species an established plant or animal not native to the **ecosystem**, region, or country

introgression the natural movement of the **gene**(s) from one **species** or **population** to another through hybridization and successive **backcrossing** of the **hybrids** —*see* **ecological niche, hybrid swarm, migration**

inventory —*see* **forest inventory**

inversion —*see* **air temperature inversion**

in vitro in glass; in aseptic culture under laboratory conditions —*see* *in vivo*

in vivo within a living organism or under natural conditions —*see* *in vitro*

IPM —*see* **integrated pest management**

Ips **beetle** a **bark beetle** in the genus *Ips* whose adults and **larvae** scar the outer surface of the xylem of the **host** when constructing galleries, which are often Y- or H-shaped with a nuptial chamber in the center —*note* initial attack is by males —*synonym Ips* engraver beetle

IR —*see* **infrared imagery**

iron oxide the oxides and hydroxides of iron —*note* iron oxides are sometimes referred to as **sesquioxides** or iron hydrous oxides

irradiance the total radiant flux received on a unit area of a given real or imaginary surface

irregular *of a regeneration method (e.g., irregular shelterwood)* characterized by variation in age structure (usually uneven-aged) or in spatial arrangement of trees —*see* **uniform, regeneration method**

irretrievable commitment an action or inaction that cannot be reversed within a reasonable time —*synonym* irreversible commitment

irrigation the intentional application of water to the soil, usually for the purpose of crop production

IRS —*see* **Indian remote sensing satellite**

island 1. a tract of land completely surrounded by water **2.** a vegetative unit completely surrounded by distinctly different vegetation **cover 3.** *urban forestry* —*see* **heat island**

island biogeography the study of theories relating to the rates of colonization and extinction on ecological islands and how the rates vary with island size and distance from the source of colonists

isobar a line of equal or constant pressure, i.e., an isopleth of pressure

isocenter the point at which the bisector of the angle between the plumb line and the photograph perpendicular intersects the plane of the photograph —*note* **tilt**-caused displacements of **images** radiate from the isocenter

isolate 1. *pathology* to accomplish isolation **2.** *pathology* a pure culture and any subcultures derived from it made by **isolation**

isolation 1. *genetics* a condition that prevents or limits **breeding** among **populations**, e.g., phenological differences in **flowering** time, **chromosome** difference, or distance —*see* **allopatric, incompatibility, phenology, sterility 2.** *pathology* the process of placing an organism in pure culture by separating it from **host** tissues or surfaces, contaminants, **infestations**, and secondary pathogens —*note* isolation is usually done for purposes of identification and by means of culture

isoquant map a contour map of a firm's production function —*note 1.* the contours show the alternative combinations of inputs that can be used to produce a given level of **output,** e.g., chips from various combinations of hardwood species require different amounts and types of glue to manufacture flakeboard meeting certain strength properties —*note 2.* an isoquant map shows the relative substitutability for certain production inputs

isotach a line in a given surface connecting points with equal wind speed

isotropic pertaining to a body that, with respect to one or more characteristics, possesses the same properties in all directions —*note* wood (in contrast to, e.g., steel) is markedly anisotropic, particularly in its strength and elastic properties, which differ in three directions according to three mutually perpendicular axes of symmetry (longitudinal, radial, and tangential) that correspond to the main features of wood structure and the marked anisotropy of the **cellulose** long-chain molecules

issue a matter of controversy or dispute over resource management activities that is well defined or topically discrete and addressed in the design of a planning alternative —*note* the term is used in land-use planning and assessments

ITUM —*see* **integrated terrain unit mapping**

J

jaggies *GIS jargon* curved lines that have a stepped or sawtooth appearance on a display device

jammer *harvesting* a lightweight, two-drum yarder on a truck or sled with a **spar** and boom used for both short-distance **yard**ing and loading of logs —*see* **loader**

Japan earth resources satellite (JERS) Japan's dedicated earth resources satellite system consisting of an L-**band** (23 cm or 9.8 in) synthetic aperture **radar** and a multispectral scanner —*note* JERS data have a spatial resolution of approximately 18 m (59 ft) and are designed to observe earth's entire land area, including Antarctica, to obtain data useful for land survey, agriculture, **forestry**, fisheries, environmental protection, disaster prevention, and coastal monitoring

jeopardy a finding made through consultation under the Endangered Species Act of 1976 that the action of a federal agency is likely to jeopardize the continued existence of a threatened or **endangered species** —*see* **threatened species**

jeopardy biological opinion the document resulting from formal consultation that states the opinion of the Fish and Wildlife Service or National Marine Fisheries Service as to whether federal action is likely to jeopardize the continued existence of listed species or to result in destruction or adverse modification of critical habitat —*synonym* biological opinion

JERS —*see* **Japan earth resources satellite**

join *GIS* 1. to connect two or more geographic data sets 2. to connect, through a **key,** two or more **table**s

J-root a root that is bent into a J-shape because the seedling was improperly planted in a hole or slit that was too shallow or narrow

jump spot *fire* an elected landing area for **smoke jumper**s or **helijumper**s

juvenile distinguishable from adults by external characters but of less than breeding age —*see* **immature**

juvenile phase the period during the life of a tree before flowering or before a mature type of foliage appears —*see* **maturation, maturity**

juvenile wood the **xylem** formed in the first 10 to 15 rings nearest to the **pith**, which is strongly controlled by growth regulators from the crown and which, in **softwood**s, has lower specific gravity, lower **fiber** length, lower **cellulose** content, higher **microfibril** angle, higher longitudinal shrinkage, and lower strength —*synonym* crownwood

K

kairomone a **semiochemical** emitted from one species that is adaptively advantageous to another species, e.g., a **predator** responding to the pheromone of its prey —*see* **allomone, pheromone, synomone**

kame a low mound or short irregular ridge composed of stratified gravels deposited by a subglacial stream or on the surface of stagnant glacial ice

kaolin 1. a class of soil minerals containing aluminum and silica in a 1:1 layer structure —*note* kaolin is composed of several minerals, the most common of which is **kaolinite,** and including halloysite and dickite 2. a soft, usually white, rock composed largely of kaolinite —*note* kaolinite is common in Georgia, where it is mined and sold to the paper industry for use as a coating on magazine-type paper to improve printability

kaolinite a clay mineral of the **kaolin** subgroup with a 1:1 layer structure composed of shared sheets of Si-O tetrahedrons and Al-(O, OH) octahedrons with very little isomorphous substitution

karst topography with sinkholes, caves, and underground drainage that is formed by dissolution in limestone, gypsum, or other rocks

karyotype the characteristic **chromosome** complement of an individual, **race,** or **species** as defined by their number, size, shape, etc. —*see* **chromosome number, chromosome set**

katabatic wind any wind blowing down an incline —*antonym* **anabatic wind**

Kelvin temperature scale an absolute temperature scale independent of the thermometric properties of the working substance —*note* Kelvin temperatures are expressed in °K

kerf the width of the cut made by a saw blade —*see* **saw**

key *computers* a **column** within a **relational database management system (RDBMS)** that contains a unique value for each record in the database

key species *range management* 1. a forage **species** of sufficient abundance and palatability to justify its use as an indicator to the degree of use of associated species 2. a species which must, because of its importance, be considered in the management program

keystone species a **species** that increases or decreases the diversity of a system —*note 1.* these species are competitively superior species —*note 2.* a species that increase the diversity of a system by selective predation is considered a **keystone** predator

KG blade a blade on a crawler tractor used in **site**

preparation to clear unwanted vegetation prior to planting tree seedlings

kiln a chambèr for drying sawn lumber having controlled temperature and humidity, forced air circulation and ventilation

kiln-drying a process in which wood or lumber is dried in a **kiln**, usually to below 20 percent **moisture content**, using controlled heat and, usually, forced air and steam or water sprays to control humidity —*synonym* kiln-seasoning —*see* **drying** —*note* kilns are usually fully automated to maintain programmed conditions of temperature, airflow, and humidity for each stage of drying

kindling point the lowest temperature at which sustained **combustion** can be initiated for a specified substance —*synonym* ignition temperature

knot a (usually) cross-section of a branch that is imbedded in lumber or other wood product —*note 1.* a knot may be regarded as either a decorative feaure or a **defect** —*note 2.* a sound knot (live knot, tight knot) occurs if the branch was living when the tree was cut; a loose knot, so called because the knot commonly falls out of the lumber, occurs if the branch was dead when the tree was cut —*see* **sucker knot**

knuckleboom *harvesting* —*see* **loader**

kraft paper a comparatively coarse, strong paper made primarily from wood pulp produced by the sulfate pulping process —*note* unbleached grades of kraft paper are used primarily as a wrapping or packaging material

kraft pulp —*see* **pulp**

kriging *GIS* an interpolation technique based on the premise that spatial variation continues with the same pattern

krummholz the **shrub**by, multistemmed form assumed by trees near the treeline —*see* **elfin forest**

k-selection *ecology* the selection of life-history **traits** that promote an ability to make a large proportionate contribution to a **population** that stays close to its **carrying capacity**

kurtosis a measure of the degree of flatness or peakedness of a **frequency distribution** as compared to the **normal distribution** —*see* **skew**

L

LAC —*see* **limits of acceptable change**

lace bug a member of the family Tingidae (Hemiptera) —*note* lace bugs may seriously infest North American ornamental *Acer* and *Platanus* trees, e.g., *Corythucha ciliata*

lacustrine relating to a lake or a standing body of water

ladder fuel —*see* **fuel type**

lag the distance between two subregions in geostatistical analysis

lagoon 1. a small, pondlike body of water, usually connected to a larger body of water **2.** an area of shallow water separated from the sea by a low bank —*see* **estuarine zone 3.** a settling pond for treatment of wastewater

lagtime 1. *flood irrigation* the period between the time that the irrigation stream is turned off at the upper end of an irrigation area and the time that water disappears from the surface at the point or points of application **2.** *hydrology* —*see* **watershed lag**

LAI —*see* **leaf area index**

Lamarckism the theory that **evolution** proceeds as the result of inheritance of acquired characteristics —*note* Lamarckism, named for J.B. de Monet Larmarck (d. 1829), who proposed the concept in 1809, is not accepted in modern genetics

laminated root disease a serious disease caused by the fungus *Phellinus weirii* on all species of Pinaceae native to the Pacific Northwest and the northern Rocky Mountains, especially Douglas-fir —*note* laminated root disease persists saprophytically in stumps and roots for many decades, reinfecting successive generations of trees —*synonym* yellow laminated root disease

laminated veneer lumber —*see* **engineered wood composite**

Lammas shoot abnormal late-season growth from a previously dormant bud, commonly caused by excess moisture —*note* Lammas Day, traditionally August 1, celebrated the first bread made from that year's grain

LAN —*see* **local area network**

land area the area of dry land and land temporarily or partly covered by water, such as marshes, swamps, and river floodplains; streams, sloughs, estuaries, and canals < 200 ft (61 m) wide; and lakes, reservoirs, and ponds < 4.5 ac (1.8 ha) in area

land breeze the complete cycle of diurnal local winds occurring on sea coasts due to differences in surface temperature of land —*note* the term sea breeze is used similarly

land classification the process of generating and applying land strata that are sufficiently homogenous with respect to physical, vegetative, and development attributes that the face validity of **models** and projections based on such strata is not threatened

land cover the ecological state and physical appearance of the land surface, e.g., forest and grassland —*note* land cover may be changed by human intervention, natural disturbances, or plant succession — *see* **land use**

landing a cleared area in the forest to which logs are yarded or skidded for loading onto trucks for transport

land management planning *Forest Service* a formal process of management planning involving four iterative steps: monitoring, assessment, decision making, and implementation —*see* **adaptive management**

land race a **population** of plants, usually exotic, that has become adapted to a specific environment

Landsat™ (land satellite) one of a series of US satellites designed (in 1972) to transmit multispectral **images** of portions of the earth's surface to ground stations —*note* the current Landsat Thematic Mapper sensor has seven broad wave **band**s, a spatial resolution of 30 m or 98 ft (for all bands except the thermal infrared), and a footprint of 185 by 170 km (115 by 106 mi)

landscape a spatial mosaic of several **ecosystem**s, landforms, and plant communities across a defined area irrespective of ownership or other artificial boundaries and repeated in similar form throughout

landscape architecture the planning and designing of outdoor space for human use and enjoyment

landscape buffer a natural or planted perennial system in a position in the landscape to mitigate any of a number of undesirable environmental impacts, e.g., runoff, wind, noise, dust, snow

landscape pattern the number, frequency, size, and juxtaposition of landscape elements (stands and patches) that are important to the determination or interpretation of ecological processes

landslide the fall or slide of a hillslope which results in the rapid or slow *en masse* movement of soil, organic debris, and rock down a slope —*see* **erosion**

land use the purpose for which land is used by humans, e.g., reserved areas, forest products, row-crop agriculture, pasture, and human settlement —*note* change in land use may not cause a significant change in **land cover,** e.g., change from some types of managed forest to reserved forest may not

cause a significant change in cover compared with change from forest to cultivated land

lapse rate the decrease of atmospheric temperature with height ($\delta T/\delta z < 0.0$) where T is the air temperature and z is height —*see* **air temperature inversion, saturation-adiabatic lapse rate;** kinds of lapse rate include the following:

—**dry-adiabatic lapse rate** the theoretical decrease of air temperature with altitude of a parcel of unsaturated air which is lifted adiabatically (no energy gained or lost), the temperature changing in response to decreasing pressure; the rate is $\delta T/\delta z = -9.77°C/1,000$ m ($-5.4°F/1,000$ ft) —*note* the term adiabatic gradient denotes the difference in temperature between two elevations and is used to calculate evapotranspiration or heat flux; the term lapse is generally used to describe the larger condition of the atmospheric surface layer

—**environmental lapse rate** the actual decrease of temperature with altitude —*note* if the environmental lapse rate is more negative than the (dry-) adiabatic lapse rate (air temperature decreases with altitude faster than the [dry-] adiabatic lapse rate), the air is unstable; if the environmental lapse rate is less negative than the (dry-) adiabatic lapse rate (air temperature decreases with altitude slower than the [dry-] adiabatic lapse rate), the air is stable; if the environmental lapse rate is nearly the same as the (dry-) adiabatic lapse rate, the air stability is neutral

—**wet-adiabiatic lapse rate** the theoretical decrease of air temperature with altitude of a parcel of saturated air, i.e., in clouds or fog, which is lifted adiabatically (no energy gained or lost), the temperature changing in response to decreasing pressure; the rate is approximately 0.6 of the dry-adiabatic lapse rate

large fire 1. *fire* a fire burning more than a specified area of land, e.g., 300 ac (121 ha) **2.** a fire burning with such size and intensity that **fire behavior** is determined by interaction between its own **convection column** and weather conditions above the surface

large fire organization (LFO) an interagency organizational system to suppress large fires —*note 1.* LFO is a designation of the national interagency fire qualification system (NIFQS) —*note 2.* the LFO system has been replaced by the **incident command system (ICS);** LFO terms include the following:

—**crew boss** the person in supervisory charge of usually five to 30 fire fighters and responsible to the sector boss for their performance, safety, and welfare

—**division boss** the supervisory staff member responsible for all suppression activity on a fire division under general instructions from the fire boss or a line boss acting for the fire boss

large fire organization *continued*

—finance chief the staff officer responsible to the fire boss for timekeeping, compensation for injury, fiscal claims, and expenditure records

—fire boss the person responsible for all fire suppression and service activities on a fire

—general fire headquarters (GHQ) the personnel who command fire-fighting forces on a multizone **campaign fire** when the complexity of the situation requires that each zone be managed more or less as a separate major fire, each with its own camp(s) and its own **command** staff —*note* GHQ may also manage one or more small fires that are adjacent to the campaign fire and tactically related to the larger fire

—line boss the supervisory officer responsible for executing the fire suppression plan of attack adopted by the fire boss —*note* the line boss may act as coordinator between two or more divisions or may supervise three or four sector bosses if no divisions have been established

—plans chief the staff officer responsible for the compilation and analysis of data needed for developing fire suppression plans

—safety chief the person responsible to the fire boss for identifying hazards and minimizing **risk**s associated with fire suppression

—sector boss the person responsible to a division boss, line boss, or fire boss, depending on the degree of organization required, for fire suppression work on one sector of a fire —*note* a sector boss supervises two or more crew bosses

—service chief the staff officer responsible for procuring, maintaining, and distributing personnel, equipment, supplies, and facilities at the times and places specified in the fire suppression plan

large organic debris (LOD) —*see* **coarse woody debris**

large woody debris (LWD) —*see* **coarse woody debris**

larva *plural* **larvae 1.** the immature form of insects that undergo **metamorphosis 2.** *in insect larva in orders that undergo complete metamorphosis* an immature insect hatching from the egg and up to the pupal **stage** —*synonym* worm (colloquial) —*see* **caterpillar, grub, maggot 3.** the six-legged first **instar** of **mites** and ticks —*see* **adult**

laser ranging measuring distances using light pulses produced by lasers

latent heat the heat released or absorbed per unit mass by a system in a reversible, isobaric-isothermal change of phase

lateral meristem a **meristem** that is located parallel with the **stem** or root axis and that exhibits lateral cell division and cell expansion, such as the vascular **cambium** and **phellogen**

lateral yarding distance the maximum distance perpendicular to each side of a **skyline** within which a log can be attached for **yard**ing

latewood secondary **xylem** in an annual ring of wood formed late in the growing season and having cells that are relatively small in diameter, thick-walled, harder, more dense, and darker than those formed earlier —*synonym* summerwood —*see* **earlywood**

Latin square one of the basic **experimental designs** that can be used to remove from the **experimental error** two sources of variation identified with the rows and columns of the square —*note 1.* this design should be used only if all **interaction** terms can be assumed to be zero —*note 2.* a 5×5 Latin square consists of 25 plots, which need not themselves be square, arranged in five rows of five plots to the row, in such a way that each of the five treatments occurs once in each row and column

latitude a method to measure the earth representing angles of a line extending from the center of the earth to the earth's surface; with $0°$ representing the equator, angles are measured in degrees north or south until $90°$ is obtained at the north and south poles —*note* lines of latitude are often called parallels —*see* **longitude**

lattice *GIS* a surface representation that uses a rectangular array of points spaced at a constant sampling interval in the x and y directions relative to a common origin

layer *GIS* a logical set of **thematic data** —*note* layers organize data by subject matter (e.g., soils, roads, and wells), and extend over the entire geographic area

layering a form of **vegetative reproduction** in which an intact branch develops roots as the result of contact with soil or other media —*see* **air layering**

LD —*see* **lethal dose**

leaching the removal of soluble materials from one zone in soil to another via water movement in the **profile** —*see* **eluviation**

lead agency *federal land management* the agency or agencies that have taken the primary responsibility for preparing the **environmental impact statement** —*see* **notice of intent**

leader the terminal, i.e., topmost shoot, characteristic of the growth of certain plants or trees —*note* forked growth, i.e., the development of two or more leaders, is often the result of injury and sometimes of heredity

lead plane an aircraft whose pilot is responsible to the air attack boss, makes dry runs over the target area to check wing and smoke conditions and topography, leads air tankers to specific targets, and supervises their drops —*note* lead plane is an **LFO** term

leaf area index (LAI) the sum of all the upper or all-sided leaf surface areas projected downward per unit area of ground beneath the canopy —*note 1.* specific leaf area is the upper surface leaf area per unit leaf weight —*note 2.* the term has no units

leaf cast *pathology* **1.** any untimely shedding of foliage —*note* leaf cast is in contrast to natural leaf-fall **2.** any disease causing untimely shedding of foliage —*note* most leaf cast is caused by fungi including *Lophodermium* needle cast and *Rhabdocline* needle cast —*synonym* needle cast (in conifers) —*see* **defoliator**

leaf mine the space between the upper and lower epidermis of a leaf or needle caused by insect feeding —*note* leaf mines are often characterized by their form such as linear, serpentine, blotch, and digitate mines —*synonym* needle mine

leaf miner an insect whose larvae feed on the inner tissues between the upper and lower epidermis of leaves or needles —*synonym* needle miner

leaf roller a **caterpillar** that feeds on leaves or needles that it (or an adult insect) has rolled, folded, or tied together for shelter —*note* most leaf rollers are in the moth families Tortricidae and Olethreutidae; important species include the oak leaf roller (*Archils semiferana*) and **budworm**s in the third to fifth **instar**s —*synonym* leaf folder, leaftier, needle roller, needle tier

leaf spot a leaf disease characterized by numerous, generally distinct, circular or angular **lesion**s —*see* **tar spot**

leafy mistletoe a parasitic plant found mainly on the Pinaceae, especially *Abies* sp., in the northern hemisphere —*note 1. Phoradendron* sp. are found mostly on hardwoods in the East and Southwest, or on Cupressaceae and *Abies* in the Southwest and Pacific coast; they are also found in Mexico —*note 2. Viscum* sp. parasitize trees in Europe; *V. album* parasitizes hardwoods and is the most important species —*note 3. Psittacanthus* sp. are widespread and sometimes serious **pest**s on *Pinus, Abies,* or *Cupressus* sp. in Mexico and Central America —*synonym* true mistletoe —*see* **dwarf mistletoe**

leapfrog method —*see* **fire suppression**

least squares method a mathematical procedure that yields estimators for which the sum of squared differences of the sample values from estimated values is minimized —*synonym* method of least squares

leave no trace (LNT) an outdoor education program designed to improve minimum-impact backcountry behavior and build an outdoor ethic

leave strip a narrow band of **forest** trees left between cutting units or adjacent to a road or stream —*also* buffer strip, green strip, or streamside management zone

leave tree a tree (marked to be) left standing for wildlife, seed production, etc., in an area where it might otherwise be felled —*synonym* **reserve tree**

legacy tree a tree, usually mature or old-growth, that is retained on a site after harvesting or natural disturbance to provide a **biological legacy**

legend the reference on a map that lists and explains the colors, symbols, line patterns, shadings, and annotation used —*note* legends often include the scale, origin, orientation, and other map information

legitimate smoke smoke from any authorized use of fire, e.g., locomotive, industrial operations, permitted burning of debris

leisure benefit the realization of a satisfying experience that results from the possession and use of leisure resources

lentic 1. of or relating to still water **2.** of or relating to organisms living in a **swamp,** pond, lake, or any other standing water

lenticel an isolated region of the **periderm** of stems or roots with intercellular spaces through which gases pass to the soil or atmosphere

lesion a localized and delineated diseased area —*see* **necrosis**

lethal dose (LD) the amount of an **insecticide**, its active ingredient, or other toxicant necessary to kill a specified proportion of an insect population —*note* LD_{50} signifies a dose (estimated or measured) that kills half the insect population in question; LD_{99} is the highest lethal dose since no dose can guarantee a 100 percent effect —*see* **median effective dose**

lethal gene a **gene** which, when expressed, is fatal —*see* **albinism, dominance, mutation**

level an instrument used in conjunction with a graduated rod (leveling staff) for determining differences in elevation

LFO —*see* **large fire organization**

liberation a release treatment made in a **stand** not past the **sapling** stage to free the favored trees from competition with older, overtopping trees —*synonym* liberation cut —*see* **cleaning, improvement cutting, weeding**

library *GIS* **1.** a collection of repeatedly used items, such as a symbol library **2.** often-used graphics objects shown on a map, or often-used program subroutines

lichen a composite organism formed from the symbiotic association of a true fungus and an alga —*see* **nonvascular**

lidar a **remote-sensing** device or technology for measuring distances and directions —*synonym* laser radar —*note 1.* lidar systems use a light beam in place of a microwave radar beam to obtain measurements of speed, altitude, direction, and range of a target —*note 2.* airborne lidar altimeters are currently being used for producing high-resolution digital elevation **model**s and mapping change in elevation —*note 3.* other lidar sensors are used for meteorological or atmospheric studies

life cycle *entomology, pathology* **1.** the successive stages (—*see* **instar, stadium**) through which an organism passes from fertilized ovum or **spore** to the fertilized ovum or spore of the next generation —*see* **disease cycle, life history, metamorphosis 2.** the period of time taken to go through this set of changes —*see* **bivoltine, multivoltine, univoltine**

life-form 1. Raunkiaer's plant classification system based on selective morphological categories and on the position of the resting buds that survive any period(s) unfavorable to growth, e.g., a cold or a dry season **2.** one of a series of classes based on the characteristic vegetative shape and appearance of a taxon —*see* **chamaephyte, cryptophyte, geophyte, growth form, halophyte, hemicryptophyte, hydrophyte, phanerophyte, therophyte**

life history the continuous, descriptive account of an organism's habits and **life cycle**, i.e., activities and duration

life table an age-specific summary of the mortality and survivorship of a **population,** usually specifying mortality agents operating

life zone a climatically defined class that can be associated with regions of soil and biota with a high uniformity in species composition and environmental adaptation

lift to loosen and remove a plant from the ground, as typically in nurseries, usually in preparation for outplanting

light burn a degree of burn in which the soil is covered with partially charred organic material but heavy fuels are not deeply charred —*see* **fire severity, moderate burn, severe burn**

light compensation point —*see* **compensation point**

light demanding —*see* **shade intolerant**

light hand tactics methods of suppressing a forest fire that consider land and resource **objective**s and seek to minimize costs and resource damage

lightning channel the irregular path through the air along which a **lightning discharge** occurs

lightning discharge the series of electrical processes by which charge is transferred along a channel of high ion density between electric charge centers of opposite sign (a) within a thundercloud (cloud discharge), (b) in a cloud and on the earth's surface (cloud-to-ground discharge or ground-to-cloud discharge), (c) within two clouds (cloud-to-cloud discharge), or (d) in a cloud and in the air below the cloud (air discharge)

lightning fire a **wildfire** caused directly or indirectly by lightning

lightning stroke 1. any one of a series of repeated electrical discharges consisting of a single **lightning discharge** (or lightning flash) **2.** *in cloud-to-ground discharge* a leader plus its subsequent return streamer

light saturation point the level (quantity) of solar radiation beyond which further increases in solar radiation will not lead to an increase in rate of **photosynthesis**

lightwood —*see* **fatwood**

lignification the process in which plant cells become woody by conversion of certain constituents of the cell wall into **lignin** —*note* lignification is generally considered to include the hardening, compressive strengthening, and secure cementing of cell walls in the formation of wood

lignin —*see* **cells (wood)**

lignotuber *plant morphology* a woody storage structure forming a swelling, more or less at ground level, originating from the **axil**s of cotyledons or, less commonly, of one or more pairs of the earliest seedling-leaves, and from whose concealed, dormant buds a new tree can develop—*note 1.* lignotubers are characteristic of many eucalypts and other Myrtaceae and often form following severe injury—*note 2.* most eucalypts develop lignotubers at the seedling stage, but in only a few **species** do these grow to a large size and produce a number of slender stems up to approximately 10 m (33 ft) high (e.g., the mallees)

limb rust a disease of *Pinus ponderosa* and related **species** —*note 1.* limb rust is caused by a group of fungi with poorly understood taxonomy including *Peridermium filamentosum, Cronartium arizonicum, C. coleosporioides,* and probably other taxa —*note 2.* known alternate **host**s of limb rusts are in the figwort family (Scrophulariaceae), which kill branches in the crown without girdling the tree; tree mortality occurs when the crown can no longer sustain the tree or when the weakened tree is attacked by **bark beetles**

lime a soil amendment containing calcium carbonate, magnesium carbonate, and other materials used to neutralize soil acidity and furnish calcium and magnesium for plant growth

limits of acceptable change (LAC) *recreation* a planning framework that establishes (a) explicit measures of the acceptable and appropriate resource and social conditions in **recreation** settings, and (b) the appropriate management strategies for maintaining or achieving those conditions

limnetic the open water region of a body of water, specifically in areas too deep to support rooted aquatic vegetation

limnology the study of the biological, chemical, geographical, and physical features of fresh waters

line 1. *genetics* a succession of descendants from an individual, e.g., a family or race —*note* breeding crosses are made within lines and production crosses among lines, resulting in no **inbreeding** in the production population **2.** *GIS* a set of ordered coordinates representing the shape of a geographic entity too narrow to be displayed as an area, e.g., contours, street centerlines, and streams —*note* a **line** begins and ends with a **node 3.** *GIS* a line on a map, e.g., a **neatline** —*see* **string**

linear feature *GIS* a geographic feature that can be represented by a **line** or set of lines, e.g., rivers, roads, and power lines

linear function a mathematical expression in which all variables appear as separate terms (no interactions) and are raised to the first power

linear programming —*see* **programming**

linear regression equation 1. simple linear **regression** equation: a statistical **model** in which the expected value of a response **variable** is conditional on a single predictor variable and the model is linear in its parameters **2.** multiple linear regression equation: a statistical model in which the expected value of a response variable is conditional on one or more predictor variables and the model is linear in its parameters **3.** nonlinear regression equation: a statistical model in which the expected value of a response variable is conditional on one or more predictor variables and the model is nonlinear in its parameters —*see* **generalized linear models**

line boss —*see* **large fire organization**

line-in-polygon *GIS* a spatial operation in which lines in one **geographic data set** are overlaid with **polygon**s of another geographic data set to determine which **arc**s, or portions of arcs, are contained within the polygons —*see* **map extent, map unit**

line-intercept method the sampling of vegetation by recording the plants intercepted by a measured line set close to the ground, or by vertical projection from the line —*see* **transect**

line out to transplant seedlings or rooted cuttings into rows in a nursery bed

line-plot survey a sampling procedure employing lines of sample plots generally laid out at regular intervals along survey lines —*synonym* line transect —*see* **strip cruise**

linkage the association of inherited characters due to **gene**s in proximity on the same **chromosome** —*see* **genetic correlation, homologous chromosomes, linkage group, Mendel's principles, recombination**

linkage disequilibrium the nonrandom association of two or more loci, **gene**s, or **trait**s —*see* **linkage, linkage group, locus**

linkage group the **gene**s located on a single **chromosome** or the characters controlled by such genes —*note* there are at least as many linkage groups as chromosome pairs —*see* **linkage**

litter the surface layer of the forest floor that is not in an advanced stage of decomposition, usually consisting of freshly fallen leaves, needles, twigs, stems, bark, and fruits —*see* **duff**

littoral the onshore area of a body of water, extending from the shore to the limits of rooted aquatic plants

live crown ratio (crown length ratio) the ratio of crown length to total tree height —*see* **crown length**

live cull a live tree classified as a **cull** —*note* live cull volume is the net volume in live, cull trees

live skyline *harvesting* a skyline that is raised and lowered during **yard**ing to facilitate logging

livestock domestic herbivorous animals —*see* **range appraisal**

livestock reservoir a structure formed by an excavation and dam across a small drainage system to provide water for **livestock** use —*synonym* earth tank, stock pond

living fence a strip of live trees or shrubs maintained to demarcate property boundaries, serve as a barrier to livestock or blowing snow, and be a source of vegetative material to provide fuel and fodder —*synonym* live fence —*see* **shelterbelt, windbreak**

living history historical **interpretation** using role playing, performances, or craft and skill demonstrations

L layer —*see* **horizon**

loader *harvesting* a self-propelled machine with a grapple or tongs and a supporting structure designed to pick up and discharge trees or logs for the purpose of piling or loading —*note 1.* the loading operation may be swing-to-load, slide-to-load, or travel-to-load —*note 2.* a loader is known as a hydraulic loader or knuckleboom if it swings to load and has hydraulically activated boom members — *see* **jammer, shovel**

loading **1.** *logging* the act of placing material, i.e., the load, on a vehicle for further transport **2.** *mechanics* the act of applying forces externally to, or the action of forces on, a body or structure and hence inducing **stress** wihin it **3.** *utilization* the amount of preservative or other chemical absorbed by timber, generally expressed in lb/ft^3 or kg/m^3, of treated volume or, particularly in diffusion treatments, as a percent of the oven-dry weight of the piece —*see* **strain**

loam a soil textural class containing roughly equal amounts of **sand, silt,** and **clay**

local area network (LAN) computer data communications technology that connects computers at the same site —*note* computers and terminals on a LAN can freely share data and peripheral devices, such as printers and plotters; LANs are composed of cabling and special data communications hardware and software

local seed source the source of seed native to the locality in which the seedlings are to be grown, i.e., belonging to the indigenous **geographic race** —*see* **provenance, race, seed source**

locus *plural* **loci** the physical location of the **gene** within the **DNA** strand or **chromosome** —*see* **allele, linkage disequilibrium, qualitative trait locus**

locust one of a few species in the insect family Acrididae capable under certain conditions of forming large swarms that move (migrate) over wide areas causing great devastation of natural and cultivated vegetation where they feed —*note* these grasshoppers can exist in two main forms, **solitary** and **gregarious,** which are often so distinct that early taxonomists regarded them as separate species

loess material transported and deposited by wind and consisting of predominantly **silt**-sized particles

log decomposition class any of five stages of deterioration of logs in the forest ranging from sound (class 1) to almost total decomposition (class 5)

logging the **felling, skidding,** on-site processing, and loading of trees or logs onto trucks —*synonym* **harvesting**

logging residue the unused portions of trees cut or killed during logging and left in the woods

logical selection *GIS* the process of selecting a subset of features using logical selection criteria that operate on the attributes of features, e.g., AREA GT 16000 —*note* only those features whose attributes meet the selection criteria are selected —*synonym* feature selection by attribute

logistics section chief —*see* **incident command system**

log rule a formula to estimate the volume (usually in board feet) of lumber that may be sawed from logs of different sizes under various assumed conditions given their length and scaling (small end) diameter —*note* log rules are commonly divided into four groups on the basis of derivation: (a) diagram rules, (b) formula rules, (c) rules based on actual output, and (d) hybrid rules —*see* **Doyle rule, international log rule, international** ^{1}/**4-inch rule, log scale, Scribner rule**

log scale **1.** the volume of a log as determined by a **log rule 2.** any system of measuring round timber **3.** a special **scale** stick used in conjunction with log rules —*note* log **scale** is usually expressed in board feet and based on various log scaling rules —*see* **Doyle rule, international** ^{1}/**4-inch rule, Scribner rule**

log-scale board foot —*see* **board-foot log scale**

long butt **1.** a section cut from the bottom log of a tree and **culled** because of rot or other defect **2.** to cut such a section from a log

long-horned beetle an adult member of the family Cerambycidae (Coleoptera) so named because of characteristically long antennae —*note* the **larvae** of many species of long-horned beetles tunnel in the wood or cambial region mainly of weakened, dying, or dead (including felled) trees —*synonym* longhorn beetle

longitude a method to measure the earth representing angles of a line extending from the center of the earth to the earth's surface; with a line passing from the north to the south pole and passing through Greenwich, England, as 0°, angles are measured in degrees east or west until 180° is obtained at the opposite side of the earth from 0° longitude —*note* lines of longitude are often called **meridian**s —*see* **latitude**

long-range planning —*see* **planning (long-range)**

long run the period of time over which all inputs can be varied by the producer —*note* none of the costs of production are assumed fixed in the long run, e.g., new plants can be built, additional machinery purchased —*see* **short run**

longspan yarding *harvesting* a cable system capable of **yard**ing logs for 2,400 ft (732 m) or more —*synonym* longline yarding

long-term fire retardant material that inhibits combustion even after the water component has evaporated, primarily through chemical reactions between combustion materials and the applied chemicals but also by forming a film and causing intumescence —*see* **fire retardant, short-term fire retardant, slurry**

long-term sustained yield (LTSY) the highest uniform wood **yield** that may be sustained under a specific management intensity consistent with multiple-use objectives on lands being managed for timber production —*see* **sustained yield**

long ton a British unit of weight equal to 2,240 lb (1,016 kg) —*see* **short ton, metric ton**

longwood 1. stemwood > 120 in (305 cm) in length **2.** stem-length logs

longwood harvesting a timber-harvesting method in which harvested trees are moved to the **landing** either as whole trees or as topped and limbed tree-length logs —*note* at the landing, further processing such as limbing, topping, **buck**ing, chipping, or loading is carried out as necessary —*synonym* tree-length harvesting

lookout 1. a person designated to detect and report fires from a fixed vantage point —*synonym* fire lookout **2.** a location and associated structures from which fires can be detected and reported —*synonym* lookout station **3.** a member of a fire crew designated to observe the fire and warn the fire crew when there is danger of becoming trapped —*synonym* lookout observer —*see* **tower person**

lookout fire fighter a person combining the functions of lookout and **fire fighter**

lookup table *computers* **1.** a special tabular data file containing additional attributes that can be related to a data file through a **key** and a **relate 2.** a special tabular data file used to control how a digital image is modified (e.g., brightened, darkened) for viewing on a monitor

looper a **larva** of the insect family Geometridae (Lepidoptera) —*note* many looper **species** are seriously defoliators of trees, including the fall **canker**worm *(Alsophila pometaria),* spring cankerworm *(Paleacrita vernata),* elm spanworm *(Ennomos subsignarius),* and hemlock looper *(Lambdina fiscellaria fiscellaria)* —*synonym* measuringworm, spanworm, geometer, inchworm

lop to cut limbs from trees, whether standing, felled, or fallen —*synonym* prune, delimb

lop-and-scatter a hand method of removing the upward-extending branches from tops of felled trees to keep **slash** low to the ground, to increase rate of decomposition, lower fire hazard, or as a pretreatment prior to burning

lost line any part of a **fireline** rendered useless by a **breakover** of the fire

lotic 1. of or relating to flowing water such as a stream or river **2.** of or relating to organisms living in a brook, stream, or river

Lotka-Volterra equations a set of **model**s of population growth based on the logistic equation

($\delta N/\delta t = rN(1-N/K)$) and modified for the effects of competition and predation, where N = population size, r = rate of growth, and K = symptote or equilibrium population size

low forest a **forest** produced from vegetative regeneration, i.e., **coppice** or **coppice with reserves** —*see* **regeneration method, high forest**

low moor a type of **fen** composed of peat or muck soil, formed in eutrophic or mesotrophic waters (generally the drainage from a surrounding catchment area into a basin site, commonly a former lake), and therefore relatively rich in minerals, which influences the type of vegetation —*see* **high moor**

low-water bridge a concrete structure at a stream crossing with or without culverts, which allows streamflow to rise and pass over the road surface during high flow

low-water ford a place in a stream designated for vehicle crossing during low-water flow

LTSY —*see* **long-term sustained yield**

lumber the sawn product from a tree —*synonym* sawnwood —*note* dimension lumber is timber cut to specific widths, thicknesses, and lengths; **hardwood** dimension lumber is cut to the approximate sizes needed in the manufacture of furniture or other products; **softwood** dimension lumber consists of boards wth thicknesses of 1 to 5 inches that are generally used in construction and sold in various sizes, e.g., 2×4, 4×8, 2×10 —*synonym* **sawnwood, sawtimber**

lumber rule an inscribed stick used for measuring the board foot volume of dried lumber —*see* **scale stick**

lumber tally a record of sawn boards giving the number of pieces by size, grade, and species —*see* **green-chain tally**

lump-sum sale a timber sale in which the buyer and seller agree on a total price for **marked** standing trees or for trees within a defined area before the wood is removed —*note* the timber is usually paid for before harvesting begins —*see* **per-unit sale, sale schedule**

lyctus beetle —*see* **powderpost beetle**

lysimeter 1. a device for measuring percolation and leaching losses from a column of soil under controlled conditions **2.** a device for measuring gains (irrigation, **precipitation**, and condensation) and losses (**evapotranspiration**) by a column of soil

M

macro a set of instructions used by a computer program or programs —*note* a macro is usually stored in a text file and invoked from a program that reads this text file as if the commands were typed interactively

macroclimate the climate that lies just beyond the local modifying irregularities of landform and vegetation —*see* **microclimate**

macrocyclic a life cycle in **rust fungi** found with four or five types of **spore**s —*note* **fusiform rust** and white pine blister rust are caused by macrocyclic fungi —*see* **microcyclic**

macrogametophyte —*synonym* **megagametophyte**

macroinvertebrate an invertebrate animal large enough to be seen without magnification

macrometeorology the study of the largest-scale aspects of the atmosphere, such as general circulation and weather types

macronutrient a chemical element (not including carbon, hydrogen, or oxygen) needed in relatively large amounts by organisms —*note* macronutrients include N, P, K, Ca, Mg, and S

macropore a soil pore generally greater than 0.06 mm (0.002 in) in diameter —*note 1.* the demarcation between macropore and **micropore** is not clearly defined —*note 2.* macropores are formed by insect or animal burrows, old root channels, and structural cracks —*see* **capillary pore**

macropore flow (preferential flow) that part of soil water movement that bypasses the soil matrix and flows through soil macropores

MACS —*see* **multiagency coordination system**

MAFFS —*see* **modular airborne fire-fighting system**

maggot a soft-bodied, legless **larva** without a well-formed head, particularly of the true flies (Diptera)

magnetic declination the angle between the directions of true north and magnetic north at any point

MAI —*see* **mean annual increment**

main line *harvesting* **1.** the line used in cable **yard**ing to bring logs to the landing **2.** the winch line on a **skidder 3.** the main logging road in transporting logs —*synonym* main road

major gene a gene whose **allele**s demonstrate detectable **phenotypic** effects —*see* **oligogene**

male sterile incapable of producing functional **pollen**

managed stand yield —*see* **yield table**

management kinds of management include the following:

—**area** an area for which a single **management plan** is developed and applied —*see* **management unit**

—**goal** a broad, general statement, usually not quantifiable, that expresses a desired state or process to be achieved —*note* normally, a management goal is stated in terms of purpose, often not attainable in the short term, and provides the context for more specific objectives

—**indicator** a plant or animal species, community, or special **habitat** selected during planning and monitored during implementation because the effects of management on its condition and trend will suggest the condition and trend of the resource as a whole

—**intensity** a management practice or combination of management practices and associated costs designed to obtain a specific level of goods and services

—**objective** a concise, time-specific statement of measurable planned results that correspond to preestablished **goals** in achieving a desired outcome —*note* an objective commonly includes information on resources to be used, forms the basis for further planning to define the precise steps to be taken and the resources to be used and assigned responsibility in achieving the identified **goal**s

—**plan** a predetermined course of action and direction to achieve a set of results, usually specified as **goal**s, **objective**s, and policies —*note* a management plan is a working instrument that guides actions and that changes in response to feedback and changed conditions, goals, objectives, and policies —*see* **planning, planning site, public involvement**

—**policy** a definite course or method of action to guide present and future decisions or to specify in detail the ways and means to achieve **goals** and **objective**s

—**practice** a specific activity, measure, course of action, or treatment undertaken on a **forest** ownership

—**prescription** a set of management practices and intensities scheduled for application on a specific area to satisfy multiple uses or other **goals** and **objective**s

—**science** —*see* **systems analysis**

—**unit** *range management* a subdivision of a **management area** —*see* **deferred grazing**

management, direct *recreation* management that emphasizes regulating human behavior —*note* in direct management, individual choice is restricted and managers aim at controlling visitor behavior directly with regulations and use requirements —*see* **management (indirect)**

management, indirect *recreation* management that emphasizes modifying human behavior by managing factors and situations that influence their decisions —*note* in indirect management, visitors retain their freedom to choose —*see* **management (direct)**

manager —*see* **incident command system**

mangrove swamp a swampy or tidal area dominated by tropical trees or shrubs of the genera *Rhizophora, Laguncularia,* and *Avicennia*

Manning's formula *hydraulics* an equation used to predict the velocity of water in an open channel or pipeline: $V = (1.48r^{2/3} S^{1/2})/n$ where V is the mean velocity of flow (ft/sec), r is the hydraulic radius (ft), s is the slope of the energy gradient or, for assumed uniform flow, the slope of the channel (ft/ft), and n is the roughness coefficient or retardance factor of the channel lining —*see* **discharge formula**

man-passing-man *obsolete* —*see* **fire suppression, leapfrog method**

mantle the layer of fungal hyphae sheathing the root **epidermis** of an **ectomycorrhiza**

many-to-one relate *GIS* a **relate** in which many **records** in one datafile can be related to a single record in another datafile —*note* a typical **goal** in **relational database** design is many-to-one relates for reducing data storage and redundancy; the datafiles then take on a normalized form

map distance the measured distance between two points on a map —*note* map distance is used with ground distance to compute **map scale**

map extent 1. the rectangular limits (xmin,ymin and xmax,ymax) of the area of the earth's surface displayed —*note 1.* map extent is specified in the coordinate system of the geographic data set used —*note 2.* typically, the extent of the geographic database (or a portion of it defined by zoomed-in view) defines the map extent for display **2.** the geographic extent of a **geographic data set** specified by the minimum bounding rectangle, i.e., xmin,ymin and xmax,ymax —*see* **line-in-polygon**

map limits the rectangular area on the **graphics page** in which geographic features are displayed —*note 1.* all geographic data are drawn within the map limits, and no geographic data are drawn outside the map limits —*note 2.* map titles and legends can be drawn outside the map limits

map projection a **mathematical model** for converting locations on the earth's surface from spherical to planar coordinates, allowing flat maps to depict three-dimensional features —*note* some map projections preserve the integrity of shape; others preserve the accuracy of area, distance, or direction; no one projection can preserve all four spatial properties; any such representation distorts some parameter of the earth's surface, e.g., distance, area, shape, direction

map query the process of eliciting information from a GIS by asking questions of the geographic data —*note 1.* query can be spatial or logical; spatial query is the process of spatially selecting features, e.g., select all **stand**s within 300 ft (91.4 m) of another stand or set of stands; logical query is the process of selecting features whose attributes meet specific logical criteria, e.g., select all vegetation types whose value for SPECIES is ponderosa pine —*note 2.* the query process involves selecting a set of features, then performing additional operations with those features and drawing them with assigned symbols, listing their attributes, or summarizing attribute values, e.g., calculating the total or average value of an item

map reference a number or combination of letters and numbers denoting the position of a point on a map **grid** —*note* a map reference is generally formed by combining the grid coordinates into a single continuous number

map scale the extent of reduction needed to display a representation of the earth's surface on a map; a statement of a measure on the map and the equivalent measure on the earth's surface —*note 1.* map scale is often expressed as a representative fraction of distance, such as 1:24,000 (one unit of distance on the map represents 24,000 of the same units of distance on the earth) —*note 2.* map scale can also be expressed as a statement of equivalence using different units, e.g., 1 in = 1 mi

map-to-page transformation the process of positioning and scaling a map on a **graphics page** —*note 1.* the transformation controls how geographic coordinates are turned into graphics on the display screen or plotter page —*note 2.* geographic data are not maps; they contain the unscaled coordinates that GIS software uses to draw maps

map unit the coordinate unit in which a geographic data set is stored —*note* units can be inches, centimeters, feet, meters, or decimal degrees —*see* **line-in-polygon**

maquis scrub vegetation, generally rather dense, composed of much-branched, thorny, and often aromatic **shrub**s found in the Mediterranean region

marginal benefit the increase in value derived by a purchaser from buying one more unit of a good or service

marginal cost the increase in total cost incurred by producing one more unit of a good or service

marginal product the additional **output** that can be produced by one or more units of a particular input while holding all other inputs constant —*note* it is usually assumed that an input's marginal productivity diminishes as additional units of input are put into use while all other inputs are fixed

marginal rate of substitution the rate at which an individual is willing to trade one good or service for another while remaining equally well off —*note* the marginal rate of substitution is the absolute value of the slope of an **indifference curve**; it is usually assumed that the marginal rate of substitution of item X for item Y will diminish as X is substituted for Y

marginal revenue the increase in total revenue that occurs from selling one more unit of a good or service

marginal utility the extra value that an individual receives by consuming one more unit of a particular good or service

marine borer a marine organism that attacks submerged or floating wood structures in salt or brackish waters —*note 1.* two main groups of marine borers are recognized: (a) crustacean borers (e.g., from the genera *Limnoria* [gribbles], *Chelura*, *Sphaeroma*) and (b) molluscean borers (e.g., from the genera *Bankia*, *Teredo* [shipworms], and *Martesia*) —*note 2. Limnoria* tunnels just below the wood surface, causing a characteristic deterioration of the timber; *Teredo* tunnels are generally lined with calcareous material —*synonym* timber worm

mark 1. *harvesting* to select and indicate by a **blaze** or paint spot the trees to be cut or left in a timber harvesting operation **2.** *range management* to place a sign on an animal, other than a **brand**, for the purpose of identification, e.g., ear slits, tags, wattles —*see* **brand, tag, timber marking**

marker-aided selection the use of molecular markers in structured **population**s to identify and propagate superior **genotype**s —*see* **marker gene**

marker gene an **allele** or, in molecular-level study, a **DNA** fragment, used to indicate the presence of specific DNA or to locate or identify a region of a **chromosome** —*see* **marker-aided selection, qualitative trait locus**

marker symbol *GIS* a symbol used to represent a point location, e.g., an airport

market value the price that land, **stumpage**, products, etc., would bring if sold today —*note* market value depends on current market conditions such as the structure of the market (e.g., competitive versus monopolistic), the available alternative supplies offered by other sellers and the prices they would accept, the number of interested prospective purchasers and the prices they would be willing to pay for various quantities and qualities, and the availability of substitutes

Markovian decision processes an iterative representation in the form of a transition probabilities matrix that describes the probabilities of the next state for an entity given its current state, e.g., to represent ecological **succession** with various kinds of potential disturbance

marl soft and unconsolidated calcium carbonate, often derived from photosynthetic activity of algae and mollusk shells and usually mixed with varying amounts of clay or other impurities

marsh 1. a water-saturated, poorly drained **wetland** area, periodically or permanently inundated, that supports an extensive **cover** of emergent, nonwoody vegetation essentially without peatlike accumulations **2.** a wetland characterized by a predominantly inorganic soil, supporting nonwoody vegetation, characteristically rushes, reeds, cattails, or sedges —*note* the water may be salt, brackish, or fresh —*see* **bog, fen, flat, swamp**

Masonite™ —*see* **engineered wood composite**

mass attack the aggregation of **bark beetle** adults on one **host** tree in sufficient numbers to overcome the tree's defense mechanisms —*see* **initial attack, primary host selection, secondary host selection**

mass fire —*see* **fire behavior**

mass selection the process of choosing individuals solely on the basis of their **phenotype**s without regard to information about ancestors, **sibling**s, offspring, or other relatives —*see* **forest tree breeding, individual selection, recurrent selection, roguing**

mass trapping the use of synthetic **pheromone**s in combination with traps to capture a significant portion of an insect population

mass wasting —*see* **landslide**

mast the fruit of trees considered as food for livestock and certain kinds of wildlife —*note* hard mast is the fruits or nuts of trees such as oak, beech, walnut, chinquapin, and hickories; soft mast includes the fruits and berries from plants such as dogwood, viburnum, elderberry, huckleberry, hawthorn, grape, raspberry, and blackberry

mast year a year in which there is abundant production of **mast**

matching species to site *urban forestry* the process of encouraging citizens to select tree species that will adapt to a particular planting site by matching species with soil type, city infrastructure, moisture regime, light tolerance, climatic zone, and seed source

maternal effect a special case of **c-effect** due to a common maternal environment or maternally inherited nonnuclear **DNA** —*see* **cytoplasmic inheritance, paternal effect**

mathematical model a set of mathematical symbols and expressions used to represent a real or hypothetical situation including imposed **constraint**s, restrictions, or limitations —*see* **model**

mathematical programming —*see* **programming**

mating design the pattern of **pollination**s set up between individuals —*note* mating design is described, e.g., as random, systematic, diallel, or according to parental similarities —*synonym* mating system —*see* **diallel cross, forest tree breeding**

mating disruption the use of **pheromone**s to interfere with the sexual communication between males and females of a **pest** species —*note* mating disruption is usually done by saturating the area with a synthetic attractant that prevents males from locating females, or by the use of inhibitor or antiaggregation pheromones that disrupt **bark beetle** colonization processes

matrix *plural* **matrices** **1.** a rectangular array of mathematical elements consisting of *m* rows and *n* columns **2.** *management* the most extensive and connected landscape element that plays the dominant role in **landscape** functioning **3.** *management* a landscape element surrounding a **patch** **4.** *management* the nonreserved portion of the **forest** landbase—*see* **interaction matrix**

mattock —*see* **hand tool**

maturation the state of growth; a sometimes abrupt (heteroblastic) or, more commonly, an unevenly gradual (homoblastic) process of orderly development from embryonic through **juvenile** and adolescent to **adult** —*note* maturation is a change to a relatively stable condition, i.e., **maturity** —*see* **aging**

mature *of trees or stands* pertaining to a tree or **even-aged stand** that is capable of sexual reproduction (other than precocious reproduction), has attained most of its potential height growth, or has reached merchantability standards —*note* within **uneven-aged stand**s, individual trees may become mature but the stand itself consists of trees of diverse ages and stages of development —*see* **juvenile phase, old-growth forest, overmature, pole, sapling**

mature soil a soil with well-developed soil **horizon**s produced by the natural processes of soil formation and essentially in equilibrium with its present environment

maximax an optimist's approach to choosing among management alternatives under **uncertainty** by (a) noting the attribute with the best value for each alternative and (b) comparing these attributes across alternatives to choose the one with the best value —*note* to determine the attribute with the best value for each alternative and follow this decision rule, a very high degree of comparability is needed among attributes within each alternative and among alternatives —*see* **maximin, minimax regret**

maximin a pessimist's approach to choosing among management alternatives under **uncertainty** by (a) noting for each management alternative the magnitude of the worst possible outcome (i.e., when faced with the least desirable state of the world for that alternative) and (b) selecting the management alternative with the best worst-case value (which could be the highest or lowest, depending on whether the outcome attribute of concern is a "good," such as **present net worth,** or a "bad," such as the number of escaped fires) —*note* to determine the lowest-valued attribute or worst-met standard and follow this decision rule, a very high degree of comparability is needed among the attributes within each alternative and among alternatives —*see* **maximax, minimax regret**

MBF a thousand board feet —*see* **board foot**

MCD —*see* **minor civil division**

mcleod —*see* **hand tool**

MDF medium-density fiberboard —*see* **engineered wood composite**

mealybug a **scale insect** of the family Pseudococcidae (Homoptera) characterized by waxy, cottony (mealy) secretions that cover the insect

mean —*see* **arithmetic mean, geometric mean**

mean annual increment (MAI) the total **increment** of a tree or **stand** (standing crop plus thinnings) up to a given age divided by that age —*note* the MAI for a whole **rotation** is termed the final MAI —*see* **culmination of mean annual increment, current annual increment (CAI), periodic annual increment (PAI), periodic increment**

mean deviation the average value of the departure from some central value, taken irrespective of sign; a measure of **dispersion** —*synonym* mean absolute deviation —*note* the central value is generally the **arithmetic mean** but may be the **median**

mean diameter *of a group of trees, crop, or stand* **1.** quadratic mean diameter, the diameter corresponding to their mean **basal area** **2.** arithmetic(al) mean diameter, the arithmetic(al) mean of the diameters

mean radiant temperature the temperature at which an object gives out as much radiation as it receives from its surroundings

mechanical control the deliberate control of **pest**s

by mechanical means, such as by hoeing weeds or constructing barriers

mechanical girdling —*see* **girdle**

mechanical harvesting cutting with mechanized equipment such as a carrier-mounted shear or a **feller-buncher** instead of by hand with a power saw

mechanical pulp —*see* **pulp**

mechanical thinning —*see* **thinning**

mechanistic a system that can be characterized exactly by the laws of physics and chemistry —*see* **deterministic, stochastic**

median the middle measurement in a set of data —*note* if the data contain an even number of items, then the median is the average of the two middle items

median effective dose (ED$_{50}$) the dose, expressed as a proportion of body weight, that produces a designated effect (usually mortality) in 50 percent of the organisms exposed —*see* **lethal dose**

medium-density fiberboard —*see* **engineered wood composite**

medullary ray —*see* **cells (wood)**

megagametophyte the female **gametophyte** —*see* **endosperm, fertilization, zygote**

meiosis a process of two consecutive specialized nuclear divisions leading to the formation of **gametophyte**s —*note* generally, the first meiotic division reduces the **chromosome** number by half (2n to n) because, after pairing, one chromosome of each pair moves to one or the other daughter cell; in the second division, each chromosome of the newly formed **haploid** (n) daughter nuclei divides so that the end result of meiosis is four cells (the tetrad), each with half the original number of chromosomes —*see* **chromosome set, Mendel's principles, mitosis**

melting level the altitude at which ice crystals and snowflakes melt as they descend through the atmosphere

memorandum of understanding (MOU) a formal, written agreement between two or more organizations or agencies that presents the relationship between the entities for purposes of planning and management

Mendel's principles a set of standards governing inheritance of **traits** first described by Gregor Mendel (1822–1884): (a) hereditary differences result from **genes**; genes are present in pairs, each of which is called an **allele;** (b) one allele may dominate the other; (c) during reproduction, paired alleles separate, allowing segregation of alleles; (d) resulting

offspring exhibit **segregation** ratios for various **character** combinations according to laws of probability, because each segregating allele is distributed randomly to one **gamete** and independently of other genes (provided the genes are not linked), and because eggs and sperm unite randomly —*see* **epigenetic, linkage, meiosis, qualitative inheritance, simple Mendelian inheritance**

mensuration 1. a branch of mathematics dealing with the measurement of lengths of lines, areas of surfaces, and volumes of solids 2. *forestry* the determination of dimensions, form, weight, growth, volume, and age of trees, individually or collectively, and of the dimensions of their products

merchantable 1. *of trees, crops, or stands* having the size, quality, and condition suitable for marketing under a given economic condition, even if not immediately accessible for logging 2. *of a bole or stem* the part(s) suitable for sale 3. *of lumber* the commercial size or grade of round or sawn timber or of other forest produce, or the entire output of a sawmill except for mill **cull**s

merchantable height the commercial height above ground or (in some countries) above stump height, to which a tree stem is salable for a particular product

merchantable top diameter the inside- or outside-bark diameter above which a stem is considered nonmerchantable for a particular product —*synonym* merch top

meridian a line running vertically from the north pole to the south pole along which all locations have the same **longitude** —*note* the prime **meridian** (0°) runs through Greenwich, England; both east and west longitudes range from 0° to 180° relative to the prime meridian

meristem an organized, undifferentiated plant tissue with rapidly dividing cells that differentiate to form new tissues or organs —*see* **apical meristem, cells (wood)**

mesic of sites or **habitat**s characterized by intermediate moisture conditions, i.e., neither decidedly wet nor dry

mesophyte an organism that inhabits sites that are neither decidedly wet nor dry

mesotrophic 1. a **habitat** with a moderate amount of dissolved nutrients 2. a water body or **wetland** with productivity intermediate between **oligotrophic** and **eutrophic**

metadata *computers* descriptions about data, or data-about-data —*note* metadata includes documentation about lineage, **format,** dates, **accuracy, precision**, and any piece of information assisting users in fully understanding data

metalimnion the water layer of a stratified lake between the **epilimnion** and the **hypolimnion,** characterized by a steep thermal gradient

metamorphosis 1. the **ontogeny** of some animals encompassing the series of changes in shape, structure, and habits undergone from egg or embryonic **stage** into adult stage —*note 1. entomology* four kinds of metamorphosis are generally recognized: (a) no metamorphosis (ametabolous), in which the form emerging from the egg has the same morphology as the adult (e.g., springtails, proturans), (b) incomplete metamorphosis (**hemimetabolous**), in which there is no pupal stage but there is a distinct change in body form between the immature and adult stages; generally, immatures are aquatic **nymph**s with **gill**s (naiads) and adults are aerial and without gills (e.g., dragonflies), (c) gradual metamorphosis, where immature nymphs and adults occupy the same **habitat**s and feed on the same food, with a gradual change in size and body proportions and a gradual development of wings and sexual organs from one molt to the next (e.g., grasshoppers, **aphid**s, **bug**s), and (d) complete metamorphosis (**holometabolous**), in which insects develop from egg to **larva** to **pupa** to **adult** —*note 2.* some entomologists recognize only two types of metamorphosis: complete, as defined above; and simple, consisting of no, incomplete, and gradual, as defined above **2.** the change in form during the development of an insect —*see* **life cycle, stadium**

metapopulation 1. a subpopulation of a **species** linked to other subpopulations by more or less restricted **migration 2.** a **population** structure in which individual populations exist on **patch**es and are dynamic in space and time

metaxenia the effect of **pollen** on maternal tissues of the **fruit,** e.g., the development of large seeds because of stimulated seedcoat growth after certain pollinations —*see* **double fertilization, xenia**

metaxylem —*see* **cells (wood)**

metric ton a unit of weight equal to 1000 kg (2,204 lb) —*see* **short ton, long ton**

metropolitan statistical area (MSA) a single county (or group of contiguous counties) that define a metropolitan region, usually with a central city with at least 50,000 inhabitants —*note* previously, these have been called standard metropolitan statistical areas (SMSA) and standard metropolitan areas (SMA); the precise definitions and changes therein are established by the US Office of Management and Budget

mica a layered, structured aluminosilicate mineral group of the 2:1 type that is characterized by its nonexpandability and high layer charge —*note* major types are muscovite, biotite, and phlogopite

micelle —*see* **cells (wood)**

microbial ecology the ecology of microorganisms, especially their roles in nutrient cycling, decomposition, and plant growth

microbial insecticide a microorganism applied as a **pesticide,** e.g., *Bacillus thuringiensis (Bt)*

microclimate 1. *ecology* the climate of small areas, such as under a plant or other **cover,** differing in extremes of temperature and moisture from the climate outside that cover **2.** *meteorology* the fine-scale climate of the air space from the surface of the earth to an altitude where the effects of the underlying surface no longer create conditions distinguishable from the general local climate (the mesoclimate or **macroclimate**)

microcyclic a type of life cycle in **rust fungi** with two, occasionally three, **spore** states —*see* **macrocyclic**

microfibril —*see* **cells (wood)**

microhabitat the specific combination of **habitat** elements in the locations selected by an organism for specific purposes or events —*note* the term expresses the more specific and functional aspects of habitat and cover; distinctive physical characteristics distinguish the microhabitats within an organism's habitat

micrometeorology that portion of the science of meteorology that deals with the observation and explanation of the smallest-scale physical and dynamic occurrences within the atmosphere

micropore a soil pore generally less than 0.06 mm (0.002 in) in diameter —*note* the demarcation between micropore and **macropore** is not clearly defined —*see* **capillary, pore, microspore**

micropropagation the *in vitro* **vegetative propagation** of plants producing plantlets, micropropagules, or **somatic** embryos

microspore the male **haploid** cell produced by sexual cell division (**meiosis**) and maturing to a **pollen** grain

microsporogenesis the development of **pollen**

mid-diameter 1. *of a tree* the stem diameter at half tree height ($d_{0.5h}$) **2.** *of a fallen or felled stem or a log* the diameter halfway along its length

midrange planning —*see* **planning**

migration 1. *ecology* —*see* **dispersal 2.** *genetics* the movement of **gene**s from one **population** to another —*see* **evolution, introgression, gene frequency, gene flow**

milacre an area of 1/1000 ac (0.0004 ha) —*note* a milacre is equivalent to, e.g., 0.1×0.1 chain, 6.6×6.6 ft, or 0.02×0.02 m

mill tally the actual board foot volume produced from a log at a given mill before drying and surfacing —*see* **overrun, underrun, utilization percent**

mimicry the common resemblance of one species (the mimic), usually in color, pattern, form, smell, sound, or behavior, to another species (the model) which is protected by unpalatability, toxicity, etc., existing in the same area —*note 1*. in Batesian mimicry, the mimic is palatable and the model unpalatable or venomous —*note 2*. in Müllerian mimicry, a group of relatively unrelated insect species, all distasteful or protected, come to resemble each other —*note 3*. in Wasmannian mimicry, a **parasite** or **predator** species comes to resemble its **host**

mineralization the conversion of an element from an organic form to an inorganic state as a result of microbial activity

mineral soil a soil consisting predominantly of, and having its properties determined predominantly by, mineral matter

minerotrophic pertaining to a **wetland** receiving water and minerals from surrounding physiographic regions, not just from **precipitation**

minimal area *ecology* the smallest area that displays the characteristic features of a plant **community** —*note* in European ecology, minimal area is often the smallest area on which the **species** of a plant community are adequately represented and is much smaller in extent than in the North American definition

minimax regret a "politician's" approach to choosing a management alternative under **uncertainty** in which, for each combination of management alternative and ensuing state-of-nature, the maximum regret is computed as the difference between the outcome of that combination and the best outcome for that state-of-nature —*note* this approach leads to choosing the decision alternative that minimizes the maximum regret, i.e., minimizing the difference between the decision and what the decision, in hindsight, should have been —*see* **maximax, maximin**

minimum bounding rectangle *GIS* the rectangle defined by the map **extent** of a geographic data set and specified by two coordinates: xmin, ymin and xmax, ymax

minimum-damage fire protection theory a concept postulating that the object of fire protection is to minimize fire damage regardless of cost

minimum diameter **1.** *of standing trees* a prescribed (generally breast height) outside-bark diameter below which felling is not allowed —*note* minimum diameter may be a qualified limit for harvest cuttings or an absolute limit for protection

of a species **2.** a lower limit for inclusion in a cruise or inventory

minimum-impact suppression tactic (MIST) *fire management* the least amount of force necessary to achieve fire management objectives

minimum mapping units *GIS* the minimum sizes or dimensions for features to be mapped as lines or areas for a given map scale —*note* long, narrow features such as streams and rivers are represented as lines if their width is less than 0.10 in (0.25 cm); a **polygon** smaller than 0.125 in (0.32 cm) on a side will be represented as a **point**

minimum streamflow the quantity of water needed to maintain the existing or planned in-place uses of water in or along a stream channel or other water bodies, and to maintain the natural character of the aquatic system and its dependent systems

minimum tool *wilderness management* use of the tool, force, regulation, instrument, or practice with the least impact necessary to bring about a desired result

minimum top diameter the inside- or outside-bark stem diameter for products such as sawlogs or pulpwood

minirhizotron a piece of equipment in which root dynamics are observed using cylindrical tubes with a periscope, and documented with a camera system —*see* **rhizotron**

minor civil division (MCD) the primary political or administrative subdivision of a county

miombo a deciduous or semideciduous open forest of *Brachystegia* or *Isoberlinia* species with a grassy root, widely distributed in Africa south of the equator

MIP —*see* **mixed integer programming**

mire a slimy soil or deep mud; **swamp**y ground, **bog**s, or **marsh**es

MIST —*see* **minimum-impact suppression tactic**

mistletoe, true —*see* **dwarf mistletoe, leafy mistletoe**

mite a small Arachnid of the order Acarina having no obvious demarcation between the various parts of its body —*note* some species of mites inhabit the soil, feeding on organic matter, e.g., decaying wood and leaves, and others are predacious or feed on plants, e.g., the spider mite, which may seriously parasitize trees —*see* **miticide**

miticide a **pesticide** used specifically to control mites —*see* **acaride**

mitigation **1.** action taken to alleviate potential adverse effects of natural or human-caused disturbances **2.** compensation for damage done —*note* in this usage, in-kind mitigation is replacement of a lost resource with one similar (stream for stream or **species** for species), while out-of-kind is replacement of one kind with another (lake for stream or one species for another)

mitosis the normal division of a **nucleus** into two identical daughter nuclei by a process of duplication and separation of **chromosomes**, so maintaining the **diploid** condition —*see* **meiosis, vegetative cell**

mixed *of a forest, crop, or stand* composed of two or more prominent species —*see* **pure**

mixed farming cropping systems that involve the raising of crops, animals, and trees

mixed integer programming (MIP) a form of **integer linear programming** in which some, but not all, of the **decision variable**s are constrained to be positive integers

mixed intercropping growing two or more crops simultaneously with no distinct row arrangement

mixing ratio *in a system of moist air* the dimensionless ratio of the mass of water vapor to the mass of dry air

MMBF a million board feet of wood in logs or lumber —*see* **board foot**

MMCF a million cubic feet of wood in logs or lumber

mobile yarder *harvesting* a self-propelled machine for cable logging using a tower that is either an integral part of the machine or a separate structure — *synonym* **yarder**

mobilization an action required to expand or create a fire organization to handle a **campaign fire** or a **conflagration** —*see* **demobilization**

mode the value occurring most frequently in a data set —*see* **arithmetic mean, geometric mean**

model **1.** an abstract representation of objects and events from the real world for the purpose of simulating a process, predicting an outcome, or characterizing a phenomenon —*note* types of models include mental models (a set of rules that may or may not lend themselves to formalization and transfer among experts), quantitative models (which capture relationships as mathematical equations), data models (which capture relationships among data, often diagramatically), spatial models (e.g., GIS, paper maps), physical models (e.g., fuel beds in wind tunnels, sand and water hydrologic models), and financial models (which emphasize the timing and magnitudes of costs and benfits) **2.** *GIS* data representation of reality, e.g., spatial data models, include the **arc-node, georelational model, raster**s or **grid**s, **polygon**, and **TIN**s —*note* the terms modeling and analysis are often used interchangeably, although the former is more limited in scope

model validation the testing of a **model** by comparing model results with observations not used to develop the model

moderate burn a degree of burn in which all organic material is burned away from the surface of the soil, which is not discolored by heat, and any remaining fuel is deeply charred —*note* in a moderate burn, organic matter remains in the soil immediately below the surface —*see* **fire severity, light burn, severe burn**

modular airborne fire-fighting system (MAFFS) a manufactured unit consisting of five interconnecting tanks, a control pallet, and a nozzle pallet, with a capacity of 3,000 gal (11,356 l) designed to be rapidly mounted inside an unmodified C-130 (Hercules) cargo aircraft for use in **cascading fire retardant** on wildfires

modulus **1.** the measure of a quantity that depends on two or more other quantities **2.** a constant indicating the relation between the amount of physical effect (**strain**) and that of the forces producing it (**loading, stress**)

modulus of elasticity a measure of wood deformation under an applied load equal to the ratio of **stress** to **strain** within the elastic range (when strain is proportional to the applied stress) —*note* modulus of elasticity is an indication of **stiffness;** modulus of elasticity (E) = normal stress/normal strain —*synonym* Young's modulus (of elasticity), coefficient of elasticity —*see* **modulus of rigidity, modulus of rupture, moment of inertia of cross section**

modulus of rigidity the shearing **stress** required to produce a shearing **strain** of unity, i.e., modulus of rigidity (G) = shearing stress/shearing strain —*synonym* modulus of elasaticity in shear, shear modulus —*see* **modulus of elasticity, modulus of rupture**

modulus of rupture a measure of the maximum wood fiber stress at failure (compression or tension) under an applied bending load —*see* **modulus of elasticity, modulus of rigidity**

moisture content the percentage of water in a substance —*note* the moisture content of wood is normally calculated as a percentage of oven-dry weight for solid wood products and as a percentage of total or green weight for paper or wood fuel products

mold a fungus with a visible surface growth of **mycelium** or **spore**s —*note* molds are commonly woolly or powdery

mollic epipedon a surface **horizon** of mineral soil that is dark and relatively thick, contains at least 5.8 g kg^{-1} of organic carbon, is not massive and hard or very hard when dry, has a **base saturation** of > 50 percent, has < 110 mg P kg^{-1} soluble in

0.05 M citric acid, and is dominantly saturated with divalent cations

molt —*see* **ecdysis**

moment of inertia of cross section a factor related to the size and shape of the cross section of a beam; for a rectangular cross section it is equal to breadth × depth ÷ ¹/4 —*note* the product of the **modulus of elasticity** × moment of inertia of cross section is termed the flexural rigidity, which for a given span and **loading** determines the deflection of the beam —*see* **stiffness**

monitoring the collection of information over time, generally on a sample basis by measuring change in an indicator or **variable,** to determine the effects of resource management treatments in the long term —*see* **adaptive management, criteria and indicators**

monocarpic fruiting only once in its life, e.g., **annuals**

monoclimax theory the hypothesis that in any one environment, there can be only one **climax** community —*see* **polyclimax theory**

monoclonal blocks a deployment option for **clones** (or similarly for families in monofamily blocks) in which each clone (**family**) is established in a pure **block**

monocotyledon a plant whose seedling normally has a single seed leaf (**cotyledon**); a division of the **Angiospermae** —*note* monocotyledons are mainly herbaceous plants but include bamboos and palms —*see* **dicotyledon**

monoculture a **stand** of a single **species**, generally even-aged

monoecious a **population** or **species** having functional male and female **flowers** (or strobili) in separate places on the same plant —*see* **bisexual, dichogamy, dioecious, strobilus**

monopoly an industry in which there is only a single seller of a good or service —*note* the single seller can negotiate different prices with different purchasers and, at the extreme, can capture the surplus of all consumers

monsoon forest an open **woodland** in a tropical area that has a long dry season followed by a season of heavy rainfall —*synonym* tropical deciduous **forest** —*note 1.* trees in a monsoon forest usually shed their leaves during the dry season and come into leaf at the start of the rainy season —*note 2.* many lianas (woody vines) and herbaceous **epiphytes** are present in such forests —*note 3.* monsoon forests are especially well developed in Southeast Asia and are typified by tall teak trees and thickets of bamboo —*see* **rainforest**

montane 1. relating to mountains 2. pertaining to climate, **ecosystems**, or mountain species —*note* afromontane refers to the temperate South and East African **rainforests** that occur from Western Cape Province (where they grow at sea level) in the south to Ethiopia in the north

Monte Carlo method an analysis of data or simulation that relies on random sampling to generate values for probabilistic components

montmorillonite an aluminum silicate (**smectite**) with a 2:1 layer structure composed of two silica tetrahedral sheets and a shared aluminum and magnesium octahedral sheet —*note* montmorillonite has a permanent negative charge that attracts interlayer cations that exist in various degrees of hydration, thus causing expansion and collapse of the structure, i.e., shrink-swell

moor an open, uncultivated tract with a more or less peaty soil supporting low vegetation, typically coarse grasses and sedges, and with sphagnum and cotton "grasses" at higher and wetter elevations; less dry than **heath** and at its wettest, a **bog**

mop-up —*see* **fire suppression**

mop-up time —*see* **elapsed time**

mor an acid forest **humus** characterized by an accumulation of organic matter on the soil surface in matted **Oe** (F) **horizons**, reflecting the dominant mycogenous decomposers —*note 1.* the boundary between the organic horizon and the underlying mineral soil is abrupt —*note 2.* mors may form peat and are sometimes differentiated into the following groups: hemimor, humimor, resimor, lignomor, hydromor, fibrimor, and mesimor —*see* **mull**

moraine an accumulation of **drift,** with an initial topographic expression of its own, built chiefly by the direct action of glacial ice —*note* types of moraines include end, ground, lateral, recessional, and terminal

morph 1. a physiologically and morphologically distinct form of the same **species** 2. an individual of one particular form —*see* **dimorphism**

morphogenesis the process of differentiation of cells into different tissues or structures

morphology 1. the external and internal form and structure of whole plants, organs, tissues, or cells 2. the study of such form and structure, including life cycles of organisms —*note* internal morphology is often known as anatomy —*see* **phenotype, physiological character, taxonomy**

mortality 1. *silviculture* trees dying from natural causes, usually by size class in relation to sequential inventories or subsequent to incidents such as storms, wildfire, or insect and disease epidemics 2. *wildlife* the loss to a population from all lethal causes, i.e., hunter kill, poaching, predation, accident, and disease —*note* mortality is a statistic generally expressed as a mortality rate (death rate, casualty rate) per 1,000, derived from the mean number of deaths divided by the mean population —*see* **recruitment, turnover**

mosaic, aerial an assemblage of overlapping aerial or space photographs or **images** whose edges have been matched to form a continuous representation of a portion of the earth's surface

mottle *soils* a spot or blotch of a different color or shade of color interspersed with the dominant color —*see* **redoximorphic feature**

MOU —*see* **memorandum of understanding**

mound planting **1.** setting out young trees on a small heap of soil to promote aeration and free drainage (particularly on wet sites) and reduce competition —*see* **bed** **2.** on dry ground, setting out young trees with the roots spread over a cone of soil at the bottom of a dug hole

mountain and valley winds a system of diurnal winds along the axis of a valley, blowing uphill and upvalley by day and downhill and downvalley by night —*note* such winds prevail mostly in calm, clear weather —*see* **canyon wind, chinook**

mountain wind —*see* **mountain and valley winds**

move-up *fire* a system of redistributing remaining personnel and equipment following dispatch of other forces among a network of fire stations, to prepare for possible new emergencies

MPT —*see* **multipurpose tree**

MSA —*see* **metropolitan statistical area**

MSS —*see* **multispectral sensor**

muck soil an **organic soil** in which the plant residues have been altered beyond recognition

mulch any loose covering on the surface of the soil whether natural, such as litter, or deliberately applied organic residues like cut grass, straw, foliage, bark, or sawdust, or artificial materials like cellophane, glass-wool, metal foil, paper, plastic, or fiber —*note* mulch is used mainly to conserve moisture and check weed growth

mull a forest **humus** characterized by intimate incorporation of organic matter into the upper mineral soil, i.e., a well-developed **A horizon**, in contrast to accumulation on the surface —*note* mulls are sometimes differentiated into the following groups: vermimull, rhizomull, and hydromull —*see* **mor**

multiaged (multicohort) stand a **stand** with two or more age classes or cohorts —*see* **age class, cohort, uneven-aged stand**

multiagency coordination system (MACS) a combination of facilities, equipment, personnel, procedures, and communications responsible for coordi-

nating **resources** from assisting agencies and for providing support to multiagency emergency operations —*note* MACS is an **ICS** term

multiclonal mixture a mixture of **clones** in (usually) equal proportions for use in forest **plantations**

multidisciplinary team a group of experts in which each member independently develops and contributes specific assigned pieces of information toward the resolution of a problem —*see* **interdisciplinary team**

multiline a **subline** of the general **breeding population** purposefully selected for different sets of **traits** or deployment destinations —*synonym* breeding group —*see* **production population**

multinodal pertaining to conifers that form more than one whorl of branches each year —*see* foxtail, **uninodal**

multiparasitization the simultaneous **infestation** of an individual **host** by two or more species of primary **parasites** —*synonym* multiparasitism —*see* **hyperparasitization**

multiple cropping cropping patterns in which more than one crop is cultivated in a field in the same year, e.g., intercropping or sequential intercropping —*synonym* polyculture —*see* **multistory cropping**

multiple objective programming —*see* **programming**

multiple regression equation a statistical formulation with two or more independent **variables** —*note* when there are exactly two independent variables, the relationship between the dependent variable and the two independent variables can be represented graphically by a plane in a three-dimensional space —*see* **regression**

multiple-stage breeding —*see* **sequential testing, combined test**

multiple use *Federal Land Policy and Management Act of 1976* the management of the public lands and their various resource values so that they are utilized in the combination that will best meet the present and future **needs** of the American people; making the most judicious use of the land for some or all of these resources or related services over areas large enough to provide sufficient latitude for periodic adjustments in use to conform to changing needs and conditions; the use of some land for less than all of the resources; a combination of balanced and diverse resource uses that takes into account the long-term needs of future generations for **renewable** and **nonrenewable resource**s including, but not limited to, recreation, range, timber, minerals, watershed, wildlife and fish, and natural scenic, scientific, and historic values; harmonious and coordinated management of the various resources without permanent impairment of the productivity of the land and the quality of the environment; this combination is not necessarily the one that will give the greatest economic return or the greatest unit output

multiple-use forestry any practice of **forestry** fulfilling two or more objectives of management —*note 1.* multiple uses may be integrated at one site or segregated from each other —*note 2.* the Multiple-Use Sustained Yield Act of 1960 identified the following multiple uses: timber, **range,** watershed, wildlife and fish, and outdoor recreation —*synonym* multiple-purpose forestry, multiple-resource forestry —*see* **national forest**

multiplier the numerical coefficient showing how much one measure will increase from a unit increase in a second measure —*note 1.* e.g., if an increase in exports or in investment of $100,000 raises the national income by $500,000, the multiplier is 5.0 —*note 2.* the two measures used to define the multiplier must be linked in a cause-effect relationship —*note 3.* the concept was developed by John M. Keynes (1883–1946) and popularized as a way of comparing the impact of investments on creating additional national income —*see* **accelerator**

multipopulation breeding —*see* **multiline**

multipurpose tree (MPT) a tree or **shrub** that is deliberately kept and managed for more than one preferred use, product, or service

multispan skyline *harvesting* a skyline having one or more intermediate supports

multispectral scanner (MSS) an imaging system for recording the brightness of earth surface features within several spectral **band**s simultaneously —*see* **hyperspectral scanner**

multistory cropping the cultivation of a large variety of mostly multipurpose plants in various vegetation layers to maximize the use of environmental factors such as water, nutrients, and sunlight —*synonym* multistoried system —*see* **multiple cropping**

multivariate analysis the branch of statistics concerned with analyzing multiple measurements that have been made on one or several individuals —*synonym* multivariate data analysis

multivoltine a life cycle in which more than two **brood**s or generations are produced in a single year —*see* **bivoltine, univoltine**

Munsell color system a system that specifies the relative degrees of the three variables of color: **hue** (red, yellow, green, blue, and purple), **value** (lightness), and **chroma** (strength or departure from

neutral) —*note* e.g., 10YR 6/4 is a color (of soil) whose hue = 10YR, value = 6, and chroma = 4

muskeg 1. a **bog,** usually a sphagnum bog, frequently with tussocks of deep accumulations of organic material, growing in wet, poorly drained **boreal** areas, often areas of permafrost **2.** a tract of partly forested peatland supporting mosses (particularly sphagnum), **shrubby** plants (particularly Ericaceae) and scattered *Picea* and *Larix* trees **3.** the peat itself on such a tract

mutation a heritable change in the genetic constitution often recognized as a sudden deviation from the ancestral **phenotype** —*note* a changed individual or part is also known as a mutation or mutant —*see* **adaptation, chromosome, ecological niche, evolution, gene, lethal gene, polyploid, recombination**

mutation rate the frequency with which a **gene** or **chromosome** changes its **DNA** sequence —*see* **evolution, mutation**

mutualism an interaction between the individuals of two or more **species** in which the growth, growth rate, or population size of both are increased in a reciprocally beneficial association

mutual threat zone *fire* **1.** an area in which a fire would endanger two or more surrounding jurisdictions and prompt them to mount an initial attack —*synonym* mutual response zone, initial attack zone **2.** a predetermined area that spans both sides of a protection boundary, such that a fire burning on one side and under the jurisdiction of one agency would threaten the other side, which is under the jurisdiction of another agency

mycelial form one of several specialized forms of a **mycelium** (a) mycelial fan: a fan-shaped mass of hyphae formed between bark layers or between the bark and wood of trees, (b) mycelial felt, plaque, plate, or fungal mat: the hyphae aggregate into dense, compact masses resembling felt cloth or paper, occupy cracks or cavities in the **host** tissue, are usually thicker than mycelial fans, and are common in *Fomes laricis*, (c) mycelial cord or strand: an aggregation of mycelia into filamentous strands, (d) rhizomorph: an aggregation of mycelia into cordlike or tapelike strands with a melanized outer layer and a specialized cortex, e.g., *Armillaria* root disease, (e) sclerotium: a densely compacted mass of hyphae varying in size from minute to several inches in diameter

mycelium *plural* **mycelia** the vegetative part of a fungus, composed of **hyphae** and forming a **thallus** —*see* **rhizomorph, sclerotium**

mycology the science dealing with fungi

mycorrhiza *plural* **mycorrhizae** the usually symbiotic association between higher plant roots (**host**) and mycelia of specific fungi that aid plants in the uptake of water and certain nutrients and may offer protection against other soil-borne organisms —*note* mycorrhizal types include ectotrophic (**ectomycorrhiza**), endotrophic (**endomycorrhiza**), and **ectendomycorrhiza** —*see* **rhizomorph**

myrmecophyte **1.** a plant that offers specialized shelter or food for ants **2.** a plant pollinated by ants

N

narrow-sense heritability the ratio of **additive genetic variance** to phenotypic **variance** —*note* narrow-sense heritability is useful in predicting the response of a **population** to **natural selection** or to **pick-the-winner selection** —*see* **breeding value, heritability, phenotype**

narrow-spectrum pesticide a selective **pesticide** (usually an **insecticide**) that is toxic to one or a few **species** or species groups —*synonym* selective pesticide —*see* **broad-spectrum pesticide**

national fire danger rating system (NFDRS) a multiple index to assess various aspects of **fire danger** on a day-to-day basis

national forest a federal reservation, generally **forest, range,** or other **wildland,** that is designated by Executive Order or statute as a national forest or purchase unit, and other lands under the administration of the USDA Forest Service, including experimental areas and Bankhead-Jones Title III lands —*note* the Forest Service administers national forests under a program of multiple use and **sustained yield** for timber, range, watershed, wildlife and fish, and outdoor recreation —*see* **forest reserve, multiple use, multiple-use forestry**

national historical trail a trail having historical qualities that give it **recreational** potential of national significance —*note* a national historical trail must be established by historic use and can be designated only by Congress under the National Trail System Act of 1968

national historic park a federal area established to preserve and make available to the public evidence of historic events and places

national interagency fire qualification system (NIFQS) the acceptable standards for experience, training, and physical fitness required for principal jobs within a large **fire suppression** organization —*note* when coupled with a **large fire organization,** NIFQS provides a complete system for **fire management**

national interagency incident management system (NIIMS) a common **command** system for day-to-day operational procedures that can be expanded to manage major single or multijurisdictional emergencies —*see* **incident command system**

national military park a federal area established to preserve battlefields significant to the nation's military history

national monument a federal area established under the Antiquities Act of 1906 to preserve and make available to the public a resource of archaeological, scientific, historic, or aesthetic interest

national park a federal area administered by the

National Park Service of the US Department of the Interior to conserve the scenery, the flora and fauna, and any natural and historic objects within its boundaries for public enjoyment in perpetuity

national recreation trail a trail with recreation potential —*note* a national recreation trail may be designated by the Secretaries of Agriculture and Interior under the National Trails System Act of 1968

national scenic trail a trail with natural or scenic qualities that give it **recreation** potential —*note* a national scenic trail has national significance and can be established only by Congress under the National Trails System Act of 1968

national wildfire coordinating group (NWCG) a national interagency operational group authorized by the US Secretaries of Agriculture and Interior and designed to coordinate **fire management** programs of participating federal, state, local, and private agencies to avoid wasteful duplication and to facilitate working together —*note* the group provides a formalized system to agree on standards of organization, training, equipment, operations, and other facets of fire management

native species 1. an indigenous **species** that is normally found as part of a particular **ecosystem 2.** a species that was present in a defined area prior to European settlement

natural area a physical and biological area in nearly natural condition that exemplifies an ecological community and its associated vegetation and other biotic, soil, geologic, and aquatic features —*note* a natural area is maintained in a natural condition by allowing physical and biological processes to operate, usually without direct human intervention, but treatments such as fire suppression or **prescribed burn**ing may be permitted

natural fire any fire of natural origin (e.g., lightning, spontaneous combustion, and volcanic activity), which is allowed to burn because it is accomplishing one or more resource management objectives —*see* **forest fire, prescribed natural fire, wildfire**

natural fuel —*see* **fuel type**

naturalize *of an alien or exotic species* to establish, grow, reproduce, and maintain itself in an area where it did not originally grow

natural pruning the process of branch death and shedding caused by physical and biotic agents, such as shading, fungi, and wind, snow, or ice breakage —*synonym* self-pruning —*see* **habitat, pruning**

natural range the geographical and elevational limits within which an organism occurs naturally —*see* **habitat, home range**

natural regeneration the establishment of a plant or

a plant age class from natural **seeding,** sprouting, suckering, or layering

natural resin 1. secretions of certain trees, or of insects feeding on them, which are oxidation or polymerization products of terpenes, consisting of mixtures of aromatic acids and esters insoluble in water but soluble in ether, alcohol, or other organic solvents —*note 1.* natural resins often exude from wounds and are obtained commercially by tapping or by extraction with solvents —*note 2.* natural resins are sometimes designated hard (having little **essential oil** and high melting points, like copal) or soft (with considerable amounts of essential oil and lower melting points, like **oleoresin** and balsam) **2.** the resin actually present in the living tree, in contrast to the exuded resin, which is subject to immediate chemical change —*synonym* **pitch** —*see* **wound gum**

natural selection the process by which the genetic makeup of a population changes under natural conditions, without human interference, on the basis of its ability to become better adapted, survive, or reproduce in a particular set of environmental conditions —*see* **selection**

natural-seminatural area an area dominated by native or naturalized vegetation that has not been cultivated or treated with any annual management or manipulation regime —*note* where it cannot be assessed whether the vegetation was originally planted or cultivated by humans, the vegetation is considered natural-seminatural

naval stores gum naval stores include pine **oleoresins** such as pitch, tar, spirits of turpentine, and **rosin;** wood naval stores include products extracted by solvents and steam from wood or from pitch-soaked stumps (**fatwood**) —*note* the term is still in current use although mainly of historical interest

navigable 1. capable of being used by humans for water-borne transportation **2.** *legal* (a) interstate waters, intrastate lakes, rivers, and streams which are utilized by interstate travelers for recreational or other purposes; (b) intrastate lakes, rivers, and streams from which fish or shellfish are taken and sold in interstate commerce; and (c) intrastate lakes, rivers, and streams that are utilized for industrial purposes by industries in interstate commerce

neatline *GIS* a line commonly drawn around the extent of a map to enclose the map, legend, scale, title, and other information, keeping all the information pertaining to that map in one so-called neatbox

necrosis the death of a cell or tissue while still part of a living organism —*see* **lesion**

needle cast —*see* **leaf cast**

needle hole —*see* **insect hole**

needle mine —*see* **leaf mine**

needle roller —*see* **leaf roller**

needs the fundamental physical or mental motivations and requirements of people —*note* needs are differentiated from wants or desires

nematode a primitive, slender, unsegmented worm, circular in cross section, of the phylum Nematoda —*note* some species of nematodes are parasitic on animals or plants, including pinewood **nematode** *(Bursaphelenchus xylophilus)* —*synonym* eelworm, roundworm

NEPA procedures the process by which a US federal resource agency complies with the requirements of the National Environmental Policy Act of 1969

net annual growth the average annual net increase in the volume of trees during the period between inventories —*note* components of net annual growth include the increment in net volume of trees at the beginning of the period surviving to the end of the period, plus the net volume of trees reaching the minimum size class during the year, minus the volume of trees that died and the net volume of trees that became cull during the period

net present value —*see* **present net worth**

net primary production 1. the gross primary production minus biomass used in respiration by primary producers **2.** the amount of food in an **ecosystem** available for primary consumers —*see* **gross primary production**

net public benefit the overall long-term value to the nation of all outputs and positive effects (benefits), less all associated inputs and negative effects (costs), whether they can be quantitatively valued or not —*note* net public benefits are measured using both quantitative and qualitative criteria rather than by a single measure or index

net scale the actual amount of merchantable wood contained in a log (as opposed to gross scale, which includes defect) —*synonym* net volume

net value change (NVC) the sum of changes resulting from increases (benefits) and decreases (damages) in the value of outputs from the area affected as a result of fire

network 1. *GIS* a system of interconnected elements through which resources can be passed or transmitted, e.g., a road network with cars as the resource or stream network with sediment as the resource **2.** *computers* the means by which computers connect and communicate with each other or with peripherals

network analysis an approach commonly used to address transportation, assignment, and transshipment problems, involving graphical representation of the relationships with the system entities as numbered circles (nodes) interconnected by a series of directional (arrowheaded) lines (arcs)

neutral allele an **allele** subject to no (or very weak) selection pressure —*note* a neutral allele is useful as an evolutionary benchmark for **mating-system** estimation and similar studies requiring the absence of **selection**

neutralism the lack of interaction between two organisms (or species); neither has any effect on the other

neutral stability the state of an unsaturated or saturated column of air in the atmosphere when its environmental lapse rate of temperature is equal to the **dry-adiabatic lapse rate** or the **saturation-adiabatic lapse rate,** respectively

NFDRS —*see* **national fire danger rating system**

niche 1. the ultimate unit of the **habitat,** i.e., the specific spot occupied by an individual organism **2.** by extension, the more or less specialized relationships existing between an organism, individual or **synusia,** and its environment **3.** the specific set of environmental and habitat conditions that permit the full development and completion of the life cycle of an organism —*note* the ecological niche of a **species** is the functional role of the species in a **community**; the fundamental niche is the totality of environmental variables and functional roles to which a species is adapted; the realized niche is the niche a species normally occupies

NIFQS —*see* **national interagency fire qualification system**

NIIMS —*see* **national interagency incident management system**

NIPF —*see* **nonindustrial private forest**

nitrate reduction the process whereby nitrate is reduced by plants and microorganisms to ammonium for cell synthesis (nitrate assimilation, assimilatory nitrate reduction) or to nitrite by bacteria using nitrate as the terminal electron acceptor in **anaerobic** respiration (respiratory nitrate reduction, dissimilatory nitrate reduction) —*note* the term is sometimes used synonymously with denitrification

nitrification biological oxidation of ammonium to nitrite and nitrate, or a biologically induced increase in the oxidation state of nitrogen

nitrogen fixation the conversion of elemental nitrogen (N_2) from the atmosphere to organic combinations or to forms readily utilizable in biological processes —*note* symbiotic nitrogen fixation is accomplished by nodule bacteria in legumes, by other microorganisms in certain nodulated nonlegumes, and by blue-green algae in some lichens

node **1.** the slightly enlarged portion of the stem from which branches, leaves, or flowers originate —*see* **whorl 2.** *GIS* the beginning and ending locations of an **arc 3.** *GIS* the location where lines connect **4.** *graph theory* the location at which three or more **lines** connect **5.** *computers* the point at which one computer attaches to a communication network **6.** the three corner points of each triangle in a **triangulated irregular network (TIN);** every sample point input to a TIN becomes a node in the triangulation; a triangle **node** is topologically linked to all triangles that meet at the node

node match tolerance *GIS* the minimum radial distance within which two nodes will be joined (matched) to form one node

nodum any abstract classificatory unit of vegetation, irrespective of category or hierarchy; analogous to taxon in systematic botany —*see* **community**

NOI —*see* **notice of intent**

NOMEX® the trade name of a fire-resistant synthetic material used for the clothing of **fire fighters** —*note* the generic name for NOMEX is aramid

nominal density density based on **oven-dry** weight and the volume when tested, commonly when the wood is green or at 50 percent or 12 percent moisture content but also when air-dry

nominal size *utilization* **1.** the dimensions of lumber before machining **2.** the dimensions of lumber after sawing or machining, having recognized tolerances —*synonym* nominal measure

nomogram a form of line chart for the graphical solution of equations, on which scales for the variables involved in a particular formula are so set that corresponding values for each variable lie on a straight line intersecting all the scales —*synonym* **alignment chart**

nonadditive gene effects —*see* **dominance, epistasis**

nonadditive genetic variation the proportion of genetic variation that causes specific pair-wise crosses to depart from performance values predicted by the **breeding value**s of the parents —*see* **additive genetic variation**

nonattainment the failure of a geographic area to attain or maintain compliance with National Ambient Air Quality Standards (NAAQS) as defined by the Clear Air Act (1990 revision)

nonattainment area a geographic area that has failed to attain or maintain compliance with air quality standards —*note 1.* boundaries of nonattainment areas are commonly the same as city, standard metropolitan statistical area, or county boundaries —*note 2.* nonattainment areas often limit the use of prescribed fire or "let burn" practices

nonchargeable volume timber harvest not included in the **allowable sale quantity** calculations

nonconsumptive use use that does not reduce the supply or capability of production of resources

nondeclining yield a flow of goods or services from a **forest** that does not decrease in successive periods —*note* the sequential flow pattern specifying the percent increase or decrease in successive periods is $H_j+1 \geq (1 - \alpha) H_j$ where H = level of **yield,** j = period (year), and α = percentage decrease in yield from the subsequent period (ranging between 0 and 1) —*see* **evenflow yield**

nonfeasible solution a combination of **decision variable**s in which at least one **constraint** is violated —*synonym* in**feasible solution**

nonindustrial private forest (NIPF) forest land that is privately owned by individuals or corporations other than **forest** industry and where management may include objectives other than timber production —*see* **industrial forest**

nonlinear programming —*see* **programming**

nonnative a plant grown outside its natural range —*see* **escape, exotic, indigenous, seed source**

nonorthogonal data data that lead to estimates of various effects not independent of one another, or possibly of other features such as **block** differences that complicate the analysis —*note* the disadvantage of such material is that the effects thus mixed up may prove inextricable or may require a complicated technique for their disentanglement —*see* **principal component analysis, orthogonality**

nonpoint source pollution —*see* **pollution**

nonpored wood wood devoid of **vessel**s and therefore of pores —*note* nonpored wood is characteristic of all **conifer**s and a few woody dicotyledons —*see* **softwood**

nonrenewable resource a resource whose total physical quantity does not increase significantly with time and consequently is diminished through use —*note* in an economic sense, a resource may be nonrenewable when costs of further production are larger than potential revenues —*see* **renewable resource**

nontarget species a plant or animal species against which a suppression measure or **pesticide** is not directed —*see* **target species**

nontimber forest products all forest products except timber, including resins, oils, leaves, bark, plants other than trees, fungi, and animals or animal products —*synonym* special forest products —*see* **forest farming**

nonuse **1.** *management planning* forest resource values such as **environmental and amenity value**s, nonconsumptive user values, existence values, bequest values, and option values **2.** *range management* absence of grazing use on the current year's forage production **3.** *range management* lack of exercise, temporarily, of a grazing privilege on grazing lands **4.** *range management* an authorization to temporarily refrain from placing **livestock** on public **range**s without loss of preference for future consideration —*see* **permit holder, stocking**

nonvascular relating to a plants not having phloem- and xylem-conducting elements —*see* **bryophyte, lichen** —*note* in some regions, cover of nonvascular **species** may exceed that of trees, **shrub**s, dwarf shrubs, and **herb**s

nonvegetated a class with less than 1 percent vegetation **cover** naturally or from which vegetation is removed and replaced by human-made surfaces or structures

nonwoody root a root lacking **secondary xylem**

normal *meteorology* the average value of a weather variable (such as temperature, humidity, wind, sunshine, and pollutants) at a given location, used in the context of climate, and calculated over periods of 30 years or more unless otherwise stated

normal curve a symmetrical, statistical distribution applicable to many continuous variables —*note* a normal distribution produces a bell-shaped curve when frequency is plotted against observed values

normal diameter *of a standing tree* the estimated diameter of a tree at breast height after allowance has been made for buttresses

normal distribution a commonly used **probability** distribution whose probability density function is symmetric and defined by two parameters, the mean and the **variance** —*synonym* **Gaussian distribution**, normal frequency distribution —*note* the wide utility of the normal distribution is a direct consequence of the central limit theorem

normal forest *obsolete* a **forest,** composed of **normal stand**s, that has reached a conceptual ideal in **stocking** and age- and size-class distribution — *note 1.* a particular forest can be compared with a normal forest to identify treatments that may be needed for sustained timber management —*note 2.* a normal forest has a normal age-class distribution, i.e., a complete series of age classes that permits equal volume (normal) **yield**s from annual or periodic fellings under the given **rotation** and silvicultural system; the growth of a normal forest is called the normal increment

normalize *computers* a method by which a datafile within an **RDBMS** is decomposed or divided into smaller, yet related tables

normal stand a growing area whose space is assumed to be fully occupied but which has ample room for the development of crop trees —*note* a normal **stand** is assumed to have average maximum competition or the average density of a fully stocked stand

normal strain —*see* **strain**

normal stress —*see* **strees**

normal yield table —*see* **yield table**

northings the y-coordinates in a plane-coordinate system —*see* **eastings**

nosebar *papermaking* a bar used to compress the wood of a peeler log ahead of the cutting edge of a lathe —*synonym* pressure bar

notice of intent (NOI) *federal land management* the first formal step in the **environmental impact statement** process, consisting of a notice with the following information: a description of the proposed action and alternatives; a description of the agency's proposed scoping process, including scoping meetings; and the name and address of the persons to contact within the **lead agency** regarding the environmental impact statement

noxious plant (weed) a plant specified by law as being especially undesirable, troublesome, and difficult to control

nucleotide the building block of **DNA** and **RNA,** consisting of a phosphate group, a sugar, and a purine or pyrimidine base

nucleus the component of a cell that is made up chiefly of **chromosomes** —*see* **cytoplasm, double fertilization, mitosis**

null hypothesis *in a statistical test of significance* the **assumption** that states a parameter's relationship (usually equivalence) to a fixed value or to another parameter —*note* in order to reject the null hypothesis, a test statistic must indicate a sufficiently low **probability** (usually 0.05 or 0.01) of observing the sample data under the null hypothesis

nuptial chamber a cell or chamber excavated by certain **bark beetles** under the **host** bark, in which mating takes place

nuptial flight a mating flight, usually in reference to ants, bees, or **termite**s

nursery an area set aside for the raising of young trees (the nursery stock) including **bare-root** and **container** seedlings for outplanting, having seedling or transplant beds or both —*see* **field nursery**

nursery bed a specially prepared plot in a **nursery** where seed is sown or into which transplants or cuttings are put

nurse tanker a water tank truck used to supply one or more ground tankers stationed at a fire —*synonym* mother tanker

nurse tree a tree, group, or crop of trees, shrubs or other plants, either naturally occurring or introduced, used to nurture, improve survival, or improve the form of a more desirable tree or crop when young by protecting it from frost, insolation, wind, or insect attack —*synonym* nurse crop

nutrient budget a statement of gains or losses of all the nutrients for a given area —*note* a nutrient budget sometimes includes an indication of the distribution of the nutrients among such categories as soil, parent material, stream water, vegetation, fauna, and atmosphere

nutrient cycle the exchange or transformation of elements among the living (organic and biotic) and nonliving (inorganic and abiotic) components of an **ecosystem**

nutrient deficiency the level within a plant at which any decline in concentration of a specific nutrient reduces growth or normal plant function —*note* nutrient deficiencies can result from an imbalance in nutrient ratios

nutrient status a measure of the degree to which the nutritional requirements of an organism are satisfied under a given set of conditions

nutritive ratio *range management* the proportion of digestible crude protein in a **livestock** feed relative to the combined digestible carbohydrates and fat

NVC —*see* **net value change**

NWCG —*see* **national wildfire coordinating group**

nymph **1.** *insects* the immature **stage** of an insect with incomplete **metamorphosis,** having all adult structures but differing from the adult mainly in its incompletely developed wings and genitalia **2.** *Acari (mites and ticks)* the immature stage that has eight legs —*see* **adult, nymph**

O

Oa horizon —*see* **horizon**

oak apple —*see* **gall wasp**

object *computers* a software packet containing a collection of related data (in the form of variables) and methods (procedures) for operating on those data —*note* the term is used inconsistently, referring sometimes to instances (a particular set of variables and procedures) and other times to **class**es (a group of instances)

object database management system (ODBMS) a database management system built specifically to store and retrieve objects rather than simple data types

objective —*see* **management objective**

objective function a mathematical expression used to represent a criterion for evaluating solutions to a problem —*note* an objective function is either maximized or minimized in the solution to the problem

obligate relating to a species that is limited in its **habitat** to few, specific environmental conditions, or a parasite or pathogen to a specific host —*note* the term is usually used in reference to a species that occurs in a **wetland** or upland habitat; if the species is very likely (> 99 percent frequency) to be found in a wetland, it would be called an **obligate** wetland species; if the species is very likely (> 99 percent frequency) to be found in an upland, it would be called an obligate upland species —*see* **facultative**

obligate parasite a **parasite** incapable of existing independent of a host —*see* **facultative parasite**

oblique aerial photograph an aerial photograph taken with some angular deviation from the vertical —*note* a high oblique includes the apparent horizon of the earth; a low oblique does not show the horizon

observation well a hole bored to a desired depth below the ground surface, used for observing the water table or **piezometric surface**

occluded front *meteorology* a composite of two **front**s formed when a cold front overtakes a warm front or a quasi-stationary front

occlusion the healing over (closing) of wounds on tree stems —*see* **callus**

ochric epipedon a surface **horizon** of mineral soil that is too light in color, too high in **chroma,** too low in organic carbon, or too thin to be a **plaggen, mollic, umbric, anthropic,** or **histic epipedon**

ocular-estimate-by-plot method a technique for determining the **cover** and composition of **range** vegetation in rangeland surveys by use of plots on which the area occupied by each species per unit area is estimated by eye —*note* this method is contrasted with the weight method —*synonym* ocular plot estimate, plot estimate method, square-foot method

Oe horizon —*see* **horizon**

off-highway vehicle (OHV) —*see* **off-road vehicle (ORV)**

off-road vehicle (ORV) a vehicle operated away from roads or on secondary roads such as forest roads for **recreation** experience or for access for other activities —*note* state vehicle operator licenses and equipment requirements may not be required for ORVs —*synonym* off-highway vehicle (OHV) —*see* **all-terrain vehicle (ATV)**

ogee profile of a weir, overflow dam, or spillway shaped as a compound reverse S curve with the crest being a convex curve and the outfall section being a concave curve

O horizon —*see* **horizon**

Oi horizon —*see* **horizon**

old-growth forest the (usually) late **successional** stage of **forest** development —*note 1.* old-growth forests are defined in many ways; generally, structural characteristics used to describe old-growth forests include (a) live trees: number and minimum size of both seral and **climax** dominants, (b) canopy conditions: commonly including multilayering, (c) snags: minimum number of specific size, and (d) down logs and **coarse woody debris:** minimum tonnage and numbers of pieces of specific size —*note 2.* old-growth forests generally contain trees that are large for their species and site and sometimes decadent (**overmature**) with broken tops, often a variety of tree sizes, large snags and logs, and a developed and often patchy understory —*note 3.* stand age, although a useful indicator of old growth, is often considered less important than structure because (a) the rate of stand development depends more on environment and stand history than age alone, and (b) **dominants** are often multiaged —*note 4.* due to large differences in forest types, climate, **site quality,** and natural disturbance history (e.g., fire, wind, and disease and insect epidemics), old-growth forests vary extensively in tree size, age classes, presence and abundance of structural elements, stability, and presence of understory —*note 5.* the minimum area needed for an old-growth forest to be a functional ecological unit depends on the nature and management of surrounding areas; small areas often do not contain all old-growth elements —*note 6.* an old-growth forest is commonly perceived as an uncut, virgin forest with very little human-caused disturbance; some believe that the time taken for stands to develop old-growth structure can be shortened by silvicultural treatments

aimed at producing the above characteristics —*synonym* primary forest —*see* **mature, second-growth forest, virgin forest**

oleoresin a group of soft **natural resins** consisting of a viscous mixture of **essential oil** (e.g., turpentine) and nonvolatile solids (e.g., **rosin**) secreted by the resin-forming cells of the pines and certain other coniferous and broad-leaved trees —*see* **naval stores**

oligogene a major **gene** that controls a **trait** —*see* **polygene, qualitative trait locus, simple Mendelian inheritance**

oligotrophic a **habitat** low in basic nutrients —*note* an oligotrophic habit is usually characterized by a low accumulation of dissolved nutrient salts, supporting only plant and animal life, having a high oxygen content owing to the low organic content, and with no marked stratification

ombrotrophic a **wetland** receiving hydrologic and mineral input from **precipitation** only

omnivory 1. the consumption by an animal of both plants and other animals **2.** the feeding on prey from more than one **trophic** level

one-lick method —*see* **fire suppression**

one-to-many *GIS* a type of relate connecting a unique value in one file to many records (that have the same value) in another file

on-grade 1. timber free from decay **2.** timber free from any defect not acceptable in the appropriate grade or for the particular end use —*synonym* clear, sound

ontogeny the developmental history of an individual organism over its **life cycle** from the **zygote** to maturity —*note* ontogeny is often interpreted to cover that of a taxonomic group, e.g., **species** —*see* **phylogeny**

open defect 1. *in veneer* any irregularity, e.g., checks, splits, open joints, cracks, knot holes, or loose knots, that interrupts the smooth, even surface of the veneer **2.** *in solid timber* any hole or split, natural or otherwise, that can be detected by the naked eye

open herding the act of allowing a herd to spread naturally while grazing —*see* **close herding, trail herding, open range**

open-pollinated progeny offspring from a mating where **pollination** is not controlled —*see* **open pollination**

open pollination a type of **pollination** in which a mixture of related and unrelated **pollen** is delivered by wind, insects, etc., and is usually not directly influenced by people —*note* as a **progeny-test** method, open pollination may provide information on **general combining ability** of the seed parents

—see **combining ability, controlled pollination, improved, open-pollinated progeny, wind pollination**

open range 1. grazing land that has not been fenced into **management units 2.** all suitable grazing land on which grazing is permitted **3.** untimbered **range**land **4.** grazing land on which the **livestock** owner has unlimited access without benefit of landownership or leasing *—see* **open herding**

operating system (OS) computer software that allows communication between the computer and the user by controlling the flow of data, the interpretation of other programs, the organization and management of files, and the display of information *—note 1.* for larger computers the operating system is usually supplied by the manufacturer *— note 2.* commonly known operating systems are VMS, VM/IS, UNIX, Windows, and NT, but there are many others

operations research the scientific approach to **decision making** that involves the operations of organizational systems *—see* **forest management, forest regulation**

operations section chief *—see* **incident command system**

opportunity cost the true cost of any action or item that can be measured by the value of the best alternative action or substitute item that must be foregone when the action is taken or the item is acquired

optical square a simple hand-held instrument, based on prisms or mirrors, for setting out right angles and establishing alignments

optimal solution the specific **decision variable** value or values that provide the "best" output for the **model**

optimum land use that feasible use which in the opinion of the decision maker provides the greatest increment of public welfare

optimum road spacing the distance between parallel roads giving the lowest combined cost of extraction and road construction per unit of log volume

oral toxicity the toxicity of a compound that, when given orally in a single dose, kills 50 percent of the ingesting animals *—note* oral toxicity is usually expressed as milligrams of chemical per kilogram of body weight of the animal

organ a differentiated structure of cells or tissues, which performs specific functions

organic pesticide a **pesticide** with organic compounds (containing carbon) including the **organochlorine** (chlorinated) **insecticide**s (e.g., DDT, chlordane) and the **organophosphate**s that

are derived from phosphoric acid esters (e.g., malathion, diazinon) *—see* **inorganic pesticide**

organic soil a soil in which the sum of the thicknesses of layers containing organic soil materials is generally greater than the sum of the thickness of mineral layers

organochlorine an **organic pesticide**, usually an **insecticide**, containing chlorine and hydrogen, including chlorinated hydrocarbons (e.g., DDT), cyclohexane derivatives (e.g., lindane), cyclodienes (e.g., chlordane), and polychloroterpenes *—note* organochlorine pesticides are toxic to vertebrates, persist in the environment, and accumulate in the food chain

organogenesis the process of differentiation of organs from cells and tissues

organophosphate an organic **pesticide**, usually an **insecticide**, derived from phosphoric acid, e.g., malathion and parathion *—note* organophosphates are environmentally hazardous but short-lived and nonpersistent *—synonym* organic phosphate, phosphorous insecticide

organosulfur an organic pesticide, usually an **acaricide** and miticide, that contains sulfur

oriented-strand board (OSB) *—see* **engineered wood composite**

original source the location of a native plant or plants from which seed or **propagule**s were collected

ornithophily pollination by birds *—see* **anemophily, entomophily**

orographic precipitation precipitation which results from the lifting of moist air over an orographic barrier such as a mountain range

orophyte a plant inhabiting hills and mountains

ortet the original plant (ancestor) from which a vegetatively propagated **clone** has been derived *—see* **ramet, vegetative propagation**

orthogonality 1. *in experimental design* the property that ensures that the various effects to be measured are not entangled in any way and the means are direct estimates of these effects **2.** the statistical independence of two variates or two linear functions of variates *—see* **canonical correlation analysis, nonorthogonal data, principal component analysis**

orthophotograph a photograph prepared from a perspective photograph by removing those displacements of points caused by **tilt**, relief, and central projection (perspective) *—note* displacement is radial from the **photograph nadir** that defines the geometry of the perspective or central projection

orthophotomap a map made by assembling a number of **orthophotograph**s into a single, composite picture with (usually) a **grid** added —*synonym* orthophotomosaic —*note* the map may be further improved by photographically emphasizing edges in the picture by adding color, symbols, etc.

orthotropism the tendency for a **propagule** to grow vertically —*see* **plagiotropism**

ortstein a cemented **spodic horizon**

ORV —*see* **off-road vehicle**

OS —*see* **operating system**

OSB oriented-strand board —*see* **engineered wood composite**

outcrossing mating unrelated individuals —*synonym* outbreeding —*see* **crossability, cross-pollination**

outfall the point at which water flows from a conduit, stream, or drain

outlet the point of water disposal from a stream, river, lake, tidewater, or artificial drain

outplanting the planting of seedlings raised in a greenhouse or nursery planting bed into the field

output 1. *economics* all the goods and services resulting from the economic activity of an individual, a firm, an industry, or a country —*note* the goods and services of others used in the process can be deducted to give the (economically more useful) net output —*see* **input 2.** *computers* the result of processing data **3.** *planning* any result, product, or service that a process or activity produces

output and substitution effects two effects that occur jointly when the price of an item changes; an output effect is the change in a firm's profitability resulting from a price change for a particular input or component; a substitution effect is the change in input mix adopted in response to an output effect to regain or increase profitability —*note* substitution effects result in a shift along the same isoquant whereas output effects cause the firm to move to a different isoquant —*see* **income and substitution effects, isoquant map**

outwash stratified detritus (chiefly **sand** and gravel) removed or "washed out" from a glacier by meltwater streams and deposited in front of or beyond the end **moraine** or the margin of an active glacier —*note* the coarser material is deposited nearer to the ice

outwash plain a flat area formed by sedimentation, carried to the site from a glacier, and deposited by changes in stream **carrying capacity**

ovary the female part of a **flower** that contains the ovules and develops into the **fruit**

oven-dry pertaining to wood that is dried to a constant weight in a ventilated oven at a temperature usually above the boiling point of water, generally $103° ± 2°C$ —*see* **normal density**

over-all application —*see* **broadcast**

overbrowsing repeated feeding on leaves and twigs of woody vegetation by ungulates that results in close-cropping and destruction of regeneration and even of the browse itself —*see* **browse line** —*note* excessive **grazing** is similarly termed **overgrazing**

overcut the harvesting of a quantity of timber in excess of the **allowable cut** —*see* **high grading, overrun, undercut, underrun**

overdominance *genetics* a special case of **dominance** in which the heterozygote is, on average, better than the best of the two homozygotes —*see* **heterosis, heterozygous, homozygous**

overgrazing continued heavy **grazing** that exceeds the recovery capacity of the community and creates a deteriorated **range**

overhead *fire* **1.** the supervisory or specialist personnel working in some capacity related to the control of a **going fire** (or fires) but not including leaders of regularly organized fire crews and equipment operators while engaged in their regularly assigned duties **2.** personnel assigned to supervisory positions, including incident commander, **command staff**, general staff, directors, supervisors, and unit leaders —*see* **incident command system, incident overhead**

overhead cost a cost that is not directly attributable to specific units of production, mainly **fixed costs** and **common costs** —*see* **short run**

overland flow water that travels over the ground surface to a point of concentration where turbulent flow occurs —*synonym* surface runoff

overlap those portions of an **aerial photograph** covering a ground area appearing on an adjacent aerial photograph, i.e., duplicated (a) along the **flight line** (forward overlap or endlap) and (b) between flight lines (lateral overlap or sidelap)

overlay 1. *GIS* a spatial operation such as a transparency superimposed on a map or a procedure using computers that combines two or more data sets —*note* e.g., an overlay can be performed between management units and soil data showing how much area of each management unit lies on which soil types, or vice versa **2.** a sheet material, e.g., plastic, bonded to the surface of (mainly) panel products, to provide a protective or decorative increase in strength, or a base for painting **3.** one or more sheets of paper impregnated with resin and used as face material, mainly over plywood but also on lumber or other products —*note* overlays can be classified as masking, decorative, or structural, depending on their purpose

overmature *of trees or stands* **1.** a tree or **even-aged stand** that has reached that stage of development when it is declining in vigor and health and reaching the end of its natural life span **2.** a tree or even-aged stand that has begun to lessen in commercial value because of size, age, decay, or other factors —*note* the term has little applicability to **uneven-aged stands**, which consist of trees of diverse ages and stages of development —*see* **mature, old-growth forest**

overrun the difference between the greater volume actually sawn over the lesser estimated **log scale** volume —*note* overruns are generally expressed as a percent of the log-scale volume —*see* **mill tally, overcut, underrun, utilization percent**

overshoot *GIS* that portion of a **line** digitized past its intersection with another line —*synonym* dangling line —*see* **spike**

overstory that portion of the trees, in a forest of more than one story, forming the upper or uppermost canopy layer, e.g., in a two-storied forest, seed bearers over regeneration, or standards over **coppice**

overstory removal the cutting of trees constituting an upper canopy layer to release trees or other vegetation in an understory —*see* **regeneration method**

overtopped —*see* **crown class**

overwintering fire a fire that persists through the winter months until the beginning of fire season —*see* **holdover fire**

ovicide an **insecticide** or other chemical that kills an organism's eggs

oviparous producing eggs that hatch outside the body of the female —*see* **viviparous, ovoviviparous**

ovoviviparous producing living young by the hatching of eggs while still within the female —*note* the term is used in contrast to **oviparous** and **viviparous**

ovulate having seed-bearing organs only —*note* ovulate may apply to individual **flowers**, strobili, or to female parts of **dioecious** species —*see* **pistillate, staminate, strobilus**

ovule **1.** the part of an ovary containing an egg cell and developing into a seed **2.** an immature seed —*see* **flower**

oxic horizon a mineral soil **horizon** at least 30 cm (11.8 in) thick and characterized by the virtual absence of weatherable primary minerals or 2:1 layer silicate **clays**, the presence of 1:1 layer silicate clays and highly insoluble minerals such as quartz **sand**, the presence of hydrated oxides of iron and aluminum, the absence of water dispersible clay and the presence of low **cation exchange capacity,** and the presence of small amounts of exchangeable bases

oxygen demand the amount of oxygen required by all the biological and chemical processes that occur in water —*see* **biochemical (biological) oxygen demand, chemical oxygen demand**

P

packing a temporary influx of organisms of various sex and age classes into remaining suitable habitat as previously available habitat is changed to unsuitable conditions

pack test *fire* a physical fitness test consisting of a 3 mi (4.8 km) hike with a 45 lb (20.5 kg) pack over level terrain to measure fitness for prolonged arduous work; a score of 45 minutes on the pack test approximates an aerobic fitness score of 45 (ml of oxygen per kg of body weight per min) —*synonym* work capacity —*see* **step test, work capacity**

PAI —*see* **periodic annual increment**

palatability the acceptability of a particular plant **species** or plant part to a herbivore —*note* palatability may vary with the season of the year —*see* **grazing preference** —*antonym* nonpalatability, unpalatability —*see* **proper-use factor**

paleoclimate the climate of a time period in the geologic past, e.g., a prehistoric climate

paleoecology the study of the relationships of past organisms and the environment in which they lived —*also* palaeoecology

palustrine pertaining to a marsh

pan *GIS* to move spatial data through the monitor window without changing the scale such that the viewable area is constantly changing

pandemic an **epidemic** that occurs simultaneously over a very large geographic area, particularly occurring in several parts of the world

panoramic photograph *fire* a photograph taken from a lookout point that includes **azimuth** and vertical angle scales to assist in locating fires with a **firefinder**

PAR —*see* **photosynthetically active radiation**

paradigm an acquired way of thinking about something that shapes thought and action in ways that are both conscious and unconscious —*note* paradigms provide a culturally shared **model** for how to think and act, but they can present major obstacles to adopting newer, better approaches

paradigm shift a transition from one **paradigm** to another —*note* paradigm shifts typically meet with considerable resistance followed by gradual acceptance as the superiority of the new paradigm becomes apparent

parallax *aerial survey* the algebraic difference (measured parallel to the **flight line**, positive in the direction of flight) between the distances of the **principal points** from corresponding **image** points in a stereoscopic pair of **aerial photographs**

—*synonym* X-parallax, absolute parallax —*see* **Y-parallax**

parallax bar a micrometer device used in conjunction with a stereoscope for measuring **parallax differences** —*note* a parallax bar incorporates two reference marks that can be usually fused to form a floating mark

parallax difference the difference in the **parallax** of two points **imaged** on an overlapping pair of **aerial photographs**, from which differences in elevation can be determined by means of **parallax bars** or **parallax wedges**

parallax wedge a simplified stereometer for measuring object heights on stereoscopic pairs of photographs —*note* a parallax wedge consists of two slightly converging rows of dots or graduated lines printed on a transparent base that can be stereoscopically fused into a single row or line for making **parallax** measurements to the nearest 0.002 in (0.005 cm)

parallel 1. a property of two or more lines that are separated at all points by the same distance 2. a horizontal line encircling the earth at a constant **latitude** —*note* the equator is a parallel with a latitude of 0°; measures of latitude are positive up to 90° above the equator and negative below

parallel attack —*see* **fire suppression**

parasite an organism that, for at least part of its life cycle, lives on or within a plant or animal of another **species** (the **host**) and derives subsistence from it without returning any benefit —*see* **epiphyte, parasitoid, pathogen, predator, saprophyte**

parasitism 1. the mode of life of a **parasite** 2. the relationship between an organism (**parasite**) that derives benefits from, and at the expense of, another organism (host) —*see* **commensalism, parasitization**

parasitization the act or state of **infestation** by one or more **parasites**

parasitoid an insect that hatches within a **host**, usually another insect, feeds on it during the **larval** stage, and becomes free-living when the host dies —*note 1.* parasitoid behavior is intermediate between **parasitism** and predation —*note 2.* parasitoids are sometimes considered **parasites** or **predators**

parenchyma —*see* **aerenchyma, cells (wood)**

parent material the unconsolidated and more or less chemically weathered mineral or organic matter from which the **solum** of the soil is developed by pedogenic processes —*see* **pedon**

pareto optimality an **allocation** of resources in which no individual can be made better off without making someone else worse off

parkland system *agroforestry* intercropping under scattered trees —*see* **agroforestry**

parthenocarpy the development of **fruit** without **fertilization,** as in the banana —*note* similar development of a (seedless) cone has been termed parthenocony —*see* **apomixis, incompatibility, parthenogenesis, sterility**

parthenogenesis reproduction from an unfertilized egg; a type of **apomixis** —*note* the resultant embryo from parthenogenesis may be either **haploid** or **diploid 2.** *pathology* the development of sexual reproduction from female **gamet**es alone —*see* **asexual reproduction, fertilization, parthenocarpy**

partial cutting removal of only part of a **stand** for purposes other than regenerating a new age class —*note* partial cutting is not considered a **regeneration method** —*synonym* **selective cutting** —*see* **harvest system, variable retention**

partial log suspension the lifting of one end of the log above the ground during **yard**ing operations

participatory forestry —*see* **social forestry**

particle board —*see* **engineered wood composite**

particle size distribution the fractions of the various soil separates (**sand, silt, clay**) in a soil sample, often expressed as mass percentages

partnership a relationship between different components of the public and private sectors to achieve mutually beneficial objectives

pasture 1. a grazing area enclosed and separated from other areas by fencing or other barriers; the **management unit** for grazing land **2.** the forage plants used as food for grazing animals **3.** any area devoted to the production of forage, native or introduced, and harvested by grazing **4.** a group of subunits grazed within a **rotational grazing** system **5.** to feed on pasture; to use as a pasture —*see* **grassland, range**

patana a xerophytic grassy slope in the Sri Lanka upland

patch 1. a small part of a stand or forest —*see* **group 2.** an **ecosystem** element, e.g., an area of vegetation, that is relatively homogeneous internally and differs from surrounding elements

patch cutting —see **regeneration method**

paternal effect a genetic difference resulting from the male (**pollen**) parent —*see* **c-effect, cytoplasmic inheritance, maternal effect**

pathfinding *GIS* the process by which a least-cost path is determined through a network or **grid** —*note* the cost element may be any descriptor such as slope, miles, or any other **impedance**

pathname *computers* the direction(s) to a file or directory location on a disk —*note 1.* pathnames are always specific to the computer operating system —*note 2.* computer operating systems use directories and files to organize data, and treelike, each branch on the tree represents a subdirectory or file; pathnames indicate locations in this hierarchy

pathogen a parasitic organism directly capable of causing disease

pathogenicity the ability of an organism to cause disease —*see* **virulence**

pathological disease a disease caused by a living organism

patrol *fire* **1.** to travel over a specified route to prevent, detect, and suppress fires **2.** to go back and forth vigilantly over a length of **control line** during or after construction to prevent **breakover**s, suppress **spot fire**s, and extinguish overlooked **hot spot**s **3.** to vigilantly check a **fireline** following **mop-up** until the fire is extinguished or considered safe from the danger of **escape 4.** a person or group of persons who carry out patrol actions —*see* **fire guard**

patrol time —*see* **elapsed time**

pattern *ecology* the spatial arrangement of **landscape** elements (**patch**es, **corridor**s, **matrices**) that determines the function of a landscape as an ecological system

payload 1. the gross weight of a loaded vehicle minus the weight of the vehicle itself **2.** *cable logging* the weight supported by the cables —*note* when logs are dragged, some weight is supported by the ground

PCT —*see* **precommercial thinning**

P/E —see **precipitation-evaporation ratio**

peak discharge —*see* **flood peak**

peak flow —*see* **flood peak**

peat organic soil material in which the original plant parts are recognizable (fibric material)

peat bog a bog with the dominant underlying material of peat —*see* **bog**

peavey *harvesting* a stout wooden lever fitted with a strong, sharp spike, used for rolling logs —*see* **cant hook**

ped a unit of soil **structure** such as a block, column, granule, plate, or prism, formed by natural processes —*note* peds are in contrast with clods, which are formed artificially

pedalfer a subdivision of a soil order comprising a large group of soils in which **sesquioxide**s increased relative to silica during soil formation —*note* this term is not used in the current US system of soil taxonomy —*see* **soil order**

pedigree a record of parentage, often including data on performance of the parents and of other relatives

pedocal a subdivision of a soil order comprising a large group of soils in which calcium accumulated during soil formation —*note* this term is not used in the current US system of soil taxonomy —*see* **soil order**

pedogenesis the process whereby soil is formed from parent material, i.e., rocks —*note* a pedogenic process is any process related to soil formation —*see* **solum**

pedon a three-dimensional body of soil with lateral dimensions large enough to permit the study of **horizon** shapes and relations —*note* its area ranges from 1 to 10 m² (10.8 to 107.6 ft²) —*see* **inclusion, parent material**

peduncle the stalk of a single **flower** or **fruit,** or the main stalk of a cluster of flowers or fruits —*see* **inflorescence, infructescence**

peel to convert wood into **veneer** by rotary cutting on a lathe

peeler a high-grade log from which **veneer** is **pee**led on a lathe or sliced for the production of **plywood**

peg-raker saw —*see* **saw**

peg-tooth saw —*see* **saw**

pelagic 1. relating to the open ocean **2.** relating to open water areas away from the shore and the bottom **3.** growing at or near the surface in water away from the shore

pellet 1. a mass of undigested hair, bones, feathers, elytra, etc. (from prey), regurgitated by a carnivorous bird or mammal **2.** any discrete dropping, typically of deer or sheep

peneplain a land surface eroded to almost a plain

perched groundwater groundwater that is separated from the main body of **groundwater** by unsaturated material —*see* **perched water table, water table**

perched water table a saturated layer of soil that is separated from any underlying saturated layers by an unsaturated layer —*see* **perched groundwater, water table**

percolation the downward movement of water through soil, especially the downward flow of water in saturated or nearly saturated soil, at hydraulic gradients of the order of 1.0 or less —*note* measures of percolation are unitless, i.e., cm/cm, mm/mm, or in/in

perennial stream a stream that has running water on a year-round basis under normal climatic conditions

perfect stage *pathology* the sexual **stage;** the phase in the life history of a fungus in which sexual **spore**s are formed

periderm —*see* **cells (wood)**

periodic annual increment (PAI) the growth of a tree or **stand** observed over a specific time period divided by the length of the period —*see* **mean annual increment (MAI), current annual increment (CAI), periodic increment**

periodic grazing the intermittent **grazing** of an area —*synonym* intermittent grazing —*note 1.* the term **periodic browsing** is used similarly —*note 2.* if the intermission is regular, the entire **range** is under rotational grazing —*note 3.* if the periods roughly correspond to one or more of the recognized seasons of the year, the grazing is termed seasonal grazing —*see* **grazing season**

periodic increment the growth of a tree or stand during any specified period, commonly 10 or 20 years —*see* **mean annual increment, periodic annual increment**

peripheral *computers* a component such as a **digitizer**, plotter, or printer that is not part of the central computer but is attached with communication cables —*synonym* peripheral devices

periphyton attached microscopic organisms growing on a lake bottom, or on other submerged substrates —*synonym* aufwuchs

permafrost 1. permanently frozen material underlying the **solum 2.** a perennially frozen soil **horizon** —*see* **taiga**

permanent wilting point the amount of water in a soil below which insignificant plant water uptake occurs —*note* permanent wilting point is generally regarded as the point at which soil matric potential is –1.5 MPa or –15 bars —*see* **available water**

permeability *soil* **1.** the ease with which gases, liquids, or plant roots penetrate or pass through a bulk mass of soil or a layer of soil —*note* since soil **horizon**s vary in permeability, permeability should be indicated for each horizon rather than for the soil as a whole **2.** the property of a porous medium itself that expresses the ease with which gases, liquids, or other substances can flow through it, and is the same as intrinsic permeability denoted by k —*note* permeability is measured by the rate at which a fluid of standard viscosity can move through material in a given interval of time under a given hydraulic gradient

permit holder —*see* **permittee**

permittee one who holds a permit to graze **livestock** or build or use roads on state, federal, or privately owned lands —*synonym* lessee, permit holder —*see* **grazing allotment, grazing fee, nonuse**

permutations all possible arrangements that may be formed from a given number of objects or elements

personal protective equipment (PPE) *fire* the equipment and clothing required to mitigate the risk of injury from or exposure to hazardous conditions encountered during firefighting —*note* personal protective equipment includes fire-resistant clothing, hard hat, flight helmet, shroud, goggles, gloves, respirator, hearing protection, chainsaw chaps, and shelter —*synonym* flame-resistant equipment

PERT —*see* **program evaluation and review technique**

per unit sale a timber sale in which the buyer and the seller negotiate a set price per unit of harvested wood, usually based on wood volume or weight and product class —*note* the buyer pays for the timber after it has been cut and the weight or volume has been determined —*synonym* pay-by-scale, pay-as-cut —*see* **lump-sum sale, sale schedule**

pest 1. an organism that is undesirable or detrimental to the interests of humans **2.** an organism capable of causing injury or damage —*note* although neither archaic nor inaccurate, the term pest has no ecological significance and its use today to describe insects and **pathogen**s is sometimes discouraged given these agents' ecological functions; however, a simple connotation-free term has not emerged to replace it

pesticide a chemical preparation used to control individuals or populations of injurious organisms —*see* **nontarget species, slurry, target species**

pest management the application of approved strategies to maintain a **pest**'s population within tolerable levels —*see* **integrated control, integrated pest management, plant health care**

pH *soil* the pH of a solution in equilibrium with soil —*note* pH is determined by means of a glass, quinhydrone, or other suitable electrode or indicator at a specified soil-solution ratio in a specified solution, usually distilled water, 0.01 M $CaCl_2$, or 1 M KCl —*see* **soil reaction**

phanerophyte 1. a land plant whose buds and shoot apices survive the unfavorable season and project on above-ground stems that persist from year to year and often for many years —*note* the phanerophyte is one of the major (noncryptophytic) life-forms of Raunkiaer **2.** of subdivisions by size, a phanerophyte 2 m (6.6 ft) high is termed a nanophanerophyte and one > 30 m (98.4 ft) a megaphanerophyte —*see* **cryptophyte, life-form**

phellem —*see* **cells (wood)**

phelloderm —*see* **cells (wood)**

phellogen —*see* **cells (wood)**

phenology the study of the time of appearance of characteristic periodic phenomena in the life cycle of organisms in nature, e.g., **migration** in birds and flowering and leaf-fall in plants, particularly as these phenomena are influenced by environmental factors —*note* phenology especially involves the effects of temperature or day length —*see* **isolation**

phenotype 1. the observed state, description, or degree of expression of a **character** or **trait 2.** the product of the interaction of the **gene**s of an organism (**genotype**) with the environment —*note* when the total character expressions of an individual are considered, the phenotype describes the individual —*see* **broad-sensed heritability, combining ability, dominance, geographic variation, heritability, heterosis, individual selection, morphology, pleiotropism, seed production area, selection, selection index, superior**

pheromone a **semiochemical** secreted into the environment by one individual for the purpose of influencing the behavior of other individuals of the same species —*note* females emit sex pheromones to attract mates —*see* **hormone, kairomone, semiochemical, synomone**

phloem —*see* **cells (wood)**

photo base the line between the **principal point**s of two adjacent photographs in a series of vertical **aerial photograph**s

photo distance the measured distance between two points on a photograph, used with ground distance to compute photo scale

photogrammetry the science and art of measuring or deducing the physical dimensions of objects from measurements on photographs

photograph nadir that point on an **aerial photograph** at which a vertical line through the perspective center of the camera lens (termed the plumb line) intersects the plane of the photograph

photo index map an index made by marking the position of the **principal point**s, or the outlines of each **aerial photograph**, on an existing map

photo interpretation a determination of the nature of objects whose **image**s appear on a photograph

photo map a **mosaic** of vertical **aerial photograph**s that is georeferenced and annotated —*note* photo maps are generally used as a navigation aid and a general mapping tool in support of field operations

photoperiodism the physiological response of an organism to the periodicity and duration of light and darkness —*note* photoperiodism affects many processes, including the growth, flowering, and germination of plants —*see* **cold hardening**

photo rectification the process of projecting a tilted **aerial photograph** onto a horizontal plane, so as to correct **tilt** displacement

photo scale reciprocal the ratio of the ground distance divided by the photo distance, providing that all distances are expressed in the same measurement units

photosynthesis the manufacture of organic compounds, particularly carbohydrates, in the **chlorophyll** cells of plants from carbon dioxide, water, and enzymes in the presence of light as the energy source —*note 1.* the process releases oxygen and water vapor —*note 2.* photosynthesis is dependent on favorable temperature and moisture conditions as well as on adequate atmospheric carbon dioxide concentration

photosynthetically active radiation (PAR) the portion of the solar radiation spectrum that is active in the photosynthetic process —*note* PAR wavelengths are approximately 0.4 to 0.7 mm

phototropism the growth or change in position of plant organs in response to the direction of light —*note* phototropism is positive when the response is toward the light and negative when away from it —*see* **chemotropism, geotropism, hydrotropism, tropism**

phreatic related to **groundwater** and the **zone of saturation** —*see* **vadose zon**e

phreatophyte a plant that derives its water supply from groundwater and is more or less independent of **precipitation**, e.g., **riparian** vegetation, particularly trees

phyllosilicate minerals soil minerals containing layer structures composed of shared octahedral and tetrahedral sheets of primarily Al and Si

phyllosphere the microenvironment of leaves

phylogeny the evolutionary history of an organism or a taxonomic group, e.g., a **species** —*see* **evolution, ontogeny, taxon, taxonomy**

physical rotation —*see* **rotation**

physiognomic class a level in the classification hierarchy defined by the relative percent **canopy cover** of the tree, shrub, dwarf shrub, herb, and nonvascular life-form (in the uppermost strata) during the peak of the growing season

physiognomic group a level in the classification heirarchy defined by a combination of climate, leaf morphology, and leaf phenology —*note* different variables are applied to this hierarchical level in the sparsely vegetated class

physiognomic subclass a level in the classification hierarchy determined by the predominant leaf phenology of classes defined by tree, shrub, or dwarf shrub stratum (evergreen, deciduous, mixed ever-green-deciduous) and the average vegetation height for the herbaceous stratum (tall, medium, short) —*note* different variables are applied to this hierarchical level in the sparsely vegetated class

physiognomy the structure and life-form of a plant **community**

physiography landform, including surface geometry and underlying geologic material

physiological character an attribute related to the life processes of an organism; a function in contrast to form or structure —*see* **ecotype, morphology**

physiologically mature exhibiting mature plant **trait**s —*note* physiological maturity may or may not be associated with chronological age

physiology the science dealing with the life processes and functions of organisms, their cells, tissues, and organs

phytocide a chemical preparation used to kill or inhibit the growth of plants, their **spore**s or seed —*note* phytocides include arboricides and silvicides (used against trees and woody plants), **herbicide**s (used against herbs, forbs, and grasses), and fungicides (used against fungi)

phytograph a polygonal figure depicting the role of a species in a plant community, the polygon being formed by straight lines connecting points representing values on each of the chosen axes —*note* the axes may represent such pertinent quantitative data as basal area, frequency, canopy density, and for trees, size class

phytophagous herbivorous, feeding on plants —*note* a phytophagous animal is termed a phytophage —*see* **carnivore**

phytotoxic poisonous to plants

pick-the-winner selection *genetics* choosing the most desirable phenotypes for a given selection **trait**

picnic area a **recreation** site providing such facilities as tables, benches, fireplaces, and sanitation for daytime use only

piece rate payment for labor where income is related to output

piezometer a tube for measuring the pressure (piezometric) head or potential of a fluid

piezometric surface the surface to which water in a well will rise above an aquifer

pine oil a distillate having a higher boiling range than wood turpentine, obtained from resinous conifer wood by destructive steam distillation —*note* pine oil was originally obtained from pines; uses include dispensing and **wetting agent**s and disinfectants —*see* **essential oil, natural resin, tung oil**

pine reproduction weevil —*see* **terminal weevil**

ping-pong ball system —*see* **ignition tool**

pinhole 1. the cross section of a **gallery** made by an ambrosia beetle adult **2.** tiny holes in leaves caused by insect feeding or by disease —*see* **insect hole**

pintle hook *harvesting* a hooking device normally found on the rear of a piece of equipment and used to pull or attach a cable or trailer

pioneer *ecology* **1.** a plant capable of invading bare sites, e.g., newly exposed soil, and persisting there or colonizing them until supplanted by **succes**sional species —*note* pioneers often invade in large numbers and over considerable areas **2.** by extension, any new arrival in the early stages of succession, with particular reference to certain species whose presence appears to promote the establishment of more exacting species —*see* **ecolysis, primary host selection, ruderal**

pioneer root a relatively large-diameter, long, rapidly elongating lateral root with two or more proto**xylem** poles and without short roots or daughter lateral roots

pistil the female portion of a **flower** comprising a **stigma**, **style**, and **ovary** —*note* collectively, the pistils are called the **gynoecium** —*see* **stamen**

pistillate having female organs only —*note* pistillate may apply to individual **flower**s or **inflorescence**s, or to plants of a **dioecious** species —*see* **ovulate, staminate**

pit —*see* **cells (wood)**

pitch 1. a viscous, dark residue consisting of many organic compounds, mainly hydrocarbons, obtained by the distillation of tar **2.** *construction* the ratio of the rise of a roof relative to its span **3.** *utilization* in a **saw** having teeth of a uniform type, the distance (circumferential for circular saws and linear for others) between the points of teeth of similar type **4.** *wood* —*see* **natural resin, naval stores**

pitch canker an important fungal disease of pines, particularly southern pines, caused by *Fusarium subglutinans* —*note* pitch canker is characterized by flagging of girdled branches (often the terminal leader), sunken **canker**s, copious resin flow from the cankers, and resin-soaked wood in the cankered area; **infection** occurs through wounds and is usually vectored by insects or weather-related injuries

pitch midge —*see* **gall midge**

pitchout the physical expulsion or drowning of an attacking **bark beetle** by the strong flow of resin from the **host** tree —*see* **pitch tube, resinosis**

pitch tube a tubular mass of resin, boring dust, and **frass** that forms on the surface of the bark at the entrance holes of **bark beetle**s (e.g., the southern

pine beetle) or other insects —*note* pitch tubes are caused by the severing of resin ducts by the insects' boring activity —*synonym* resin tube —*see* **pitchout**

pith —*see* **cells (wood)**

pixel 1. *remote sensing* the smallest information-containing element (picture element) of an **image** that has been electronically coded in an array **2.** *GIS* one picture element of a uniform **raster** or **grid** file; the intersection of a row and column within the raster file —*synonym* **cell**

plaggen epipedon an artificial surface **horizon** more than 50 cm (19.7 in) thick that is formed by long-term manuring and mixing

plagiotropism the tendency for a **propagule** to grow at an angle similar to a branch, in contrast to vertical (orthotropic) growth —*see* **orthotropism**

plan —*see* **management plan**

plane-coordinate system a system for determining location in which two groups of straight lines intersect at right angles and have as a point of origin a selected perpendicular intersection

planer saw —*see* **saw**

planimeter an instrument used to mechanically measure an area by tracing the perimeter on a scaled map, drawing, or photo

planimetric map a large-scale map with all features projected perpendicularly onto a horizontal datum plane so that horizontal distances can be measured on the map with accuracy

plankton microorganisms suspended in the water having little or no power of locomotion, carried by waves, currents, and other movements of water —*note* phytoplankton are microscopic floating aquatic plants; zooplankton are microscopic floating aquatic animals; aeroplankton are spores, pollen, and microorganisms floating in air; macroplankton are > 500 μ, microplankton are 50 to 500 μ, nanoplankton are 10 to 50 μ, ultraplankton are 0.5 to 10 μ

planning components of **management plan**s include the following:

—**area** all the lands addressed in a land management plan

—**horizon** the overall time period considered in the planning process that spans all activities covered in the analysis or plan and all future conditions and effects of proposed actions that would influence the planning decisions

—**level** the scale of the planning effort, usually denoted by the size of the land area involved or by the level in the organization at which the planning is being done

planning *continued*

—**period** the time interval within the **planning horizon** that is used to show incremental changes in **yield**s, costs, effects, and benefits

—**process** the activities necessary to develop information, options, alternatives, and recommendations for decision making —*note* a planning process includes: (a) identifying problems, opportunities, and issues, (b) collecting, analyzing, and interpretating data, (c) formulating potential and appropriate alternatives courses of action, (d) evaluating the effects and consequences of the alternatives, (e) selecting the plan, (f) implementing the plan, and (g) monitoring and adjusting the plan

planning, long-range the identification and selection of overall **goals** and **objective**s for present and immediately foreseeable actions, using the best possible knowledge of future conditions and human **needs** to achieve desired results 10 or more years in the future —*see* **management plan, planning (short-range)**

planning, midrange planning that combines the results from early implementation of short-range plans with expected actions in the five- to 10-year period to enhance achievement of long-term goals —see **management plan**

planning section chief —*see* **incident command system**

planning, short-range planning and control for usually less than five years —*see* **management plan, planning (long-range)**

planning, site the planning, organization, and disposition of objects and activities at a given location at the largest scale subject to unified control —*see* **management plan**

plan of attack *fire* a selected course of action and organization of personnel and equipment in **fire suppression** that is applied to a particular fire or to all fires of a specific type —*see* **tactics**

plan of operations *management* a statement, usually tabular, showing the order and extent of all work to be carried out during one year (the annual program of work) or over a few years —*note* a plan of operations is commonly based on the prescriptions of a management plan, including financial provisions —*synonym* operating plan

plans chief —*see* **large fire organization**

plant association a plant community type based on land management potential, successional patterns, and species composition —*synonym* association, community —*note* a plant association usually has floristic uniformity in all layers

plantation a **stand** composed primarily of trees established by planting or artificial seeding —*note 1.*

a plantation may have tree or understory components that have resulted from natural regeneration —*note 2.* depending on management objectives, a plantation may be pure or mixed species, treated to have uniform or diverse structure and age classes, and have wildlife species commensurate with its stage of development and structure —*note 3.* plantations may be grown on short **rotation**s for biomass, energy, or fiber production, on rotations of varying length for timber production, or indefinitely for other values

plantation maintenance intermediate treatments in a recently planted or seeded **plantation** to promote the survival and growth of desired trees

plant class a subdivision of a **biome** based on dominant growth form and **cover** of the plants that dominate the vegetation —*see* **plant subclass**

plant formation a subdivision of a **plant subclass** based on size, shape, and structure

plant growth regulator a naturally occurring, organic substance that influences physiological processes at low concentrations, e.g., auxin, gibberellic acid, cytokinins, abscisic acid —*synonym* hormone

plant health care *urban forestry* the wise observation, assessment, and environmentally and economically sound prescription of recommendations for maintaining vigorous landscapes and plant communities —*see* **pest management**

planting bar a long-handled, tapered spade used to make narrow, relatively deep planting holes or slits

planting stock seedlings, transplants, cuttings, and occasionally wildlings, for use in planting —*synonym* **nursery stock** —*see* **dibble, hoedad, J-root, reforestation**

plantlet a plant produced *in vitro*

plant percent the proportion of seeds in a given sample that develop into seedlings at the end of a given period, generally the first growing season —*note* the percentage includes both **cull**s and plantable seedlings

plant series a subdivision of a **plant formation** based on individual dominant plant species of the **community**

plant subclass a subdivision of a **plant class** based on morphological characters, such as evergreen and **deciduous** habitat, or on adaptation to temperature or water —*see* **plant formation**

plasticity 1. the extent to which a **genotype** may vary in **phenotype** in different environments **2.** the phenotypic or genotypic variation in a **species** or **population**

platform the type of vehicle holding the **remote sensing** device, generally an airplane or a satellite

playa a shallow basin with a clay soil bottom, forming **ephemeral** lakes and **wetlands** during wet cycles —*note* playas are found in Texas, Oklahoma, New Mexico, Colorado, and Kansas

pleiotropism the capacity of a **gene** to affect a number of characteristics —*see* **phenotype**

plinthite a weakly cemented, iron-rich, **humus**-poor mixture of **clay** with other dilutants that commonly occurs as dark red redox concentrations that form platy, polygonal, or reticulate patterns —*see* **redox potential** —*note* plinthite changes irreversibly to ironstone **hardpans** or irregular aggregates on exposure to repeated wetting and drying

plot 1. the **experimental unit** to which a treatment is randomly assigned 2. *genetics* the largest part of a test **plantation,** nursery, or greenhouse experiment consisting of a single seedlot or clone and treatment

plow line a **fireline** constructed by a fire plow —*note* the plow is usually drawn by a **tractor** or other motorized equipment

PLSS —*see* **public land survey system**

plug a seedling with its roots still surrounded by the planting medium, grown in a plug container

plumule the stem apex of the seed embryo from which the primary plant shoot develops —*see* **epicotyl, hypocotyl, radicle**

plus *genetics* appearing distinctly **superior** to the average —*note 1.* the term describes **phenotypes** of both **stands** and single trees —*note 2.* the superior **character**(s) is usually specified, i.e., relative to volume, quality, **pest** resistance, or a combination of characters —*see* **elite**

plus tree a tree selected on the basis of its outstanding **phenotype** but not yet clonally or **progeny tested** —*see* **clone, elite, superior**

plywood —*see* **engineered wood composite**

pneumatophore a specialized aerial outgrowth from the submerged roots of certain swamp or estuarine trees (e.g., mangroves and certain palms) containing **aerenchyma** —*see* **stilt root**

PNW —*see* **present net worth**

pocket rot any wood decay localized in small areas —*note* pocket rot generally forms rounded or lens-shaped cavities, which in the early stages of decay may be filled with whitish fibers but later are empty —*syn,* peck rot, peckiness, pit rot, pitting

pocosin an upland **swamp** or **bog** of the coastal plain of the southeastern United States

podzolization a process of soil formation resulting in the genesis of Podzols and Podzolic soils characterized by the **eluviation** of iron, aluminum, and organic matter from the surface **horizon,** which results in the formation of a highly leached, whitish gray **E horizon** and a dark reddish brown to black **B horizon**

point *GIS* 1. a single x,y coordinate that represents a geographic feature too small to be displayed as a **line** or **area,** e.g., the location of a mountain peak or a building location on a small-scale map 2. used in some **GIS** systems to identify the interior of a **polygon**

point density the **basal area** per unit of area, as determined by point sampling

point sampling a type of **forest** sampling in which the sample is selected with a **probability** proportional to tree size —*note 1.* the variable plot size is proportional to the size of the tree being sampled —*note 2.* an angle device (prism) is used to project a constant angle, and all trees wider than that angle are tallied —*synonym* angle-count method, angle-gauge sampling, Bitterlich sampling, prism-count sampling, horizontal point sampling, plotless sampling, point cruising, prism cruising, **variable plot cruising,** variable-radius plot sampling —*see* **angle-count method, forest inventory, relaskop, sample**

point source pollution —*see* **pollution**

Poisson distribution a discrete **frequency distribution** of the number of events occurring in periods of equal time or space, on the **assumption** that the probability of an event in a very short time or limited space is small, constant, and independent of any other event —*note* the Poisson distribution may approach the binomial distribution under certain conditions

polar 1. *geography* relating to regions where the average temperature is $< 50°F$ ($< 10°C$) in all months 2. relating to areas within the polar circles (66.5° N and S latitude)

pole a tree of a size between a **sapling** and a **mature tree** —*note* the size of a pole varies by region

policy —*see* **management policy**

pollarding the practice of radically pruning fast-growing trees to produce a close head of shoots (pollards) —*note 1.* pollarding is done for either commercial or aesthetic purposes —*note 2.* pollarding should not be confused with tree topping, which is an improper pruning technique that leaves the tree in a weakened and vulnerable condition that allows for insect, disease, and wind breakage problems

pollen a mass of **pollen grains** —*see* **strobilus**

pollen grain a microscopic, usually yellow particle which is the male **gametophyte** and which may result in seed formation after it fertilizes an ovum in the female **flower**

pollen tube an outgrowth of a germinating **pollen grain** through which the sperm cell passes to **fertilize** the egg —*see* **germ tube**

pollination deposition of **pollen** on the receptive part of the female **flower** or **strobilus** —*note* in angiosperms this is the **stigmatic** surface; in gymnosperms, the ovule tip —*see* **controlled pollination, fertilization, receptivity**

pollution the condition caused by the presence in the environment of substances of such character, location, and quantity that the quality of the environment is impaired or rendered offensive to life —*see* **best management practices, forest decline;** kinds of pollution include the following:

—**point source pollution** pollution that arises from a well-defined origin, such as discharge from an industrial plant or runoff from a beef cattle feedlot

—**nonpoint source pollution** pollution that arises from an ill-defined and diffuse source, such as runoff from cultivated fields, agricultural lands, urban areas, or **forests** and **wildlands**

polyclimax theory the hypothesis that in any one environment there can be, or can be attained, more than one **climax** community —*see* **monoclimax theory**

polycross —*see* **polymix cross**

polycross test a progeny test to assess general combining ability from crosses among parents —*note* in a polycross test, a mixture of **pollen** from several male parents is used and **progeny** identities can be maintained only for the seed parents —*see* **combining ability, cross-pollination, diallel cross, topcross test**

polygene a **gene** determining a quantitative **trait** and having a small additive effect —*see* **additive gene, oligogene, quantitative inheritance**

polygon *GIS* **1.** a **vector** representation of the boundary and interior of an enclosed area, described by a sequential list of vertices or mathematical functions —*see* **vertex 2.** a type of **model** that stores all area **features** as closed loops or **lines** —*note* with all lines that describe the boundary of two or more polygons, the coordinates describing that line will be represented (and stored) as many times as that line is used

polymix cross a **mating** scheme in which several **pollen** sources (usually unrelated to each other) are mixed and used to control pollinate a series of females that are (usually) unrelated to any of the pollen parents —*synonym* polycross —*see* **topcross test**

polymorphism 1. the condition of individuals having several distinct forms (**morphs**) in the adult **stage** in the same **habitat** at the same time, usually with the rarer form at or above some minimum frequency —*note 1.* polymorphism may be limited to color intensity or patterns, such as in snow geese and many butterflies, or may involve morphology and physiology such as in honeybees and ants —*note 2.* the term polyphenic is used if the condition is genetically predetermined rather than environmentally induced —*see* **dimorphism 2.** nonproportionality of the members of a system of site index or height growth curves

polypedon a group of contiguous similar soil **pedons** —*note* the limits of a polypedon are reached at a place where there is no soil or where pedons have characteristics that differ significantly

polyphagy feeding behavior in which a wide range of food is accepted —*note* in polyphagy, some preferences may be exhibited within that range, e.g., migratory **locusts**

polyploid an organism with more than twice the basic number n of **chromosomes** of the ancestral **species** in its vegetative cells —*note* a cell, tissue, or organism having three sets ($3n$) is called triploid, four sets ($4n$) tetraploid, and six sets ($6n$) hexaploid —*see* **aneuploid, chromosome number, diploid, haploid, mutation, xenia**

population 1. *genetics* a group of similar individuals sharing a common **gene** pool, delimited in range by environmental or endogenous factors, and considered a unit —*note* in crossbred organisms, the population is often defined as the interbreeding group —*see* **character, cline, ecotype, subpopulation 2.** *biometrics* the aggregate of all units, finite or infinite, forming the subject of study —*synonym* universe; kinds of population include the following:

—**density** the number of individuals of a **species** per unit area —*see* **frequency, severity**

—**dynamics** the aggregate of changes that occur during the life of a population, including all phases of **recruitment** and growth, senility, mortality, seasonal fluctuations in the biomass, and persistence of each year class and its relative dominance, plus the effects that these factors exert on the population —*see* **epidemic**

—**index** any indicator of the size of a population —*note* an index may be, e.g., animal tracks per mile, dead rabbits per mile of road, or pellet counts per unit of area —*see* **standing crop**

—**persistence** the capacity of a population to maintain sufficient density to persist, well distributed, over time

—**pressure** the combined effect of a population on the other plants and animals and the environment —*note* high pressure may lead to dispersal, interference with **recruitment**, malnutrition, over-

population *continued*

browsing, etc. —*see* **concentration area, hunting pressure**

—**viability** the probability that a population will persist for a specified period across its range despite normal fluctuations in the population and in its associated environmental conditions

pore —*see* **cells (wood)**

porosity the volume of pores in a soil sample (nonsolid volume) divided by the bulk volume of the sample —*see* **bulk density**

pot planting the setting out of young trees in receptacles having closed or perforated bottoms in which they have been raised from seed or to which they have been transferred from the seed bed; a type of container planting —*note 1.* pots are made of various materials, e.g., peat, concrete, or tin plate; polythene pots are often termed polypots, or polybags —*note 2.* this method is generally used for establishing trees in semiarid regions —*see* **container nursery, container seedling, tube planting**

potential evapotranspiration the amount of moisture which, if available, would be removed from a given land area by **evapotranspiration** —*note* potential evapotranspiration is expressed in units of water depth

potential temperature the temperature a parcel of dry air would have if brought adiabatically from its initial state to the (arbitrarily selected) standard pressure of 10,000 mb

potential vegetation vegetation that would develop if all successional sequences were completed under present site conditions —*see* **habitat type**

powderpost beetle a member of the family Lyctidae (true powderpost beetles) or Bostrichidae (false powderpost beetles) —*note 1.* the **larvae** of powderpost beetles tunnel in the sapwood of partially or completely dry timber and wood products, mainly hardwoods, leaving a fine powdery bore dust, Lyctus beetles (*Lyctus* sp.) being particularly destructive —*note 2.* Bostrychidae that make augerlike tunnels, mainly in the sapwood of hardwoods, are termed auger beetles —*see* **ambrosia beetle, wood borer**

powdery mildew an obligate plant **parasite** of the order Erysiphales with superficial **mycelium** that attaches to the **host** plant and gains nourishment from it by means of haustoria —*note* leaves infected by powdery mildew look as though they were dusted with powder —*see* **haustorium**

prairie an extensive tract of level or rolling land that was originally treeless and grass covered —*note 1.* a prairie is generally characterized by a deep fertile soil —*note 2.* similar but generally infertile tracts

in South America are termed llano north of the Amazon and pampa south of it; in Asia, steppe; in South Africa, high veld(t) —*see* **savanna, savanna woodland**

prairie pothole a pothole **marsh** or depression formed by glaciers and located in Minnesota, Iowa, North Dakota, and South Dakota in the United States and in Alberta, Saskatchewan, and Manitoba in Canada

preattack *fire* a planned, systematic procedure for collecting, recording, and evaluating prefire and fire management intelligence data for a specified planning unit or preattack block —*note* in preattack, a planning phase is usually followed by a construction and development program integrated with other resources and activities

precipitable water the total atmospheric water vapor contained in a vertical column of unit cross-sectional area extending between any two specified levels

precipitation 1. any or all forms of liquid or solid water particles that fall from the atmosphere and reach the earth's surface, including drizzle, rain, snow, snow pellets, snow grains, ice crystals, ice pellets, and hail —*note* the ratio of precipitation to evaporation is the most important factor in the distribution of vegetation zones 2. a measure of the quantity, expressed in inches, centimeters, or milliliters of liquid water depth, of the water substance that has fallen at a given location in a specified amount of time —*see* **precipitation gauge, recording rain gauge**

precipitation-evaporation ratio (P/E) an empirical expression devised for the purpose of classifying climates numerically on the basis of **precipitation** and evaporation for a given locality and month

precipitation gauge any device that measures the amount of precipitation, e.g., a rain gauge or snow gauge

precipitation intensity the rate of **precipitation**, usually expressed in in/hour or mm/hour

precision 1. the closeness to each other of repeated measurements of the same quantity —*see* **accuracy** 2. the exactness of measurement —*note* e.g., the measurement 134.98 is more precise than the measurement 134.9 3. the statistical representation for the standard deviation of a number of measurements —*see* **accuracy, double-precision, single-precision**

precocious *genetics* predictably producing offspring at an early age

precommercial thinning (PCT) the removal of trees not for immediate financial return but to reduce **stocking** to concentrate growth on the more desirable trees —*synonym* respacing, **thinning**-to-waste

predation 1. the mode of life of a **predator 2.** the act of catching and killing the prey organism

predator an organism that feeds externally on other organisms —*note* the term predator usually refers to a free-living animal that hunts, kills, and generally eats other animals that are usually smaller and weaker than itself (prey) but also includes the relationship between herbivores and plants —*see* **buffer, parasite, parasitoid**

predator-mediated coexistence the coexistence of species in a community, one or more of which would have become competitively excluded were it not for the presence of a **keystone** predator

predisposition the influence of environment on the susceptibility of a plant or animal to disease or insect attack —*note* predisposition may include prior **infection** or **infestation** —*see* **primary insect, primary pathogen, secondary insect, secondary pathogen**

predominant —*see* **crown class**

preemergence application an application of a pesticide (usually an **herbicide**) after sowing but before the crop to be protected emerges from the soil; or, with an established perennial crop, before shoot emergence

premature grazing grazing before **range** readiness

preparatory cut —*see* **regeneration method, shelterwood**

prescribed burn to deliberately burn **wildland** fuels in either their natural or their modified state and under specified environmental conditions, which allows the fire to be confined to a predetermined area and produces the **fireline** intensity and rate of spread required to attain planned resource management objectives —*synonym* controlled burn, prescribed fire —*see* **broadcast burn, smoke management;** kinds of prescribed burn include the following:

—**prescribed managed fire** a fire ignited by management to meet specific objectives —*note* a written prescribed fire plan must be approved and all legal requirements (e.g., NEPA in federal situations) met prior to ignition

—**prescribed natural fire** a naturally ignited **wildland** fire that burns under specified conditions where the fire is confined to a predetermined area and produces the fire behavior and fire characteristics to attain planned fire treatment and resource management objectives

prescription 1. *fire* a written statement defining the objectives to be attained as well as the conditions of temperature, humidity, wind direction and speed, fuel moisture, and soil moisture under which a fire will be allowed to burn —*note* a prescription is generally expressed as acceptable

ranges of the prescription elements and the limit of the geographic area to be covered; prescription criteria may include safety, economic, public health, environmental, geographic, administrative, social, or legal considerations **2.** *silviculture* a planned series of treatments designed to change current **stand** structure to one that meets management **goals** —*note* the prescription normally considers ecological, economic, and societal **constraints 3.** *management* —*see* **management prescription**

present net worth (PNW) the residual when the present value of costs is deducted from the present value of benefits —*note* if the present value of costs exceeds the present value of benefits, the residual is shown as a negative number —*synonym* net present worth, net present value, present net value

preserve 1. any area protected from treatment **2.** *wildlife* an area managed essentially for its game and fish, the stocks of which may often be replenished artificially —*note* a wildlife preserve is generally private land that may or may not be managed for profit —*synonym* refuge —*see* **sanctuary**

pressure bar —*see* **nosebar**

presuppression fire activities undertaken in advance of a fire to help ensure more effective fire suppression, including overall planning, recruitment and training of fire personnel, procurement and maintenance of fire-fighting equipment and supplies, fuel treatment, and creating, maintaining, and improving a system of fuelbreaks, roads, water sources, and control lines —*see* **fire suppression**

prevention 1. *fire* —*see* **fire prevention 2.** *vegetation management* the prescriptions or strategies used to ameliorate conditions that cause or favor the presence of competing, unwanted, or noxious vegetation —*see* **suppression**

prevention guard a **fire guard** (or **fire fighter**) who helps prevent fires by contacting land users and inspecting the fire prevention measures and fire equipment of industrial operations in the field —*synonym* fire prevention technician, prevention patrol

price deflator a measure of change in the purchasing power of money used to adjust money incomes, wages, etc., to compare their real values over a number of time periods

price-size curve the relationship between price per unit volume (or other relevant measure of quantity) and the volume (or other measure of size) of a tree or log

pricking out the transplanting of individual seedlings that are too small to be handled by conventional lining-out methods into boxes, flats, tubes, etc., or into nursery beds

primary forest —*see* **old-growth forest, virgin forest**

primary growth tree growth from a bud, root tip, or other apical meristem —*see* **secondary growth**

primary host 1. *entomology* the **host** on which the sexual form is found in those insects with alternating sexual and parthenogenic generations **2.** *in rust fungi* the sexual or telial host —*note* the pycnia and aecia of primary hosts form on the alternate or **secondary host** —*see* **aecium, pycnium 3.** *in common (usually incorrect) usage with rust fungi* the economically important host **4.** the principal host

primary host selection *entomology* the location and identification of a susceptible **host** tree by a small number of adult beetles, particularly **bark beetles** —*synonym* (usually) initial attack —*see* **mass attack, pioneer, secondary host selection**

primary insect an insect, particularly a **bark beetle**, that can kill healthy plants —*see* **predisposition, primary pathogen, secondary insect, secondary pathogen**

primary key *computers* the central **column** within an **RDBMS** that contains a unique value for each **record** in the datafile —*note* a primary key is the unique number assigned to each parcel within a county

primary lookout *fire* a **lookout point** that must be staffed during the fire season to meet planned minimum seen area coverage in a given locality —*note* the primary lookout person is not sent to fires

primary meristem the meristematic tissue derived from an **apical meristem**

primary mineral a mineral that has not been altered chemically since deposition and crystallization from molten lava

primary parasite a **parasite** whose **host** is not a parasite —*see* **hyperparasitization**

primary pathogen a **pathogen** that can infect the **host** and induce disease without the involvement of insects or other (secondary) pathogens —*see* **predisposition, primary insect**

primary root growth the developmental processes that result in the transformation of a **root primordium** into a root with **epidermis, cortex,** pericycle, and **vascular cylinder (stele)**

prime rate the rate of interest charged by large corporate banks to their best customers —*note 1.* generally, the prime rate represents the rate charged for loans fully secured by highly liquid assets and having the least **risk** —*note 2.* often, interest rates charged to other clients or for loans with higher risk are expressed as prime plus x percent, where x represents the interest required to offset perceived risk of the loan's not being repaid

principal component analysis a statistical method for reducing the dimensionality of a set of **multivariate** observations —*note* each principal component is a specific linear combination of the original variables such that all principal components are orthogonal and successive principal components account for a smaller proportion of the original variation —*see* **orthogonality, nonorthogonal data**

principal host the **host** on which a particular **parasite** most frequently occurs

principal point the point on an **aerial photograph** at which the optical axis of the camera intersects it —*note* provided the camera is in perfect adjustment, this is the geometrical center of the photograph, defined by the **fiducial marks**

principal species the **species** to which the **silviculture** of a mixed forest is primarily directed, for either economic or protective value —*note* a species of intrinsically higher economic value than another may be less economically important because of its lower frequency of occurrence and therefore is not the principal species

priority animal taxa a species or subspecies with special significance for management, including endangered, threatened, and special status species —*see* **endangered species, threatened species**

prism cruising the use of a glass wedge or prism of known angle to estimate basal area of a forest stand from which volumes can be estimated —*see* **anglecount method, cruise, point sampling, relaskop, three-P sampling**

probabilistic model —*see* **stochastic model**

probability the relative **frequency** of a specific event, expressed as a proportion or percent of the total number of events —*see* **confidence limits**

processor *harvesting* a machine that performs two or more functions on a felled tree, including delimbing, debarking, bucking, measuring, or chipping —*see* **harvester**

producer any individual or firm engaged in harvesting roundwood or chips and converting them into various products —*note 1.* primary producers include loggers and chip harvesters, saw millers, plywood producers, pulp manufacturers, and paper makers who produce the initial merchantable products —*note 2.* secondary producers buy products from primary producers and manufacture additional products, such as furniture parts, paper bags or boxes, and modular housing —*note 3.* the line between primary and secondary producers is fuzzy; generally, the initial breakdown of roundwood or chips into salable products is regarded as primary processing and the firm that does that is called the primary producer

production 1. *ecology* the process of producing organic material **2.** *ecology* the increase in biomass by individuals, species, or species groupings over time **3.** *management* the amount of goods or services produced by an area over a given time

production population *genetics* a highly selected subset of the **breeding population** parents or **clones** that is propagated sexually or vegetatively for **reforestation** —*see* **multiline**

production possibility frontier the locus of all the alternative quantities of several outputs and the total costs of producing the outputs

productivity 1. *ecology* the rate at which biomass is produced per unit area by any class of organisms **2.** *ecology* the rate of new tissue formation or energy utilization by one or more organisms **3.** *ecology* the capacity or ability of an environmental unit to produce organic material **4.** *ecology* the ability of a population to recruit new members by reproduction **5.** *management* the relative capacity of an area to sustain a supply of goods or services in the long run —*see* **site quality**

productivity class a classification of forest land in terms of potential annual cubic volume growth per unit area at **culmination of mean annual increment** in fully stocked natural stands

profile *soils* a vertical section of soil showing **horizon**s

profit the difference between the total revenue a firm receives from selling its outputs and its total costs of producing the outputs

profundal the deep, bottom-water area beyond the depth of effective light penetration; all of the lake floor beneath the hypolimnion —*see* **aphytal, hypolimnion**

progenic causing improvement of genetic qualities in natural or production **population**s of a **species** —*see* **eugenic**

progeny the offspring of a particular tree or mating —*see* **general combining ability**

progeny test a planting generally designed to evaluate parents by comparing the performance of their offspring or to provide for **selection** of future parents from within the planting itself —*see* **clonal test, combining ability, elite, genetic test, genotype-environment interaction, provenance test, roguing, seed zone**

program an activity or combination of activities carried out to meet an **objective** or set of objectives

program evaluation and review technique (PERT) a **network analysis** model that seeks to estimate variances associated with the expected times of completion of the total project and its subprojects —*see* **critical path method**

programmatic environmental assessment or impact statement —*see* **environmental assessment, environmental impact statement**

programming, mathematical a mathematical technique used to determine the optimum **allocation** of resources to maximize an **objective function** where the problem involves either a sequence of decisions or a situation that can be treated as if the decisions were sequential in time —*note* kinds of mathematical programs include the following:

—**dynamic programming** a generalized approach to solving optimization problems in which a sequence or set of interrelated parts (e.g., multistage problems) is solved before the final solution is developed —*note* dynamic programming problems often deal with a time-based sequence of decisions (e.g., multiple **thinnings**, construction of roads) that are decomposed and solved; the problems may involve linear or nonlinear relationships

—**goal programming** a multicriterion mathematical programming formulation designed to minimize the (usually weighted) deviations from preset management targets

—**integer linear programming** a special case of linear programming in which some or all of the **decision variables** are constrained to have positive integer values

—**linear programming** a **mathematical model** for representing a decision problem characterized by a set of **decision variables**, a linear **objective function** of those decision variables representing the system component that is to be maximized or minimized (e.g., harvest volume, **present net worth**, sediment pollution, and cost), and a set of linear **constraints** that satisfy the **assumptions** of **additivity, proportionality, determinism**, and **divisibility** —*note 1.* linear programming assumes that the contribution of all activities to the objective function is the sum of the contribution of each activity (additivity), that all variables are continuous and can have any positive value (divisibility), that the contribution of any activity to the objective function is directly proportional to the level of that activity (proportionality), and that all coefficients can be represented as known with certainty (determinism); linear programming is used to help decide the most profitable combination of products that a given machine, factory, or forest can yield, or the best combination of factors of production or of machines and equipment to produce a given **output** —*note 2.* linear programming is used extensively in scheduling periodic harvests based on management objectives; the objective function (e.g., maximize net present value, minimize cost, maximize timber volume) and **constraint**s (e.g., land area, harvest flow) are formulated and solved as linear equations—*see* **assignment problem**

programming *continued*

—multiple objective programming a mathematical formulation designed to evaluate **trade-off**s between two or more objectives

—nonlinear programming a mathematical **algorithm** in which the **objective function** (e.g., maximize net present value, minimize cost, maximize timber volume) and the **constraint**s (e.g., land area, harvest flow) are formulated and solved as nonlinear equations —*note* nonlinear programming helps to decide the most profitable combination of products that a given machine, factory, or forest can yield, or the best combination of factors of production or of machines and equipment to produce a given output; it is used less extensively than linear programming in scheduling periodic harvests based on management objectives

progressive clearcut system a system whereby all trees are harvested in a sequence of strips —*note* the direction of felling (felling sequence) may advance toward prevailing winds to reduce **windthrow** losses —*see* **regeneration methods (clearcutting)**

projection —*see* **map projection**

propagule 1. a plant part such as a bud, tuber, root, shoot, or spore used to propagate an individual vegetatively **2.** the individual resulting from **vegetative propagation** —*see* **asexual reproduction, ramet**

property rights the legal specification of ownership and of the rights that landowners have —*note* property rights are codified in laws and regulations and, in some cases, are affected by cultural preferences of neighboring landowners

proper-use factor *range management* an index to the **grazing** use that may be made of a specific forage species, based on a system of **range** management that will maintain the economically important forage species or achieve other management objectives, such as maintenance of watersheds and recreation values —*see* **allowable use, stocking** —*note* the estimated factor for each forage species contributes to a weighted average for the range type —*see* **palatability**

proprietary jurisdiction a law enforcement jurisdiction where the state has not ceded authority to another level of government —*note* under proprietary jurisdiction, authority is equivalent to that for any landowner

protandry the shedding of **pollen** prior to female receptivity on the same plant or **flower** —*see* **dichogamy, protogyny, receptivity**

protectant a **pesticide** that prevents the attacking organism from establishing itself on the surface of its host —*see* **fungistat**

protection boundary *fire* the limits of an area within which a specified fire agency has assumed a degree of responsibility for fire protection

protection forest an area, wholly or partly covered with trees, managed primarily to regulate stream flow, maintain water quality, minimize **erosion**, stabilize drifting sand, conserve **ecosystem**s, or provide other benefits via protection

protein bank the cultivation of trees or shrubs for the purpose of providing fodder for animals kept in stalls —*synonym* cut-and-carry system

protogyny the receptivity of the female prior to the shedding of **pollen** on the same plant or **flower** —*see* **dichogamy, protandry**

protoplast a plant cell excluding the cell wall —*note* a protoplast may be produced by enzymatically removing the cell wall

protoxylem —*see* **cells (wood)**

provenance the original geographic source of seed, **pollen**, or **propagules** —*see* **geographic race, local seed source**

provenance test a planting in which **population** samples from **stand**s of known geographic origins are grown together in one or more locations —*see* **progeny test, seed source**

pruning 1. the removal, close to the branch collar or flush with the stem, of side branches (live or dead) and multiple leaders from a standing tree —*note 1.* pruning is generally done on **plantation** trees to improve the tree or its timber, or on urban and rural trees to improve their aesthetics or health —*note 2.* green pruning is the removal of live branches, dry pruning is the removal of dead branches, and chemical pruning is the application of chemicals, e.g., plant-growth regulators, to the living tree to kill, suppress, or inhibit lateral shoots —*see* **brashing, bud pruning, natural pruning 2.** clipping to shape, e.g., for the Christmas tree market or for a topiary —*see* **shearing**

pruning lift pruning to a specified height or stem diameter in one operation or stage

psammophyte a plant growing in sands or sandy soils

pseudorandom number a computer-generated number developed from mathematical expressions with the property of a random number

psychrometric table a table prepared from the psychrometric formula and used to obtain vapor pressure, **relative humidity,** and **dew point** from values of wet-bulb and dry-bulb temperature

public domain lands the original holdings of the United States never granted or conveyed to other jurisdictions or reacquired by exchange for other public lands

public involvement the use of appropriate procedures for informing the public and in obtaining early and continuing participation in planning and decision making —*note* the public(s) may refer to individuals, local, state, regional, and national public service and interest groups, as well as public agencies that have knowledge, expertise, or jurisdiction relevant to the decisions being contemplated —*synonym* public participation

public lands *Federal Land Policy Management Act (FLPMA) of 1976* any lands and interest in land owned by the United States within several states and administered by the Secretary of the Interior through the Bureau of Land Management without regard to how the United States acquired ownership

public land survey system (PLSS) a rectangular survey system that utilizes 6-square-mile townships as its basic survey unit —*note 1.* the location of townships is controlled by baselines and meridians running parallel to **latitude** and **longitude** lines; townships are defined by range lines running parallel (north-south) to **meridians** and township lines running parallel (east-west) to baselines — *note 2.* the PLSS was established in the United States by the Land Ordinance of 1785

public participation —*see* **public involvement**

pulaski —*see* **hand tool**

pulling tops *fire* the dragging of unutilized treetops with branches attached and accumulations of other **slash** away from seed trees or advanced regeneration —*note* pulling tops is a protective measure in timber harvesting, aimed at reducing damage in case of accidental fires

pulp separated wood fibers used in manufacturing paper and allied products —*see* **defibration, pulpwood;** pulp types include the following:

—**chemical pulp** a pulp resulting from the reduction of wood or other fibrous material into its component parts by cooking with various chemicals, typically under pressure, in such processes as sulfate, sulfite, etc.

—**dissolving pulp** a very pure, fully bleached chemical pulp with a high alpha cellulose content, made specifically for dissolving in suitable solvents for regeneration to form cellophane, rayon, etc., or processing further to form acetate, nitrates, etc.

—**elemental chlorine-free (ECF) pulp** wood pulp that is free from elemental chlorine

—**kraft pulp** a strong papermaking fiber produced by the kraft process in which the principal cooking agent is a mixture of sodium sulfide and sodium hydroxide—*synonym* sulfate pulp

—**mechanical pulp** any wood pulp manufactured wholly or in part by a mechanical process in which

pulp *continued*

fibers are separated by grinding or refining —*note* groundwood pulp is a type of mechanical pulp obtained by grinding wood against revolving cylinders so that its **fibers** or fiber bundles are separated but remain chemically unchanged; groundwood pulp is used mainly for newsprint; chemigroundwood pulp is obtained by treating wood with chemical solutions under pressure before grinding

—**sulfate pulp** —*see* **kraft pulp**

—**sulfite pulp** a pulp produced by cooking fibers mainly using magnesium bisulfite or sodium sulfite

—**thermomechanical (TMP) pulp** a high-yield pulp produced by a process in which wood particles are softened by preheating under pressure prior to a primary pressurized refining stage

—**total chlorine-free (TCF) pulp** wood pulp that is totally free from chlorine

pulping the separation of wood fibers by mechanical or chemical action

pulpwood roundwood, whole-tree chips, or **wood residue**s that are used for the production of wood pulp

punk a soft, weak, spongy wood condition caused by decay

pupa *plural* **pupae** *insects* the immature, generally immobile, transformation **stage** between the insect **larva** and the **adult** of insects with complete **metamorphosis** —*note* the hard-shelled pupa of a Lepidoptera is termed a chrysalis

pupation *entomology* the transformation of a **larva** into a **pupa** and the development changes within the pupa of insects with complete **metamorphosis**

pure *of a forest, crop, or stand* composed principally of one **species,** conventionally at least 80 percent based on numbers, basal areas, or volumes —*see* **mixed**

pycniospore a spore that functions as a **gamete** in the **rust fungi,** fusing with a receptive hypha —*note* a pycniospore is borne in a **pycnium**

pycnium *plural* **pycnia** a spherical fruiting structure of the **rust fungi** in which receptive **hyphae** and **pycniospore**s are produced —*see* **primary host**

pyrophyte a plant **species** that is adapted to survive or benefit from some type of fire regime —*see* **fire climax**

Q

QDT —*see* **quality development time**

QTL —*see* **quantitative trait locus**

quad **1.** one quadrillion (1×10^{15}) BTU **2.** *sawmilling* having a main saw consisting of a bank of four saw blades, e.g., quad mill

quadrangle *GIS* a four-sided area, usually bounded by a pair of **meridian**s and a pair of **parallel**s

quadrat a small, clearly demarcated, sample area of any shape but known size on which ecological observations are made —*see* **random quadrat**

quadratic mean diameter —*see* **mean diameter**

quadtree *GIS* a spatial index that breaks a spatial data set into homogeneous **cell**s of regularly decreasing size; each decrement in size is one-fourth the area of the previous cell —*note 1.* the quadtree segmentation process continues until the entire map is partitioned —*note 2.* quadtrees are often used for storing **raster** data and typically have significantly fewer storage requirements than raster data

quaking bog an accumulation of organic matter and living organisms in the **littoral** zone that eventually floats on open water —*see* **bog**

qualitative inheritance the inheritance of a character such as resistance to white pine blister rust that is controlled by one or a few **gene**s, resulting in a discontinuous **phenotypic effect** —*see* **Mendel's principles, simple Mendelian inheritance**

quality development time (QDT) the time spent working with a **GIS** when no specific product is being created, but technique, skills, knowledge, and general acceptance of the GIS are increased —*note* since many GISs have numerous components, such as data entry, data conversion, data cleaning, data management, data analysis, and data output, and there are many variations of each component, QDT; allows procedures to be developed for each variation desired

quality of life a measure of the degree to which society offers effective opportunity to enjoy a combination of goods, services, and experiences —*note* quality of life is a subjective judgment and may be based on individual opinion or on community consensus

quantitative inheritance the inheritance of a **character,** such as size, which varies continuously (quantitatively) —*note* **gene**s act cumulatively and cannot generally be detected at the **phenotypic** level by their individual effects —*see* **additive genes, alleles, polygene, simple Mendelian inheritance**

quantitative trait locus (QTL) a position within a **genome** typically associated with a particular **phenotype** and commonly identified by a molecular marker —*see* **locus, marker gene, oligogene**

quarter-sawn a sawn board in which the growth rings meet the face and back sides at angles of greater than 45°, i.e., the face of the board parallels the stem radius —*see* **flat-sawn, radially sawn**

query —*see* **map query**

queueing theory the body of knowledge dealing with waiting in lines —*see* **interarrival time**

quiescence *insects* a temporary cessation of development as a response to immediate adverse conditions —*note 1.* development resumes as soon as conditions are favorable —*note 2.* quiescence is the simplest type of **dormancy** —*see* **diapause**

quiescent center the area of slowly dividing cells between the **apical meristem** and the **root cap** of plant roots that regenerates damaged apical **meristem** and rootcap cells —*see* **elongation zone**

R

race a **population** that exists within a **species** and exhibits general genetic characteristics discontinuous and distinct from other populations —*note* when the distinguishing characteristics of a race are adaptive, the term is synonymous with **ecotype** —*see* **cline, geographic race, line, local seed source, variety**

radar a method, system, or technique for using beam, reflected, and timed electromagnetic radiation to detect, locate, and track objects, to measure distance (altitude), and to acquire terrain **imag**ery —*note 1.* radar is an acronym from RAdio Detection And Ranging —*note 2.* in remote sensing, radar refers to active microwave systems (from about 1 GHz to 100 GHz; the majority of current instruments operate below 10 GHz)

radial-arm saw —*see* **saw**

radial section a longitudinal section of a tree stem that passes along the radius of the stem from the pith

radially sawn a sawn board in which the face of the board is along the radius of the stem from pith to bark —*see* **flat-sawn, quarter-sawn**

radian a unit of angular measure whose intercepted arc on a circle is equal in length to the radius of the circle

radiance a measure of the intrinsic radiant intensity emitted by a radiator in a given direction

radiation the process by which electromagnetic radiation is propagated through free space by virtue of joint undulatory variations in the electric and magnetic fields in space

radiational cooling the cooling of the earth's surface and adjacent air accomplished (mainly at night) whenever the earth's surface suffers a net loss of heat due to terrestrial radiation

radiation fog a major type of **fog,** produced over a land area when radiational cooling reduces the air temperature to or below its **dew point** —*see* **steam fog**

radicle 1. the root of a seed embryo from which the primary root develops —*see* **tap root, plumule** 2. the germinating rootlike structure of a **dwarf mistletoe** seed —*see* **hypocotyl** —*synonym* primary root

radiometry the process of measuring the values of a **pixel** in one band of a remotely sensed image that represent the amount of light in that wavelength — *note* given a range of values from 0 to 255, a value of 0 measures no light and is represented as black, and a value of 127 is medium gray

radiosonde a balloon-borne instrument for the simultaneous measurement and transmission of meteorological data

rainfall duration the time during which rainfall occurs, exceeds a given intensity, or maintains a given intensity

rainfall frequency the frequency, usually expressed in years, at which a given rainfall intensity and duration can be expected to be equaled or exceeded

rainforest an evergreen **forest** associated with a climate characterized by continual high humidity and abundant rainfall (> 60 in or > 1524 mm per year) and a short or no dry season —*note* the term is commonly applied, in a restricted sense, to tropical forests with an annual rainfall > 80 in (> 2032 mm) and abundant **epiphyte**s and climbers —*see* **monsoon forest, montane**

rain shadow an area to the leeward of a high land mass, particularly a mountain range, which receives less rain than would be expected had the high land mass not been upwind of it —*note* what the area receives is mainly the residue of orographic rain

raised bog an accumulation of organic matter with enough capillarity to raise the water level in the mat and thereby lift the **bog** above the original soil surface

raker (tooth) a square-fronted sawtooth carrying no **set,** interposed between groups of other teeth, e.g., peg teeth, to remove from the **kerf** the sawdust these produce —*see* **saw**

ramet an individual member of a **clone** vegetatively propagated from an **ortet** —*see* **propagule**

ramicorn a large, high-angled branch that often results when one member of a fork is partly suppressed by the more dominant member —*note* when boards are sawn from a stem where a ramicorn originates, the resulting **knot** is called a **sucker knot**

randomization the process of assigning treatments to experimental material that uses a chance device, such as flipping a coin or the use of random number tables —*see* **random sample**

randomized block an experimental design in which each **block** contains a complete **replication** of treatments allocated to the units within the blocks in a nonsystematic fashion, thus allowing un**bias**ed estimates of **experimental error** to be made —*synonym* randomized complete-block design

random mating *genetics* an act of pairing in which each individual in the population has the same probability of mating with every other individual

random quadrat a random placement of fixed sampling area for ecological research —*see* **quadrat**

random sample a portion of a **population** (sample) selected in such a manner that all possible samples of the same size have an equal chance of being chosen —*synonym* simple random sample —*see* **randomization**

random variable a quantity that may take any one of a specified set of values with a specified **probability** —*synonym* variate —*see* **stochastic**

range 1. *ecology* the area in which a plant naturally lives and reproduces **2.** *ecology* the known geographical distribution of a plant or animal during a defined time **3.** *wildlife, range management* the area in which an animal seeks food and water **4.** *biometrics* an elementary measure of the dispersion of a set of random variables, equal to the largest minus the smallest **5.** *range management* any land supporting vegetation suitable for grazing, including rangeland, grazable **woodland** and shrubland —*note* range is not a use —*see* **habitat, pasture, grassland, herbland, year-long range 6.** *range management* modifies resources, products, activities, practices, and phenomena pertaining to rangeland

range appraisal the classification and valuation of **range**land from an economic or production standpoint —*note* a range **appraisal** includes considerations such as the relationship to other feed sources and facilities for handling —*see* **appraisal, livestock, range survey**

range finder an optical or electronic instrument for measuring distances to an object

range management a discipline founded on ecological principles and dealing with the use of rangelands and **range** resources for a variety of purposes including watersheds, wildlife **habitat**, grazing by **livestock**, recreation, and aesthetics —*see* **range survey**

range plant an herbaceous or **shrub**by plant growing on **range** or **forest** land —*synonym* fodder, **forage** —*note* the four major categories recognized are grasses, grasslike plants, **forb**s, and browse —*see* **browse, feed**

ranger district an administrative subdivision of a USDA Forest Service **national forest** —*note* a ranger district is managed by a district ranger

range reseeding the process of establishing vegetation by the artificial dissemination of seed —*see* **interseeding, range**

range site *range management* an area of **range**land that has the potential to produce and sustain distinctive kinds and amounts of vegetation to result in a characteristic plant community under its particular combination of environmental factors, particularly climate, soils, and associated native biota —*note 1.* range site is synonymous with ecological

site when referring to rangeland —*note 2.* some agencies use range site based on the **climax** concept, not potential natural community

range survey 1. the systematic acquisition and analysis of resource information needed for planning and for management of **range**lands —*synonym* range inventory **2.** a survey to determine, on a given area, such data as soil condition and topography, together with the extent, composition, and condition of the range plant **cover**, as a basis for management plans —*see* **range appraisal, range management**

rappelling *fire* a technique of landing **firefighter**s from hovering helicopters that involves sliding down ropes with the aid of friction-producing devices to control the rate of descent

raster *GIS* a cellular data structure composed of rows and columns in which groups of cells represent features —*note 1.* the value of each **cell** represents the value of the feature —*note 2.* **image** data are stored using this structure —*see* **grid**

raster data *GIS* machine-readable data that represent values usually stored for maps or **image**s and organized sequentially by rows and **column**s —*note* each **cell** must be rectangular, but not necessarily square, as with **grid** data

rate of production transformation 1. the rate at which one output can be traded for another in a production process while holding the total quantities of inputs constant **2.** the absolute value of the slope of the **production possibility frontier**

rate of spread the relative speed with which a fire increases in size —*note* the rate of spread is usually expressed as the rate of increase of the perimeter or area, or the rate of advance of its **head** in chains/hour (m/hour) or ac/hour (ha/hour) for a specific period in the fire's history

rate of technical substitution 1. the rate at which one input may be traded off against another in the production process while holding output constant **2.** the absolute value of the slope of an **isoquant**

rate of use the amount of use per unit of time —*see* **use (cumulative)**

rating curve a graphic or sometimes tabular representation of performance or output under a stated series of conditions, e.g., a rating curve for a flume shows volume of flow per unit time at various stages or depths of flow

ray —*see* **cells (wood)**

RDBMS —*see* **relational database management system**

reaction wood wood with distinctive anatomical and physical characteristics, formed typically in parts of leaning or crooked stems and in branches, that tends to restore the branch or stem to its original position —*note* reaction wood is known as **tension wood** in broad-leaved trees and **compression wood** in conifers

rear —*see* **forest fire**

rearing habitat *aquatics* areas in rivers or streams where juvenile salmon and trout find food and shelter to live and grow

reburn 1. the repeat burning of an area over which a fire has previously passed but has left unburnt **fuel 2.** the area reburned

receptivity *genetics* the condition of the reproductive organs of a female **flower** that permits effective **pollination** —*see* **anthesis, fertilization, protandry**

recession curve *hydraulics* —*see* **depletion curve**

recessive gene an **allele** without **phenotypic** effect when present in the **heterozygous** state —*see* **dominance, dominant gene**

recharge the process by which water is added to the **zone of saturation,** as recharge of an aquifer

reciprocal cross the repetition of a cross in which the sexual function of the parents is reversed, i.e., female B × male A is the reciprocal of female A × male B —*see* **cross-pollination**

reciprocal recurrent selection a breeding scheme in which **selection** within each of two independent **lines** is based on **progeny tests** of crosses between the lines —*note* reciprocal recurrent selection is meant to select for both **additive** and **nonadditive genetic variation**

recombinant 1. an organism containing a different combination of alleles than its parent, resulting from either crossing-over events or from the independent assortment of **chromosome**s at **meiosis 2.** having new combinations of the **genes** (**alleles**) of the parent(s) —*note* the term is often used when the genes are **linked**

recombination 1. the formation in the **progeny** of new combinations of linked genes not present in either parent **2.** a new combination in the absence of linkage —*see* **mutation**

reconnaissance a preliminary inspection or survey of a **forest** or **range** area to gain general information (e.g., timber volumes) useful for future management —*see* **cruise**

reconstruction *recreation* the rebuilding of a structure of cultural or historical significance, typically using contemporary methods and materials

record 1. *GIS* in an attribute table, a single row of thematic descriptors —*see* **descriptive data 2.** a logical unit of data in a file —*synonym* tuple

recording rain gauge a rain gauge that automatically records the amount of precipitation collected in a period of time —*see* **precipitation gauge**

record of decision (ROD) *federal land management* a public document separate from but associated with an **environmental impact statement** that identifies all alternatives, provides the agency's final decision, the rationale behind that decision, and the agency's commitments to monitoring and mitigation

recovery (recovery rate) 1. *utilization* —*see* **utilization percent 2.** *wildlife management* any action that is necessary to reduce or resolve the threats that caused a species to be listed within the Endangered Species Act of 1976 as threatened or endangered —*see* **endangered species, threatened species**

recreation an activity pursued during leisure time and by free choice that provides its own satisfaction

recreation facility the improvements within a developed recreation site offered for visitors' enjoyment

recreation opportunity spectrum (ROS) a planning approach identifying a range of recreational environments from urban **recreation** areas to **wilderness**

recreation resource management the management of recreational opportunities by means of resource, social, and managerial inputs to produce recreational experiences that result in user satisfaction

recreation river *Wild and Scenic Rivers Act of 1968* a river or section of river that is readily accessible by road or railroad, may have some development along its shoreline, and may have undergone some impoundment or diversion in the past

recreation site a land or water area having characteristics that make it suitable for development for public enjoyment, such as camping, picnicking, and water sports

recruitment 1. *silviculture* regeneration; the additional trees moving from one size class to another **2.** *wildlife* the addition to a population from all causes, i.e., reproduction, immigration, and **stocking**—*note* recruitment may refer to numbers born or hatched, or to numbers at a specified stage of life-breeding age, weaning age, etc. —*see* **breeding potential, mortality**

recruitment period the time between a tree's entering and leaving any specified diameter class

rectify *GIS* the process by which an **image** or **grid** is converted from image coordinates to real-world coordinates —*note* rectification typically involves rotation and scaling of **cells** and thus requires re-sampling of values

recurrence interval the average time between actual occurrences of an event of a given or greater magnitude

recurrent breeding the process of improving a set of value **traits** through **selection, breeding,** and testing in repeated cycles (generations) —*synonym* recurrent improvement

recurrent selection *genetics* the process of selecting individuals or families and intermating them or allowing them to interpollinate to produce the next generation —*note* the new generations are generally used as foundation populations in which to start repeated cycles of **selection** and **breeding** —*see* **mass selection**

red-belt —*see* **winter injury**

red card a card issued to a person showing his or her qualifications to fill a specified **fire suppression** position in a large fire suppression organization and identifying training needs —*note* the qualified person is designated as fire rated

red flag cancellation —*see* **fire weather forecast**

red flag warning —*see* **fire weather forecast**

red flag watch —*see* **fire weather forecast**

redoximorphic feature a soil property, associated with wetness, which results from the reduction and oxidation of iron and manganese compounds in the soil after saturation with water and desaturation, respectively —*note* **mottle**s are common redoximorphic features of soils

redox potential (E_H) the potential that is generated between an oxidation or reduction half-reaction and the standard hydrogen electrode (0.0v at pH = 0) —*note* in soils it is the potential created by oxidation-reduction reactions that take place on the surface of a platinum electrode measured against a reference electrode minus the E_H of the reference electrode; this is a measure of the oxidation-reduction potential of electrode reactive components in the soil —*see* **plinthite, soil reaction**

red ring decay a disease caused by the fungus *Phellinus pini* in living conifers in the northern hemisphere —*see* **heart decay** —*synonym* red ring **rot,** red heart, ring scale, **conk** rot, white **pocket rot** —*see* **red rot**

red rot a wound decay caused by the **white rot** fungus *Stereum sanguinolentum* —*note* red rots cause severe heart rot in living conifers, especially balsam fir and spruces in temperate forests of the northern hemisphere —*synonym* red **heart decay** —*see* **red ring decay**

reduced cost the amount by which an **objective function** coefficient would have to improve (in-crease for a maximization problem, decrease for a minimization problem) before the corresponding **decision variable** would take on a positive value in the **optimal solution**

re-entrant an introversion of land levels as exemplified by bays, inlets, and valleys and delineated in map contours —*note* re-entrants are in contrast to their extroversion, i.e., extension, as in capes, promontories and spurs

reference level the absolute **stand** density normally expected in a stand of given characteristics under some standard condition, e.g., average maximum competition (normal stands), no competition, or maximum density —*see* **relative stand density**

refilling the restocking of failed areas in a stand by further plantings or sawings —*see* **beating up, enrichment planting, high forest method, improvement planting**

reforestation the reestablishment of forest cover either naturally (by natural seeding, **coppice,** or root suckers) or artificially (by direct **seeding** or planting) —*note* reforestation usually maintains the same forest type and is done promptly after the previous **stand** or forest was removed —*synonym* **regeneration** —*see* **afforestation, deforestation, dibble, hoedad, J-root, stand establishment**

refugium *plural* **refugia** 1. *ecology, wildlife, and botany* locations and habitats that support populations of organisms that are limited to small fragments of their previous geographic range 2. *pest management* a location and **habitat,** such as uncultivated margins of crop fields, that support small populations of interest, usually **pest** species or natural enemies of pest species

regeneration 1. *genetics* the production of organs, embryos, or whole plants by tissue culture, usually as a morphogenic response to stimulus 2. *ecology* the established progeny from a parent plant 3. *silviculture* seedlings or **saplings** existing in a **stand** —*synonym (obsolete)* reproduction 4. *silviculture* the act of renewing tree cover by establishing young trees naturally or artificially —*note 1.* regeneration usually maintains the same forest type and is done promptly after the previous stand or forest was removed —*note 2.* regeneration may be artificial (direct **seeding** or planting) or natural (natural seeding, **coppice,** or root suckers) —*synonym* **reforestation** —*see* **afforestation, deforestation, dibble, hoedad, J-root, reforestation, stand establishment**

regeneration cut(ting) any removal of trees intended to assist **regeneration** already present or to make regeneration possible —*synonym* regeneration felling

regeneration interval —*see* **regeneration period**

regeneration method a cutting procedure by which a new age class is created; the major methods are **clearcutting, seed tree, shelterwood, selection,** and **coppice** —*synonym* reproduction method —*see* **biological legacy, harvesting method, irregular, variable retention harvest system;** regeneration methods are grouped in four categories: coppice, even-aged, two-aged, and uneven-aged

1. coppice methods achieve the majority of **regeneration** from stump sprouts or root suckers —*synonym* **low forest** methods

> **coppice** all trees in the previous **stand** are cut and the majority of regeneration is from sprouts or root suckers

> **coppice selection** only selected stems of merchantable size are cut at each felling, giving **uneven-aged stands**

> **coppice with reserves** reserve trees are retained to attain **goals** other than regeneration —*synonym* **coppice** with standards —*note* the method normally creates a two-aged **stand**

2. even-aged methods regenerate and maintain a **stand** with a single age class

> **clearcutting** the cutting of essentially all trees, producing a fully exposed microclimate for the development of a new age class —*note 1.* **regeneration** can be from natural **seeding**, direct seeding, planted seedlings, or advance reproduction —*note 2.* cutting may be done in **groups** or patches (group or patch clearcutting), or in strips (strip clearcutting) —*note 3.* the management unit or stand in which regeneration, growth, and **yield** are regulated consists of the individual clearcut stand —*see* **4. uneven-aged methods (group selection)** —*note 4.* when the primary source of regeneration is advance reproduction, the preferred term is **overstory removal**

> **clearcutting with reserves** —*see* **3. two-aged methods**

> **seed tree** the cutting of all trees except for a small number of widely dispersed trees retained for seed production and to produce a new age class in fully exposed microenvironment —*note* seed trees are usually removed after regeneration is established —*also* **seed tree with reserves** —*see* **3. two-aged methods**

> **shelterwood** the cutting of most trees, leaving those needed to produce sufficient shade to produce a new age class in a moderated microenvironment —*note* the sequence of treatments can include three types of cuttings: (a) an optional preparatory cut to enhance conditions for seed production, (b) an establishment cut to prepare the seed bed and to create a new age class, and (c) a removal cut to release established **regeneration** from competition with the overwood; cut-

ting may be done uniformly throughout the stand (uniform shelterwood), in **group**s or patches (group shelterwood), or in strips (strip shelterwood); in a strip shelterwood, regeneration cuttings may progress against the prevailing wind

> **shelterwood with reserves** —*see* **3. two-aged methods, wedge system**

3. two-aged methods regenerate and maintain **stand**s with two age classes —*note* the resulting stand may be two-aged or tend towards an uneven-aged condition as a consequence of both an extended period of **regeneration** establishment and the retention of reserve (green) trees that may represent one or more age classes

> **clearcutting with reserves** a clearcutting in which varying numbers of reserve trees are not harvested to attain **goals** other than regeneration

> **seed tree with reserves** some or all of the seed trees are retained after regeneration has become established to attain **goals** other than regeneration

> **shelterwood with reserves** some or all of the shelter trees are retained after regeneration has become established to attain **goals** other than regeneration

4. uneven-aged (selection) methods regenerate and maintain a multiaged structure by removing some trees in all size classes either singly, in small **group**s, or in strips —*synonym* all-aged methods —*see* **all-aged stand**

> **group selection** trees are removed and new age classes are established in small **group**s —*note 1.* the width of groups is commonly approximately twice the height of the mature trees with smaller openings providing microenvironments suitable for tolerant **regeneration** and larger openings providing conditions suitable for more intolerant regeneration —*note 2.* the management unit or **stand** in which regeneration, growth, and **yield** are regulated consists of an aggregation of groups —*see* **2. even-aged methods (clearcutting)**

> **group selection with reserves** some trees within the **group** are not cut to attain **goals** other than regeneration within the group

> **single tree selection** individual trees of all size classes are removed more or less uniformly throughout the **stand,** to promote growth of remaining trees and to provide space for **regeneration** —*synonym* individual tree selection

regeneration period the time between the initial **regeneration cut**ting and the successful reestablishment of a new age class by natural means, planting, or direct **seeding** —*synonym* reproduction period

regeneration weevil —*see* **terminal weevil**

regime *hydrology* a pattern in which streams make part of their boundaries from their transported load and part of their transported load from their boundaries, carrying out the process at different places and times in the stream in a balanced or alternating manner that permits unlimited growth or removal of boundaries

regimen *hydrology* the stability of a stream and its channel —*note* a river or canal is in regimen if its channel has reached a stable form as the result of its flow characteristics

regression a statistical measure of the amount of change in a dependent variable and one or more independent variables —*note* regression is generally expressed as a regression equation —*see* **multiple regression equation**

regression coefficient the multiplier of an independent variable in a **regression** equation

regular —*see* **uniform**

regular uneven-aged stand a group of trees in which three or more distinct age classes occupy approximately equal areas and provide a balanced distribution of diameter classes —*synonym* balanced **stand**

regulation —*see* **forest regulation**

reinforcement planting —*see* **enrichment planting**

rejuvenation *genetics* a change in a tissue or an organism from a more mature state to a more juvenile state

relaskop an instrument designed for use as an angle gauge in the Bitterlich angle method of forest sampling —*synonym* Spiegelrelaskop, relascope — *note* the instrument can also be used to directly measure tree diameter, tree height, slope, and horizontal distance

relate *GIS* an operation that connects corresponding **record**s in two tables using a **column** common to both —*note* each record in one table is connected to those records in the other that share the same value for a common column —*see* **relate key, relational join**

relate key *GIS* the common set of columns used to relate two attribute tables —*note* the column in the table to be related from is called the foreign key; the column in the table to be related to is called the primary key

relational *GIS* a type of data storage involving tabular data in which the storage structure is independent of the relations

relational constraint the relation between one set of **decision variable**s to another in **mathematical programming** formulations —*note* e.g., in relating volume harvested in period n to that in period

n-1, a relational **constraint** could set these as equal or to no more than a 20 percent decline

relational database *computers* a method of structuring data as collections of tables that are logically associated to each other by shared **attribute**s —*note* any data element can be found in a relation by knowing the name of the table, the attribute (column) name, and the value of the primary key —*see* **relate, relate key, relational join**

relational database management system (RDBMS) a type of database management system able to access data organized in tabular files that can be related together by a common field (**column**) —*note* the system can recombine the data columns from different files

relational join *GIS* the operation of relating and physically merging two **attribute** tables using their common item

relative humidity the (dimensionless) ratio of the actual vapor pressure of the air to the saturation vapor pressure

relative stand density the ratio, proportion, or percent of absolute **stand** density to a reference level defined by some standard level of competition —*see* **reference level, stand density**

relative thinning intensity the periodic (annual) **yield** of a **stand** from **thinning**s, expressed as a percentage of its periodic annual increment —*see* **thinning intensity**

release-kill ratio *obsolete* the ratio of **stocking** to hunter kill

release (release operation) a treatment designed to free young trees from undesirable, usually overtopping, competing vegetation —*note* treatments include **cleaning, liberation**, and **weeding** —*see* **stand improvement**

releve method 1. a method of vegetation classification that groups classes by presence and abundance of characteristic species that are neither ubiquitous nor rare —*note* the releve method is typically European (Braun-Blanquet method) 2. a method of systematic and comprehensive searches through an area to collect complete information on species diversity

relief displacement the displacement of **image**s radially from the **photograph nadir,** caused by differences in elevation of the corresponding ground objects

relog to salvage small timber, **cull**s, and other residuals following the main logging operation —*see* **salvage cutting**

remote sensing the science and art of obtaining information about an object, area, or phenomenon through the analysis of data acquired by a device that is not in contact with the object —*note* methods include aerial photography, radar, and satellite imaging —*see* **image, image footprint, scene**

removal cut —*see* **regeneration method (3. uneven-aged methods, shelterwood)**

renewable resource a resource whose supply becomes available for use at different time intervals and in which present use does not diminish future supply —*note* two types of renewable resources are: (a) those that are not dependent on or affected by human activity, such as wind and (b) those that may be increased or decreased by human activity, such as timber growth and soil productivity —*see* **nonrenewable resource, Resources Planning Act**

repellent a substance that deters animals from eating or damaging the seeds or plants to which it has been applied —*see* **attractant**

repetition repeating a treatment or set of treatments at different points in space or time, as distinct from **replication**

replacement value the estimated cost at present prices of replacing a tree, **stand**, or **forest** with one of equivalent value, or converting it to capital equipment or other goods

replication repeated sampling under similar conditions, or applying a treatment or set of treatments more than once at one place and, so far as possible, at one period of time to increase the **precision** of comparisons and to provide an assessment of the variability among experimental units treated alike —*see* **repetition**

report time —*see* **elapsed time**

representative fraction (RF) a fraction expressing the ratio between linear measurements on a map or photograph and the corresponding distance on the ground —*note* the RF numerator is always unity, and numerator and denominator are in the same units

representativeness a criterion for assessing how adequately an area of interest represents the range of variation in a region

reproduction —*see* **regeneration**

reproductive cell —*see* **germ cell**

reproductive material all plant tissue produced by sexual or asexual means used for production —*see* **germplasm**

resample to calculate the value of a **pixel** in a **raster data** file during a rectification or **rubber sheeting** process —*note* common methods are nearest neighbor, bilinear interpolation, and cubic convolution, depending on whether the file is continuous or discrete —*see* **rectify**

resaw —*see* **saw**

reserve tree a tree, **pole**-sized or larger, retained in either a dispersed or aggregated manner after the **regeneration** period under the **clearcutting, seed tree, shelterwood, group selection,** or **coppice** methods —*synonym* **standard, green tree retention**

residence time 1. *fire* the time required for a fire front to pass a stationary point; numerically, the flame depth divided by the rate of spread 2. *pesticide* the time a chemical remains in the **ecosystem**

residual 1. *silviculture* a tree or **snag** remaining after an intermediate or **partial cutting** of a **stand** 2. *biometrics* the difference between an observed data point and that generated by a **mathematical model**

residual soil a soil formed from, or resting on, consolidated rock of the same kind as that from which it was formed and in the same location —*note* the term is not used in the current US system of soil taxonomy

residual stand a **stand** composed of trees remaining after any type of intermediate harvest

residue 1. the wood or bark that is left after harvesting or a manufacturing process, e.g., slabs, edgings, trimmings, miscuts, sawdust, shavings, veneer cores and clippings, pulp screenings, and logging slash —*note* residues may be separated into logging residues and mill residues 2. *in pesticide applications* a pesticide or its derivatives remaining in the environment or on the crop after treatment —*see* **residence time**

residuum unconsolidated, weathered, or partly weathered mineral material that accumulates by disintegration of bedrock in place

resilience 1. *ecology* the capacity of a (plant) community or **ecosystem** to maintain or regain normal function and development following disturbance —*see* **forest health** 2. *utilization* the property whereby a **strain**ed body gives up its stored energy (if possessing **elasticity,** by doing work as it returns to its original shape, dimensions, or position) on the removal of the deforming force; the stored energy itself

resin —*see* **natural resin**

resin canker a **canker** associated with a dwarf mistletoe **infection** in which the sapwood is heavily infiltrated with resin

resinosis 1. a copious flow or exudation of **oleoresin** on the bark commonly in response to infection, injury, or insect attack —*synonym* bleeding, resin flow —*see* **natural resin, pitchout 2.** the impregnation of wood tissues with oleoresin —*see* **fatwood**

resin tube —*see* **pitch tube**

resistance 1. *ecology* the ability of a **community** to avoid alteration of its present state by a disturbance **2.** *pesticides* the ability of an individual or strains of organisms to survive normally lethal doses of pesticides —*note* resistance results from genetic selection over multiple generations of the population to repeated exposure to the toxicant **3.** *entomology and pathology* the ability of plants to avoid, suppress, prevent, overcome, or tolerate insect or **pathogen** attack or to adversely affect the attacking insects or pathogens —*note* resistance may be none (death), partial, or complete (immune) —*see* **escape, susceptibility**

resistance to control the relative difficulty of constructing and holding a **control line** as affected by **fire behavior** and resistance to line construction — *synonym* difficulty of control

resolution 1. *GIS* the accuracy at which the location and shape of map features can be depicted for a given map scale —*note* at a map scale of 1:63,360 (1 in = 1 mi), it is difficult to represent areas smaller than 1/10-mi (0.16 km) wide or 1/10-mi (0.16 km) in length because they are only 1/10-in (0.25 cm) wide or long on the map; in a larger-scale map there is less reduction, so feature resolution more closely matches real-world features; as map scale decreases, resolution also diminishes, because feature boundaries must be smoothed, simplified, or not shown at all **2.** the size of the smallest feature that can be represented on a map **3.** *GIS* the number of points in x and y in a grid, e.g., the resolution of a one-degree **digital elevation model (DEM)** is 1,201 × 1,201 mesh points **4.** *remote sensing* the measure of the finest geometric, spectral, radiometric, and temporal detail that can be distinguished in an **image**d object or phenomenon

resources 1. the natural resources of an area, e.g., timber, grass, watershed values, recreation values, wildlife **habitat 2.** *fire* all personnel and major items of equipment available or potentially available for fire-fighting tasks on which status is maintained —*note* resources is an **ICS** term

Resources Planning Act (RPA) Assessment and Program the assessment and program are two components of the US Forest and Rangelands Renewable Resources Planning Act (RPA) of 1974; the assessment is prepared every 10 years and describes the potential of the nation's **forest**s and **range**lands to provide a sustained flow of goods and services; the program is prepared every five years to chart the long-term course of the USDA Forest Service's management of the national forests, assistance to state and private landowners, and research —*see* **renewable resource, nonrenewable resource**

respiration a process in plants involving the breakdown of carbon-containing compounds (mainte-

nance or growth respiration) or competitive reactions during **photosynthesis** (photorespiration) resulting in the release of carbon dioxide

restoration 1. *ecology* the process of returning **ecosystem**s or **habitat**s to their original structure and **species** composition **2.** *recreation* the removal of nonhistorical elements from a historic structure and the replacement of any missing elements

rest-rotation a grazing-management scheme in which rest periods for individual pastures, paddocks, or grazing units, generally for the full growing season, are incorporated into a **grazing** rotation —*see* **grazing system, rotational stocking**

retardant —*see* **fire retardant**

retardant drop a **fire retardant** that is **cascaded** from an **air tanker** or **helitank**er

reticulate mottling a network of **mottles** with no dominant color most commonly found in deeper **horizon**s of soils containing **plinthite**

return flow the portion of the water diverted from a stream that finds its way back to the stream channel, either as surface or underground flow

returns to scale a way of classifying production functions that records how output responds to proportional increases in all inputs —*note* if a proportional increase in all inputs causes output to increase by a smaller proportion, the production function exhibits decreasing returns to scale; if output increases by a greater proportion than the inputs, the production function exhibits increasing returns to scale; constant returns to scale is the middle ground

revegetation the reestablishment and development of vegetation

RF —*see* **representative fraction**

RGP —*see* **root growth potential**

rhizobia 1. bacteria able to live symbiotically in roots of leguminous plants from which they receive energy and often utilize molecular nitrogen **2.** the collective common name for the genus *Rhizobium*

Rhizobium the genus of nitrogen-fixing bacteria which, through initial colonization of fine roots, forms root nodules on the root system of a symbiotic host in the legume family

rhizome a modified **stem** that grows below ground, commonly stores food materials, and produces roots, scale leaves, and suckers irregularly along its length and not just at nodes —*note* rhizomatous plants include bamboo, horsetail, and bracken fern —*see* **stolon**

rhizomorph a rootlike strand of fungal **hyphae**, often much branched —*see* **mycelial form, mycelium, mycorrhiza**

rhizosphere the zone of soil immediately surrounding plant roots that is significantly influenced by the presence of the root, enriched with carbon from the root, and characterized by more intensive microorganismal activity than nonrhizosphere soil

rhizotron a window or chamber from which the dynamics and interactions of roots can be observed through glass or Plexiglas® —*see* **minirhizotron**

ribonucleic acid (RNA) a single-strand nucleic acid found in the protoplasm and partially controlling cellular chemical activities —*note* the major function of RNA is to carry the genetic message from the nuclear **DNA** to the **ribosome**s where proteins are synthesized

ribosome a protoplasmic granule containing ribonucleic acid where protein synthesis occurs —*see* **ribonucleic acid, translation**

richness —*see* **species richness**

rich tool —*see* **hand tool**

rick a pile of evenly stacked cordwood, staves, bolts, or other short-length wood —*see* **cord**

riffle a fast section of a stream where shallow water races over stones and gravel —*note* riffles usually support a wider variety of bottom organisms than other stream sections —*synonym* rift

rift valley a long, narrow valley resulting from subsidence of strata between more or less parallel faults or from the elevation of strata outside parallel faults

rig *harvesting* **1.** to prepare a tailhold, spar, or tower for **yard**ing by guying and anchoring it, attaching all rigging, and stringing the lines **2.** a truck or pickup

rigging *harvesting* cables, **blocks**, and other equipment used in **yard**ing and loading logs

right-of-way (ROW) 1. a legal right of passage over another person's land **2.** a path or thoroughfare that one may lawfully use **3.** a strip of land that is managed specifically for access or the construction and maintenance of electric, telephone, water, other domestic utilities, streets, roads, and highways

rill —*see* **gully**

rill erosion —*see* **erosion**

ring fire —*see* **firing technique**

ring-porous pertaining to wood of hardwoods in which the **earlywood** of the annual ring forms a well-defined zone or ring and has larger-diameter pores than those of the **latewood** —*note* ring-porous woods include ash and oak —*see* **diffuse porous**

ring rot any **rot** localized mainly in the early wood of the growth rings, giving a concentric pattern of decayed wood in cross-section, e.g., of **red ring decay**

riparian related to, living, or located in conjunction with a wetland, on the bank of a river or stream but also at the edge of a lake or tidewater —*note* the riparian community significantly influences, and is significantly influenced by, the neighboring body of water —*see* **riverine**

riparian zone a terrestrial area, other than a coastal area, of variable width adjacent to and influenced by a perennial or intermittent body of water —*note 1.* the riparian zone contributes organic matter to the river or stream and may be influenced by periodic surface or subsurface water —*note 2.* riparian zones provide a functional linkage between terrestrial and aquatic **ecosystem**s through coarse and fine organic matter input, bank stability, water temperature regulation, sediment and nutrient flow regulation, maintenance of unique wildlife **habitat,** and in limiting or mitigating **nonpoint source pollution** —*note 3.* the management of a riparian zone is commonly constrained or modified to retain particular **ecosystem** values and functions; the term is used in management plans, legislation, regulation, and government policy in which riparian zone width is variably defined —*synonym* **riparian** area, riparian buffer zone, riparian habitat

ripper 1. a toothed blade or set of heavy tines mounted at the front or rear of a vehicle, e.g., a tractor or bulldozer, or trailed from it, for breaking up soft rock and hard ground and tearing out stumps and boulders **2.** a vehicle so equipped

riprap rocks, pieces of used concrete, or other material of various sizes placed firmly or loosely on river banks to prevent scouring by the river, or on slopes or road cuts to prevent **erosion** —*see* **gabion**

rip saw —*see* **saw**

risk 1. *management, operations research* the relative probability of any of several alternative outcomes as determined or estimated by a decision maker when the actual outcome of an event or series of events is not known **2.** *management, operations research* the product of the probability of the event taking place, the probability of being exposed to the event, and the probability of certain outcomes if exposure to the event occurs **3.** *entomology, pathology* the probability that an insect population or outbreak will occur in a particular stand, watershed, or forest, or that a particular tree will be severely damaged under a given set of conditions; e.g., with bark beetles, risk is the short-term expectation of tree mortality in a stand as a result of a **bark beetle** infestation —*note* risk is not related to the extent of damage —*see* **hazard 4.** the probability that a tree will die within a specified time period **5.** *fire* —*see* **fire risk, hazard, uncertainty**

risk-rating system 1. a ranking of trees or forest **stand**s according to the probability of attack or outbreak by one or more insects or **pathogen**s **2.** a prediction of the probability that a tree will die within a specified period of time

riverain relating to watercourses or small islands in river beds —*note* riverain describes vegetation growing close to water —*see* **riverine**

riverine relating to rivers and streams —*see* **riparian, riverain** —*note* the term riverine is used commonly in classifying and delineating **wetland**s and deepwater **habitat**s

R layer hard bedrock including granite, basalt, quartzite, and indurated limestone or sandstone that is sufficiently coherent to make hand digging impractical

RMS error —*see* **root mean square error (RMS)**

RNA —*see* **ribonucleic acid**

ROD —*see* **record of decision**

rod a graduated measuring stick used with various leveling instruments to determine differences in elevation between two points

roguing systematic removal of individuals not desired for the perpetuation of a **population**, e.g., from a seed stand, nursery, or genetic test —*synonym* **cull**ing —*note* roguing is usually based on data from genetic tests—*see* **eugenic, genetic test, mass selection, progeny test, seed orchard**

root biomass the standing crop of live plus dead roots expressed per volume or area of soil

root cap a mass of cells, distal to the **apical meristem**, which originates in the apical meristem, protects it, and secretes mucigel

root channel a location in the soil where a living root died and left a cavity or area in the soil that is high in organic matter and low in bulk density

root collar the location on a plant where the primary vascular anatomy changes from that of a **stem** to that of a root —*note* in some species the root collar is clearly defined, but in others the position of the stem-root junction is not clear and may be defined at an arbitrary distance below the cotyledonary node

root collar weevil —*see* **terminal weevil**

root core a core of soil that is removed from the soil profile using a metal cylinder or auger and used to quantify fine root biomass on a volumetric basis

root disease a disease of the root system mostly caused by root-inhabiting Basidiomycotina fungi,

some of which can persist for long periods as **saprophyte**s on dead plant material —*note* root diseases include *Armillaria* root rot, *Annosus* root rot, *Phellinus* root disease, and the *Phytophthora* root rots —*synonym* root decay, root rot —*see* **infection center**

root growth potential (RGP) the ability to grow new roots quickly, as measured under standard growing conditions and used as an indicator of planting stock quality —*synonym* root growth capacity

root hair a microscopic, hairlike protuberance extending from an epidermal cell forming a trichome (threadlike root) in a young root —*see* **epidermis**

root length density the length of roots per volume of soil

root mean square error (RMS error) 1. the square root of the average of the squared differences of values from their mean **2.** *GIS* the square root of the mean error between the "known" and digitized coordinate locations—*note 1.* RMS error is calculated when **tic**s are used to register a map on the **digitizer**; the lower the RMS error, the more accurate the digitizing or transformation —*synonym* tic registration error —*note 2.* for highly accurate geographic data, the RMS error should be kept under 0.004 in (0.01 cm); for less accurate data, the value may be higher —*see* **accuracy, tic**

root nodule a protuberance on the roots of leguminous plant species such as *Robinia* in which *Rhizobium* species metabolize atmospheric nitrogen to form ammonia nitrogen

root pressure a force developed in the roots of certain plants at certain times causing water to move into the xylary system —*see* **cells (wood)**

root primordium an organized group of root cells at the early stage of differentiation within the pericycle that develops into a lateral root

root pruning the cutting of seedling roots, with minimum disturbance, in a nursery bed to limit their vertical or lateral growth —*note* root pruning is usually done by a horizontal blade drawn by a tractor at a prescribed depth —*synonym* undercutting —*see* **wrenching**

rootrake a set of tines, either mounted on the front of a tractor or trailed from it, for collecting stumps and **slash** —*see* **windrow**

rootstock the root-bearing plant or plant part, usually stem or root, onto which another plant part (**scion**) is **graft**ed —*see* **bud, stock**

ROPS a rollover protective structure, such as a roll bar, that protects the operator if a machine overturns

ROS —*see* **recreation opportunity spectrum**

rosin the solid residue after evaporation and distillation of turpentine from the **oleoresin** of various pines, consisting mainly of rosin acids (abietic acid and primaric acid) —*see* **essential oil, natural resin, naval stores**

rosser a machine that peels bark using knives mounted on a head

rot an advanced and obvious stage of **decay** —*note* the term designates both the causal organism and its effect, i.e., **dry rot, soft rot**

rotation in even-aged systems, the period between **regeneration** establishment and final cutting —*note* rotation may be based on many criteria including mean size, age, **culmination of mean annual increment**, attainment of particular minimum physical or value growth rate, and biological condition —*see* **financial maturity, soil rent(al)**

rotation(al) grazing a grazing-management system in which animals are moved from one grazing unit (pasture or paddock) to another in the same group of grazing units without regard to specific graze or rest periods or levels of plant defoliation —*synonym* cyclic grazing —*see* **grazing system, pasture**

rotational stocking a **grazing method** that alternates periods of grazing and rest among two or more pastures or paddocks in a grazing **management unit** throughout the period when grazing is allowed —*note* words such as controlled or intensive are sometimes used to describe the degree of **grazing management** applied but are not synonyms of rotational stocking —*see* **continuous stocking, rest rotation, set stocking**

rotation pasture a cultivated area utilized as pasture for one or a few years, as part of an agricultural crop rotation —*see* **rotational grazing**

roughage plant materials containing a low proportion of nutrients per unit of weight and usually bulky and coarse, high in fiber, and low in total digestible nutrients —*note* roughage may be classed as either dry or green

rough grazing a pasture in its wild state, e.g., on moorland or **scrub** —*synonym* unimproved grazing

roundheaded borer a member of the family Cerambycidae, which are phloem borers —*note 1*. neither the **larvae** nor the adults of roundheaded borers have round heads; the term may refer to the round emergence holes of some species —*note 2*. some species of roundheaded borers are important **pests**, e.g., the southern pine sawyer, *Monochamus titillator* —*synonym* roundheaded phloem borer —*see* **flatheaded borer**

roundheaded pine beetle a **bark beetle** (*Dendroctonus adjunctus*) that attacks pines in the Southwest, particularly those in the smaller diameter classes

roundup the purposeful gathering of animals into a herd by humans —*synonym* muster

roundwood a length of cut tree generally having a round cross section, such as a log or bolt

roundworm —*see* **nematode**

route *GIS* a process that establishes connections through a **network** or **grid** from a source to a destination —*note 1*. a route could be established through a network of streets from a fire station to the fire; a grid example would be to move soil particles from a ridgetop to a stream based on equations developed by soil scientists —*note 2*. the determination of routes usually takes into consideration **impedance**s

ROW —*see* **right-of-way**

row **1.** *computers* a **record** in a relational table **2.** *GIS* a horizontal group of **cell**s in a **grid,** or **pixels** in an **image**

royalty *United Kingdom and other countries* payment to be made to the owner or lessor of a forest for the right of harvesting, generally based on a rate per unit of produce removed —*see* **stumpage**

RPA —*see* **Resources Planning Act (RPA) Assessment and Program**

r-selection *ecology* selection of life-history **trait**s that promote an ability to rapidly multiply in numbers

rubber sheeting *GIS* a procedure to adjust the entities of a geographic data set in a nonuniform manner, by defining the polynomial (using a set of known from- and to-coordinates) used to calculate the new coordinates from the old, and determining the value of the new coordinates (resampling)

rub tree a tree used as pivot to protect the remaining **stand** during extraction

ruderal a plant that grows on wasteland, old fields, waysides, or highly disturbed sites —*see* **pioneer**

running fire —*see* **fire behavior**

running line a cable that moves during harvesting —*see* **standing line**

running skyline *harvesting* a system of two or more suspended moving lines, generally referred to as **main lines** and **haulback lines** —*note* a running skyline provides lift and travel to the load carrier when tension is properly applied

runoff that portion of the precipitation on a drainage area that is discharged from the area in stream channels —*note* types include surface runoff, **groundwater** runoff, or seepage

runt any animal, particularly **livestock**, of inferior size and condition, and by extension, of inferior breeding

rural (development) forestry —*see* **social forestry**

rust 1. a **rust fungus 2.** a disease caused by a rust fungus —*note* an example is white pine blister rust, *Cronartium ribicola* **3.** masses of brown, orange, or black **spore**s of a rust fungus on the surface of a plant

rust fungus a fungus in the order Uredinales, characterized by obligate **parasitism** and complex life cycles —*note* rust fungi have as many as five **spore** forms, frequently with alternate **host**s

S

safety chief —*see* **large fire organization**

safety guy *harvesting* a line rigged under the **bull block** to take it to the ground if the holding straps break

safety island *fire* an area cleared of flammable material that can be used with relative safety by **fire fighter**s and their equipment in the event of a nearby **blowup**, or used for escape if the **control line** is outflanked or a **spot fire** causes **fuel**s outside the control line to render the line unsafe —*note 1.* in firing operations, crews progress to maintain a safety island nearby —*note 2.* large safety islands may also be constructed as integral parts of **fuelbreak**s

safety officer —*see* **incident command system**

sale schedule the quantity of timber planned for sale by time period from an area of suitable land covered by a forest plan —*note* in a sale schedule the first period, usually a decade, provides the **allowable sale quantity;** future periods are shown to establish that long-term **sustained yield** will be achieved and maintained —*see* **lump-sum sale, per unit sale**

saline soil a non**sodic soil** containing sufficient soluble salt to adversely affect the growth of most crop plants —*note* the lower limit of saturation extract electrical conductivity of such soils is conventionally set at 4 dS m^{-1} (at 25°C or 77°F); sensitive plants are affected at half this salinity and highly tolerant ones, at about twice this salinity (dS = decisiemen)

salting 1. providing salt as a mineral supplement for animals **2.** placing salt on the **range** to improve distribution of **livestock** grazing

salvage cutting the removal of dead trees or trees damaged or dying because of injurious agents other than competition, to recover economic value that would otherwise be lost —*synonym* salvage felling, salvage logging

sample 1. a part of a population consisting of one or more sampling units selected and examined as representative of the whole **2.** to select and measure or record a sample of a population —*see* **point sampling**

sample fraction the proportion of a **population,** stratum, or multistage unit included in a sample

sample mean the **arithmetic mean** of a **random variable** in a sample, calculated by dividing the sum of the observations by their number

sample plot an area of a **stand** or **forest** chosen as representative of a much larger area —*note* sample plots are used in inventories, in studies of growth, or the effects of treatments —*see* **experimental plot, experimental unit**

sample, proportional a sampling procedure in which the selection of the sampling unit is proportional to the particular parameter being sampled —*see* **point sampling, three-P sampling, variable-radius plot sampling**

sample, stratified a sample taken by selecting sample units from each of several strata

sample, systematic a sample consisting of units selected according to a geometric or other nonrandom procedure —*note* the first sampling unit is often selected randomly

sampling error the difference between a **population** value and a sample estimate that is attributable to the sample, as distinct from errors due to **bias** in estimation, errors in observation, etc. —*note* sampling error is measured as the standard error of the sample estimate

sampling unit an entity measured that may be a subset of an **experimental unit**, e.g., in a fertilizer treatment the plots are the experimental units and the trees are the sampling units

sanctuary an area set aside for the complete protection of all forms of wildlife from hunting, other anthropogenic disturbance, and occasionally from specified predators and parasites —*see* **preserve**

sand 1. a soil separate having an effective diameter of 0.05 to 2.00 mm (0.002 to 0.08 in) **2.** a soil textural class defined by soil material that contains 85 percent or more of sand; the percentage of **silt,** plus 1.5 times the percentage of **clay,** does not exceed 15

sanitation cutting the removal of trees to improve **stand** health by stopping or reducing the actual or anticipated spread of insects and disease —*see* **stand improvement**

sap the fluid contents circulating through dead **xylem** cells or canals, i.e., **apoplast** —*see* **sapwood, translocation**

sapling a usually young tree larger than a seedling but smaller than a **pole** —*note* size varies by region —*see* **mature**

saprophyte an organism that lives on dead organic matter and gains its nutrition from this substrate —*see* **parasite**

sap rot any rot characteristically confined to the sapwood

sapwood the outer layers of a stem, which in a live tree are composed of living cells and conduct water up the tree —*note* sapwood is generally lighter in color than **heartwood** —*see* **sap, translocation**

SAR —*see* **synthetic aperture radar**

saturated air moist air in a state of equilibrium with a plane surface of pure water or ice at the same time temperature and pressure, i.e., air whose vapor pressure is the saturation vapor pressure —*note* the **relative humidity** of saturated air is 100 percent

saturated flow the liquid flow of water in soils that occurs when the soil pores in the wettest part of the soil are completely filled with water and the direction of flow is from the wettest zone of higher potential to one of lower potential

saturation-adiabatic lapse rate the rate of decrease of temperature with height of an air parcel lifted in a saturation-adiabatic process through an atmosphere in hydrostatic equilibrium —*note* this is a special case of process lapse rate

saturation deficit the difference between the actual vapor pressure and the saturation vapor pressure at the existing temperature

savanna a lowland, tropical or subtropical grassland, generally with a scattering of trees or shrubs —*note* if woody growth is absent, such an area is termed grass savanna; with **shrubs** and widely, irregularly scattered trees, it is called a tree savanna —*see* **derived savanna, prairie, savanna woodland**

savanna woodland a more or less open tropical or subtropical **woodland** having an undergrowth mainly of grasses, the trees being of moderate height and generally deciduous or, if evergreen, tending to have small leaves —*see* **prairie, savanna**

saw kinds of saw include the following:

—**band saw** an endless beltlike strip of steel, toothed along one or both edges and running unidirectionally between two pulleys, used to saw logs —*note* more than one band saw may be mounted to provide, e.g., a twin-band or a triple-band saw

—**bow saw** a hand frame saw in which the narrow, striplike blade is fitted in a stiff bow-shaped frame and commonly used for felling small trees and crosscutting small logs

—**breaking-down saw** a saw used in the initial operation of converting a log by sawing the log longitudinally into **cants** —*synonym* breakdown saw, headsaw, headrig

—**chain saw** a saw that is powered by a gasoline, hydraulic, or electric motor, with cutting elements on an endless chain

—**Chip-n-Saw**™ a machine that makes small logs into **cants**, converting part of the outside of the log directly into chips without producing any sawdust —*note* cants are then sawn into lumber as part of the same operation

saw *continued*

—**circular saw** a circular steel plate (disk) having cutting teeth on the circumference and rotating on a saw **arbor** —*note* if the plate retains its full thickness throughout, the saw is termed a plate saw as distinct from a concave, ground-off, hollow-ground, **single-conical,** or **double-conical** saw —*see* **pitch**

—**crosscut saw** any saw with teeth specifically designed (or set) for cutting across the grain

—**double-conical saw** a **swage-set** circular saw whose plate tapers on both sides from near the center (collar) to the rim —*synonym* taper-ground saw, double swage-set saw

—**edger saw** a machine used to square-edge **waney** lumber

—**gang saw** a machine in which two or more circular saws are mounted together on the same **arbor** —*synonym* frame saw

—**head** the principal saw (either circular or band) in a sawmill, used for the initial breakdown of logs by sawing along their length —*note* logs are first cut into **cants** on the headrig before being sent on to other saws for further processing —*synonym* headsaw, breaking-down saw

—**peg-raker saw** any saw having cutting teeth in pairs, each pair separated by a **raker** tooth —*synonym* clearer tooth

—**peg-tooth saw** a circular saw having triangular teeth, i.e., peg teeth, generally used for crosscutting as distinct from **ripping**

—**planer saw** a hollow-ground **circular** saw having teeth of special design, commonly sets of four peg teeth and one **raker**, to produce a particularly smooth cut

—**radial-arm saw** a machine fitted with a small-diameter **circular** saw attached to a motor that is suspended through adjustable mountings from an overhead arm, so that the saw can cut in any desired plane —*note* a radial-arm saw can be used for crosscutting, ripping, bevel and angle cutting, molding, etc.

—**resaw** a machine fitted with either **band** or **circular** saws to convert **cants** and other large lumber into smaller sizes

—**rip saw** any saw with teeth specially designed for cutting along the grain (ripping) —*synonym* ripper

—**single-conical saw** a **swage-set** circular saw whose plate is wholly flat on one side but tapers from the central portion (collar) to the rim on the other side

sawfly a gregarious, defoliating insect mostly in the families Diprionidae and Tenthredinidae whose larvae feed generally on conifer foliage —*note* sawflies that are important forest defoliators include European spruce sawfly *(Gilpinia hercyniae),* jack pine sawfly *(Neodiprion pratti banksianae),* larch sawfly *(Pristiphora erichsonii),* and red pine sawfly *(Neodiprion nanulus nanulus)*

sawlog a log that meets minimum regional standards of diameter, length, and defect, intended for sawing

sawlog top diameter the diameter outside bark (DOB) at the top of the sawlog length of the bole

sawnwood the sawn product from a tree —*synonym* **lumber**

sawtimber trees or logs cut from trees with minimum diameter and length and with stem quality suitable for conversion to **lumber** —*see* **sawlog**

sawyer one who cuts logs into boards in a sawmill or who cuts felled trees into logs —*see* **bucker**

SCA —*see* **specific combining ability**

scalariform pit —*see* **cells (wood)**

scale 1. the relationship between a distance on a map and the corresponding distance on the earth —*note* e.g., a scale of 1:24,000 means that 1 unit of measurement on the map equals 24,000 of the same units on the earth's surface **2.** *ecology* the level of spatial resolution perceived or considered **3.** *entomology* —*see* **scale insect 4.** *utilization* to measure the weight or volume of a log, load of logs, or stacked fuelwood —*note* the person who measures is a scaler —*see* **checkscaler, grading**

scale bar a map element that shows the map scale graphically

scale insect *also* **scale** a plant-juice sucker whose small, wingless female nymphs secrete a protective covering —*note* scales may be soft, e.g., the cottony maple scale *(Pulvinaria innumerabilis);* hard (armored), e.g., the oystershell scale *(Lepidosaphes ulmi);* or waxy (mealy), e.g., the **mealybugs** (family Pseudococcidae)

scale stick a graduated rule for measuring the small-end diameters of logs under bark and estimating the board-foot volume or heights of trees or logs —*note 1.* the scale stick is usually marked in 1-in (2.54 cm) diameter classes to 40 in (101.6 cm) **DBH**, tree heights up to five 16-ft (4.87 m) logs, and board-foot volumes for various log lengths and common **log scales** —*note 2.* a **log rule** is generally reproduced on it (**log scale**) so that lumber contents can be read off directly (log scale) —*note 3.* a stick fitted with calipers and graduated for the volumes of logs of different lengths is a **caliper** scale —*synonym* scaling stick —*see* **lumber rule**

scaling the measurement or estimation of the quantity or quality of felled timber

scaling diameter the inside-bark diameter at the small end of a log

scalp to remove vegetation and other organic or inorganic material to expose underlying mineral soil and prepare an area for planting or **seeding** —*note* scalping is usually done by hand rather than by machine —*see* **grub, scarification, screef, site preparation**

scanner an active or passive remote-sensing device for imaging a region of interest —*see* **digitizer**

scanning *GIS* a process by which information in hard copy format (paper print, Mylar™ transparencies, microfilm aperture cards) can be rapidly converted to digital raster form (**pixels**) using optical readers —*synonym* automated digitizing, scan digitizing —*see* **digitize**

scarification 1. mechanical removal of competing vegetation or interfering debris, or disturbance of the soil surface, to enhance **reforestation** —*see* **scalp, screef 2.** chemical, mechanical, heat, or moisture treatment of seeds to make the seed coat permeable and improve **germination**

scarp an escarpment, cliff, or steep slope of some extent along the margin of a plateau, mesa, terrace, or structural bench

scatterometer a nonimaging radar device that quantitatively records backscatter from microwave pulses transmitted as a function of incidence angle

scavenger an organism that consumes dead animals or dead organic material —*see* **carnivore, herbivore**

scenario a word picture of a fixed sequence of future events in a defined environment —*note* a scenario is normally used to focus attention on causal processes, decision points, and potential consequences

scene the area covered by a remotely sensed image —*see* **remote sensing**

scenic river a river or segment of river, as defined by the Wild and Scenic Rivers Act of 1968, that is free of impoundments, with a shoreline or watershed still largely primitive, and that is undeveloped but accessible in places by roads

schoolmarm a tree that initially had a single trunk that later divided into two separate trunks partway up

scion an aerial plant part, often a branch tip, that is grafted onto the root-bearing part (rootstock) of another plant —*see* **graft, rootstock, vegetative propagation**

sclereid —*see* **cells (wood)**

sclerophyllous forest a **forest** characterized by the prevalence of **species** with leathery, generally small leaves, commonly in a climate with relatively hot and dry seasons

sclerophyte a generally small, evergreen, and xerophytic plant with thick, hard leaves —*see* **xeromorphic, xerophyte**

sclerosis the hardening of cell walls of wood by lignification —*see* **lignin**

sclerotium *plural* **sclerotia** a compact hardened body of densely woven **hyphae** —*note 1.* sclerotia generally act as resting bodies during periods of unfavorable conditions —*note 2.* active mycelia develop once conditions are favorable —*see* **mycelium**

scope *federal land management* the types of actions to be included in a project, the range of alternatives, and the impacts to be considered

scorch an injury to bark, foliage, flowers, or fruit from (a) excessive heat, whether from fires or sunlight (insolation), (b) hot, freezing, salt-laden, fume-laden, or unduly strong winds, or (c) unbalanced nutrition or poisoning, e.g., from the misapplication of a pesticide —*see* **sunscald, windblast, winter sunscald**

SCORP —*see* **state comprehensive outdoor recreation plan**

scratch file *GIS* a temporary file holding intermediate calculations —*note* a scratch file is used, e.g., when calculating **arc** intersections or building feature topology

scratch line an unfinished preliminary **fireline** hastily established or constructed as an emergency measure to check fire spread —*see* **barrier, firebreak, fuelbreak**

screef to prepare a **forest** soil for planting or **seeding** by pushing aside the **humus** layer to expose mineral soil —*see* **scalp, scarification**

scribe a tool for marking trees or round timber by scoring the outer surface

Scribner decimal C log rule a modification of the **Scribner rule** in which the board foot volume is taken to the closest 10 bd ft and then the last digit is dropped —see **Doyle rule, Doyle-Scribner rule, international log rule, international 1/4-inch rule, log scale**

Scribner rule a diagram **log rule** that assumes 1-in (2.54-cm) boards and 0.25-in (0.64 cm) kerf, is based on diameter at the small end of the log, disregards taper, and does not provide for **overrun** —*note* the Scribner rule underestimates lumber **yield** on small logs and on long logs with taper —*see* **Doyle rule, Doyle-Scribner rule, Scribner decimal C log rule**

scrub 1. small or stunted trees or **shrubs**, generally of unmerchantable species —*note* where such trees are sufficiently numerous, the vegetation is termed a scrub forest **2.** any woody growth of low economic potentiality

sea-level pressure the atmospheric pressure at mean sea level

seasoning —*see* **drying**

secondary dormancy a relapse into **dormancy** of seeds or spores after initial dormancy has been broken, either naturally or after artificial treatment

secondary forest —*see* **second-growth forest**

secondary growth growth from the cambium responsible for thickening of tree stems, branches, and roots —*see* **primary growth**

secondary host 1. *entomology* in insects with complex life cycles, the **host** on which only asexual reproduction occurs **2.** *pathology* in the **rust fungi,** the host of the pycnial and aecial forms —*see* **aecium, pycnium 3.** a host species attacked less frequently than the principal host —*see* **primary host, rust fungus**

secondary host selection the aggregating response of adult insects, particularly **bark beetles,** usually in large numbers, to pheromones produced by pioneers and sometimes also to attractive **host**-produced volatile compounds—*synonym* secondary attraction —*see* **initial attack, mass attack, primary host selection**

secondary insect an insect that can successfully attack only plants that are already weakened, diseased, dying, or dead, e.g., many *Scolytus* **bark beetles** —*see* **predisposition, primary insect, primary pathogen, secondary pathogen, secondary pest**

secondary line any **fireline** constructed at a distance from the fire perimeter concurrently with or after a primary control line has been constructed on or near the perimeter —*note* a secondary line is generally constructed as an insurance measure in case the fire jumps the primary line

secondary mineral a mineral resulting from the decomposition of a primary mineral or from the reprecipitation of the products of decomposition of a primary mineral

secondary parasite a **hyperparasite**

secondary pathogen a **pathogen** that can invade the **host** only after establishment of a primary pathogen —*note 1.* once established, secondary pathogens may or may not be able to induce disease on their own —*note 2.* secondary pathogens may include pathogens that can invade the host after insect **infestation,** particularly by **bark beetles** —*see* **predisposition, primary insect, primary pathogen, secondary insect, secondary pest**

secondary pest an insect or **pathogen** whose population levels are not normally damaging but which reach damaging levels when their natural enemy populations are disrupted by preventive or suppressive treatments targeted toward another **pest** (or pests) —*see* **secondary insect, secondary pathogen**

secondary phloem the **phloem** tissue formed by the **vascular cambium** during secondary growth in a vascular plant

secondary root growth the development of a primary root into a woody root with the formation of a **vascular cambium** between the primary **phloem** and primary **xylem** and the further development of secondary vascular tissues

secondary xylem **xylem** tissue formed by the **vascular cambium** during secondary growth in a vascular plant

second-growth forest a relatively young **forest** that has been regenerated naturally or artificially after some drastic interference such as extensive cutting, wildfire, insect or disease attack, or blowdown —*synonym* secondary forest, young-growth forest —*see* **old-growth forest**

section 1. *surveying* a land survey subdivision, usually one square mile (640 ac or 259 ha) **2.** *fire* —*see* **incident command system**

sector *fire* a designated segment of the perimeter or **control line** comprising the **fire suppression** work unit for two or more crews under one **sector boss** —*note* an **LFO** term

sector boss —*see* **large fire organization**

sediment 1. solid material, both mineral and organic, that is in suspension and being transported from its site of origin by the forces of air, water, gravity, or ice **2.** material thus carried that has come to rest on the earth's surface either above or below sea level

sedimentation the process of **sediment** deposition, usually resulting from **erosion**

sediment discharge the quantity of **sediment** transported through a stream cross-section in a given time —*note* sediment discharge is measured in dry weight or by volume and consists of both suspended load and bedload —*synonym* sediment yield

sediment yield —*see* **sediment discharge**

seed 1. the ripened **ovule** of a plant containing an embryo, seed coat, and nutritive tissue **2.** in **dwarf mistletoe,** a propagating structure made up of endosperm and embryo, lacking a true seed coat but encased in the fruit's endocarp

seed and cone insect an insect whose **larvae, nymph**s, or adults feed on the flowers, cones, or seeds of trees —*note* such insects include cone beetles (*Conophthorus* sp.) and seed chalcids (*Megastigmus* sp.)

seed bearer 1. any tree (capable of) producing seed **2.** any tree retained to provide seed for natural **regeneration**, e.g., during seed cuttings

seed bed 1. *natural regeneration* the soil or forest floor on which seed falls **2.** *nursery practice* a prepared area over which seed is sown

seed certification the process of guaranteeing by an accredited agency of the origin (geographic, genetic), purity, quality, clean condition, etc., of a given lot of seed —*note* such lots may include **source-identified, selected,** certified, or tested seed

seed collection zone —*see* **seed zone**

seed efficiency the percentage of pure live seed in a given lot or sample that develops into plantable seedlings (non**cull**s) at the end of a predetermined period —*note* the term generally refers to greenhouse and nursery results

seeding 1. the production or shedding of seed by a plant **2.** the distribution of seed by hand or machine in **regeneration** —*synonym* direct seeding, sowing

seedlot a collection of seeds, usually of known origin

seed orchard a **plantation** consisting of **clones** or seedlings from selected trees for early and abundant production of seed and to promote balanced, random mating (panmixis) —*note* seed orchards may attempt isolation to reduce **pollination** from outside sources, and more advanced techniques may seek to skew mating to the most desirable clones —*see* **breeding arboretum, isolation, roguing, seed production area**

seed production area an existing **stand** that is usually upgraded and opened by removal of phenotypically undesirable trees and then cultured for early and abundant seed production —*see* **phenotype, seed orchard**

seed purity the percentage by weight of clean, full seed of the desired **species** in a batch —*see* **germinative capacity, germinative energy, seed quality**

seed quality the percentage, by weight or number, of clean, sound, full-sized seed in a batch —*see* **germinative capacity, germinative energy, seed purity**

seed source 1. the locality where a seed lot was collected —*synonym* **seed zone 2.** the seed itself —*note* if the **stand** from which collections were made was in turn from nonnative ancestors, the original seed source is recorded and designated as

the **provenance** —*see* **geographic race, local seed source, nonnative, provenance test, race, source-identified seed (plant)**

seed spot a prepared, limited space, e.g., a small, cultivated patch, within which (tree) seeds are sown —*note* the operation is called spot **seeding** —*see* **spot planting**

seed trap a device for catching the seeds falling on an area —*note* a seed trap is used to determine the amount of seed fall and the time, period, rate, and distance of dissemination

seed tree 1. a tree left standing for the sole or primary purpose of providing seed **2.** a method of natural regeneration —*see* **regeneration method**

seed year a year in which trees or other plants produce abundant seed as individuals or as a **stand**

seed zone a designated area, usually with definite topographic bounds, climate, and growing conditions, containing trees with relatively uniform genetic (racial) composition as determined by progeny-testing various seed sources —*note* a single geographic **race** may be divided into several seed zones —*see* **geographic race, progeny test, seed source**

seen area *fire* an area that is directly visible under specified atmospheric conditions from an established or proposed lookout point or aerial detection flight route —*synonym* direct(ly) visible area, visible area —*see* **blind area**

seepage 1. water escaping through or emerging from the ground along an extensive line or surface, as contrasted with a spring where the water emerges from a localized spot **2.** *percolation* the slow movement of gravitational water through the soil

segregation the separation of **homologous chromosomes** and their accompanying **gene**s at **meiosis** —*see* **Mendel's principles**

seiche a sudden oscillation in water levels of a lake, bay, etc., caused by wind, earthquakes, and other extreme weather conditions

selected seed (plant) a seed lot or a plant derived from clearly defined and carefully chosen natural **stand**s or **plantation**s that conform to specified standards and have been approved and registered by a designated authority —*note* selected seed is also normally harvested, processed, and stored, and plants are also raised, under the supervision of a designated authority —*see* **seed certification, source-identified seed (plant)**

select grade high-quality lumber

selection 1. the nonrandom differential production of different **genotypes** —*synonym* artificial selection —*note* in (artificial) selection, the breeder chooses individuals for propagation from a larger

population 2. a plant that displays one or more desirable characteristics and is selected for a specific use —*see* **evolution, natural selection, phenotype, progeny test, selection intensity**

selection differential the difference between the mean of the whole **population** and the mean of the selected group —*see* **selection intensity**

selection forest a **forest** treated and managed under the selection system —*see* **regeneration method (selection method)**

selection index a numerical value that expresses the overall desirability of individuals based on a group of **characters** —*note* the value, or total score, depends on the character's phenotypic value, **heritability**, genetic correlations with other characters, and economic value —*see* **phenotype**

selection intensity 1. the standardized selection differential between the average of the selected individuals and the average of the **population 2.** the percentage of individuals selected from a candidate population —*see* **genetic gain, selection**

selection method (selection felling) —*see* **regeneration method (uneven-aged methods)**

selection thinning —*see* **thinning**

selective cutting a cutting that removes only a portion of trees in a **stand** —*see* **partial cutting** —*synonym* selective felling —*note* selective cutting is a general term that should not be confused with cutting done in accordance with the **selection method**

selective pesticide —*see* **narrow-spectrum pesticide**

self 1. to place pollen from a male **flower** (or **strobilus**) onto a female flower (or strobilus) of the same tree or clone **2.** the offspring resulting from such a **pollination** —*see* **inbred line, self-pollination**

self-loader *harvesting* a logging truck with a loading device, generally a knuckleboom **loader,** mounted behind the cab

self-pollination pollination of a **flower** (or **strobilus**) with **pollen** from the same tree or clone —*see* **cross-pollination, diallel cross, F_1, F_2, inbreeding, inbred line, self**

semiochemical a chemical produced by one organism that incites a response in another —*note* semiochemicals are usually volatile and include **allomones, kairomones,** and **pheromones** —*see* **hormone**

senescence the life phase of an organism or a part of the organism that precedes natural death, usually involving a decreased ability to repair damage and degradation

sensible heat flow the transfer of sensible heat (enthalpy) from one region of a fluid to another by fluid motion

sensitive species those species that (a) have appeared in the Federal Register as proposed for classification and are under consideration for official listing as endangered or threatened, (b) are on an official state list of endangered or **threatened species,** or (c) are recognized by a management agency as needing special management to prevent their being placed on federal or state lists —*see* **endangered species**

sensitivity analysis an evaluation of how changes in the coefficients of a **linear programming** problem affect the **optimal solution** to the problem

sensor a device that responds perceptibly to a stimulus without being in contact with the source of the stimulus; in particular, to a stimulus that is far from the device

sequential intercropping growing two or more crops in sequence on the same field

sequential sampling a progressive process in which the number of samples taken is determined by the degree of **precision** attained as sampling proceeds

sequential testing a testing approach in which large numbers of genetic entries are tested in few replications in the early stages, with progressively fewer entries tested in more replications or in larger plots during the later stages —*synonym* stepwise testing —*see* **combined testing, multiple-stage breeding**

seral stage a temporal and intermediate stage in the process of **succession** —*see* **climax, subclimax**

sere the individual sequential stages in forest **succession**

serotinous 1. pertaining to fruit or cones that remain on a tree without opening for one or more years —*note* in some species (e.g., *Pinus contorta*) cones open and seeds are shed when heat is provided by fires or hot and dry conditions **2.** pertaining to a plant or a plant species that flowers or fruits late in the season or to late bud opening and leaf shedding —*see* **case hardening**

service chief —*see* **large fire organization**

sesquioxide a general term for oxides and hydroxides of iron and aluminum

sessile permanently attached, not freely moving, e.g., many **scale insects,** rooted plants, and stalkless structures

set 1. *logging* a cutting crew, generally composed of two workers, a faller and a bucker **2.** the lateral projection, or spread, given to the teeth of a **saw** to provide clearance for the plate or band when sawing —*see* **kerf 3.** *utilization* a localized change in dimension in wood caused by internal stresses on drying

set stocking the practice of allowing a fixed number of animals on a fixed area during the time when grazing is allowed —*see* **range management, continuous stocking, rotational stocking**

setting 1. *logging* the area logged or **yard**ed to one landing —*see* **block 2.** *utilization* —*see* **set**

setworks the mechanism on a log **carriage** that serves to advance the knees toward, or withdraw from, the sawline, so regulating the thickness of the board being cut —*note* the operation is termed **setting**

severance tax a tax imposed on a fixed natural resource on its removal from its natural site —*note* e.g., timber is tax free until harvest, at which time the act of severing a tree from its root system creates the tax liability —*see* **specific tax, yield tax**

severe burn a degree of burn in which all organic material is removed from the soil surface and the soil surface is discolored (usually red) by heat —*note* in a severe burn, organic material below the surface is consumed or charred —*see* **fire severity, light burn, moderate burn**

severity 1. *fire* —*see* **fire severity 2.** *pathology* the amount of disease per unit examined —*note* severity is usually expressed as a percentage or as the number of **lesion**s, **canker**s, **gall**s, etc., per unit —*see* **frequency, incidence, population density**

sex ratio the ratio of males to females at some point in development —*note* on a **monoecious** tree, the term refers to the ratio of male to female **flower**s (or strobili) —*see* **strobilus**

shackle *harvesting* a clevis or U-shaped metal connector with a pin or threaded bolt through the ends, used to connect cables, etc.

shade density the complement of the percent of light intercepted by crowns, assuming that uninterrupted light has, at the time of measurement, a value of 100 percent —*see* **crown density**

shade intolerant having the capacity to compete for survival under direct sunlight conditions —*synonym* light demanding —*see* **shade tolerant, tolerance**

shade symbol *GIS* a pattern used to shade **polygon**s in a **GIS** —*note* e.g., crosshatch, repeating, and solid fill are commonly used **shade** symbols —*see* **text symbol**

shade tolerant having the capacity to compete for survival under shaded conditions —*synonym* shade demanding —*see* **shade intolerant, tolerance**

shade tree system intercropping of trees (often nitrogen-fixing) with crops that benefit from the provision of shade

shadow price —*see* **dual price**

shake 1. a fissure or crack in a log or stem that follows a growth ring for some distance **2.** a longitudinal fissure or crack in lumber resulting from stresses that caused the wood fibers to separate along the grain and not extending in the converted piece from one surface to another —*see* **growth stress 3.** a thin section split from a **bolt** used for roofing or weatherboarding —*see* **shingle** —*see* **windshake**

Shannon-Weiner diversity index *also* **Shannon-Weaver diversity index** a measure of the diversity of a **community:**

$$H' = -\sum_{i=1}^{s} p_i \ln p_i$$

where H' is the Shannon-Weiner diversity index, s is **species** richness (number of species), and p_i is proportion **abundance** contributed by the ith species to the total —*see* **Simpson's diversity index, diversity index**

shear *harvesting* an hydraulically operated, scissor-like device for falling a tree or crosscutting its stem —*see* **feller-buncher**

shearing the shaping of a Christmas tree using a long-handled knife —*see* **pruning**

shearing strength the capacity of an object or soil to resist shearing stresses

sheave *harvesting* a grooved wheel —*synonym* pulley

sheepsfoot roller a steel drum surfaced with short metal rods sometimes shaped like a sheep's foot —*note* a sheepsfoot roller is used for compacting soil, e.g., in road making

sheet erosion —*see* **erosion**

shelterbelt a strip of trees or **shrub**s maintained mainly to alter windflow and microclimates in the sheltered zone, usually agricultural fields —*see* **living fence, timberbelt, windbreak**

shelterwood —*see* **regeneration method**

shepherd's crook a leader or branch with a downward-curved tip that is a characteristic symptom of attack by certain insects or **pathogen**s, e.g., white pine weevil (*Pissodes strobi*)

shifting cultivation a primitive, more or less unregulated method of cyclical cultivation, still widely practiced in the tropics, whereby cultivators cut some or all of the tree crop, burn it, and raise agricultural crops for one or more years before moving on to another site and repeating the process —*note*

1. shifting cultivation has numerous native names including *chena* (Sri Lanka), *kaingin* (Philippines), *kumri* (India), *ladang* (Malaysia), *parcelero* (Puerto Rico), *shamba* (Kenya), and *taungya* (Myanmar) —*note 2.* if practiced from a fixed settlement on a fairly regular cycle, shifting cultivation is termed the bush fallow system (mainly Africa), a form of land rotation —*see* **slash and burn, transhumance**

shingle a short, thin, oblong piece of wood, generally tapering in thickness along the grain, used for roofing or weatherboarding —*see* **shake**

shipping tally a tally of lumber or of timber made after drying and preparation for shipment

shoestring root rot —*see Armillaria* **root disease**

shoot 1. any young, slender, aerial outgrowth from a plant body, particularly a sprouting stem or branchlet, often including its leaves **2.** the aboveground, generally ascending axis of a plant including, in the seedling and transplant stages, any branches and leaves

shoot borer *entomology* an insect that bores into the phloem or wood of growing shoots —*note* larvae of **tip moth**s and **terminal weevil**s are shoot borers —*see* **insect hole, terminal borer, wood borer**

shoot moth —*see* **tip moth**

shoot weevil —*see* **terminal weevil**

short-duration grazing a form of **grazing management** whereby relatively short periods (days) of **grazing** and associated nongrazing are applied to **range** or pasture units —*note 1.* periods of **grazing** and nongrazing are based on plant growth characteristics —*note 2.* the term has nothing to do with intensity of grazing use —*see* **grazing system**

short-range planning —*see* **planning (short-range)**

short root an ephemeral root, typically the site of **ectomycorrhiza**e formation, that does not contain proto**xylem** poles or elongate beyond a minimum uniform length —*synonym* feeder root

short run a period of time during which some inputs are regarded as fixed in quantity or quality —*note* e.g., a new plant cannot be built and new machinery cannot be purchased in the short run —*see* **long run, overhead cost**

short-term fire retardant a chemical that inhibits **combustion** primarily by the cooling and smothering action of water —*note* a short-term retardant may be added to water to alter its viscosity or retard its evaporation, thereby increasing its effectiveness —*see* **long-term fire retardant, slurry, viscous water, wetting agent**

short ton a US measure of weight equal to 2,000 lb (907 kg) —*see* **long ton, metric ton**

shortwood stem wood < 120 in (305 cm) in length

shotgun *harvesting* a two-drum, live **skyline** yarding system used in uphill logging in which the carriage moves down the skyline by gravity, is lowered to attach logs, and is then raised and pulled to the landing by the **main line**

shothole a type of **leaf spot** in which the necrotic tissue falls out, leaving a hole in the leaf —*see* **ambrosia beetle, insect hole**

shovel *harvesting* a knuckleboom **loader** outfitted to maneuver through a harvest area, typically with tracks

shovel logging *harvesting* **skid**ding performed by swing machines successively moving trees or stems from one pile to another in the direction of the skid

show any unit of operation in the woods associated with timber harvesting

shrinkage the decrease in wood dimensions due to loss of water in the wood cell walls, expressed as a percentage of the green wood dimensions —*note* shrinkage across the grain of wood occurs when the moisture content falls below 30 percent, the **fiber saturation point;** below the fiber saturation point, shrinkage is generally proportional to moisture content, down to a moisture content of 0 percent

shrub a woody, perennial plant differing from a perennial **herb** in its persistent and woody stem, and less definitely from a tree in its lower stature and the general absence of a well-defined main stem —*see* **brush tree**

sib an offspring that has one or both parents in common with another individual —*note* full sibs have both parents in common, half sibs only one —*synonym* sibling —*see* **full-sib progeny, half-sib progeny**

side a logging job including the personnel and equipment needed to operate it —*note* a harvesting operation may consist of several sides —*synonym* chance, **show**

side rod the person in charge of a **side**

sieve cell —*see* **cells (wood)**

silica-sesquioxide ratio the molecules of silicon dioxide (SiO_2) per molecule of aluminum oxide (Al_2O_3) plus ferric oxide (FO_3) in clay minerals or in soils

silt 1. a soil separate having an effective diameter of 0.002 to 0.05 mm (0.00008 to 0.002 in) **2.** a soil textural class defined by soil material that contains 80 percent or more silt and < 12 percent **clay** —*see* **sand**

silvics the study of the life history and general characteristics of **forest** trees and **stand**s, with particular reference to environmental factors, as a basis for the practice of **silviculture**

silvicultural prescription —*see* **prescription**

silvicultural system a planned series of treatments for tending, harvesting, and re-establishing a **stand** —*note* the system name is based on the number of age classes (**coppice, even-aged, two-aged, uneven-aged**) or the **regeneration method** (**clearcutting, seed tree, shelterwood, selection, coppice, coppice with reserves**) used

silviculture the art and science of controlling the establishment, growth, composition, health, and quality of **forests** and **woodlands** to meet the diverse **needs** and values of landowners and society on a sustainable basis —*see* **silvics**

silvopastoralism —*also* silvipastoralism a form of **agroforestry** system consisting of the trees (woody perennials) and pasture and animal components —*synonym* silvopastoral system —*see* **agrosilviculture, agrosilvopastoralism**

simple Mendelian inheritance the inheritance of **gene**s for discrete **character**s, e.g., the presence or absence of pigments —*note* simple Mendelian inheritance is controlled by one or a few major genes whose effects are discontinuous and sufficiently pronounced to be detected in the **phenotype** —*see* **dominance, Mendel's principles, oligogene, qualitative inheritance, quantitative inheritance**

simplex method an algebraic procedure for solving **linear programming** problems in which elementary row operations are used to iterate from one basic **feasible solution** (extreme point) to another until the **optimal solution** is reached

Simpson's diversity index a measure of the diversity of a **community:**

$$D = 1 / \sum_{i=1}^{s} p_i^2$$

where D is Simpson's diversity index, s is **species** richness (number of species), and p_i is the proportion **abundance** contributed to the ith species —*see* **Shannon-Weiner diversity index, diversity index**

simulation an operations research technique that represents physical, natural, social, and economic systems by **model**s (generally mathematical and processed by computer) in order to study the factors affecting the system and to aid **decision making**

single-conical saw —*see* **saw**

single precision a lower level of numeric representation based on the possible number of significant digits that can be stored for the number —*note* single-precision numbers can store up to seven signif-

icant digits and thus retain a precision of ±5 m (16.4 ft) in an extent of 1,000,000 m (3,280,840 ft) —*see* **double-precision, precision**

single-span skyline *harvesting* a **skyline** without intermediate support **spar**s

single tree selection —*see* **regeneration method**

sink 1. *ecology* a depression or hole in a low-lying, poorly drained area formed by the dissolution of underlying rock, where waters collect or disappear by sinking down into the ground or by evaporation **2.** *physiology* any region in the tissues of an organism with a high requirement for nutrients or other substances, which therefore move preferentially toward it

sinker root 1. a root other than a **taproot** that grows straight downward **2.** a secondary root from the cortical system (**cortex**) in some (semi)parasitic plants, e.g., *Viscum* and *Loranthus,* that grows directly downward into the tissues of the host —*synonym* sinker —*see* **haustorium**

sinker root system a rooting habit of trees in which a strong **taproot** is absent but large lateral roots radiate horizontally from the base of the tree, from which vertical **sinker root**s elongate downward —*synonym* flat root system

sinking fund a fund accumulated from profits by setting aside regular (generally annual) installments sufficient, at compound interest, to replace the capital value of a depreciating asset, e.g., a piece of machinery, at the end of its useful life (when it is written off) or to meet a known, future liability, e.g., repayment of a loan, or to recover an investment, e.g., a leasehold interest in property —*note* a sinking fund is a form of **amortization**

SIP —*see* **state implementation plan, stewardship incentive program**

site the area in which a plant or **stand** grows, considered in terms of its environment, particularly as this determines the type and quality of the vegetation the area can carry —*note* sites are classified either qualitatively, by their climate, soil, and vegetation, into site types, or quantitatively, by their potential wood production, into **site class**es —*see* **habitat**

site class a classification of **site quality**, usually expressed in terms of ranges of dominant tree height at a given age or potential mean annual increment at culmination

site height the average height of trees used to estimate **site index** in an even-aged stand —*see* **top height**

site index a species-specific measure of actual or potential **forest** productivity (**site quality,** usually for **even-aged stand**s), expressed in terms of the average height of trees included in a specified stand component (defined as a certain number of **dominants, codominants,** or the largest and tallest trees per unit area) at a specified index or base age —*see* site index is used as an indicator of site quality —*see* **top height**

site index curve a curve showing the expected height growth pattern for trees of the specified stand component in even-aged stands of a given site index

site planning —*see* **planning (site)**

site preparation hand or mechanized manipulation of a site, designed to enhance the success of **regeneration** —*note* treatments may include bedding, burning, chemical spraying, chopping, disking, drainage, raking, and scarifying and are designed to modify the soil, litter, or vegetation and to create microclimate conditions conducive to the establishment and growth of desired species —*see* **chopper, disk, grub, scalp, windrow**

site productivity class a species-specific classification of forest land in terms of inherent capacity to grow crops of industrial, commercial wood —*note* the site productivity class is usually derived from the **site index**

site quality the productive capacity of a site, usually expressed as volume production of a given species —*synonym* site productivity

situation analysis *fire* an analysis of factors which influence suppression of an **escaped fire** from which alternative strategies of **fire suppression** will be developed and evaluated —*synonym* escaped fire situation analysis (EFSA)

sizing *utilization* an agent added to the internal structure or surface of paper to make it more impervious to ink or moisture and eliminate ink feathering and bleed-through, usually by aqueous substances

skeletonizing the result of an insect's feeding on the soft material of a leaf, leaving the veins as a skeleton —*note* birch leaf skeletonizer and oak leaf skeletonizer are misnomers because these insects are actually **window-feeding** insects —*synonym* leaf skeletonizing

sketchmaster, vertical a simple form of rectifier in which the **image** of a vertical **aerial photograph** can be viewed superimposed on a map of the same area, and additional details can be transferred from there to the map in their correct relative positions

skew(ness) a relative measure of asymmetry of a **frequency distribution** as compared with the **normal distribution** —*note* a distribution with positive skew exhibits a long right-hand or positive tail, and a distribution with a negative skew exhibits a long left-hand or negative tail —*see* **kurtosis**

skid **1.** to haul a log from the stump to a collection point (landing) by a **skidder** —*see* **yard, forward** **2.** a load pulled by the **skidder**

skidder *harvesting* a self-propelled machine, often articulated (hinged) in the center, for dragging trees or logs —*note* a skidder may be cable (using a main winch cable and cable **choker**s to assemble and hold a load), clam-bunk (using an integrally mounted loader to assemble the load and a clam or top-opening jaws to hold it), or **grapple** (using a grapple or bottom-opening jaws to assemble and hold a load) —*see* **arch**

skid road an access cut through the woods for skidding —*synonym* skid trail

skyline *harvesting* a cableway stretched tautly between two points, such as **yard**ing tower and stump anchor, and used as a track for a block or **skyline carriage**

skyline carriage *harvesting* —*see* **carriage**

skyline road the area bounded by the lateral **yard**ing distance on both sides of the **skyline** and the **external yarding distance**

slab the rounded side of a log removed in the first cut of the breaking-down saw

slack **1.** the length of time an activity can be delayed without affecting the project completion time **2.** *synonym* **slack variable** in a mathematical **programming** problem and solution

slackline system *harvesting* a live **skyline** system employing a **carriage**, skyline, **main line**, and **haul-back line** —*note* in a slackline system, both main and haulback lines attach directly to the **carriage**; the skyline is lowered by slackening the skyline to permit the chokers to be attached to the carriage; the **turn** is brought to the landing by the main line; lateral movement is provided by side blocking

slack variable a variable added (explicitly by the user or implicitly by the **algorithm**) to the left-hand side of a less-than-or-equal-to **constraint** in a mathematical **programming** problem specification to convert the constraint into an equality —*note* the value of this variable can usually be interpreted as the amount of unused resource —*see* **surplus variable**

slash the residue, e.g., treetops and branches, left on the ground after logging or accumulating as a result of storm, fire, **girdling**, or delimbing

slash and burn the cutting and burning of vegetation, primarily in tropical areas, prior to using the land for agriculture —*see* **shifting cultivation**

slash chopper a set of blades mounted on a horizontal, power-driven shaft to reduce the bulk of **slash** after felling, thus facilitating planting or reducing fire hazard —*synonym* brash chopper

slasher *harvesting* a mobile machine that cuts felled trees to a predetermined length with a shear or saw —*see* **bucker**

slashing cutting back the less tough, competing vegetation in **plantations** with a **slasher** or similar light cutting tool or machine; a form of **cleaning**

slick spot an area of soil with a puddled or crusted, very smooth, nearly impervious surface —*note* the underlying material is dense and massive

slickenside stress surfaces that are polished and striated, produced by one mass sliding past another —*note* slickensides are common in clay soils below a depth of 50 cm (19.7 in) and are caused by the shrinking and swelling of the clay; the stress occurs because the expanding clay is under pressure in the soil

slime flux —*see* **wetwood**

slime mold a nonchlorophyll group of phagotrophic organisms whose vegetative structures lack cell walls and that reproduce by **spore**s —*note* slime molds are believed to be primitive fungi; they derive nourishment by ingesting microorganisms

sling psychrometer a **psychrometer** in which the wet- and dry-bulb thermometers are mounted on a frame connected to a handle at one end by means of a bearing or a length of chain —*note* swinging the sling psychrometer causes maximum differences between the wet-bulb and dry-bulb temperatures due to evaporation from the wet bulb

sling thermometer a thermometer mounted on a frame connected to a handle at one end by means of a bearing or length of chain —*note* the thermometer may be whirled by hand to provide ventilation

slip erosion —*see* **erosion**

slit planting inserting a seedling in a cut made in the soil by a spade, mattock, or planting bar (bar planting), then closing the cut by foot pressure

sliver polygon *GIS* a relatively narrow **feature,** commonly occurring along the borders of **polygon**s following the **overlay** of two or more geographic data sets; this feature also occurs along map borders when two maps are joined, as a result of inaccuracies of the coordinates in either or both maps

slope a measure of change in surface value over distance, expressed in degrees or as a percentage —*note 1.* e.g., a rise of 2 m over a distance of 100 m (or 2 ft over 100 ft) describes a 2 percent slope with an angle of 1.15° —*note 2.* mathematically, slope is referred to as the first derivative of the surface

slough 1. a low, swampy ground or overflow channel where water flows sluggishly for considerable distances **2.** a channel of sluggish water, such as a side channel of a stream, in which water flows slowly through low, swampy ground, or through a section of an abandoned stream channel containing water most or all of the year, but with flow only at high water, and occurring in a **floodplain** or delta **3.** a marshy tract lying in a shallow, undrained depression on a piece of dry ground **4.** a creek or body of sluggish water in a bottomland

slurry 1. a suspension of insoluble matter in water **2.** *fire* a short- or long-term retardant after the mixing process has been completed **3.** a **pesticide** suspension formulated as a thin fluid such as liquid mud in order to produce a thick coating or to reduce dust —*see* **fire retardant**

small end the end of a log having the smaller cross section —*note* the small end is nearly always the upper, younger end

smallwood round timber below a certain diameter or circumference (girth), but sometimes also not less than a certain minimum —*note* the dimension may be either outside- or inside-bark

smear a preparation and staining procedure for studying **chromosome**s in which tissues are spread apart by pressure —*synonym* squash —*note* smears are often made of cells during **meiosis** or **mitosis**

smectite a group of 2:1 layer silicates with high **cation exchange capacity** and variable interlayer spacing —*note* smectite was formerly called the **montmorillonite** group

smoke jumper a **fire fighter** who travels to fires by fixed-wing aircraft and parachute —*see* **helijumper**

smoke management conducting a prescribed fire under suitable fuel moisture and meteorological conditions with **firing technique**s that keep smoke impact within designated areas and below violations of air quality standards or within visibility protection guidelines —*see* **prescribed burn**

smoldering fire —*see* **fire behavior**

smoothing *GIS* a process to generalize data and remove variation

smut 1. a fungus characterized by having sooty **spore** masses —*note* although many smuts cause agriculturally important diseases, none cause tree diseases **2.** the area on a **host** plant infected by a smut fungus

SMZ —*see* **streamside management zone**

snag 1. a standing, generally unmerchantable dead tree from which the leaves and most of the branches have fallen —*note* for wildlife **habitat** purposes, a snag is sometimes regarded as being at least 10 in (25.4 cm) in diameter at breast height and at least 6 ft (1.8 m) tall; a hard snag is composed primarily of sound wood, generally merchantable, and a soft snag is composed primarily of wood in advanced stages of decay and deterioration —*see* **biological legacy, cull 2.** a standing section of the stem of a tree, broken off usually below the crown **3.** a sunken log or a submerged stump or tree **4.** the projecting base of a broken or cut branch on a tree stem

snapping *GIS* the process of moving a feature to coincide exactly with the coordinates of another feature within a specified distance or tolerance

snowbreak 1. a windbreak or other barrier (natural or artificial) maintained to trap blowing snow and thereby prevent excessive accumulations on roadways, etc. —*also* snowfence —*see* **shelterbelt 2.** the damage to trees from snow loading —*synonym* snow breakage

snow mold a fungus that grows best at temperatures slightly above freezing —*note* some snow molds cause diseases of foliage and twigs under snow cover —*synonym* snow **blight**

snubbing line *harvesting* a line used to retard a load

sociability *ecology* the tendency of organisms to grow together with others of the same kind —*note* the degree of sociability is expressed by Braun-Blanquet on an arbitrary numerical scale from one (growing singly) to five (growing in great crowds or pure populations)

social *entomology* pertaining to organisms living in more or less organized communities of individuals —*note* truly social (eusocial) insects possess three **trait**s as defined by E.O. Wilson (1971): (a) cooperation among individuals in caring for the young, (b) "reproductive division of labor with more or less sterile individuals working on behalf of fecund individuals," and (c) "an overlap of at least two generations in life **stage** capable of contributing to colony labor so that offspring assist parents during some period of their life" —*antonym* **solitary**

social benefit the nonmonetary and rarely calculable returns to society arising from any form of economic activity, e.g., those from creating a town recreation park —*note* a social benefit is a positive **externality,** often created as a direct result of deliberate public policy —*see* **social cost**

social cost the nonmonetary and rarely calculable toll on society arising from any form of economic activity, e.g., from smoke pollution over and above the cost of the goods and services causing the smoke —*note* a social cost is a negative **externality,** often created as a direct result of loopholes in current laws, regulations, or public policy —*see* **social benefit**

social forestry *international forestry* **afforestation, reforestation,** and other **forestry** programs that purposely and directly involve local people, their values, and their institutions —*synonym* participa-

tory forestry, rural (development) forestry —*see* **communal forest, community forest**

society *ecology* a localized **climax** plant community, occurring within an area controlled by a single or a few **dominant** species, that is characterized by a single **subdominant** species —*note* a society may constitute a seasonal aspect or a **synusia** of the larger community of which it is a component —*see* **association**

sod grass a **stolon**iferous or rhizomatous grass that forms a sod or turf —*synonym* turf grass —*see* **bunch grass, stem grass**

sodic soil a nonsaline soil containing sufficient exchangeable sodium to adversely affect crop production and soil **structure**

softcopy photogrammetry —*see* **digital photogrammetry**

soft rot a type of decay that develops under very wet conditions in the outer wood layers —*note* soft rots are caused by cellulose-destroying fungi, e.g., in the family Xylariaceae, that attack the secondary cell walls and not the intercellular layer —*see* **spongy rot**

software a computer program that provides the instructions necessary for the hardware to operate correctly and to perform the desired functions, e.g., operating system, utility, and application

softwood the **xylem** and trees of the **Gymnospermae** —*note 1.* commercial softwood timbers are practically confined to the order Coniferales —*note 2.* softwood is relatively uniform in structure and is composed mostly of longitudinal **tracheid**s and a small amount of **rays** and resin ducts —*see* **hardwood, lumber, nonpored wood**

soil the unconsolidated mineral or organic material on the immediate surface of the earth that serves as the natural medium for the growth of land plants

soil compaction the process by which the soil grains are rearranged, resulting in a decrease in void space and causing closer contact with one another, thereby increasing bulk density —*note 1.* soil compaction can result from applied loads, vibration, or pressure from harvesting or site-preparation equipment —*note 2.* compaction can cause decreased tree growth, increased water runoff, and soil **erosion**

soil consistence the attributes of soil material as expressed in degree of cohesion and adhesion or in resistance to deformation or rupture

soil drainage class one of seven classes of natural soil drainage referring to the frequency and duration of periods of saturation or partial saturation —*note* soil drainage classes may range from excessively drained to very poorly drained

soil ecology the study of soil organisms, their activities, and their interactions within the soil environment and with each other

soil horizon —*see* **horizon**

soil map a map showing the distribution of soils or other soil map units in relation to the prominent physical and cultural features of the earth's surface

soil moisture the water content stored in a soil — *note 1.* measured by volume (Mv), soil moisture is the volume of water per unit of soil, usually expressed as a percentage —*note 2.* measured by weight (Mw), it is the weight of water per unit oven-dry weight of the soil; Mv = Mw multiplied by bulk density of the soil

soil order a group of soils in the broadest category, differentiated by the presence or absence of diagnostic **horizons**; in the current US system of soil taxonomy there are 11 soil orders: Alfisol, Andisol, Aridisol, Entisol, Histosol, Enceptisol, Mollisol, Oxisol, Spodosol, Ultisol, and Vertisol —*see* **alluvial soil, intrazonal soil, pedalfer, pedocal, zonal soil**

soil quality the capacity of a soil to function within **ecosystem** boundaries to sustain biological productivity, maintain environmental quality, and promote plant and animal health —*synonym* soil productivity

soil reaction the degree of acidity or alkalinity of a soil, usually expressed as a **pH** value —*note* descriptive terms commonly associated with certain ranges in pH are extremely acid, < 4.5; very strongly acid, 4.5 to 5.0; strongly acid, 5.1 to 5.5; moderately acid, 5.6 to 6.0; slightly acid, 6.1 to 6.5; neutral, 6.6 to 7.3; slightly alkaline, 7.4 to 7.8; moderately alkaline, 7.9 to 8.4; strongly alkaline, 8.5 to 9.0; and very strongly alkaline, > 9.1 —*see* **acid soil, base saturation, buffer power, cation exchange capacity, humic acid**

soil rent(al) the net financial **yield** of an even-aged **stand** converted into its equivalent in annual income on bare **forest** soil previous to the establishment of **regeneration** —*note 1.* the soil rent concept extends the **financial maturity** concept by including in the decision about rotation length of the current stand those changes in the **net present value** of future stands induced by the decision to harvest now or extend the current rotation —*note 2.* the soil rent approach gives the highest financial returns from timber production under a management program that will produce a succession of rotations —*see* **forest rent(al)**

soil separates mineral particles, < 2.0 mm (0.08 in) in equivalent diameter, ranging between specified size limits —*note* the names and size limits of separates recognized in the US are very coarse **sand,** 2.0 to 1.0 mm (0.08 to 0.04 in); coarse sand,

1.0 to 0.5 mm (0.04 to 0.02 in); medium sand, 0.5 to 0.25 mm (0.02 to 0.01 in); fine sand, 0.25 to 0.10 mm (0.01 to 0.004 in); very fine sand, 0.10 to 0.05 mm (0.004 to 0.002 in); **silt,** 0.05 to 0.002 mm (0.002 to 0.00008 in); and **clay,** < 0.002 mm (< 0.00008 in)

soil series the lowest or most basic category of the US system of soil taxonomy; a conceptualized class of soil bodies (**polypedon**s) that have limits and ranges more restrictive than all higher taxa —*note 1.* soil series are commonly used to name dominant or codominant polypedons represented on detailed soil maps —*note 2.* soil series serve as a major vehicle to transfer soil information and research knowledge from one soil area to another

soil solution the aqueous liquid phase of the soil and its solutes

soil structure the physical combination or arrangement of primary soil particles into secondary aggregates or **ped**s —*note 1.* the principal forms of soil structure are platy (laminated), prismatic (vertical axis of aggregates longer than horizontal), columnar (prisms with rounded tops), blocky (angular or subangular), and granular —*note 2.* structureless soils are either single-grained (as in a dune sand) or massive —*see* **clod**

soil texture a characteristic consistency of soil determined by the relative proportions of the various **soil separates** —*note 1.* textural classes may indicate the presence of substantial amounts of rock fragments, e.g., stony **silt** loam —*note 2.* **sand, loam**y sand, and sandy loam are further subdivided on the basis of the proportions of the various sand separates present —*see* **clay**

soil type 1. the lowest or most basic unit in the natural system of soil classification; a subdivision of a soil series and consisting of or describing soils that are alike in all characteristics including the texture of the **A horizon** or plow layer —*note* the term was used in the US soil classification systems prior to publication of USDA's *Soil Taxonomy* (1975) **2.** in Europe, soil type is roughly equivalent to a great soil group

solar constant the rate at which solar radiation is received outside the earth's atmosphere on a surface normal to the incident radiation and at the earth's mean distance from the sun

solitary *entomology* showing none of the **trait**s of **social** behavior

solum *plural* **sola** a set of **horizon**s that are related through the same cycle of **ped**ogenic processes; the A, E, and B horizons —*see* **pedogenesis**

somaclonal variation the variation arising in tissue culture of **somatic cell**s, often due to higher than average rates of gene **mutation**, transpositions, and various **chromosome** abnormalities

somatic cell a **diploid** (*2n*) cell —*see* **gamete, germ cell, vegetative cell**

somatic crossing over an exchange of genetic material between homologous **chromosome**s during **mitosis** in **somatic cell**s

somatic embryogenesis a process by which **somatic cell**s are differentiated into somatic embryos

sooty-bark canker a disease caused by the fungus *Encoelia pruinosa* —*note* sooty-bark cankers are important **pathogen**s causing rapidly growing blackish diffuse **canker**s (sooty bark) on the main stems of *Populus*

sooty mold **1.** an epiphytic fungus that lives on **honeydew** excreted by insects, particularly **aphid**s —*note 1.* sooty molds are usually dark or black and are **pathogen**ic when they screen sunlight from the leaves **2.** the mycelial covering on a surface produced by a sooty mold fungus

soundex *GIS* a phonetic spelling (up to six characters) of a street name, used for address matching —*note 1.* each of the 26 letters in the alphabet corresponds to a letter in the soundex equivalent: English: A = A, B = B, C = C, D = D, E = A, F = B, G = C, H = H, I = A, J = C, K = C, L = L, M = M, N = M, O = A, P = B, Q = , R = R, S = C, T = D, U = A, V = B, W = W, X = C, Y = A, Z = C —*note 2.* where possible, geocoding uses a soundex equivalent of road names for faster processing; during geocoding, initial candidate road names are found using soundex, then real names are compared and verified

sound knot an intergrown knot free from decay, solid across its face, and at least as hard as the surrounding wood

source-identified seed (plant) a seed lot or plant derived from a defined area **(seed source)** registered by a designated authority —*note* source-identified seed is normally harvested, processed, and stored, and plants raised, under the supervision of a designated authority —*see* **seed-certification, selected seed (plant)**

space photography oblique or vertical photography acquired from spacecraft such as the space shuttle

span the horizontal distance between two adjacent **skyline** supports —*see* **chord**

spar *harvesting* a standing or raised tree or steel **tower** used to provide lift for rigging in **cable logging** systems

sparsely vegetated having 1 to 10 percent vegetation **cover** over the landscape at the peak of the growing season

spatial analysis **1.** the process of **model**ing, examining, and interpreting model results **2.** the process of extracting or creating new information about a set of geographic features —*note 1.* spatial analysis is useful for evaluating suitability and capability, for estimating and predicting, and for interpreting and understanding —*note 2.* in **GIS** there are four traditional types of spatial analysis: spatial overlay and contiguity analysis, surface analysis, linear analysis, and **raster** analysis —*synonym* **modeling**

spatial data information about the location and shape of, and relationships among, geographic features, usually stored as coordinates and topology

spatial index *GIS* a geographic-based, sequential numbering system that accelerates the drawing, spatial selection, and identification of entities

spatial model *GIS* a set of analytical procedures applied with a **GIS** —*note* there are three categories of spatial **model**ing functions that can be applied to geographic data objects within a GIS: (a) geometric models (such as calculation of Euclidean distance between objects, buffer generation, and area and perimeter calculations); (b) coincidence models (such as polygon **overlay**, **line** on polygon overlay, and **point** on line overlay); and (c) adjacency models (such as **pathfinding,** redistricting, and **allocation**); all three model categories support operations on geographic data objects such as **point**s, **line**s, **polygon**s, **TIN**s, and **grid**s; functions are organized in a sequence of steps to derive the desired information for analysis

special forest products —*see* **nontimber forest products**

species *biology* the main category of taxonomic classification into which genera are subdivided, comprising a group of similar interbreeding individuals sharing a common morphology, physiology, and reproductive process —*note 1.* there is generally a sterility barrier between species, or at least reduced fertility in interspecific **hybrid**s — *note 2.* the species is the basic unit of taxonomy on which the binomial system has been established; the lower taxonomic hierarchy is species, subspecies, variety, and forma

species-area curve the graph of species versus area that describes the asymptotic growth in number of species encountered as the area sampled increases

species hybrid the offspring produced by crossing two **species** —*see* **crossability, cross-pollination, hybrid, interspecific hybrid, sympatric**

species invasion the immigration and establishment of a **species** in an area it did not previously occupy

species richness a measure of the number of **species**

present in a **community, ecosystem, landscape,** region, etc.

specific combining ability (SCA) the degree to which the average performance of a specific family (usually full sibs) departs from the average of its parental breeding values —*note* specific combining ability is sometimes used to denote the departure of an individual **clone** from the performance of its **sib**s —*see* **combining ability, full-sib progeny, general combining ability**

specific gravity the ratio of the density (weight per unit volume) of an object (such as wood) to the density of water at 4° C (39.2° F) as the reference

specific tax a tax based on a physical rather than a value unit, e.g., a timber severance tax per 1,000 bd ft —*see* **ad valorem tax, severance tax, yield tax**

spectral reflectance the reflectance of electromagnetic energy at specified wavelength intervals

speed of attack *fire* 1. the **elapsed time** from fire origin to arrival of the first **resources** 2. with strength of attack specified, the elapsed time from fire origin to arrival of **resources** necessary to contain the fire at an acceptable or predetermined limit within a specified **fuel type** —*see* **elapsed time**

spider mite —*see* **mite**

spike *GIS* 1. an **overshoot** line created erroneously by a **scanner** and its **raster** software 2. an anomalous data point that protrudes above or below an interpolated surface representing the distribution of the value of an **attribute** over an area

spike camp a **fire camp** with minimum facilities established along a **fireline** for the subsistence and equipping of **fire fighter**s assigned to that portion of the perimeter —*synonym* line camp, side camp

spillway an open or closed channel, or both, used to convey excess water from a reservoir —*note* a spillway may contain gates, either manually or automatically controlled, to regulate the discharge of excess water

spiral grain wood in which the **fiber**s are arranged spirally around the stem axis —*note* lumber made from trees with spiral grain has a grain direction that is not parallel to the board length, resulting in loss of strength and a tendency to twist on drying —*see* **grain**

spittlebug a member of some genera in the family Cercopidae whose **nymph**s feed on plants and live in a white frothy mass (spittle) consisting of air bubbles and partially digested sap expelled from the anus —*note* several species of spittlebugs are serious **pest**s of pines and other conifers, including the Saratoga **spittlebug** *(Aphrophora saratogensis)* and the pine spittlebug *(A. parallela)*

splash erosion —*see* **erosion**

spline to mathematically smooth spatial variation by adding **vertices** along a line —*see* **densify** for a slightly different method for adding vertices

split-plot design a factorial experiment in which additional or subsidiary factors are introduced by dividing each experimental plot into two or more portions —*note* the design may be adopted either to increase precision on subplot comparisons at the expense of main-plot comparisons, or because some treatments cannot be applied satisfactorily to small plots

spodic horizon a mineral soil **horizon** characterized by the illuvial accumulation of amorphous materials composed of aluminum and organic carbon with or without iron —*see* **illuviation**

spongy rot any decay or rot in wood that becomes soft and yielding in texture in its advanced stage —*see* **soft rot**

sporangiospore an asexual **spore** within a **sporangium**

sporangium *plural* **sporangia** a fruiting body that produces **endogenous** asexual **spore**s —*see* **sporocarp, sporophore**

spore a propagative body in fungi consisting of one to many cells, each cell capable of germinating and reproducing the organism but not containing a preformed embryo —*note* spores can live in a dormant state once liberated from the **mycelium**

sporidium *plural* **sporidia** a **basidiospore** in the **rust** and **smut** fungi

sporocarp a large, multicellular structure in the higher fungi that produces **spore**s —*see* **sporangium**

sporophore a special reproductive structure in fungi that produces **spore**s or spore-supporting hypha, particularly a **conidiophore** —*see* **fructification, sporangium**

sporophyll special leaves on which spores are produced; modified sporophylls (scales) are grouped at the ends of stems to form cones or strobili —*see* **strobilus**

sporophyte the **diploid** (2N) spore-producing phase or generation in organisms

SPOT a French satellite carrying two imaging systems: (a) a three-**band** multispectral sensor with 20-m (65.6-ft) spatial resolution and (b) a panchromatic sensor with 10-m (32.8-ft) resolution —*note* the sensors are pointable so that stereo coverage is possible

spot burn a **prescribed burn** in which fuels or accumulations of **slash** are burnt in localized areas —*note* spot burning is a modified form of **broadcast burn**ing

spot fire —*see* **fire behavior**

spot planting setting out young trees in small, prepared patches —*see* **seed spot**

spreader a solid or liquid **adjuvant** added to a **pesticide** to improve its ability to spread over the surfaces on which it is deposited —*see* **surfactant**

spring-set to set saw teeth by bending alternate teeth in different sideways directions —*note* spring-setting ensures clearance between the saw plate and the cut made by the saw —*see* **swage-set**

springwood —*see* **earlywood**

sprout generally, a shoot arising from the base of a (woody) plant, whether from the **stool** (a stool shoot) or as a sucker

spud *harvesting* a tool with a narrow, curved blade used in removing bark by hand —*synonym* barking iron

spur road a short, low-standard road that supports a low level of traffic such as serving one or two **landings**

SQL —*see* **structured query language**

stability 1. *ecology* the extent to which the variation in an individual characteristic of an ecological system is less than the variation in the environmental variables that influence that characteristic —*see* **static stability** 2. *genetics* the degree to which genetic entities (individuals, families, **clones**, etc.) demonstrate little response to environmental changes —*note* stable clones or families show relatively constant rankings across different environments —*see* **family**

stabilization *recreation* the strengthening and securing of a historic structure with only minor replacement of missing elements

stabilizer a solid or liquid substance added to a **pesticide** or **herbicide** to ensure that the formulation's components neither separate nor deteriorate

stadium *entomology* the period between insect molts —*see* **instar, life cycle, metamorphosis, stage**

stage *entomology, pathology* a distinct period in the development of a fungus or insect marked by distinctiveness of form, e.g., egg stage and **larval** stage —*see* **instar, metamorphosis, stadium** —*note* in entomology, the terms stadium, stage, and instar are used interchangeably to indicate the form an insect takes during that period

stage structure *ecology* the demographic distribution of a population based on developmental stages rather than absolute age

staging area *fire* 1. an area within a **fire camp** where personnel and equipment are assembled for transportation to the **fireline** 2. a temporary on-**incident** location where **resources** are assigned on a three-minute availability basis —*note* staging area is an **ICS** term

stain a discoloration of wood, usually only the sapwood, in live or recently cut trees (including timber, chips, and pulp) caused by certain fungi, particularly *Ceratosystis* sp., sometimes **vector**ed by insects, particularly bark beetles and ambrosia beetles —*note* stains may occur in a variety of colors but blue, green, and black are most common

staking supporting plants or cuttings with stakes to protect against wind-rocking and promote straight growth

stamen the organ of a **flower** (anther) that produces male **gametes** —*see* **pistil**

staminate having pollen-bearing organs (**stamen**s) only —*note* the term may apply to individual male plants of a **dioecious** species or to **flowers**, **inflorescences**, and strobili —*see* **dioecious, ovulate, pistillate, strobilus**

stand 1. *ecology* a contiguous group of similar plants 2. *silviculture* a contiguous group of trees sufficiently uniform in age-class distribution, composition, and structure, and growing on a site of sufficiently uniform quality, to be a distinguishable unit —*see* **all-aged stand, mixed, pure, even-aged**, and **uneven-aged stand**s —*note 1.* a **mixed stand** is composed of a mixture of **species** —*note 2.* a **pure stand** is composed of essentially a single species —*note 3.* in a **stratified mixture** stand different species occupy different strata of the total crown canopy 3. *wildlife* a place from which game is shot (at) and past which game is generally driven —*synonym* hide —*see* **blind**

stand age 1. the mean age of the dominant and codominant trees in an even-aged **stand** 2. the mean age of a specified number of the largest trees per unit area (usually 40 ac or 100 ha) in an even-aged stand —*note* the concept of stand age is complex in the case of two-aged stands, **uneven-aged** stands, or stands with residual green trees

standard —*see* **regeneration method (coppice with reserves), reserve tree**

standard atmosphere a hypothetical vertical distribution of atmospheric temperature, pressure, and density which, by international agreement, is taken to be representative of the atmosphere for purposes of pressure altimeter calibrations, aircraft performance calculations, aircraft and missile design, ballistic tables, etc.

standard deviation a measure of the **dispersion** about the mean of a **population** or sample, i.e., the positive square root of the variance

standard error the **standard deviation** of a distribution of means or other statistic determined from samples —*note* the standard error of the mean is estimated by dividing the standard deviation by the square root of the number of observations

standard error of estimate the **standard deviation** of a distribution of observed values about a **regression** line computed as the square root of the residual mean square and generally representing an estimate of the variation likely to be encountered in making predictions from the regression equation

standard firefighting orders a list of 10 safety orders that are memorized and followed by **fire fighters** —*note* the orders: fight fire aggressively but provide for safety first; initiate all action based on current and expected **fire behavior;** recognize current weather conditions and obtain forecasts; ensure instructions are given and understood; obtain current information on fire status; remain in communication with crew members, your supervisor, and adjoining forces; determine safety zones and escape routes; establish **lookouts** in potentially hazardous situations; retain control at all times; stay alert, keep calm, think clearly, act decisively —*see* **watch-out situations**

standard knot a sound knot that is not greater than 1.5 in (3.81 cm) in diameter (with hardwoods not greater than 1.25 in or 3.18 cm in diameter) —*note* the diameter range includes a pin knot at not greater than 0.5 in (1.27 cm), a small knot at not greater than 0.75 in (1.90 cm), a medium knot at not greater than 1.5 in (3.81 cm), and a large knot at greater than 1.5 in (3.81 cm)

standard pressure the arbitrarily selected atmospheric pressure of 1,000 mb to which adiabatic processes are referred for definitions of potential temperature, equivalent potential temperature, etc.

stand average height the average height of all trees calculated either as the arithmetic mean or, more frequently, as the estimated height corresponding to the quadratic **mean diameter** (tree of mean **basal area**)

standby crew a group of trained **fire fighters** stationed at a dispatch point for rapid deployment

stand composition —*see* **composition**

stand density 1. a quantitative measure of **stocking** expressed either absolutely in terms of number of trees, **basal area,** or volume per unit area or relative to some standard condition 2. a measure of the degree of crowding of trees within stocked areas commonly expressed by various growing space ratios, e.g., height/spacing —*see* **relative stand density, stand density, stand density index**

stand density index (SDI) 1. a widely used measure developed by Reineke (1933) that expresses **rela-**

tive **stand density** in terms of the relationship of a number of trees to stand quadratic **mean diameter** 2. any index that expresses **relative stand density** based on a comparison of measured stand values with some standard condition

stand development changes in forest **stand** structure over time

stand establishment the initiation of tree cover, either by **afforestation, reforestation,** or **regeneration** —*see* **intolerant, tolerant**

stand height the mean height of the dominant trees in a **stand** or crop, generally based on a predetermined number of the thickest or tallest stems —*see* **site height, stand average height, top height**

stand improvement an intermediate treatment made to improve the composition, structure, condition, health, and growth of even- or **uneven-aged stands** —*see* **release**

standing crop 1. *silviculture* the forest **stand** 2. *wildlife* the total number or the total weight (biomass) of certain species or all species of animals present in an area at a given time —*see* **population index**

standing dead tree a dead tree of at least **breast height** that is free standing

standing line *harvesting* a fixed cable that does not move during logging operations, e.g., a **skyline** anchored at both ends —*see* **running line**

stand origin the apparent source of vegetation on the location

stand simulator —*see* **yield table**

stand structure 1. *ecology* the physical and temporal distribution of plants in a **stand** 2. *silviculture* the horizontal and vertical distribution of components of a forest **stand** including the height, diameter, crown layers, and stems of trees, **shrub**s, herbaceous understory, snags, and down woody debris

stand table a listing of the number of trees by species and diameter classes, generally per unit area —*note* such data may be presented in the form of a frequency distribution of diameter classes —*see* **stock table**

stand type a class of **stand** defined for silvicultural or management purposes, usually according to composition, structure, and age —*see* **forest type**

starch a mixture of polysaccharides, composed of glucose units, which forms the reserve food material of most plants —*note* starch is present in the sapwood of many **hardwood**s, which are consequently susceptible to attack by certain wood-boring insects that depend on starch for their nutrition

state comprehensive outdoor recreation plan (SCORP) a state **recreation** plan that assesses recreation supply and demand within a state —*note* a SCORP typically includes an action plan to address identified **needs**

state implementation plan (SIP) a state document, required by the Clean Air Act of 1955 as amended, describing a comprehensive plan of action for achieving specified air-quality objectives and standards for a particular locality or region within a specified time, as enforced by the state and approved by the Environmental Protection Agency

states of nature the uncontrollable future events that affect the payoff associated with a decision alternative

static stability the **stability** of an atmosphere in hydrostatic equilibrium with respect to vertical displacements, usually considered by the parcel method

station *ecology* **1.** the exact place of occurrence of a **species** or individual within a given **habitat 2.** a circumscribed area representing a complete and definite ensemble of conditions of existence, as reflected in the uniformity of the vegetation

station pressure the atmospheric pressure computed for the level of the station elevation

statistic any function of the sample observations; often an estimator of some **population** parameter

statistical fire an **actionable fire** on which a fire agency reports and maintains specified information, e.g., cause, date and point of origin, size, **fire damage**

steam fog the **fog** formed when water vapor is added to air that is much colder than the vapor's source — *note* steam fog most commonly occurs when very cold air drifts across relatively warm water —*see* **radiation fog**

Stefan-Boltzmann law a radiation law stating that the amount of energy radiated per unit time from a unit surface area of an ideal black body is proportional to the fourth power of the absolute temperature of the black body —*see* **black-body radiation**

stele the vascular cylinder of a **primary root**

stem the principal axis of a plant from which buds and shoots develop —*note* stems in woody species may be of any age or width —*see* **bole, branch, burl, tree**

stem analysis the analysis of a complete tree stem by counting and measuring the annual growth rings on a series of cross sections taken at different heights to determine its past rates of growth and changes in stem form, and to develop taper and volume equations —*see* **stump analysis**

stem class 1. any class into which the trees forming a crop or **stand** may be divided on the basis of some quality or condition of the stem **2.** the trees falling into such a class —*see* **crown class, diameter class**

stemflow precipitation that is intercepted by vegetation and subsequently flows down to the ground via the **stems** of plants —*see* **interception**

stem grass a grass characterized by its habit of developing separate and more or less isolated stems —*see* **bunch grass, sod grass**

stem map a map or set of coordinates specifying the physical location of each tree within some limited area, commonly a research plot

stemwood the wood of the **stem**(s) of a tree, i.e., of its main axis (or axes) as distinct from the branches (branchwood), stump (stumpwood), or roots —*note* stemwood is not to be confused with logwood, which is the dye-yielding wood of *Haemotoxylon campechianum*

stenothermic having or tolerating a small range of temperature

stepped leader 1. the initial streamer of a lightning discharge **2.** an intermittently advancing column of high ion density that establishes the channel for subsequent return streamers and **dart leaders**

step test *fire* a five-minute test measuring aerobic capacity and used to predict a person's ability to perform arduous work —*note 1.* a numerical scoring system that rates fitness on postexercise pulse rate, body weight, and age, in terms of milliliters of oxygen consumed per kg of body weight per minute —*note 2.* **fire suppression** jobs have been assigned fitness scores starting at a score of 45 for **fireline** construction and other strenuous work —*note 3.* applicants must attain the necessary test score to qualify —*see* **pack test, work capacity**

stereogram a stereoscopic pair of photographs or drawings correctly oriented and mounted or projected for stereoscopic viewing

stereometer any stereoscope with special attachments for measuring **parallax** or, more particularly, the attachments themselves, e.g., a **parallax bar** or **parallax wedge**

stereoplotter a photogrammetric instrument combining a stereoscopic measuring device with either a plotter (for transfer to maps) or a digital recorder (for input into **GIS, CAD,** or other software for eventual plotting)

stereoscope a binocular instrument used to view overlapping aerial photographs in three dimensions

stereoscopic pair aerial photographs with sufficient overlap and consequent duplication of detail to make possible stereoscopic examination of an object or area common to both

stereoscopic vision the particular application of binocular vision that enables the observer to view an object simultaneously from two perspectives, e.g., two photographs taken from different camera stations, and so obtain the mental impression of a three-dimensional **model**

sterility an absence or defectiveness of **pollen**, eggs, embryo, or **endosperm** that prevents sexual reproduction —*see* **crossability, incompatibility, isolation, parthenocarpy**

stewardship the administration of land and associated resources in a manner that enables their passing on to future generations in a healthy condition

stewardship incentive program (SIP) a cost-share program administered by the USDA that funds **forestry** practices prescribed in an official landowner Forest Stewardship Plan

sticker **1.** *pesticide* an ingredient added to a **pesticide** spray or dust to improve its adherence to the target surface —*note* a sticker is usually an **adjuvant** for improving adherence to plants **2.** *utilization* a spacing board used to separate courses of lumber to enhance air circulation in both air- and **kiln-drying** —*see* **drying**

sticky point **1.** a condition of consistency at which a soil barely fails to stick to a foreign object **2.** specifically and numerically, the water mass content of a well-mixed kneaded soil that barely fails to adhere to a polished nickel or stainless steel surface when the shearing speed is 50 mm s^{-1} (1.97 in s^{-1})

stiffness the capacity of a body to withstand deformation, particularly bending, as measured by the **modulus of elasticity** —*see* **moment of inertia of cross section**

stigma *in angiosperms* the uppermost portion of the **carpel** where **pollen grains** germinate —*see* **flower**

stilling well a pipe, chamber, or compartment having closed sides and bottom except for a comparatively small inlet, or inlets, connected to the main body of water —*note 1.* a stilling well is used for attenuating waves or surges while permitting the water level within the well to rise and fall with major fluctuations of the main body —*note 2.* a stilling well is used with water-measuring devices to improve accuracy of measurement

stilt root an **adventitious** root (a type of aerial root) that develops from the butt of a tree above ground level so that the tree appears as if supported on stilts —*note* plants with stilt roots include mangroves of the genus *Rhizophora* and some palms (*Pandanus* sp.) —*synonym* prop root —*see* **pneumataphore**

stipe *in fungi* the stem of a mushroom

stippling injury small dead spots on the leaves caused by feeding by **mites** and insects with piercing-sucking mouthparts —*note* in stippling injury, the small dead spot (toxemia) is due to loss of sap and to the toxic effect of saliva on the leaf tissue

stochastic **1.** referring to patterns resulting from random effects **2.** not characterized exactly; containing element(s) of chance (randomness) or probability —*see* **deterministic, mechanistic, random variable**

stochastic model a **model** in which at least one input varies with some degree of randomness such that model output will vary when the model is run repeatedly with the same input —*synonym* probabilistic model

stochastic process a system that changes in time or space according to probabilistic laws

stock **1.** the plant material used for establishment of genetic tests, **plantations**, etc. **2.** the material onto which part of another plant is grafted —*see* **graft, rootstock**

stocked quadrat *regeneration survey* a quadrat having (usually) at least one live tree seedling or regrowth

stocking **1.** *biometrics* the amount of anything on a given area, particularly in relation to what is considered optimum **2.** *silviculture* an indication of growing-space occupancy relative to a preestablished standard —*note* common indices of stocking are based on percent occupancy, **basal area**, relative density, **stand density index,** and crown competition factor —*see* **stand density 3.** *wildlife management* releasing wildlife, particularly mammals, birds, and fish, specifically reared or captured elsewhere, into a given **habitat** for replenishment purposes **4.** *wildlife management* the relative amount of animals, birds, and fish in a given habitat **5.** *range management* the number of specific kinds and classes of animals **grazing** or utilizing a unit of land for a specified time period —*note 1.* stocking may be expressed as animal unit months (AUM) or animal unit days per acre, hectare, or section, or the reciprocal (area of land per animal unit month or day) —*note 2.* when dual use is practiced (e.g., cattle and sheep), stocking rate is often expressed as AUMs per unit of land or the reciprocal —*see* **allowable use, continuous stocking, nonuse, proper-use factor, rotational stocking, set stocking, target stocking**

stocking percent the extent to which a given **stand** density meets a management objective, expressed as a percent

stock table a listing showing the proportions of total

volume within a **stand** by diameter classes —*see* **stand table**

stolon a stem or branch that grows along the ground surface and takes root at its nodes, e.g., strawberry and *Hedera* sp. —*see* **rhizome**

stomata the pores in plant leaves that control the gas exchange (CO_2 and O_2) and transpiration of a plant

stool a living stump (capable of) producing sprouts —*see* **coppice**

storied high forest trees in which the canopy can be differentiated into one or more layers (**story** or **stratum**) —*note* in a natural **forest,** the dominant species generally differ in each layer

stormflow that part of streamflow that occurs in direct response to precipitation —*note* stormflow is the sum of surface and subsurface flow

storm track the path followed by a center of low atmospheric pressure

story —*see* **stratum**

strain 1. *genetics* a group of trees related by common descent but different in some respect from the main body of the **species 2.** *utilization* the deformation resulting from a **stress,** e.g., tension and compression, measured as a change in specimen length per unit of total length —*note* normal strain is any compressive or tensile strain —*see* **deformation, loading, modulus**

strangulation the constriction of the stem or other part of a living tree by climbing plants or by artificial means —*note* strangulation with a metal band is sometimes done to stimulate flowering and seed production

strategic planning a disciplined effort to produce the basic decisions that shape and guide an organization and determine what it is, what it does, and why —*note* a strategic plan lays out organizational **goals**, examines the internal and external environment and influences that will affect these goals, and selects the most strategic objectives that will achieve the goals; progress toward the defined goals is continually monitored and adjustments are made as needed —*see* **comprehensive planning, incremental planning**

strategy *fire* an overall plan of attack for fighting a fire based on the most cost-efficient use of personnel and equipment in consideration of values threatened, **fire behavior,** legal **constraint**s, and objectives established for management of natural resources —*note* strategy leaves decisions on tactical use of suppression personnel and equipment to line commanders —*see* **tactics**

stratification 1. *biometrics* the subdivision of a **population** into strata, i.e., **block**s, before sampling, each of which is more homogeneous for the vari-

able being measured than the population as a whole **2.** *silviculture* the exposure of seed to a cold, moist treatment to overcome **dormancy** and promote **germination** —*see* **afterripening, vernalization**

stratified random sample a sample drawn from a stratified **population** consisting of a random sample from each stratum and permitting the sampling fraction to vary by **stratum** to (a) improve efficiency of sampling, (b) obtain separate estimates for strata, or (c) improve the **precision** of the population estimate

stratum *plural* **strata 1.** a distinct layer of vegetation within a forest community —*synonym* canopy layer **2.** a subdivision of a **population,** used in stratified sampling —*see* **stratification**

straw line *harvesting* a lightweight **wire rope** used to string heavier lines in **cable yarding** systems

streambank erosion —*see* **erosion**

streambed erosion —*see* **erosion**

stream gradient the change in elevation per unit distance along a stream channel —*note* stream gradient is usually expressed in units of percent or length/length (i.e., m/m) —*synonym* stream slope

stream order *ecology, silviculture* a hierarchical ordering of streams based on the degree of branching —*note 1.* a first-order stream is an unforked or unbranched stream —*note 2.* two first-order streams flow together to make a second-order stream; two second-order streams combine to make a third-order stream, etc.

streamside management zone (SMZ) a strip of land adjacent to a stream or river and managed in a way that meets water quality and productivity **goal**s

stress *utilization* a distributed force per unit area, e.g., where a beam transfers a load to a column —*note* normal stress is any compressive or tensile stress—*see* **deformation, elastic limit, loading, modulus, strain**

stress grading a system of classifying structural lumber in which grades are either visually, mechanically, or electronically established on a range of strength standards

strike team —*see* **incident command system**

string *biometrics* a set of alphanumeric characters, e.g., Ab& xy(+ —*see* **line**

stringy rot any decay or rot in wood that in its advanced state becomes fibrous or strandlike —*note* e.g., *Armillaria* in conifers is a form of stringy rot

strip burning —*see* **firing technique**

strip count 1. a tally of pieces of surfaced timber according to the width and length of the rough material from which they were made **2.** any complete count or tally taken on a sample strip through a **stand** or nursery bed —*synonym* strip tally

strip cruise a survey of one or more sample strips commonly based on regularly spaced, open traverses or transects along which recording of data is continuous —*see* **line-plot survey**

strip cutting —*see* **clearcutting, regeneration method, shelterwood**

strobilus *plural* **strobili** a **cone** of a conifer —*note* pines are **monoecious,** with male cones usually borne in the lower crown and female cones in the upper crown of the same tree —*see* **conelet, controlled pollination, dioecious, flower, fruit, Gymnospermae, inflorescence, ovulate, pollen, sex ratio, sporophyll, staminate**

stroma *plural* **stromata** *in fungi* a compact mass of hyphae on or within which fruiting structures are formed

structure —*see* **soil structure, stand structure**

structured query language (SQL) *biometrics* a syntax for defining and manipulating data from a **relational database** —*note* developed by IBM in the 1970s, SQL has since become an industry standard for query languages in most **relational database management system**s **(RDBMS)**

stubble the basal portion of **herbaceous** plants remaining after the top portion has been harvested either artificially or by **grazing** animals —*see* **aftermath**

stuffing material of little or no nutritive value, eaten by starving game in the absence of better food

stumpage 1. standing timber as viewed by a commercial cutter **2.** the value of timber as it stands uncut in terms of an amount per unit area —*synonym* stumpage value —*see* **royalty**

stump analysis the analysis of a stump cross section by counting and measuring annual growth rings to estimate the age of the tree and its past rates of radial growth —*see* **stem analysis**

stump height 1. the height of the top of a stump above ground level —*note* the point(s) of measurement selected as **ground level** will govern the point(s) along the stump rim taken as top **2.** *timber* —*see* **at the stump**

stump scale 1. the volume of pulpwood as stacked at the stump **2.** a tree volume table based on stump diameter

stump sprout regeneration of shoot growth from either adventitious or dormant buds from a cut tree stump

style *in angiosperms* the middle portion of the **carpel,** between the **stigma** and **ovary** —*see* **flower**

subalpine relating to the highest mountainous areas that can support forests

subclimax the (seral) stage in plant **succession,** immediately preceding the **climax** —*see* **seral stage**

subdominant 1. *ecology* a component of a **community,** typically a **species** which, though locally (co)dominant, exerts much less dominance than does the widespread **dominant 2.** *silviculture* —*see* **crown class**

suberin a fatty or waxy substance in the cell walls of the **phellem** and **casparian strip** of the **endodermis** —*see* **cutin**

suberized a condition of plant cells caused by the deposition of **suberin** in the cell walls

sublimation the transition of a substance (such as water) from the solid phase (ice) directly to the vapor phase, or *vice versa*, without passing through an intermediate liquid phase —*see* **ablation**

subline a division of a **line** within a **breeding population,** each with the same breeding objective —*see* **multiline**

sublittoral zone the part of a shore from the lowest water level to the lower boundary of terrestrial plant growth; the transition zone from the **littoral** to the **profundal**

subpolar relating to regions in which only one month has an average temperature of ± 50°F (10°C)

subpopulation a well-defined set of interacting individuals that constitute a proportion of a large, interbreeding **population** —*see* **subspecies**

subspecies a category usually intermediate between **species** and **variety,** based on fewer correlated characters than are used to differentiate species but more correlated characters than are used to differentiate varieties —*note* subspecies are generally identified by their geographical or ecological occurrence —*see* **subpopulation**

substitute one of two goods or services such that, when the price of one increases, the quantity demanded of the other increases, e.g., wooden and steel studs —*antonym* **complement**

substrate 1. that which is laid or spread under an underlying layer, such as the subsoil **2.** the substance, base, or nutrient on which an organism grows **3.** compounds or substances that are acted on by enzymes or catalysts and changed to other compounds in the chemical reaction

subsurface flow shallow lateral flow through a hillslope along an impermeable or slowly permeable layer above the groundwater table —*note* subsurface flow occurs early during storms and contributes to stormflow —*synonym* interflow, throughflow

subtropical relating to regions in which the average temperature is ± 50°F (10°C) for five to eight months of the year

succession the gradual supplanting of one community of plants by another —*note 1.* the sequence of communities is called a **sere**, or seral stage —*note 2.* a sere whose first stage is open water is termed a **hydrosere,** one whose first stage is dry ground, a **xerosere** —*note 3.* succession is primary (by **pioneers**) on sites that have not previously borne vegetation, secondary after the whole or part of the original vegetation has been supplanted, **allogenic** when the causes of succession are external to and independent of the community (e.g., accretion of soil by wind or water, or a change of climate), and **autogenic** when the developing vegetation is itself the cause

sucker a shoot arising from below ground level either from a **rhizome** (e.g., bamboos) or from a root (e.g., *Populus* sp.) —*see* **coppice**

sucker knot a **knot** sawn from a log that contains the origin of a forked top or **ramicorn**

suitability the appropriateness of applying certain resource management practices to a particular area of land, as determined by an analysis of the social, economic, and environmental consequences and the alternative uses foregone —*note* a unit of land may be suitable for a variety of individual or combined management practices

sulfate pulp —*see* **pulp**

sulfite pulp —*see* **pulp**

summerwood —*see* **latewood**

sunscald localized injury to **bark** and **cambium** caused by a sudden increase in exposure of a stem or branch to intense sunlight (insolation) and high temperatures —*synonym* bark scorch, white spot — *see* **winter sunscald**

superior *genetics* phenotypically better than the average of the **population** but not yet tested for genetic worth —*see* **elite, plus, phenotype, plus tree**

superparasitization the simultaneous **infestation** of an individual **host** by two or more individuals of the same parasitic **species** —*see* **hyperparasitization, multiparasitization**

supersaturation *meteorology* the condition existing in a given portion of the atmosphere (or other space) when the **relative humidity** is greater than 100 percent, i.e., when it contains more water vapor than is needed to produce saturation with respect to a plane surface, pure water, or pure ice

supplement *range management* a nutritional additive (salt, protein, phosphorus, etc.) intended to remedy deficiencies of the **range** diet for **livestock** —*synonym* supplementary feed

supply **1.** the functional relationship between the price of a given commodity or service and the quantity that sellers would be willing and able to sell in a given market during a specified time period —*note* supply is typically expressed as a mathematical equation (showing quantity supplied as a function of price) or as a curve showing price per unit plotted over quantity **2.** the actual quantity of a commodity or service offered by sellers in the market over a specified time period —*see* **demand**

suppressed —*see* **crown class, overtopped**

suppression **1.** *silviculture* the process whereby a tree or other vegetation loses vigor and may die when growing space is not sufficient to provide photosynthate or moisture to support adequate growth **2.** *entomology* the regulation or modification of an insect population that is causing intolerable effects **3.** *fire* —*see* **fire prevention, fire suppression**

supralittoral zone the portion of the shore adjacent to the water's edge

surface *GIS* a representation of geographic information as a set of continuous data in which the map features are not spatially discrete, i.e., there is an infinite set of values between any two locations —*note* there are no clear or well-defined breaks between possible values of the geographic feature; surfaces can be represented by **models** built from regularly or irregularly spaced sample points on the surface

surface body layer the thin layer of air adjacent to the earth's surface and extending up to the so-called anemometer level (the base of the Ekman layer)

surface chart an analyzed **synoptic chart** of surface weather observations

surface fire —*see* **forest fire**

surface friction the drag or skin friction of the earth on the atmosphere —*note* usually expressed in terms of the shearing stress of the wind on the earth's surface, i.e., the aerodynamic force per unit area

surface fuel —*see* **fuel type**

surface inversion a temperature inversion based at the earth's surface, i.e., an increase of temperature with elevation beginning at the ground level —*see* **temperature inversion**

surface model *GIS* digital abstraction or approximation of a surface —*note* because a surface contains an infinite number of **points**, some subset of points must be used to represent the surface; each **model** contains a formalized data structure, rules, and x,y,z point measurements that can be used to represent a surface

surface runoff —*see* **overland flow, runoff**

surface soil the uppermost part of the soil, ordinarily moved in **tillage** or its equivalent in uncultivated soils, and ranging in depth from 7 to 25 cm (2.8 to 9.8 in) —*synonym* plow layer, surface layer, Ap layer, Ap **horizon** —*see* **topsoil**

surface wind a wind measured at a surface observing station, customarily at some distance (usually 20 ft or 6 m) above the ground to minimize the distorting effects of local obstacles and terrain

surfactant an ingredient in a **pesticide** formulation that modifies the relationship between the surfaces of a liquid and another liquid or surface, e.g., **emulsifier, wetting agent, spreader**

surplus variable a variable subtracted (explicitly by the user or implicitly by the **algorithm**) from the left-hand side of a greater-than-or-equal-to **constraint** in a **mathematical programming** problem specification to convert the constraint into an equality —*note* the value of this variable can usually be interpreted as the amount over and above some required minimum level —*see* **slack variable**

survivorship curve *ecology* a plot of percent survival in a **cohort** over time resulting in a curve whose shape identifies the competitive strategy (r- or K-selection) of a species

susceptibility *entomology, pathology* 1. the probability that a tree or **stand** will be attacked by, or incur an outbreak of, an insect or **pathogen** —*see* **immunity, resistance** 2. the suitability of a habitat for an insect or pathogen or for populations of insects or pathogens 3. the inability to avoid or withstand attack by a **parasite**, usually a matter of degree —*see* **hazard, tolerance**

suspect *pathology* any likely **host**, especially with respect to a **pathogen**

suspended sediment the very fine soil particles that remain in suspension in water for a considerable time —*note* sediment is maintained in suspension by the upward components of turbulent currents or may be fine enough to form a colloidal suspension

suspended solid any solid substance present in water in an undissolved state, usually contributing directly to turbidity

sustainability the capacity of **forests**, ranging from **stands** to **ecoregions**, to maintain their health, productivity, diversity, and overall integrity, in the long run, in the context of human activity and use

sustainable forest management (sustainable forestry) (SFM) *this evolving concept has several definitions* 1. the practice of meeting the **forest** resource **needs** and values of the present without compromising the similar capability of future generations —*note* sustainable **forest management** involves practicing a land stewardship ethic that integrates the **reforestation**, managing, growing, nurturing, and harvesting of trees for useful products with the **conservation** of soil, air and water quality, wildlife and fish **habitat**, and aesthetics (UN Conference on Environment and Development, Rio De Janeiro, 1992) 2. the stewardship and use of forests and forest lands in a way, and at a rate, that maintains their **biodiversity, productivity, regeneration** capacity, vitality, and potential to fulfill, now and in the future, relevant ecological, economic, and social functions at local, national, and global levels, and that does not cause damage to other **ecosystem**s (the Ministerial Conference on the Protection of Forests in Europe, Helsinki, 1993) —*note* criteria for sustainable **forestry** include (a) conservation of biological diversity, (b) maintenance of productive capacity of forest ecosystems, (c) maintenance of forest ecosystem health and vitality, (d) conservation and maintenance of soil and water resources, (e) maintenance of forest contributions to global carbon cycles, (f) maintenance and enhancement of long-term multiple socioeconomic benefits to meet the needs of societies, and (g) a legal, institutional, and economic framework for forest conservation and sustainable management (Montréal Process, 1993) —*see* **biological legacy, certify, chain of custody, criteria and indicators, criterion, ecosystem management**

sustained yield 1. the **yield** that a **forest** can produce continuously at a given intensity of management —*note* sustained-yield management implies continuous production so planned as to achieve, at the earliest practical time, a balance between increment and cutting 2. the achievement and maintenance in perpetuity of a high-level annual or regular periodic output of the various **renewable resources** without impairment of the productivity of the land —*see* **ecosystem management, long-term sustained yield (LTSY)**

swage-set to set saw teeth by broadening and sharpening the tip of each tooth —*note* swage-setting ensures clearance between the saw plate and the cut made by the saw —*see* **saw, spring-set**

swamp 1. a tract generally characterized by a soil that is slightly acid, neutral, or slightly alkaline, and a water table at or above the soil surface (the water often moving perceptibly), supporting not only low vegetation, e.g. sedges, but also reeds and woody vegetation, including trees —*note* in tidal areas, such a tract is termed a tidal swamp —*see* **bog, marsh** 2. a tree- or tall **shrub**-dominated **wetland,** characterized by periodic flooding and nearly permanent subsurface water flow through mixtures of mineral sediments and organic materials, essentially without peat accumulation

sweep the extent to which the lower portion of a tree's stem diverges from straight, usually measured in degrees —*note 1.* sweep applies to both trees and cut logs —*note 2.* a tree with sweep is distinct from a leaning stem

symbiosis a mutually beneficial association between two or more organisms (symbionts) —*note* in obligatory symbiosis the mutual association is necessary for all symbionts; a nonobligatory relationship may be called protocooperation; in conjunctive symbiosis the symbionts form a single body or organ, as in **mycorrhizae** and **lichens** —*see* **commensalism**

symbol a graphic pattern used to represent a feature —*note 1. GIS* **line** symbols represent **arc** features, marker symbols represent **points**, shaded symbols represent **polygons**, and text symbols represent **annotation** —*note 2.* many characteristics define symbols, including color, size, angle, and pattern —*see* **marker symbol, shade symbol, text symbol**

sympatric the capacity for **species** or **populations** to inhabit the same or overlapping geographic areas —*see* **allopatric, species hybrid**

symplast a network of connected axial and radial **parenchyma** cells in **sapwood** and inner bark —*note* symplasts store energy reserves —*see* **apoplast**

symptom *entomology, pathology* any observable change in **host** structure or character caused by disease or insect **infestation**, e.g., chlorosis, **wilt**ing, **gall**s

syndrome 1. symptoms that together are characteristic of a specific disease **2.** a predictable, characteristic condition or pattern that tends to occur under certain circumstances, whether visible or not, and whether the causal agent(s) is known or not —*see* **decline**

synecology the study of biotic communities and the interaction of organisms that compose them

synergist a chemical substance that, when used with a pesticide or drug, will increase the total effect over the sum of their individual effects —*see* **adjuvant**

synomone a **semiochemical** that is adaptively advantageous to both the emitting and the receiving organism —*see* **kairomone, pheromone**

synoptic chart any chart or map on which data and analyses are presented that describe the state of the atmosphere over a large area at a given moment in time —*see* **high**

synoptic weather observation a surface weather observation, made at periodic times (usually at three-hour and six-hour intervals, as specified by the World Meteorological Organization), of sky cover, state of the sky, cloud height, atmospheric

pressure reduced to sea level, temperature, **dew point,** wind speed and direction, amount of precipitation, hydrometeors and lithometeors, and special phenomena that prevail at the time of the observation or have been observed since the previous specified observation

syntax *GIS* a set of rules governing the way statements can be used in a computer language

synthetic aperture radar (SAR) a specific microwave radar sensor in which an effective antenna is emulated by storing and comparing the **Doppler shift** signals received while the aircraft travels along its flight path —*note 1.* this synthetic antenna (or array) is many times longer than a physical antenna, thus sharpening the effective beam width and improving azimuth resolution —*note 2.* good-quality SAR imagery can be obtained regardless of time of day or weather, thus offering an alternative electro-optical imagery for **remote sensing** of cloudy regions

synusia any component of a **community** of one or more **species**, belonging to the same life-form, having similar environmental requirements and occurring in similar **habitat**, e.g., a layer of moss plants

systematics the study of biological diversity and evolutionary relationships among organisms —*note* the term is sometimes used interchangeably with taxonomy

systematic sample —*see* **sample (systematic)**

systemic 1. a **pathogen** capable of spreading throughout its **host 2.** a **pesticide** that is absorbed by and permeates some or all of the host tissues, and that is more toxic to the target insects and pathogens than to the host **3.** a pesticide that is absorbed by and permeates some or all of the host tissues and is toxic to the absorbing organism

systemic infection 1. an **infection** in which the **parasite** is found generally throughout the **host** tissue **2.** a **dwarf mistletoe** infection in which the endophytic system is in the terminal bud and keeps pace with the apex of the host, generally with little **hypertrophy** or **hyperplasia** —*see* **endophyte**

systems analysis the theory and practice of quantitatively analyzing the relationships within a system, both to better understand system structure and to produce predictive **models** of system behavior under multiple **scenario**s, some of which may not yet have occurred —*note* systems range widely in spatial and temporal extent and complexity, but include forests, transportation, and initial attack on wildfires —*synonym* **operations research,** management science

T

table *GIS* **1.** the datafile in which the relational data reside —*synonym* relational table —*see* **relational database 2.** a file that contains **ASCII** or other data in some sort of **row** and **column** order

tackle *harvesting* a system of blocks and lines arranged to gain mechanical advantage for hoisting and pulling

tactics *fire* planned operational actions that determine where and how to build a **fireline** and what other **fire suppression** measures are necessary to extinguish a fire —*note* tactics must be consistent with the **strategy** established for suppressing the fire —*see* **plan of attack**

tag *range management* **1.** to attach identifying tags to animals —*synonym* mark, **brand 2.** to clip manured and dirty locks from sheep

tagline *harvesting* an extra length of line attached to the end of any drum line to extend the operating distance —*note* a tagline is used as an extension for carrying additional **choker** hooks or to dampen the swing of a bucket or **grapple** on a boom-type **loader**

taiga a subarctic, coniferous **forest** that is typically of open, slow-growing spruces, interspersed with bogs, and characteristic of Europe, Asia, and North America —*note* taiga forms a transition zone between the denser, **boreal forests** to the south and the **tundra** to the north and has a vegetation pattern that is closely related to the presence of **permafrost** and to fire history —*see* **boreal, tundra**

tail block *harvesting* **1.** a block fixed to a stump at the outer edge of a setting through which the **haulback line** is run for returning the **main line** and **carriage** or **butt rigging** to the loading point **2.** a block that supports the **skyline** in skyline logging

tail hold *harvesting* **1.** the anchor at the end of the **skyline** away from the landing **2.** a line securing a **tail block** to a stump

tailwater 1. *hydraulics* water in a river or channel immediately downstream from a structure **2.** *irrigation* water that reaches the lower end of a field

taking 1. the reduction of private property rights (and associated property value) due to government policy or regulation —*synonym* take —*note 1.* in the United States, this is a violation of the US Constitution's provision, "...nor shall private property be taken for public use without just compensation...," caused by landuse regulation **2.** under the Endangered Species Act of 1976, a taking or take is to harass, harm, pursue, hunt, shoot, wound, kill, trap, capture, or collect an animal or to attempt to engage in any such conduct —*see* **incidental take**

talus a slope landform typically covered by coarse rock debris forming a more or less continuous layer that may or may not be covered by duff and litter

taper the decrease in thickness, generally in terms of diameter, of a tree stem or log from the base upwards or from the larger diameter end to the smaller end in logs —*synonym* **form** —*see* **form class**

taper curve (function) a curve or mathematical equation that describes the shape of a tree bole —*note* the taper curve is often used for computing tree volumes to different top diameters

tap root 1. the primary plant root developing from the **radicle 2.** the main descending root of a plant **3.** the dominant root of a seedling or tree root system that is a direct continuation of the radicle or, if the radicle is absent, a direct continuation of a dominant first-order lateral root

taproot system a rooting habit of trees in which the main root elongates downward and from which other roots develop

target canker a perennial **canker** characterized by prominent, concentrically arranged zones of callus that mark alternate outgrowth and death of the edge of living tissues surrounding the wound

target species a plant or animal species against which a suppression measure or **pesticide** is directed —*see* **nontarget species**

target stocking the desirable number of well-spaced trees per unit area in an even-aged stand at the age of first commercial thinning or harvest —*see* **stocking**

tarif table a series of harmonized single-entry volume tables applicable only to even-aged **stand**s —*note 1.* the volume of a tree with a basal area of 1 ft^2 (0.09 m^2) is often used as the index to the tables and is called the tarif number of that table —*note 2.* the choice of any tarif for a given tree or crop depends either on the mean volume of a small sample of trees or on some index of site or height derived from examining (a small sample of) the crop itself —*note 3.* tarifs may be general or local, and also compound (i.e., site classes differentiated) or simple (site classes undifferentiated)

tar spot a leaf-spot disease of *Acer* caused by species of the fungus *Rhytisma* —*note* a particularly important tar-spot disease is the **leaf spot** of *Acer pseudoplatanus* caused by *R. acerinum*

taungya —*see* **shifting cultivation**

taxol 1. a compound among the group of taxanes derived from the bark and other organs of the Pacific yew *(Taxus brevifolia)* and other yews used as a drug for the treatment of advanced ovarian cancer

2. the drug paclitaxel with a complex ring structure ($C_{47}H_{51}NO_{14}$), used in medicine and having the registered name Taxol®

taxon *plural* **taxa** any formal taxonomic category, e.g., genus, **variety** —*see* **cline, dioecious, monoecious, phylogeny, taxonomy**

taxonomy the classification of organisms, including identification and nomenclature (naming) —*see* **morphology, phylogeny, taxon, variety**

TCF total chlorine-free pulp —*see* **pulp**

TDS —*see* **total dissolved solids**

technical rotation —*see* **rotation**

technology transfer the transfer of ideas, information, methods, procedures, techniques, tools, or technology from the developers to potential users —*note* methods of technology transfer include scientific publications in peer-reviewed journals, articles in management-oriented publications, computer programs, training sessions, tours, workshops, etc.

teliospore the resting **spore** in **rust fungi** in which the male and female nuclei fuse and from which the **perfect stage** of pro**mycelium** or **basidium** arises

telium *plural* **telia** a **spore** in **rust fungi** containing the **teliospores** —*see* **uredinium**

temperate relating to regions in which the average temperature is ± 50°F (10°C) for two to four months of the year

temperature inversion a layer in which temperature increases with altitude —*see* **surface inversion**

template *GIS* **1.** a geographic data set containing boundaries, such as land-water boundaries, for use as a starting place in automating other geographic data sets that use this line —*note 1.* **forest management** units and soil type units both use the land-water boundary —*note 2.* templates save processing time during spatial overlays **2.** a map containing **neatlines**, north arrow, logos, and similar map elements for a common map series, but lacking the central information that makes one map unique from another **3.** an empty tabular data file containing only **column** definitions

temporal *remote sensing* pertaining to the frequency of data collection over one area by a satellite

tending —*see* **intermediate treatment**

tension wood reaction wood formed in the **Angiospermae** on the upper sides of leaning **hardwood** trees —*note* compared with normal wood, tension wood has more **cellulose**, less **lignin**, and higher density but produces weaker paper; boards cut from tension wood produce a fuzzy surface on sawing and tend to **collapse** on drying —*see* **compression wood, reaction wood**

tent caterpillar a member of the family Lasiocampidae (Lepidoptera), particularly as a **larva** which lives gregariously in the early stages, generally in a large silken nest or matting that is woven on, and sometimes envelops, the **host** plant —*note 1.* some species of tent caterpillars are serious forest defoliators, e.g., the western **tent caterpillar** *(Malacosoma californicum)* —*note 2.* some tent caterpillars do not construct true tents, e.g., the forest tent caterpillar *(M. disstria)* —*synonym* tent maker —*see* **webworm**

tenure **1.** the act of owning, using, and controlling land under certain terms and conditions **2.** the holding, particularly as to manner or term (i.e., period of time), of a post or office

terminal *computers* a device, usually a display monitor and a keyboard, used to communicate with the computer

terminal borer an insect that bores only in the terminal shoots —*note* the white pine weevil is a terminal borer —*see* **shoot borer, wood borer**

terminal value the value of all resources, including land, at the end of the planning horizon

terminal weevil a member of the family Curculionidae (Coleoptera) which causes serious damage in conifer seedlings and **saplings**, forest **regeneration** and Christmas tree **plantation**s —*synonym* shoot weevil —*note* terminal weevils are usually grouped according to their mode of injury: (a) seedling-debarking weevils (pales weevils, pitch-eating weevils), (b) pine reproduction weevils, (c) root collar weevils (pine root collar weevil, Warren's collar weevil), and (d) terminal weevil (white pine weevil)

termite a eu**social** insect of the order Isoptera that utilizes cellulose, including wood, either directly or through symbiotic fungi or protozoa, and is therefore important in recycling dead wood material and can be very destructive to wood products —*note 1.* termites have no known effective, natural enemies —*note 2.* four main **ecotype**s of termites are: (a) damp wood termites, which enter wood directly from the air (at swarming time) and are largely confined to decaying wood, (b) dry wood termites, also entirely wood inhabiting and requiring no contact with the ground can directly attack dry wood, (c) subterranean termites (also called ground termites, mound builders, and higher termites), which build extensive tunnels, and (d) powderpost termites, which usually attack dry wood and do not require ground contact

terrace **1.** a level, usually narrow, plain bordering a river or stream and lying above the current **flood-plain 2.** an abandoned floodplain

territory *wildlife* the area that an animal defends, usually during breeding season, against intruders of its own species

test fire a prescribed fire ignited to evaluate such factors as **fire behavior,** efficiency in fire detection, or **fire suppression** measures

test of significance a computation of the **probability** that an observed effect or difference may have arisen purely as a result of chance or as a result of **experimental error** —*note 1.* if this probability is less than an agreed small value (termed the level of significance and often accepted as 1:20), the effect or difference is said to be significant, leading to a decision to accept or reject the statistical hypothesis under consideration —*note 2.* a nonsignificant result does not, however, constitute a proof that the result is due to chance only —*see* **variance-ratio test**

tetraploid an organism or cell that has four times (4*n*) the **haploid** (*n*) number of **chromosomes** —*see* **polyploid**

text symbol *GIS* a text style defined by font, size, character spacing, color, etc., used to label maps —*note* e.g., *Text symbol 1,* Text symbol 2, Text symbol 3 —*see* **shade symbol, symbol**

thallus *plural* **thalli** a vegetative, often flattened structure not differentiated into **stem,** leaves, and roots —*note* a thallus forms the main body of lichens, liverworts, and fungi

thematic data —*see* **descriptive data**

thematic map a map that illustrates one subject or topic either quantitatively or qualitatively —*note* a thematic map is not to be confused with Landsat Thematic Mapper, which is a trade name for a satellite remote sensing system

theme *GIS* a collection of logically organized geographic objects defined by the user and organized logically into groups of layers or themes, e.g., streets, wells, soil types, and streams

theodolite an instrument that precisely measures horizontal and vertical angles —*see* **transit**

thermal infrared the emissive portion of the electromagnetic spectrum considered to occur from 3 to 14 mm —*note* this spectral region spans the radiant power peak of the earth

thermocline the zone of water depth within which temperature rapidly changes between the upper warm water layer (**epilimnion**) and the lower cold water layer (**hypolimnion**)

thermomechanical pulp (TMP) —*see* **pulp**

therophyte a plant that completes its life cycle, from

germination to ripe seed, within a single growth period, e.g., an **annual** —*see* **life-form**

Thiessen polygon a **polygon** having boundaries that define the area closest to each **point** relative to all other points —*note* Thiessen polygons are generated from a set of points; they are mathematically defined by the perpendicular bisectors of the lines between all points; they are created using a triangulated irregular network (**TIN**) structure —*synonym* Dirichlet tessellation

thinning a cultural treatment made to reduce **stand** density of trees primarily to improve growth, enhance **forest health,** or recover potential mortality; types of thinning include the following:

—**chemical thinning** the killing of unwanted trees by using an herbicide, e.g., including band or frill girdling

—**crown thinning** the removal of trees from the **dominant** and **codominant** crown classes in order to favor the best trees of those same crown classes —*synonym* thinning from above, high thinning

—**free thinning** the removal of trees to control **stand** spacing and favor desired trees, using a combination of thinning criteria without regard to crown position

—**low thinning** the removal of trees from the lower crown classes to favor those in the upper crown classes —*synonym* thinning from below

—**mechanical thinning** the thinning of trees in either even- or **uneven-aged stand**s, involving removal of trees in rows, strips, or by using fixed spacing intervals —*synonym* geometric thinning

—**selection thinning** the removal of trees in the dominant crown class in order to favor the lower crown classes —*synonym* dominant thinning

thinning cycle —*see* **thinning interval**

thinning from above —*see* **thinning (crown)**

thinning from below —*see* **thinning (low)**

thinning grade one of several traditional degrees of **thinning,** based essentially on dominance, crown and stem classes, and the extent to which these classes are removed (and the canopy therefore opened) at any one thinning —*see* **crown class**

thinning intensity a measure of the combined effect of **thinning** weight or severity and thinning frequency, usually in terms of the volume removed divided by the number of years between successive thinnings —*see* **relative thinning intensity**

thinning interval the period of time between successive **thinning** entries, usually used in connection with even-aged **stand**s —*synonym* thinning cycle —*see* **cutting cycle**

thinning regime a term comprising the type, grade, and frequency of **thinnings** for a given area, generally along with their year of commencement and sometimes termination

thinning weight the severity of **thinning** expressed in terms of the basal area or volume removed per unit area at any one time —*note* thinning weight is commonly expressed as light, moderate, or heavy —*see* **thinning grade**

thiocyanate an **insecticide** having a molecular structure containing thiocyanate endings, which interfere with cellular respiration and metabolism of insects

thorax the middle body region of an insect, usually composed of three **segments** (prothorax, mesothorax, metathorax), primarily functioning for locomotion, and bearing any legs and wings

threatened species 1. a plant or animal species likely to become endangered throughout all or a significant portion of its range within the foreseeable future 2. a plant or animal identified and defined in the Federal Register in accordance with the Endangered Species Act of 1976 —*see* **conservation recommendations, endangered species, habitat conservation plan, incidental take, jeopardy, priority animal taxa, recovery, taking**

three-P sampling *inventory* a modification of variable probability sampling in which the chance of a tree being selected in the sample varies directly with the size of the tree —*synonym* **3-P sampling** —*see* **angle-count method, point sampling, prism cruising, relaskop, sample, proportional**

throughfall 1. *meteorology* precipitation that falls directly through a vegetative **canopy** or is intercepted by vegetation and then drips to the ground —*see* **interception** 2. *pathology* dwarf **mistletoe** seeds that fall directly to the ground (immediately on discharge) or are intercepted by foliage but eventually reach the ground, usually because of rain

tic *GIS* registration or geographic control points representing known locations on the earth's surface —*note 1.* tics allow all features to be recorded in a common coordinate system, e.g., Universal Transverse Mercator (UTM) meters or State Plane feet —*note 2.* tics are used to register map sheets when they are mounted on a **digitizer,** and to transform the coordinates, e.g., from digitizer units (in)to UTM (m) —*see* **root mean square error**

tic match tolerance *GIS* the maximum distance allowed between an existing **tic** and a tic being digitized —*note 1.* if this distance is exceeded, the digitizing error is considered unacceptable and the map must be re-registered —*note 2.* tic match tolerance is used to ensure a low **RMS error** during map registration on a **digitizer**

tidal marsh a low, flat marshland traversed by interlaced channels and tidal **sloughs** and subject to tidal inundations —*note* normally, the only vegetation present is salt-tolerant bushes and grasses

tie-in —*see* **fire suppression**

tiering *federal land management* the process of preparing multiple levels of environmental review, typically including general matters in broad **environmental impact statements** with subsequent, narrower environmental impact statements

TIGER —*see* **topologically integrated geographic encoding and referencing data**

tightlining *harvesting* a method of **highlead yarding** in which the **haulback line** supports the **butt rigging** and makes it possible to lift the butt rigging and its load over obstacles

tile *GIS* a part of the **database** in a **GIS** representing a discrete part of the earth's surface —*note* by splitting a study area into tiles, considerable savings in access times and improvements in system performance can be achieved

till 1. unsorted and unstratified earth material, deposited by glacial ice, which consists of a mixture of **clay, silt, sand,** gravel, stones, and boulders in any proportion 2. to prepare the soil for **seeding;** to seed or cultivate the soil

tillage the mechanical manipulation of the soil profile for any purpose

tilt the distortion caused by any departure of the camera axis (the direction in which the camera is pointing) from the vertical when the photograph is taken

tilt displacement the displacement of **images** radially from the **isocenter** of an **aerial photograph,** caused by its **tilt**

tilth the physical condition of the soil as related to its ease of **tillage,** fitness as a seedbed, and impedence to seedling emergence and root penetration

timber 1. **forest** crops and **stands** containing timber 2. wood, other than fuelwood, potentially usable for lumber

timber appraisal an estimate of the monetary value of a timber **stand**

timberbelt a windbreak specifically managed for timber production —*see* **shelterbelt**

timber cruise —*see* **cruise**

timberland —*see* **commercial forest land, unreserved forest land**

timberline —*see* **tree line**

timber marking the denoting of individual trees for treatment (cutting, leaving, or pruning) using paint, flagging, or other marks

timber stand improvement (TSI) *obsolete —see* **stand improvement**

timberworm a beetle of the families Lymexylonidae and Brentidae (Coleoptera) whose **larvae** are wood borers and cause pinhole damage (referred to as wormy wood) similar to ambrosia beetles but with the galleries free of bore dust and stain *—note* timberworms such as the oak timberworm *(Arrhenodes minutus)* attack living, dying, and freshly dead hardwoods in the eastern United States *—synonym* brentid beetle

timelag the time necessary for a **wildland** fuel particle, under specified conditions, to lose 63 percent of the difference between its current moisture content and its equilibrium moisture content *—synonym* timelag period *—note* fuels are grouped into the following classes:

—one-hour timelag fuel fine combustible material consisting of dead herbaceous plants and roundwood less than 0.25-in (0.64-cm) in diameter, including the uppermost litter layer

—10-hour timelag fuel dead **fuel** consisting of roundwood 0.25- to 1-in (0.64- to 2.54-cm) in diameter and the general layer of litter extending from immediately below the surface to 0.75 in (1.90 cm) below the surface

—100-hour timelag fuel dead combustible material consisting of roundwood 1 to 3 in (2.5 to 7.6 cm) in diameter and the layer of the forest floor that extends generally from 0.75 to 4 in (1.9 to 10.2 cm) below the surface

—1,000-hour timelag fuel dead combustible material consisting of roundwood 3 to 8 in (7.6 to 20.3 cm) in diameter and the layer of the forest floor that extends 4 in (10.2 cm) below the surface

time of concentration the time required for water to flow from the most remote point of a watershed, in a hydraulic sense, to the outlet

time-preference rate the annual percent at which an individual, firm, or public agency subjectively discounts future values when making decisions about current expenditures or land-holding costs *—synonym* **alternative rate of return**

time study the assessment of the amount of time required to perform one or a series of tasks or operations, e.g., **fireline** construction, landing operations, planting, and **riparian** restoration, under specified conditions, usually to produce data in support of planning or **model**ing *—note* time studies may involve actual measurements or estimates based on expert opinion*—see* **work measurement, work study**

TIN *—see* **triangulated irregular network**

tip the fore-and-aft component of **tilt,** i.e., the departure of the camera axis from the perpendicular in the vertical plane along the **flight line**

tip moth a member of the genus *Rhyacionia* (Lepidoptera) whose **larvae** tunnel in the needle bases, terminal buds, twigs, and shoots of young pines *—note 1.* tip moths include the European pine **shoot moth,** *R. buoliana* and the pitch pine tip moth (*R. rigidana*) *—note 2.* many tip moths are **multivoltine** *—synonym* shoot moth *—see* **twig girdler**

tissue culture an aseptic cell, tissue, organ, or protoplast culture *—see* **axenic, vegetative propagation**

TMP thermomechanical pulp*—see* **pulp**

tolerance 1. *ecology* the capacity of an organism or biological process to subsist under a given set of environmental conditions *—note* the range of conditions under which it can subsist, representing its limits of tolerance, is termed its ecological amplitude **2.** *entomology, pathology* the ability of a plant to endure the development and survive the invasion of a **parasite** or **pathogen**ic organism with minimum symptoms of disease *—see* **susceptibility 3.** *human health* the amount of a pesticide that may safely and legally remain as a residue on a food plant or in meat or fat *—synonym* tolerance level **4.** *silviculture* the capacity of trees to grow satisfactorily in the shade of, and in competition with, other trees; if intolerant of shade, they are termed light demanders; if tolerant, shade bearers *—see* **shade tolerance, light demanding 5.** *wildlife* the ability of animals to adjust to different or disturbed **habitat**s

tolerant 1. a plant capable of becoming established and growing beneath overtopping vegetation *—note* the term is usually applied to shade, but may also refer to tolerance to flooding, salt, pollutants, etc. *—antonym* **intolerant 2.** pertaining to a plant having **tolerant** characteristics *—see* **stand establishment**

tone each particular shade variation from black to white distinguishable on an **photograph aerial** (monochromatic or panchromatic)

topcross test a **progeny test** derived by crossing each parent with the same tester (topcross) **pollen** *—note* in a topcross test, the pollen may be a single lot or a mixture from a number of tester trees, but should not mask the contribution of the female parents being tested *—see* **cross-pollination, diallel cross, polycross test, polymix cross**

top diameter the diameter, either inside or outside bark, of the tree stem at a point on the bole above which there is usually no merchantable portion for the product of interest, e.g., sawlog, **pole,** or pulpwood

top height the average height of the 40 trees/ac (100

trees/ha) of largest diameter —*see* **site height, stand height**

top kill gradual or sudden dieback of the uppermost portion of a plant, usually a coniferous tree —*note 1.* top kill is often caused by defoliators and *Ips* **bark beetle**s —*note 2.* a tree with top kill is termed a spike-top, spiked top, or stagheaded tree —*synonym* top-kill, **snag** top

topographic map a map that shows land forms, topographic features, and elevations, usually by means of contour lines, as well as other features, such as roads

topologically integrated geographic encoding and referencing (TIGER) data a format used by the US Census Bureau for the 1990 census to support census programs and surveys —*note* TIGER files contain stream lines and all roads found on 1:100,000 maps, as well as street address ranges along lines and census tract or block boundaries; these files enable data to be associated with map features

topology *GIS* the spatial relationships between connecting or adjacent features, e.g., **arc**s, **node**s, **polygon**s, and **point**s —*note 1.* the topology of an arc includes its from- and to-nodes and its left and right polygons, if the arcs are used to describe polygons —*note 2.* topological relationships are built from simple elements into complex elements: points (simplest elements), arcs (sets of connected points), polygons (sets of connected arcs), **route**s (sets of sections that are arcs or portions of arcs), and regions (sets of polygons) —*note 3.* redundant data (coordinates) are eliminated because an arc may represent a linear feature or part of the boundary of a polygon or part of a region boundary —*note 4.* topology is useful in GIS because many spatial **modeling** operations do not require coordinates, only topological information, e.g., to find an optimal path between two points requires a list of which arcs connect to each other and the cost of traversing along each arc in each direction; coordinates are necessary only to draw the path after it is calculated —*see* **arc-node topology**

topophysis the persistence of nongenetic effects (e.g., age, position) after rooting or **grafting** —*see* **vegetative propagation**

top rot decay localized in the upper portion of the bole

topsoil the layer of soil moved in cultivation, frequently designated as the Ap layer or Ap **horizon** —*see* **surface soil**

topworking the grafting of **scion**s into the tops of trees, usually done to induce earlier or more abundant **flower**ing of the **scion**s

total chlorine-free pulp —*see* **pulp**

total dissolved solids (TDS) the total dissolved mineral constituents of water

total yield the sum of intermediate and final products

totipotency the capacity of a nucleus, cell, or tissue to develop into a complete organism

tower *harvesting* a steel, commonly telescoping, mast used instead of a **spar** tree at the landing for **cable yarding**

tower person a **lookout** stationed at a **lookout tower**

toxicity 1. the degree of being poisonous 2. the physiological condition of an organism under the action of a poison

toxicogenic capable of producing a toxin —*note* the term toxicogenic is often used in reference to insects that introduce toxins while feeding

trace a strand of connecting vascular tissue, tissue connecting a leaf with a stem (leaf trace) or a bud with a stem (bud trace)

trace element a chemical element found in extremely small amounts in plants and animals —*note* trace elements essential for growth are termed micronutrients, e.g., Bo, Co, Cu, Fe, Mn, and Zn

tracheid —*see* **cells (wood)**

tractor *harvesting* 1. a powered vehicle mounted on crawler tracks or wheels used for **skid**ding or hauling —*note* tracklaying or crawler tractors are often fitted with various devices on the front end, such as (a) a curved, straight-bottomed blade for pushing soil, e.g., in road making, (b) a raker blade with tines on the bottom for **site preparation**, or (c) a **KG blade** for stump removal —*synonym* crawler, bulldozer 2. a short-wheelbase truck used to haul trailers

tradeoff the exchange of one thing or value in return for another, usually the loss of one benefit for the gain of a different benefit —*note* tradeoffs commonly involve weighing many different factors in the **decision-making** process, including how equity will be distributed among those who might gain or lose, costs of the tradeoff, time required to realize benefits and losses, and whether the proposed tradeoff will meet or assist in meeting management **goal**s

trail herding the work of directing and controlling the movement of a group of **livestock** on restricted overland routes —*synonym* driving, droving —see **close herding, drift, drive, open herding**

trait a characteristic of an organism which may be quantitative (continuous) or qualitative (discontinuous) —*see* **character, genotype, phenotype, variation**

transcription the enzyme-mediated process of transcribing the information contained in a **DNA** strand into a complementary **RNA** strand

transect *ecology* a narrow sample strip or a measured line laid out through vegetation specifically chosen for study —*note* transects are used in analysis, profiling, and inventorying—*see* **line-intercept method, vegetation profile**

transform *GIS* the process of converting data from one coordinate system to another through translation, rotation, and scaling —*note* in the process, the **projection** remains the same

transformation *GIS* the conversion of coordinates in one coordinate system to another

transgenic pertaining to individuals containing a foreign gene (transgene) in all of their cells, inserted by means of gene-transfer techniques —*note* the new genetic information is passed on through the **germ line** of the adult individual —*see* **chimera, genetic transformation**

transgressive segregation appearance in the F_2 or other segregating generations of individuals whose expression of some **character** (usually discrete) is more extreme than in either the parental or the F_1 generation —*see* **heterosis**

transhumance 1. the seasonal moving of **livestock,** particularly sheep, goats, and camels, to fresh **range,** generally at a different elevation —*see* **drive 2.** comparable movements of groups of people (tribes, etc.) associated with livestock herding —*see* **shifting cultivation**

transit a surveying instrument consisting of a telescopic sight mounted on a swivel to measure horizontal and vertical angles and distances —*note* a transit performs the same functions as a **theodolite** but with less precision

translation the process by which information in an **RNA** strand creates the sequence of amino acids during polypeptide (protein) synthesis —*see* **ribosome**

translocation the long-distance transport of water, minerals, and organic compounds, including plant-growth regulators within plants —*see* **sap, sapwood, transpiration**

transmissivity a measure of the amount of **radiation** propagated through a given medium, defined as the ratio of transmitted radiation to the total radiation incident on the medium

transpiration the process by which water vapor passes from the foliage or other parts of a living plant to the atmosphere —*note* transpiration refers to the upward passage of water and solutes within the plant (mainly via the **xylem** and constituting the xylem sap) from the roots to the leaves —*see* **evapotranspiration, translocation**

transpiration ratio the ratio of the weight of water transpired by a plant during its growing season to the weight of dry matter produced

transplant 1. a seedling after it has been lifted and replanted, i.e., moved one or occasionally more times in the nursery, in contrast to a seedling planted out directly from the seed bed —*note* transplants are designated using two numbers, the first figure showing the number of years in the seed bed, and the other the number of years in the transplant bed (e.g., 1-1) **2.** to move nursery stock from one part of a nursery to another, to improve its development before forest planting

trap crop a crop or other vegetation purposefully planted or maintained to divert attack by plant-feeding insects

trap tree a log or tree felled or treated in a manner to invite insect **infestation,** particularly **bark beetles** —*note* a trap tree diverts and localizes insect attack preparatory to effecting a concentrated kill of the resultant **brood**s —*synonym* trap log

traumatic ring a zone of wound (traumatic) tissue produced by an injured **cambium** —*note 1.* traumatic rings tend to be colored dark from associated gums and resins, and include traumatic parenchyma —*note 2.* intercellular canals and drought cracks may be present —*note 3.* common causes of traumatic rings are frost (or cold weather occurring after growth is initiated in the spring) and drought; other causes may be fire and lightning

travel corridor —*see* **corridor**

travel time —*see* **elapsed time**

traverse 1. to determine the relative positions of horizontal points (generally control points) by measuring the distances between successive points and the horizontal angles between, or the bearings of, successive straight lines (survey lines) joining them —*note* in a closed traverse, the first and last observations are taken at a point of known position **2.** the resulting set of connected lines

tree a woody perennial plant, typically large and with a well-defined stem or stems carrying a more or less definite crown —*note* sometimes defined as attaining a minimum diameter of 5 in (12.7 cm) and a minimum height of 15 ft (4.6 m) at maturity, with no branches within 3 ft (1 m) of the ground —*see* **branch, shrub, stem**

tree age the total age of the aboveground stem of the tree in years —*note 1.* tree age does not include the age of the rootstock or the total age from seed —*note 2.* total age is usually the annual ring count to the pith of the tree at breast height plus an estimate of the number of years it took the tree to reach breast height —*see* **breast-high age**

tree class 1. any class into which the trees forming a

crop or **stand** may be divided for a variety of purposes, e.g., for determining a type of **thinning 2.** the trees falling into such a class

tree fallow the replacement or enhancement of natural fallow vegetation by the introduction of trees or shrubs for the purpose of fallow improvement

tree farm a privately owned **woodland** in which the production of wood fiber is a primary management **goal,** as distinct from a tree nursery, fruit orchard, or landscape business —*note* a Tree Farm™ is a tree farm that is certified by the American Tree Farm System

tree improvement —*see* **forest tree improvement**

tree injection the deliberate introduction, by pressure or simple absorption, of a chemical (generally a water-soluble salt in solution) into the sapstream of a living tree —*note* the object of tree injection is to kill the tree or to prevent or control insects or diseases

tree line the limit beyond which trees cannot or do not occur, commonly at high elevation or geographical latitude but sometimes also because of aridity, flooding, or air pollution —*note* a distinction may be drawn between tree line and timberline, the latter being roughly the limit of timber rather than isolated trees —*see* **tundra**

tree maintenance *urban forestry* activities to control insect and disease problems, reduce potential hazards, and maintain **forest health;** the standard care of trees in a community

tree preservation ordinance *urban forestry* a local law to help preserve the character of the natural **ecosystem** within a community, and to preserve trees within a community

tree protection standard *urban forestry* a guideline for protecting individual trees during building construction by not allowing any activity within the **critical root zone**

tree ring —*see* **discontinuous ring, false ring, growth ring**

tree ring analysis —*see* **dendrochronology**

tree risk management *urban forestry* an evaluation and priority ranking of the health and condition of trees that could cause injury to a person or damage to property

tree tenure *agroforestry* trees that are a form of property separable from the land on which they are located —*note* the concept of tree tenure has critical importance in legal or customary property rights claims throughout much of the world

trench *fire* a ditch dug on a slope below a fire, generally as part of a **fireline,** and designed to catch rolling **firebrands** —*synonym* fire trench, gutter trench

trench planting the setting out of seedlings in single file along a continuous shallow trench or slit, either in the nursery or in the field —*see* **heeling in**

triangulated irregular network (TIN) *GIS* a representation of a surface derived from irregularly spaced sample points and breakline features —*note 1.* the TIN data set includes topological relationships between points and their proximal triangles; each sample point has an x,y coordinate and a surface or z value; these points are connected by edges to form a set of nonoverlapping triangles that can be used to represent the surface —*note 2.* TINs are also called irregular triangular mesh or irregular triangular surface **models**

triangulation a method of determining the positions of horizontal control points by observing the horizontal angles of the triangles formed by the points —*note* if the length of one triangle side (a base line) is measured, the lengths of all other sides can be calculated by trigonometry

triangulation point a point whose position is fixed by triangulation

triploid having three times ($3n$) the **haploid** (n) number of **chromosomes** —*see* **polyploid**

trophic pertaining to food and nutrition

trophic dynamics the flow of energy through a community organized into several **trophic level**s

trophic level a position in the food chain assessed by the number of energy transfer steps to reach that level

tropical relating to regions characterized by a climate with high temperature, humidity, and rainfall, and having light frosts very rarely and an average temperature of $65°F$ ($18°C$) for the coolest month

tropism the growth response of part of a plant to an external stimulus causing it to move, turn, or bend —*see* **chemotropism, geotropism, hydrotropism, phototropism**

tropophyte a plant that markedly changes its character, particularly its water requirements, with seasonal changes of climate, e.g., a deciduous tree

true-to-type having essentially the same **phenotype** as the donor plant, cultivar, or **clone**

true volume measure *round timber* the solid volume (i.e., the total wood content) of a stem or log in cubic units, obtained by multiplying length by cross-sectional area(s), the latter being located or weighted according to stem shape —*note 1.* the sectional area is commonly taken at midlength (Huber's method) or as the mean of the two endsections (Smalian's method), using the formula $\pi/4$ or $g^2/4\pi$ where d = diameter and g = girth —*note 2.* true volume measure is widely used in Europe and Asia, and for statistical research

truncated soil soil that has lost all or part of the upper soil **horizon** or horizons by soil removal, e.g., **erosion** or excavation

truncation selection the process of choosing a set of members of a candidate **population** equal to or greater than some minimum value in a **trait** or index

trunk rot —*see* **butt rot**

TSI timber stand improvement *(obsolete)* —*see* **stand improvement**

t-test a test of significance for hypotheses involving differences between two means where the test is based on Student's t-distribution

tube planting the setting out of young trees in narrow, open-ended cylinders of various materials, e.g., polythene, bamboo, bark, veneer, palm leaves, in which they have been raised from seed or into which they have been transplanted —*note 1.* such cylinders are most commonly termed planting tubes, planting sleeves, or planting cylinders —*note 2.* tube planting is a type of container planting —*see* **container nursery, container seedling, pot planting**

tuff a compacted deposit that is 50 percent or more volcanic ash and dust

tundra the zone of low, arctic vegetation between the tree line of the taiga to the south and the region of perpetual ice and snow —*note* the corresponding zone on high mountains may be termed mountain tundra —*see* **tree line, taiga, boreal, boreal forest**

tung oil a drying oil expressed or extracted with solvents from the seeds of trees of the genus *Aleurites,* native to China —*see* **essential oil, pine oil**

tuple —*synonym* **record**

turbidity 1. the cloudy condition caused by suspended solids, dissolved solids, natural or human-developed chemicals, algae, etc., in a liquid **2.** a measurement of the suspended solids in a liquid **3.** conditions in the atmosphere that reduce its transparency to **radiation**, especially to visible radiation

turbulence a state of fluid flow in which the instantaneous velocities exhibit irregular and apparently random fluctuations so that, in practice, only statistical properties can be recognized and subjected to analysis

turbulent flow a type of flow in which any particle may move in any direction with respect to any other particle and not in a fixed or regular path because the water is being agitated by cross currents and eddies

turgor the status of water content of a plant cell

turn a load of logs brought to the landing in any one trip

turnover 1. *ecology, hydrology* the complete mixing of a lake that occurs when the **epilimnion** and **hypolimnion** become isothermal **2.** *ecology, soils* the production and death of roots (usually **fine roots**) over a certain period of time **3.** *wildlife* the movement of **year class**es into, through, and out of a population —*note* the rate of movement is commonly specified by the time required for a given **year class** to die, e.g., a three-year turnover —*see* **mortality**

turn the corner *fire* to contain a fire along a **flank** of the fire and begin containing it across the **head**

turpentine beetle 1. the approved common name of the **flatheaded borer** *(Buprestis apricans)* that lays its eggs on the dried or burnt-out faces of resin-tapped trees into which the **larvae** tunnel —*note* turpentine beetles were a serious **pest** in the production of naval stores but are now minor pests associated with fire scars and mechanical wounds **2.** some *Dendroctonus* beetles, particularly the red turpentine beetle and the black turpentine beetle *(D. valens* and *D. terebrans,* respectively), are pests of pines and characterized by production of large **pitch tube**s —*note Dendroctonus* beetles prefer stumps and severely weakened trees, are often secondary to primary **bark beetle**s, but can attack healthy trees when population levels are high —*synonym* turpentine borer

tussock moth a member of the family Lymantriidae (Lepidoptera) whose larvae are serious defoliators of **forest** trees, e.g., the Douglas-fir tussock moth *(Orgyia pseudotsugata)* and the gypsy moth *(Lymantria dispar)* —*note* tussock moths are named for the tufts (horns) of long hairs on the **larva**'s thorax and abdomen —*see* **tussockosis**

tussockosis an allergic reaction in humans in response to the body hairs (**urticating hair**s) of **tussock moth** larvae —*note* the hairs are often shed by the **larva**e and carried by the wind, or left embedded in the egg masses and cast larval skins

twig girdler 1. the common name of *Oncideres cingulata* —*note* twig girdler adults girdle twigs in the autumn prior to ovipositing eggs in the distal portion of the stem, which then falls to the ground **2.** any insect whose **larvae** are borers or phloem feeders in twigs and girdle the twigs, including some **flatheaded borer**s, Cerambycid beetles, and clearwing moths, e.g., the cottonwood twig borer *(Gypsonoma haimbachiana)* —*see* **tip moth**

two-aged stand a growing area with trees of two distinct age classes separated in age by more than ± 20 percent of rotation —*see* **all-aged stand**

two-aged system a planned sequence of treatments designed to maintain and regenerate a **stand** with two age classes

tyloses —*see* **cells (wood)**

type map a map showing the distribution of various types of soil, vegetation, or **site quality** throughout a **forest**

type specimen 1. the original plant from which a description was drawn up 2. that constituent part (i.e., an individual) of a taxon to which a botanical name is permanently attached

U

ultraviolet radiation 1. electromagnetic **radiation** of shorter wavelength than visible radiation but longer than x-rays 2. radiation in the wavelength interval from 10 to 4,000 Å

umbric epipedon a surface layer of mineral soil that has the same requirements as the **mollic epipedon** with respect to color, thickness, organic carbon content, consistence, **structure,** and phosphorus content, but has a **base saturation** < 50 percent

unbundled *computer software* sold separately from hardware —*see* **bundled**

uncertainty the lack or inadequacy of knowledge needed by a decision maker to quantify the relative likelihood of alternative outcomes —*note* in a situation of uncertainty, a decision must be made before the state of nature is revealed, the decision maker must base decisions on optimistic (**maximax**), pessimistic (**maximin**), or politician (**minimax regret**) approaches or assume that all outcomes are equally likely —*see* **hazard, risk**

unconfirmed channel a channel in which lateral migration is relatively unrestricted, as on a broad **floodplain**

uncontrolled fire any fire that threatens to destroy life, property, or natural resources and (a) is not burning within the confines of **firebreak**s or (b) is burning with such intensity that it cannot be readily extinguished with ordinary tools

underburn —*see* **fire behavior**

undercut a wedge-shaped notch cut in the base of a tree to govern the direction of its fall —*synonym* box, **face,** notch

undercut line a fireline below a fire on a slope that is trenched to catch rolling firebrands—*synonym* underslung line

undercutting —*see* **root pruning, wrenching**

undergrowth the herbaceous **cover** and the lower **shrub**s, and even the lowest trees, under a **forest** canopy

underplanting the setting out of young trees, or sowing of tree seed under an existing **stand** —*note* the trees themselves are termed underplants

underrun the difference between the lesser volume actually sawn and the greater estimated **log scale** volume —*note* underruns are generally expressed as a percent of the log-scale volume —*synonym* undercut —*see* **mill tally, overcut, overrun, utilization percent**

undershoot *GIS* an **arc** that does not extend far enough to intersect another arc

understory all forest vegetation growing under an overstory

uneven-aged stand a stand with trees of three or more distinct age classes, either intimately mixed or in small groups —*see* **all-aged stand, multi-aged**

uneven-aged system a planned sequence of treatments designed to maintain and regenerate a **stand** with three or more age classes —*see* **regeneration method (4. uneven-aged methods, single tree selection** and **group selection)**

unified command —*see* **incident command system**

uniform *of a forest, crop, or stand* constituted of trees whose crowns form an ordered, even canopy; the trees are not necessarily even-aged —*see* **irregular**

uniform flow the movement of water in an open channel of constant cross-section where depth and velocity remain constant and the water surface is parallel to the streambed —*note* uniform flow is the desired condition for gauging streamflow

uninodal pertaining to forming a single whorl of branches in conifers each year —*see* **foxtail, multinodal**

unit —*see* **incident command system**

unit hydrograph a hydrograph of 1 in (2.54 cm) of direct runoff occurring uniformly on a basin at a uniform rate over a specified duration

universal soil loss equation a formula used to design water **erosion** control systems —*note* $A = RKLSPC$ wherein A is average annual soil loss (t/ac/year), R is the rainfall factor, K is the soil erodibility factor, L is the length of slope, S is the percent slope, P is the conservation practice factor, and C is the cropping and management factor

universal transverse Mercator (UTM) a widely used planar coordinate system, extending from 84° north to 80° south **latitude** and based on a specialized application of the transverse Mercator projection —*note 1.* the extent of the coordinate system is broken into sixty 6° (**longitude**) zones; within each zone, coordinates are usually expressed as meters north or south of the equator and east from a reference axis —*note 2.* for locations in the northern hemisphere, the origin is assigned a false **easting** of 500,000 and a false **northing** of 0; for locations in the southern hemisphere, the origin is assigned a false easting of 500,000 and a false northing of 10,000,000

univoltine a **life cycle** in which only one generation or **brood** is produced per year —*see* **bivoltine, multivoltine**

unreserved forest land forest land that is not withdrawn from harvest by statute or administrative regulation —*see* **timberland**

untrammeled *wilderness management* not subject to human controls and manipulations that hamper the free play of natural forces —*note* the word is used in the Wilderness Act of 1964 to describe desired state of **wilderness**

upper air *meteorology* the portion of the atmosphere that is above the lower troposphere

upwelling the rise of deeper, nutrient-rich water to the surface of the ocean along coasts

urban and community forestry statewide program a program operated in cooperation between the USDA Forest Service and the National Association of State Foresters to provide statewide leadership through information dissemination, technical assistance, grants to local units of government, and networking of resources among various levels of government

urban forestry the art, science, and technology of managing trees and **forest** resources in and around urban community **ecosystem**s for the physiological, sociological, economic, and aesthetic benefits trees provide society

urban forestry maintenance program the care of trees within a community including tree pruning, fertilization, removal of individual trees, **thinning,** exotic species eradication, and improvement of trees and **stand**s under public ownership in and around communities

urban tree ordinance a legal document used at the local level to identify who has authority to manage trees on public lands within communities and what standard of care will be expected

urban-wildland interface a **forest** or **shrub**land, commonly in the foothills of rural areas, where structures and other human development meet or intermingle with undeveloped **wildland** vegetation —*note* the junction may be well-defined or diffuse —*synonym* rural-urban interface

urediniospore a repeating asexual dikaryotic **spore** in **rust fungi** produced in a **uredinium** —*synonym* urediospore

uredinium *plural* **uredinia** a fruiting body in **rust fungi** on the **primary host** producing **urediospore**s —*note* uredinia reinfect the primary host or give rise to telia —*synonym* uredium *plural* **uredia** —*see* **telium**

urticating hair small spines (setae) on the bodies of some insects which, when broken, allow the discharge of a secretion from epidermal poison glands, causing urticaria (hives) in humans and other animals —*see* **tussockosis**

use *range management* **1.** the proportion of the current year's forage production that is consumed or destroyed by **grazing** animals —*note* use may refer either to a single species or to the vegetation

use *continued*

as a whole —*synonym* degree of use, utilization, **range** use **2.** the utilization of **range** for a purpose such as **grazing, bed**ding, shelter, trailing, watering, **watershed**, recreation, **forestry 3.** *land use* types of land use include the following:

—**compatible use** a land use that can exist without improving or detracting from the quality of another —*note* in practice compatible uses usually include those that can coexist with only slight conflict

—**competitive use** a land use that cannot occur at the same general time and in the same general place without detracting from the quality or quantity of itself or others

—**complementary use** a land use that improves its quality or quantity when in association with other uses in the same area

—**conflicting use** a land use whose quality is harmed by association with others that occur in the same area, because of competition for limited resources, use, or byproducts —*synonym* incompatible uses

—**cumulative use** the total stream of resource use over time —*see* **rate of use**

user fee a charge for the use of a facility

use rights rights for the use of forest resources that can be defined by local custom, mutual agreements, or prescribed by other entities holding access rights

utility a measure of the total worth of an outcome, reflecting a decision maker's attitude toward considerations such as profit and loss, and intangibles such as **risk**

utility corridor —*see* **corridor**

utility function the conceptual way in which individuals rank the value obtained (consumer's surplus) from alternative bundles of goods and services they can purchase

utilization cut a reduction factor applied to gross acreage of **grazing** or browsing to allow for unusable areas, e.g., eroded, inaccessible, or burned areas that are termed waste **range** —*see* **browse**

utilization percent the ratio, as a percent, between the estimated volume of a standing tree, log, or log input to a mill, and the volume of its manufactured or merchantable product(s) —*synonym* conversion factor, recovery, recovery rate, outturn —*see* **mill tally, overrun, underrun**

UTM —*see* **universal transverse Mercator**

V

vadose zone the layer of soil that is normally unsaturated by water (having soil pores containing both air and water), and that usually extends from the soil surface downward to the permanent **water table** —*note* the vadose zone may be referred to as the zone of aeration —*see* **phreatic, zone of saturation**

vagility the capacity of an organism to become widely dispersed

valley wind —*see* **canyon wind, chinook, foehn, mountain and valley winds**

value 1. *soils* the degree of lightness or darkness of a color in relation to a neutral gray scale —*note* value is on a neutral gray scale, extending from pure black to pure white **2.** *soils* one of the three variables of color used in describing soils —*see* **chroma, hue, Munsell color system 3.** *management* —*see* **environmental and amenity value, nonuse**

values at risk *fire* any or all natural resources, improvements, or other values that may be jeopardized if a fire occurs

value trait the characteristic that is an important contributor to the value of a genetic improvement program

variable 1. any quantity that varies —*synonym* random variable **2.** a quantity that may take any one of a specified set of values

variable cost the cost that changes in response to a change in the level of output produced by a firm —*note* variable costs are contrasted with **fixed cost**s that do not change in the **short run**

variable-density yield table —*see* **yield table**

variable-plot cruising —*see* **point sampling**

variable-radius plot sampling —*see* **point sampling**

variable retention harvest system an approach to harvesting based on the retention of structural elements or biological legacies (trees, snags, logs, etc.) from the harvested **stand** for integration into the new stand to achieve various ecological objectives —*note* the major variables in the variable retention harvest system are types, densities, and spatial arrangement of retained structures; aggregated retention is the retention of structures or biological legacies as (typically) small, intact forest patches within the harvest unit; dispersed retention is the retention of structures or biological legacies in a dispersed or uniform pattern —*see* **biological legacy, harvesting method, partial cutting**

variance a statistical measure of the variation of a characteristic from the **population** mean; the expected value of the squared difference between a statistic and the expected value of that statistic —*see* **variation**

variance-ratio test a test widely employed in the **analysis of variance** to appraise the homogeneity of a set of means; also used to compare the variance of two **populations** of **normal distribution** —*see* **test of significance**

variation *genetics* the occurence of differences among individuals of the same species attributable to differences in their genetic composition or the environment in which they were raised —*note* quantitative differences in a given **trait** are assessed by their **variance**

variegation the appearance of different kinds of tissue in patterns, patches, or bands, frequently caused by the presence of special pigments or the absence of normal pigments —*note* unusual pigmentation may be due to the effect of special **gene**s, disease, **albinism, chimera,** or **mutation**

variety *ecology* a category usually intermediate between **species** (or subspecies) and forma (i.e., **form**), given a Latin name preceded by "var.", based on fewer correlated characters than are used to differentiate species or subspecies, and having a more restricted geographical occurrence—see **eco-type, species, subspecies 2.** an assemblage of cultivated individuals distinguished by any useful, reproducible character(s), usually termed a **cultivar** —*see* **race, taxon, taxonomy**

varve 1. a sedimentary layer, lamina, or sequence of laminae deposited in a body of still water within one year **2.** a thin pair of graded glaciolacustrine layers seasonally deposited, usually by meltwater streams, in a glacial lake or other body of still water in front of a glacier

vascular relating to plants having phloem- and xylem-conducting elements

vascular cambium a lateral **meristem** forming the secondary vascular tissues in stems and roots

vascular cylinder the **stele** or the vascular region of **stem** and root axes

vector 1. *genetics* a carrier of a pollen or disease **2.** *genetics* a self-replicating **DNA** molecule (usually a plasmid, virus, or bacteriophage) used to move foreign DNA into a organism **3.** *zoology* any agent, particularly animals (and typically insects) but also seed, wind, and water, capable of transplanting a microorganism to a **host 4.** *entomology, pathology* to transplant a microorganism to a host **5.** *GIS* —*see* **vector data**

vector data *GIS* a coordinate-based data structure commonly used to represent map features —*note 1.* each linear feature is represented as a list of ordered x,y coordinates —*note 2.* attributes are asso-

ciated with the feature (as opposed to a **raster** data structure, which associates attributes with a grid cell) —*note 3.* traditional **vector** data structures include double-digitized **polygon**s and **arc-node** models —*see* **arc-node topology**

veering a change in wind direction in a clockwise sense (e.g., south to southwest to west) in either hemisphere of the earth —*antonym* **backing**

vegetation cover the **cover** of all vegetation occupying an area —*see* **ground cover**

vegetation profile a diagram of the aboveground portions of plants along a transect presented in elevation, i.e., in their natural positions, in contrast to a chart **quadrat** showing in plan the location of and areas covered by each plant —*see* **bisect**

vegetative cell a cell of the body tissue (soma), as distinct from a reproductive cell **(germ cell)** —*see* **chromosome set, diploid, haploid, mitosis, somatic cell**

vegetative infection a dwarf mistletoe **infection** that does not produce aerial shoots —*note* vegetative infection usually occurs on heavily shaded branches or on incompatible **host**s —*synonym* sleeper, inactive infection

vegetative propagation the propagation of a plant by asexual means, as in **budding, graft**ing, rooting, **air layering,** and **tissue or cell culture** —*note* the **genotype**s of the resulting **ramet**s are identical to those of the original plant (**ortet**) —*see* **asexual reproduction, clone, coppice, cutting, scion, topophysis**

vegetative reproduction reproduction (**regeneration**) produced by **vegetative propagation**

veneer a thin sheet of wood of uniform thickness, produced by rotary cutting (peeling) or slicing, and sometimes by sawing —*see* **peel, peeler**

vermiculite a highly charged layer silicate of the 2:1 type that is formed from **mica** and characterized by adsorption preference for potassium, ammonium, and cesium over smaller exchange cations

vernalization the exposure of seed or seedlings (e.g., of winter cereals) to a period of cold (0 to 5°C or 32 to 41°F) to hasten flowering —*see* **af-terripening, stratification**

vertex *plural* **vertices** *GIS* one **point** along a **line** —*see* **grain tolerance**

vertical aerial photograph an aerial photograph made with the optical axis of the camera approximately perpendicular to the earth's spheroid and with the film as nearly horizontal as practical

vertical exaggeration the extent to which the vertical scale appears larger than the horizontal scale in a stereo **model**

vesicle 1. an air-, resin-, or fluid-filled cavity **2.** a specialized structure of an intercellular **endomycorrhizal** fungus hypha for the storage of assimilated reserve compounds

vesicular-arbuscular mycorrhiza —*see* **endomycorrhiza**

vessel —*see* **cells (wood)**

viability 1. *botany* the capacity of a seed, spore, or pollen grain to germinate and develop under given conditions —*note* potential viability is commonly estimated by germination tests or by cutting, X-raying, or soaking in chemicals that color seed components; actual viability is determined by measuring **germinative capacity** —*see* **dormancy, germination, germinative energy 2.** *wildlife* the ability of a wildlife or plant population to maintain sufficient size to persist over time in spite of normal fluctuations in numbers —*note* viability is usually expressed as the probability of maintaining a specific population for a specified period

viewable area *computers* the portion of a digital image (stored on disk) visible in a window on a monitor —*note* the user can choose to view every **pixel** in a small area, or every second or third pixel over a larger area

viewshed the landscape that can be directly seen from a viewpoint or along a transportation corridor

virga wisps or streaks of water or ice particles falling out of a cloud but evaporating before reaching the earth's surface as precipitation

virgin forest an original **forest**, usually containing large trees, that has not been significantly disturbed or influenced by human activity —*synonym* primary forest —*see* **old-growth forest**

virtual temperature *meteorology* in a system of moist air, the temperature of dry air having the same density and pressure as the moist air

virulence the degree or measure of **pathogenicity**

virulent 1. having the capacity to cause disease **2.** strongly pathogenic

virus a submicroscopic, disease-producing, obligate intracellular **parasite** consisting of a nucleic acid surrounded by a protein coat —*note* viruses can reproduce only in living tissues; transmission is passive and most plant viruses are vectored by insects; **host** injury occurs when the host organism diverts metabolites from normal activities to the production of virus particles and to abnormal metabolic activities

viscous water *fire* water that contains a thickening agent to reduce surface runoff, improve adhesion to burning fuels, and spread several times more thickly than plain water, thereby having an increased capacity to absorb heat, cool fuel, and exclude oxygen —*synonym* thickened water, thick water —*see* **fire retardant**

visible area map *fire* a map showing the different classes of visible area covered by a lookout point or points —*note* a visible area map may differentiate between **seen area**s, indirectly visible areas, and **blind area**s, or only between seen areas and blind areas —*synonym* seen area map, visibility area map —*see* **seen area**

visible crown diameter the diameter of a tree crown as discernible on a vertical **aerial photograph**, usually measured with a template, e.g., a crown diameter wedge

visible radiation electromagnetic radiation lying within the wavelength interval to which the human eye is sensitive, the spectral interval from approximately 0.4 to 0.7 μ (4,000 to 7,000 Å)

visible tree height that part of the total height of a tree discernible on an aerial photograph, usually measured with a stereometer device, e.g., **parallax bar** or **parallax wedge**

visit *recreation* the entrance of one person or one group to a recreation site for some period of time

visitor-day *recreation* the presence of one or more persons (other than staff) on lands and waters generally recognized as providing outdoor recreation for continuous, intermittent, or simultaneous periods totaling 12 hours

viviparous bearing living young —*see* **oviparous, ovoviparous**

volume equation a mathematical expression that provides estimates of cubic or **board foot** volume of a tree, given values for diameter and height (and occasionally a measure of **form**)

volume regulation —*see* **forest regulation**

volume table a listing showing, for one or more species, the average cubic or merchantable contents of trees or logs according to easily measured tree dimensions, such as tree diameter or height —*note* such tables are constructed from samples of felled trees or from detailed tree dimensional data, and are used for estimating the timber contents of either individual trees or **stand**s —*see* **tarif table**

volumetric water content the soil water content expressed as the volume of water per unit bulk volume of soil

W

wane the remnants of the original, rounded surface of a tree, with or without bark, remaining on a sawn board

watch-out situations *fire* a list of potential situations that may be unsafe for **fire fighters** in suppressing a forest fire —*note* the situations are as follows: the fire is not scouted and sized up; the fire is in country not seen in daylight; safety zones and escape routes are not identified; you are unfamiliar with weather and local factors influencing **fire behavior;** you are uninformed on **strategy, tactics,** and hazards; instructions and assignments are not clear; you have no communication link with crew members or your supervisor; you are constructing a line without a safe anchor point; you are building a **fireline** downhill with fire below; you are attempting frontal assault on the fire; there is unburned **fuel** between you and the fire; you cannot see the main fire and are not in contact with someone who can; you are on a hillside where rolling material can ignite fuel below; the weather is becoming hotter and drier; the wind increases or changes direction; there are frequent **spot fire**s across the line; the terrain and fuels make escape to safety zones difficult; you are resting near the fireline —*see* **standard firefighting orders**

water bar a shallow channel or raised barrier of soil or other material laid diagonally across the surface of a road or skid trail to lead water off the road and prevent soil **erosion** —*synonym* cross ditch

water budget the balance of all water moving into and out of a specified area in a specified period of time

water equivalent the depth of water that would result from the melting of the snow pack or of a snow sample

water potential 1. the free energy level or ability of water to do work 2. a measure of plant water status —*synonym* **xylem pressure potential**

water quality standard the minimum requirement of purity of water for the intended use with respect to the physical, chemical, and biological characteristics

watershed a region or land area drained by a single stream, river, or drainage network —*synonym* drainage basin —*see* **catchment**

watershed analysis or **assessment** a systematic procedure for characterizing mainly biophysical watershed and ecological processes to meet specific management and social objectives —*note 1.* watershed analysis is not a formal planning process but a stratum of **ecosystem management** planning applied to watersheds of approximately 20 to 200 mi² (51.8 to 518.0 km²) and evaluating the hierarchical

relations between the watershed and its neighboring watersheds —*note 2.* watershed analysis is similar to watershed review, which is regarded as a less in-depth evaluation

watershed lag the time from the effective center of a rainfall event to the peak streamflow registered on a **hydrograph** —*see* **lagtime**

watershed review —*see* **watershed analysis**

water table 1. the upper surface of groundwater 2. that level or elevation, measured from a datum, where the water is at atmospheric pressure and below which the soil is saturated with water —*see* **groundwater, perched groundwater, perched water table**

water year a 12-month period, October 1 through September 30, designated by the calendar year in which it ends —*note* the term is used with streamflow data and analyses

weather the short-term state of the atmosphere, mainly with respect to human activities —*see* **climate**

weathering all physical and chemical changes produced in rocks, at or near the earth's surface, by atmospheric agents

webworm any gregarious caterpillar of the family Lepidoptera that builds weblike structures from silk or silk and foliage —*note* this common name is applied to several species, e.g., the fall webworm (*Hyphantria cunea*) —*see* **tent caterpillar**

wedge system a modification of the shelterwood-strip system in which cuttings begin as narrow, interior, wedge-shaped strips with the apex pointing into the prevailing wind and are then successively enlarged and advanced —*note* **regeneration** is mainly natural and fairly even-aged —*see* **regeneration method, shelterwood**

weed 1. a valueless, troublesome, or noxious plant, often exotic, growing wild, especially one growing profusely 2. a plant growing where it is not wanted —*note* what one person or group considers a weed may not be considered a weed by others

weeding a release treatment in **stand**s not past the **sapling** stage that eliminates or suppresses undesirable vegetation regardless of crown position —*see* **cleaning, improvement cutting, liberation**

weed tolerance *GIS* the minimum allowable distance between any two vertices along an **arc** —*note 1.* weed tolerance is a parameter that can be set before adding arc features —*note 2.* when adding new arcs, if an input **vertex** is within the weed distance from the last vertex it is disregarded; when weeding existing arcs, it is the tolerance used by the Douglas-Peucker **algorithm**

weed tree 1. any tree of a species having little or no

economic value on the site in question **2.** a tree of little or no economic value, more particularly when competing with one or more desirable timber trees at any stage of development and therefore due for elimination from the crop

weevil a beetle of the extensive family Curculionidae, including many species whose adults or larvae are serious forest **pest**s, particularly terminal or shoot weevils in conifers and weevils that attack hardwood seeds

weight *biometrics* the importance of a value in relation to a set of values to which it belongs —*note* weight is often a numerical coefficient attached to an observation (frequently by multiplication), such that the observation assumes a desired degree of importance in a function of all observations of the set

weighted mean a type of average that takes into account the differing **weight**s of the observations: the summed product of the values times their weights divided by the sum of the weights

weight table a listing showing for one or more species the average weight of trees, **pole**s, or logs as a function of diameter and length —*note* a weight table can be based on green or dry weights and include bole wood only (to some merchantability limit); wood and bark; wood, bark, and crown; etc.

weir 1. a notch or depression in a levee, dam, embankment, or other barrier across or bordering a stream, through which the flow of water is measured or regulated **2.** a barrier constructed across a stream to divert fish into a trap **3.** a dam (usually small) in a stream to raise the water level or divert its flow, with water flowing over the top of the structure

well distributed *wildlife* a geographic distribution of habitats that maintains a population throughout a planning area and allows for interaction of individuals through periodic interbreeding and colonization of unoccupied habitats

western spruce budworm —*see* **budworm**

wet-adiabatic lapse rate —*see* **lapse rate**

wet-bulb depression the difference in degrees between the **dry-bulb temperature** and the **wet-bulb temperature**

wet-bulb temperature the temperature an air parcel would have if cooled adiabatically to saturation at constant pressure by evaporation of water into it, all latent heat being supplied by the parcel —*see* **dry-bulb temperature, wet-bulb depression**

wetland 1. a transitional area between aquatic and terrestrial ecosystems that is inundated or saturated for periods long enough to produce hydric soils and support hydrophytic vegetation —*note* state or

federal regulations may require the use of specific agency definitions of wetlands **2.** a seasonally flooded basin or flat —*note* the period of inundation is such that the land can usually be used for agricultural purposes

wet line a line of water, or water and chemical retardant, sprayed along the ground, serving as a temporary control line from which to ignite or stop a low-intensity fire

wettable powder a **pesticide** formulation in which the pesticide is absorbed, generally on an inert carrier, together with an added **surfactant** and the whole finely ground so that it will form a short-term suspension when agitated with water

wetted perimeter the length of the wetted contact between a liquid and its containing conduit, measured along a plane at right angles to the direction of the flow

wetting agent a **surfactant** compound that reduces the surface tension of water (producing "wet water") or other liquid, causing spray solutions to spread, contact plant surfaces more thoroughly, or penetrate more effectively —*synonym* penetrant, surfactant —*see* **fire retardant, pine oil**

wetwood a water-soaked area in the **heartwood** of trees that is a symptom and condition of **infection** by certain fungi (particularly yeasts) and bacteria

whip any slender tree that the wind causes to lacerate the crowns of its neighbors

WHIP —*see* **wildlife habitat incentive program**

whitefly a sap-sucking insect of the Homoptera family Aleyrodidae related to **aphid**s —*note* though primarily greenhouse and household plant **pest**s, some whiteflies are problems on ornamental trees and **shrub**s, e.g., the azalea whitefly (*Pealius azaleae*)

white pine blister rust a **heteroecious macrocyclic** fungal disease caused by *Cronartium ribicola* that forms swollen fusiform **canker**s on stems and branches of pines throughout Asia, Europe, and North America —*note* telial **host**s of white pine blister rust include *Ribes* sp. and (in Asia) *Pedicularis* sp.; aecial hosts include pines within the foxtail, stone, and white pine groups —*see* **aecium**

white pocket rot —*see* **red ring decay**

white rot any decay or rot in wood attacking both the cellulose and the lignin, producing a generally whitish residue that may be spongy or stringy rot or occur as **pocket rot**, as with annosum root disease —*note* most root-decay fungi cause white rots —*see* **brown rot**

whole-tree harvesting —*see* **full-tree harvesting**

whorl a circle of leaves, flowers, branches, or other organs developed from one **node**

wilderness 1. *Wilderness Act of 1964* "a wilderness, in contrast with those areas where man and his works dominate the landscape, is hereby recognized as an area where the earth and its community of life are untrammeled by man, where man himself is a visitor who does not remain" **2.** roadless land legally classified as a component area of the National Wilderness Preservation System and managed to protect its qualities of naturalness, solitude, and opportunity for primitive types of recreation —*note* wilderness is usually of sufficient size to make its maintenance in such a state feasible and to provide opportunities for solitude and self-reliant recreation

wilderness study area (WSA) an area found to possess characteristics that make it eligible for **wilderness** designation and identified for formal study to assess its suitability for wilderness classification

wildfire any nonstructure fire, other than prescribed fire, occurring on **wildland** —*synonym* wildland fire —*see* **forest fire, natural fire**

wildland land other than that dedicated for other uses such as agricultural, urban, mining, or parks

wildland fire situation analysis (WFSA) a decision-making process that evaluates alternative management strategies against selected safety, environmental, social, economic, political, and resource management objectives —*see* **escaped fire situation analysis, forest fire**

wildlife 1. all nondomesticated animal life **2.** nondomesticated vertebrates, especially mammals, birds, and fish and some of the higher invertebrates, e.g., many Arthropods

wildlife corridor —*see* **corridor**

wildlife habitat incentive program (WHIP) a program created by the 1996 Farm Bill and administered by the Natural Resource Conservation Service that provides cost-share incentives and technical assistance for the development, enhancement, and restoration of wildlife habitats for both game and nongame species

wildlife management the practical application of scientific and technical principles to wildlife populations and **habitats** so as to maintain or manipulate such populations (particularly mammals, birds, and fish), essentially for recreational or scientific purposes —*note* wildlife management includes the narrower concept of game management, in which an additional purpose may be commercial, i.e., the controlled harvesting of wild game —*see* **wildlife habitat incentive program (WHIP)**

wildlife tree 1. a live or dead tree designated for wildlife **habitat** or retained to become future wildlife habitat **2.** a tree planted to become a refuge for beneficial predators of agricultural **pests**

wildling a naturally grown (in contrast to a nursery-raised) seedling, sometimes transplanted and used in **forest** planting when nursery stock is scarce

wild river *Wild and Scenic Rivers Act of 1968* a river or segment of river free from impoundments, with shorelines or a watershed that is largely primitive and undeveloped and primarily inaccessible except by trail

wilt 1. a loss of cellular turgidity that causes a plant to droop, usually as a result of water loss or disease **2.** a plant disease in which the most conspicuous symptoms are foliage chlorosis and wilting caused by disruption of normal water uptake or conduction —*note* many wilts are vectored by insects, such as Dutch elm disease, which is caused by *Ophiostoma ulmi* and vectored by Scolytid beetles

wilting point the moisture content of soil, on an oven-dry basis, at which plants wilt and fail to recover their turgidity when placed in a dark, humid atmosphere —*synonym* **permanent wilting point** —*note 1.* wilting point is a property of the soil and virtually independent of the kind of plant or environment; it corresponds to a soil moisture tension of 15 atmospheres (1.5 MPa) —*note 2.* the moisture content at the wilting point is termed the wilting coefficient and is generally expressed as a percent of soil dry weight (wilting percent) —*see* **available water**

windblast injury, essentially mechanical, to twigs, foliage, flowers, or fruit by strong winds —*see* **scorch, sunscald, winter sunscald**

windbreak a strip of trees or shrubs maintained mainly to alter windflow and microclimates in the sheltered zone, usually farm buildings —*see* **living fence, shelterbelt**

wind chill index the cooling effect of any combination of temperature and wind, expressed as the loss of body heat

windfall —*see* **blowdown**

windfirm *of trees* able to withstand strong winds and resist windthrow (**blowdown**), wind-rocking, and major breakage

window 1. a subregion of a map or a subsection of a time series from which measurements are obtained, usually for comparison with other windows **2.** a small time period when an opportunity for action is available

window feeding a type of insect feeding on only one surface of a leaf, allowing the light to penetrate through the remaining leaf layer —*see* **skeletonizing**

wind pollination natural **pollination** by wind-borne pollen —*see* **anemophily, controlled pollination, open pollination**

wind profile a graph of the value of windspeed versus height

wind rose any one of a class of diagrams designed to show the distribution of wind direction and thus the prevailing wind direction experienced at a given location over a considerable period

windrow brushwood, **slash**, etc., concentrated (usually by machine) along a line, to clear the intervening ground for **regeneration** —*see* **site preparation**

windrow burn **1.** to burn **slash** that has been piled into long continuous rows **2.** a **wildfire** in vegetation planted to protect improvements or agriculture

windshake a separation along the grain (**shakes**) in tree **stem**s caused by wind stress

wind shear the local variation of the wind vector or any of its components in a given direction

windthrow —*see* **blowdown**

winter drying the desiccation of foliage and twigs by dry winds at times when water conduction is restricted by either cold soil or by the freezing of plant tissues or the ground —*see* **winter sunscald**

winter injury the desiccation and sometimes mortality of foliage or twigs by strong dry winds at times when water conduction is restricted by cold or frozen soil or by frozen plant tissues —*note* the term red-belt refers to winter injury to conifers confined to distinct altitudinal zones or bands —*synonym* winter drying, red-belt

winter sunscald localized injury to bark and **cambium** caused by freezing following warming by the sun in late winter or early spring —*note* winter sunscald is localized on the side of the stem exposed to midday and afternoon sun, and often results in wounds or **cankers**, particularly on smooth-barked trees —*see* **scorch, sunscald, windblast, winter drying**

wire rope a flexible steel rope made up of numerous wire strands twisted helically together about a wire or fiber core

witches' broom an abnormally bushy, local growth of plant shoots on woody plants (**fasciculation**) characterized by shortening of the internodes and prolific branching —*note* witches' broom is usually caused by **dwarf mistletoe** or rust **infection** but sometimes by abiotic stress

witness tree —*see* **bearing tree**

wolf tree a generally predominant or dominant tree with a broad, spreading crown, that occupies more growing space than its more desirable neighbors —*see* **crown class**

wood **1.** a community of trees growing more or less closely together, of smaller extent than a **forest**

—*note* a wood may or may not constitute a **stand**, depending on its degree of homogeneity in one or more respects **2.** an area of **woodland** bearing a local name —*synonym* woods **3.** the material produced in the stems and branches of trees and other woody plants —*see* **cells** (**wood**)

wood borer *entomology* an insect feeding or boring into the phloem and wood, only the wood, or only the growing shoot —*see* **ambrosia beetle, powderpost beetle, shoot borer, terminal borer**

woodland **1.** a **forest** area **2.** a plant community in which, in contrast to a typical forest, the trees are often small, characteristically short-boled relative to their crown depth, and forming only an open canopy with the intervening area being occupied by lower vegetation, commonly grass

woodwasp —*see* **horntail**

wood worm a collective term for **powderpost beetle**s and **timberworm**s

woody corridor a linear grove of trees or **shrub**s of natural or planted origin —*see* **corridor**

woody debris —*see* **coarse woody debris**

woody root a root containing secondary **xylem**

woolly adelgid a member of the Homoptera family Phylloxeridae —*see* **adelgid**

work capacity *fire* the employee's ability to accomplish production goals without undue fatigue and without becoming a hazard to oneself or coworkers —*note* work capacity is a complex composite of aerobic and muscular fitness, natural abilities, intelligence, skill, experience, acclimatization, nutrition, and motivation; for prolonged, arduous work, fitness is the most important determinant of work capacity —*see* **pack test, step test**

working plan —*see* **management plan**

work measurement the application of techniques designed to establish the time required for a qualified worker to carry out a specified job at a defined level of performance —*see* **time study**

work study **1.** those techniques, particularly method study and **work measurement**, that are used in the examination of human work in all its contexts, and that lead systematically to the investigation of all factors affecting the efficiency and economy of the situation being reviewed with a view to effecting improvement **2.** an intensive inquiry into management to ensure the best possible use of human and material resources in carrying out a specified activity —*see* **time study**

wormy wood —*see* **timberworm**

worse face in grading lumber, the **face** containing the greater amount of defective material, not necessarily the more numerous defects —*note* 1.

rough timber (especially hardwoods) is generally graded on this face —*note 2.* a **cant** having four faces may also have a worst face —*see* **better face**

wound gum a dark, amorphous, gummy substance produced in the wood of **hardwood**s and some **softwood**s in response to injury, infection, or other irritation —*see* **natural resin**

wound parasite a **parasite** able to enter the **host** and establish itself only through wounds or injured tissue

wound stain a discoloration in wood originating in, or developed as a result of, a wound in the tree

wound wood a **callus** consisting of cells that are undifferentiated and lignified

wrenching the disturbance of seedling roots in a nursery bed to stimulate the development of a fibrous root system —*note 1.* usually done one or more times in a growing season, using a tilted blade drawn by a tractor at a prescribed depth —*note 2.* the tilted blade temporarily lifts the seedlings in their bed and causes root breakage —*see* **root pruning**

X

xenia an observable effect of pollen on the **endosperm** or embryo, resulting from the dominance relationships and other types of **gene** action in the **triploid endosperm** —*see* **allele, dominance, metaxenia, double fertilization, polyploid**

xeric pertaining to sites or **habitat**s characterized by decidedly dry conditions

xeromorphic having structural characteristics common among plants adapted to drought (e.g., small thick leaves with sunken stomata or revolute margins, surfaces that are heavily pubescent, waxy or highly reflective and small vein islets) —*see* **sclerophyte**

xerophyte a plant adapted to arid conditions, having **xeromorphic** characteristics —*see* **sclerophyte, xerotype**

xerosere —*see* **succession**

xerotype a plant that is adapted to dry conditions —*see* **xerophyte**

X-parallax —*see* **parallax**

xylem —*see* **cells (wood)**

xylem pressure potential an estimate of plant water potential commonly measured in the leaf petiole, needle, or plant **stem** with a pressure chamber —*synonym* **water potential**

xylometer an apparatus for determining the volumes of irregular pieces of wood by measuring the amount of liquid (generally water) displaced when immersed

Y

yard *harvesting* **1.** a place where logs are accumulated **2.** to convey logs or trees to a **landing,** particularly by cable, balloon, or helicopter logging
systems —*see* **forward, skid**

yarder *harvesting* a system of power-operated
winches and a tower used to haul logs from a
stump to a landing —*synonym* **mobile yarder**

year class *wildlife* an age class composed of animals
born in the same calendar year —*see* **turnover**

year-long grazing continuous **grazing** for a calendar year —*see* **continuous grazing**

year-long range grazing land that is, or could be,
grazed any time of year —*see* **continuous grazing**

yield **1.** *management* the amount of wood that may
be harvested from a particular type of **forest stand**
by **species,** site, **stocking,** and management regime
at various ages **2.** *utilization* the amount of product output recovered from a quantity of raw material input **3.** *wildlife* the harvest, actual or estimated, of mammals, birds, or fish, expressed by
numbers or weight, or as a proportion of the standing crop, over a given period

yield determination the calculation, by volume regulation or, less directly, by area regulation, of the
amount of timber that may be harvested annually
or periodically from a specified area over a stated
period in accordance with the management objectives

yield table a table showing the expected timber
yields by age of an **even-aged stand,** usually by
site index classes, and typically including quadratic **mean diameter (DBH),** height, number of
stems, **basal area,** and standing volume per unit
area; yield tables may also include volume of **thinnings, CAI, MAI** (*see* **increment table**), and other
data —*note* a money yield table (*synonym* financial
yield table) gives an estimate of future income if
volumes are converted to values by applying appropriate generalized prices with suitable deduc-
tions for expected losses of growing stock and
costs of sales; the types of yield table are as follows:

—**empirical yield table** a yield table, usually based
on **inventory** data, showing average volumes and
other statistics in relation to age and (sometimes)
site index classes as they are found in the existing
forest—*note* empirical yield tables are of limited
usefulness today because existing older stands do
not reflect the effects of changing management
practices applied to younger stands

—**growth-and-yield model** a set of relationships,
usually expressed as equations and embodied in a
computer program, that provides estimates of fu-

yield table *continued*

ture stand development given initial stand conditions and a specified management regime —*note*
growth-and-yield models are used to generate
managed-stand yield tables, predict future stand
conditions for management planning, update inventories, and compare predicted results of alternative possible management regimes

—**managed-yield table** a yield table, usually developed from remeasured plot data, that accounts for
the effects of differences in stand origin, **stand
density,** and effects of management treatments
such as **thinning** and **fertilization** in addition to
the variables **site index** and age

—**normal-yield table** a yield table showing the average development of well-stocked stands over
time, usually by **site index** classes —*note* in North
American usage, normal-yield tables were usually
developed from one-time measurements in unman-
aged stands of natural origin and are historically
important but of limited usefulness under modern
conditions; in European usage, normal-yield tables
do not necessarily represent stands of natural origin only and are often based on remeasured plots,
sometimes with low **thinning**

—**stand simulator** a computer program embodying
a growth-and-yield model that generates estimates
of future stand conditions given initial conditions
and a specified management regime —*note* stand
simulators are used to produce managed-stand
yield tables, update inventories, predict future conditions for management planning, and choose
among possible alternative management regimes

—**variable density yield table** a yield table that includes **stand density** in addition to **site index** and
age as classification or predictor values

yield tax a tax levied per unit of value harvested
—*note 1.* state or local governments often impose
yield taxes in combination with a low annual property tax rate to enable the property owner to postpone a portion of the annual property taxes normally due until such time as income is received
from the property (e.g., at timber harvest) —*note 2.*
a yield tax recognizes that in many years **forest**
property owners generate no income from their
lands —*see* **ad valorem tax, severance tax, specific tax**

Y-parallax the difference between the distances to
the vertical plane containing the air base of the two
images of a point on an overlapping pair of **aerial
photographs** —*note* the existence of Y-parallax is
an indication of **tilt** in either or both photographs
or a difference in flight altitudes: it confuses stereoscopic examination of the pair —*see* **parallax**

Z

zero-plane displacement 1. an empirically determined constant introduced into the logarithmic velocity profile to extend its applicability to very rough surfaces **2.** a measure of the roughness of the surface

zonal soil *obsolete* **1.** a soil characteristic of a large area or zone **2.** one of the three primary subdivisions (orders) in soil classification as used in the United States —*note 1.* the term is not used in the current US system of soil taxonomy; zonal soils include Brown Podzol, Chernozem, Chestnut, Gray-Brown Podzol, Laterite, Latosol, Podzol, Prairie, and Red-Yellow Podzolic —*see* **soil order**

zone *fire* a geographical portion of a very large fire, usually handled more or less as a separate major fire with its own **command staff** and **fire camp**s, under the supervision of a zone boss —*note 1.* coordination with adjacent zones is usually handled by the **general fire headquarters** fire boss —*note 2.* zone is an **LFO** term

zone line a narrow dark brown or black line of fungal or decomposition products, formed in wood decaying under the attack of certain wood-destroying fungi —*note* zone lines often delimit small, irregular areas of decay

zone of aeration —*see* **vadose zone, zone of saturation**

zone of saturation the layer of soil that generally extends downward from the **water table** to some soil or geologic layer that confines flow, or below which the soil is no longer saturated —*see* **vadose zone, zone of aeration**

zoning 1. *management* the demarcation of a planning area by designation, ordinance, or law into zones and the establishment of regulations to govern the use of the land and structures within each zone **2.** *recreation* the establishment of specific sites in which selected activities may occur, but from which other uses are excluded or restricted to reduce conflict between competing uses or to reduce deterioration of fragile resources

zoom *GIS* to display a smaller or larger area instead of the present spatial data set **extent** in order to show greater or lesser detail

zooplankton microscopic animals living within the water column —*see* **plankton**

zoospore a motile, flagellated **sporangiospore**

z-value *GIS* the elevation value of a surface at a particular x,y location —*synonym* spot value, spot elevation

zygospore a sexual **spore** resulting directly from the fusion of morphologically similar gametangia —*see* **gametangium**

zygote 1. the cell formed by the sexual fusion of two **gamete**s **2.** the organism developing from such a cell —*note* the zygotic **chromosome number** is normally **diploid** $(2n)$ —*see* **fertilization, megametophyte**

This dictionary is a product of the working group program of the Society of American Foresters; about 100 people over a three-year period worked to develop and refine terms and definitions specific to their disciplines. The project was managed by a subcommittee of the Forest Science and Technology Board, and initial drafts and the final product were reviewed by specialists in many areas. This collaborative work obviously involved substantial time from dedicated volunteers, and SAF and I are deeply appreciative.

ACKNOWLEDGMENTS

Working Group Contributors

The working groups named the following people as having made significant contributions to the development of the dictionary.

Ginger Anderson, Neil Armantrout, Carol Ann Bates, James Bates, Thomas Blush, Greg Booth, Bill Botti, Stephen Boyce, Jim Boyle, James Brandle, Gerald Bratton, William Brenneman, Russell Briggs, John Brissette, Marilyn Buford, John Burde, Thomas Burk, David Canavera, Lloyd Casey, Jim Chambers, Timothy Chick, David Chojnacky, Elizabeth Close, James Cook, Frank Croft, Peter Daugherty, Lester DeCoster, Jenine Derby, Paul Doruska, Matt Duvall, Sherman Finch, Thomas Fox, Jeremy Fried, Alex Friend, David Funk, Peg Gale, Charles Gay, Wayne Geyer, Michael Gold, James Granskog, Jerry Greer, Richard Guldin, Carl Haag, Mark Hansen, Wade Harrison, Jan Henderson, Frank Hershey, Reinee Hildebrandt, Steven Horsley, George Ice, Larry Irwin, Pamela Jakes, Deepak Khatry, Bruce Kessler, Fred Kinard Jr., Joe Kovach, Larry Leefers, Scott Lewis, Ann Lynch, Douglas Maguire, Craig McKinley, Ken McNabb, Will McWilliams, Ralph Meldahl, Michael Meridith, Miles Merwin, David Miller, Edwin Miller, Carl Mize, Melinda Moeur, Rose-Marie Muzika, Niki Nicholas, Kevin O'Hara, Dan Opalach, Brian Palik, Douglas Powell, Tim Resch, Robert Ricard, Carol Rice, Joe Roise, Steven Sader, Pete Schaefer, Richard Schultz, Terry Sharik, Josh Shroyer, Glen Smalley, George Smith, Joe Spruce, Kim Steiner, Donna Story, William Straw, Mary Anne Sword, Richard Thom, John Thurmes, Keith Ticknor, Marian True, Don Turton, Paul Walvatne, Bently Wigley, Andrew Youngblood, Boris Zeide

Dictionary Subcommittee

The dictionary subcommittee reviewed all working group submissions, provided initial technical editing, and resolved issues of duplicate definitions and other technical issues.

John Helms (chair), Richard Fisher, Robert Martin, Harold (Tom) Nygren, with the assistance of Robert Van Aken

Forest Science and Technology Board

The board was responsible for initiating the project and reviewed the initial, compiled dictionary.

John Helms (chair), Fred Hain, Richard Haynes, Gary Lindell, Denise Meridith, Steven Prisley, Terry Sharik

Reviewers

The complete dictionary or major portions of it were reviewed by 20 people. Their many thoughtful suggestions for improvement of definitions and addition of terms added greatly to the quality of the dictionary.

John Bissonette, James Brown, Ann Forest Burns, Robert Curtis, William Fieber, Rick Fletcher, Jerry Franklin, Sharon Haines, Tim Hardwick, Howard Heiner, Bill Hubbard, Lawrence Larson, Patricia Neenan, Douglas Powell, Sam Radcliffe, Michael Rechlin, Bryce Stokes, Ben Stringham, Michael Thompson, Ross Whaley

SAF Publications

SAF's publications staff converted the initial draft dictionary into a professional product with remarkable skill and dedication.

Sally Atwater, Mary Beth Blackmon, Nina Graves, Lynn Riley, Rebecca Staebler

To all the above people I offer my sincere thanks for transforming, on behalf of the profession, the idea for a much-needed revision of forest terminology into the reality of this dictionary.

John A. Helms, Editor
Professor emeritus, Department of Environmental Science, Policy, and Management, University of California–Berkeley, and chair, Forest Science and Technology Board, Society of American Foresters, Bethesda, Maryland

The vast majority of the 4,500 terms in this dictionary were defined by scientists in the working groups of the Society of American Foresters. There were some already-published definitions, however, on which the working groups could not improve. In other cases, the scientists felt it important to have a terminology consistent with that of related fields and therefore wanted to use what they considered standard definitions. Permission to reprint or adapt definitions from other sources has been graciously granted by the following copyright holders, who reserve all rights:

Academic Press

Blanchard, R.O., and T.A. Tattar. 1981. *Field and Laboratory Guide to Trees:* infection.

Van der Plank, J.E. 1963. *Plant Diseases: Epidemics and Control:* epidemic.

Wright, J.W. 1976. *Introduction to Forest Genetics:* acclimatization, anther, archegonium, biotype, breeding, catkin, cone, correlation analysis, cultivar, cytoplasm, deoxyribonucleic acid, dominant gene, fertile, forest genetics, general combining ability, genetic drift, genetics, genotype, hybrid index, inbreeding depression, karyotype, Lamarckism, Lammas shoot, layering, linkage group, male sterile, open pollination, outcrossing, ovary, ovule, plot, pollen grain, pollen, polygene, progeny, quantitative inheritance, ramet, regression, ribonucleic acid, ribosome, self, strain, topophysis, variance.

Addison Wesley Longman Ltd.

Lawrence, R.C., ed. 1995. *Henderson's Dictionary of Biological Terms* (11th ed.): adaptation, cline, desert, detritus, ecosystem, heath, humus, hyperparasite, lentic, lichen, lotic, mor, myrmecophyte, nematode, net primary production, nutrient cycle, selection, weed, xerophyte.

Taylor, D.A. 1990. *Object Oriented Technology: A Manager's Guide.* © Servio Corporation: class, encapsulation, expert system, fourth-generation language, northings, object, object database management system, paradigm, paradigm shift.

American Phytopathological Society

Hansen, E.M., and K.J. Lewis, eds. 1997. *Compendium of Conifer Diseases:* brown rot, Comandra blister rust, decline, gall rust, Gymnosporangium rust, limb rust, white pine blister rust, white rot.

American Society for Photogrammetry and Remote Sensing

American Society of Civil Engineers, American Congress on Surveying and Mapping, and American Society for Photogrammetry and Remote Sensing. *Glossary of the Mapping Sciences.* 1996.

Greve, C. (ed.) 1996. *Digital Photogrammetry: An Addendum to the Manual of Photogrammetry.*

Morain, S.A., and A.M. Budge. 1996. *Earth Observing Platforms and Sensors. An Illustrated CD Addendum to the Manual of Remote Sensing* (3rd ed., Version 1.0).

aerial photo coverage, air base, airborne GPS, advanced very high resolution radiometer, base-height ratio, digital image processing, digital orthophotography, digital terrain model, electronmagnetic spectrum, earth observing system, earth resources satellite, false color, flight altitude, flight line, flight strip, focal length, global positioning system, image classification, image footprint, instantaneous field of view, Indian remote sensing satellite, Japan earth resources satellite, Landsat, lidar, orthophotograph, orthophotomap, photo interpretation, photo map, photograph nadir, pixel, platform, resolution, scanner, sensor, stereoplotter, stereogram, synthetic aperture radar.

Annual Review Inc.
Meyer, W.B., and B.L. Turner II. 1992. Human population growth and global land-use/cover change. *Annual Review of Ecology and Systematics* 23:39–61: land cover, land use.

Canada Centre for Remote Sensing
CCRS Glossary on the World Wide Web
(http://www.ccrs.nrcan.gc.ca/ccrs/eduref/ref/glosndxe.html): lidar, radar, resolution, scanner, space photography, synthetic aperture radar, Y parallax.

Columbia University Press
Wilke, D.S., and J.T. Finn. 1996. *Remote Sensing Imagery for Natural Resource Monitoring.* M.C. Pearl, ed.: charge coupled device, Doppler shift, false color, multispectral scanner.

ERDAS International
ERDAS Field Guide (4th ed.). 1997: digital elevation model.

ESRI
Introduction to GIS Using ArcView®: geographic information system terms *passim.*

W.H. Freeman & Company
Ricklefs, R.E. 1990. *Ecology* (3rd ed.): acclimation, acclimatization, adaptation, alpha diversity, beta-diversity, ecotype, phenotype, stochastic, thermocline, trophic level.

Harvard University Press
Wilson, E.O. 1971. *The Insect Societies:* social insect.

Holt Rinehart Winston
Nicholson, W. 1975. *Intermediate Microeconomics and Its Application:* complement, consumers' surplus, elasticity, entry condition, equilibrium, expansion path, income and substitution effects, indifference curve, isoquant map, marginal product, marginal rate of substitution, marginal utility, opportunity cost, Pareto optimality, profit, rate of technical substitution, returns to scale, substitute, variable cost.

IEEE Press, Institute of Electrical and Electronic Engineers
Bernstein, R., ed. 1978. *Digital Image Processing for Remote Sensing:* digital image processing, geometric correction.

Kluwer Academic Publishers
Cox, D.R., and H.D. Miller. 1965. *The Theory of Stochastic Processes:* stochastic process.
Nair, P.K.R. 1993. *An Introduction to Agroforestry:* agrosilviculture, agrosilvopastoralism, hedgerow, home garden, intercropping, mixed farming, mixed intercropping, multipurpose tree, sequential intercropping, silvopastoralism.
Richards, O.W., and R.G. Davies. 1977. *Imm's General Textbook of Entomology* (10th ed.), vol. 2: *Classification and Biology:* locust.

Macmillan
Coombs, J. 1992. *Dictionary of Biotechnology* (2nd ed.): cytoplasmic inheritance

Oxford University Press

Emiliani, C. 1987. *Dictionary of the Physical Science:* peneplain.

Huxhold, W. 1991. *An Introduction to Urban Geographic Information Systems:* absolute map accuracy, cadastre, coterminous, flat file, public land survey system.

Plenum Press

Berryman, A. A. 1986. *Forest Insects: Principles and Practices of Population Management:* risk.

Prentice Hall

Monmonier, M., and G. A. Schnell. 1988. *Map Appreciation:* analog map, digital map, metropolitan statistical area, minor civil division, plane-coordinate system, planimetric map, quadrangle, thematic map, topographic map.

Society for Range Management

A Glossary of Terms Used in Range Management. 1989, 1998: allowable use, animal month, animal unit, animal-unit conversion factor, animal-unit equivalent, band, band day, basal area, bed-ground, brand, bunch grass, close herding, common use, continuous grazing, decreaser plant species, deferred grazing, deferred rotation, density, drift, drive, dry band, dual use, exclosure, forage, forb, frequency, grass, grasslike plant, grazing fee, grazing period, grazing preference, grazing season, grazing system, herb, herder, increaser plant species, interseeding, key species, management unit, mark, nonuse, open range, overgrazing, pasture, permittee, premature grazing, proper-use factor, range site, range survey, rest-rotation, rotational grazing, roundup, salting, short duration grazing, stocking, stubble, supplement, tag, trail herding, use, year-long range.

Soil and Water Conservation Society

Resource Conservation Glossary (3rd ed). 1982: acre-foot, acre-inch, aerobic, anaerobic, aquitard, available water, bank storage, bed load, bedding, best management practice, broad-crested weir, capillary pore, capillary water, channel density, chemical oxygen demand, coefficient of roughness, colloidal suspension, control section, crest-stage gauge, critical depth, critical reach, critical velocity, Darcy's law, datum, depletion curve, depression storage, depth-area-duration analysis, discharge coefficient, discharge curve, discharge formula, dissolved solids, drainage, effluent, epilimnion, erosion, erosive, flashboard, flood peak, flood routing, flume, fluvial, gauge, graded stream, greenhouse effect, gully, head, headwater, hydraulic radius, hydrologic balance, hydrologic cycle, hydrologic model, interflow, intermittent stream, lagtime, Manning's formula, observation well, ogee, organophosphate, outfall, outlet, overland flow, oxygen demand, percolation, permeability, piezometric surface, pollution, rainfall duration, rainfall frequency, rating curve, recharge, recurrence interval, regime, regimen, return flow, riffle, runoff, saturated flow, sediment, sediment discharge, seepage, soil moisture, spillway, stilling well, streamside management zone, suspended sediment, suspended solid, tailwater, time of concentration, total dissolved solids, turbidity, turbulent flow, unit hydrograph, universal soil loss equation, water quality standard, water year, wetland, wetted perimeter.

Soil Science Society of America

Glossary of Soil Science Terms. 1997: ablation till, acid soil, adsorption complex, aggregation, A horizon, albic horizon, alkaline soil, allochthonous flora, alluvial soil, apatite, aquic, available water, azonal soil, basal till, base saturation, basic slag, bedrock, B horizon, blowout, bog, breccia, buffer power, calcareous soil, calcification, caliche, cambic horizon, catena, cation exchange, cation exchange capacity, chelate, C horizon, chroma, clay, claypan, colluvial, creep, crumb structure, deflation, degradaton, desert pavement, drainage class, duff mull, ectomycorrhiza, E horizon, eluvial horizon, eluviation, endomycorrhiza, epipedon, erosion, erosion pavement, esker, fault, field capacity *in situ,* flocculation, forest floor, fragipan, gilgai, glacial drift, gleyed, gravitational water, groundwater, hardpan, hue, humic acid, humin, humus, hydric soil, hydromorphic soil, hydrophilic, hydrophobic, illite, illuvial horizon, illuviation, infiltration flux, intrazonal soil, irrigation, kaolin, kaolinite, karst, leaching, litter, loess, lysimeter, marl, mature soil, mica, mineralization, mollic epipedon, mor, moraine, mosaic (aerial), mottle, muck soil, mull, Munsell color system, mycorrhiza, nitrification, nutrient deficiency, ochric epipedon, organic soil, ortstein, outwash, oxic horizon, parent material, particle size distribution, peat, ped, pedalfer, pedocal, perched water table, permafrost, permeability, pH, phyllosilicate minerals, plaggen epipedon, plinthite, polypedon, porosity, primary mineral, redox potential, residual soil, residuum, reticulate mottling, rhizobia, rhizosphere, riparian, R layer, saline soil, sand, scarp, screef, secondary mineral, sesquioxide, silica-sesquioxide ratio, silt, slick spot, slickenside, soil horizon, soil map, soil quality, soil separates, soil series, soil solution, soil structure, soil texture, soil type, solum, splash erosion, sticky point, substrate, surface soil, till, tilth, tuff, umbric epipedon, vadose zone, value, varve, volumetric water content, water table, weathering, zonal soil.

Solano Press Books
Bass, R.E., and A.I. Herson. 1993. *Mastering NEPA: A Step-by-Step Approach:* direct effect, finding of no significant impact, indirect effect, lead agency, notice of intent, record of decision, scope.

Springer-Verlag
Rieger, R., A. Michaelis, and M.M. Green. 1991. *Glossary of Genetics, Classical and Molecular* (5th ed.): Hardy-Weinberg model.

University of British Columbia Press, Vancouver
Dunster, J., and K. Dunster. 1996. *Dictionary of Natural Resource Management:* alterne, base flow, biomass, burl, discharge, drift, flow, hydrograph, macroinvertebrate, myrmecophyte, risk, stereoscope, weir.

John Wiley and Sons
Coulson, R.N., and J.A. Witter. 1984. *Forest Entomology: Ecology and Management:* hazard, skeletonizing, stippling injury.

MacDicken, K.G., and Vergara, N.T., eds. 1990. *Agroforestry: Classification and Management:* agroforestry, tree fallow.

Pritchett, W. L. 1979. *Properties and Management of Forest Soils:* F layer, H layer, L layer.

Tainter, F.H., and F.A. Baker. *Principles of Forest Pathology:* epidemic, epidemiology, fungistatic, parthenogenesis.

Zobel, B., and J. Talbert. 1984. *Applied Forest Tree Improvement:* land race, mass selection.